ALTERNATIVE BANKING AND FINANCIAL CRISIS

BANKING, MONEY AND INTERNATIONAL FINANCE

FORTHCOMING TITLES

Financial Innovation, Regulation and Crises in History
Piet Clement, Harold James and Herman Van der Wee (eds)

ALTERNATIVE BANKING AND FINANCIAL CRISIS

EDITED BY

Olivier Butzbach and Kurt von Mettenheim

Routledge
Taylor & Francis Group

LONDON AND NEW YORK

First published 2014 by Pickering & Chatto (Publishers) Limited

Published 2016 by Routledge
2 Park Square, Milton Park, Abingdon, Oxfordshire OX14 4RN
711 Third Avenue, New York, NY 10017, USA

First issued in paperback 2015

Routledge is an imprint of the Taylor & Francis Group, an informa business

BRITISH LIBRARY CATALOGUING IN PUBLICATION DATA

Alternative banking and financial crisis. – (Banking, money and international
finance; 1)
1. Global Financial Crisis, 2008–2009. 2. Banks and banking – Europe – History – 21st century. 3. Banks and banking – United States – History – 21st
century. 4. Bank management – Europe. 5. Bank management – United States.
I. Series II. Butzbach, Olivier editor of compilation. III. Mettenheim, Kurt von,
1957– editor of compilation.
332.1'094-dc23

ISBN-13: 978-1-138-66308-4 (pbk)
ISBN-13: 978-1-8489-3447-4 (hbk)
Typeset by Pickering & Chatto (Publishers) Limited

CONTENTS

ACKNOWLEDGEMENTS

The editors thank the contributors to this volume for participating in several phases of this project and for delivering original chapters that exceeded our expectations. In particular, the editors wish to thank Reinhard H. Schmidt for pointing us in the right direction and for his unfaltering support and rigorous interest in alternative banking. We also thank our home institutions, the Getulio Vargas Foundation São Paulo Business School in Brazil and the Second University of Naples in Italy, for supporting our research and, in particular, for funding visits for teaching and brainstorming in São Paulo in July 2010 and Naples in April 2012. Thanks are also due to the Rockefeller Foundation for hosting a conference on alternative banking and social inclusion at the Bellagio Center in July 2011, followed by research residencies for the editors, during which this volume took shape. The Bellagio Center was a wonderful setting for drafting volume chapters and meeting great colleagues and new friends. We also thank fellow participants at various meetings where the ideas in this volume blossomed, especially meetings of the Society for the Advancement of Socio-Economics in Paris in 2009, Boston in 2012 and Milan in 2013.

LIST OF CONTRIBUTORS

Dilek Bülbül is Assistant Professor in the Chair of International Banking and Finance at the Goethe University House of Finance in Frankfurt. Her research focuses on efficiency and stability in banking networks, and her recent work concentrates on bank regulation. Publications include 'Determinants of Trust in Banking Networks' in the *Journal of Economic Behavior and Organization* and 'Why Do Banks Provide Leasing?' in the *Journal of Financial Service Research*. She holds an MSc degree from the University of Wales, Cardiff and a doctoral degree in finance from Goethe University Frankfurt, and she has several years of working experience in the financial industry.

Olivier Butzbach is a Researcher in Economics at the Department of Political Science of the Second University of Naples and teaches finance at King's College London. He is also a Research Associate at the London Centre for Corporate Governance and Ethics. A graduate of the Institut d'Études Politiques de Paris and of the Johns Hopkins University School of Advanced International Studies, Butzbach holds a PhD from the European University Institute in Florence. In 2006 he was awarded the European Savings Banks Institute Academic Award second prize for his research on the comparative history of French and Italian savings banks. His main research interests lie in the fields of alternative banks and the theory of banking; comparative financial systems and comparative political economy; and institutionalism. He is the author of several publications on the changing governance and strategy of French and Italian savings banks.

Luca Giordano is a Senior Economist in the Research Department at the Italian Financial Market Authority (CONSOB), where he is involved in monitoring new financial risks and drawing up research on financial market efficiency, market microstructure, systemic risk and contagion. Previously, he has worked as a financial officer at the Department of International Financial Affairs of the Italian Ministry of Economy and Finance, where he developed macroeconomic short-term analysis and provided technical support in the formulation and implementation of the government's economic and financial policy choices. He holds a PhD in economics and an MSc in economics and finance from the

University of Naples Federico II. He has published in banking, econometrics, finance and empirical macroeconomics.

Hans Groeneveld is Senior Vice President at the Directorate Cooperative & Sustainable Business at Rabobank Nederland. His main responsibilities comprise managing strategic projects and advising executive board members. Before taking up this job, he held various senior and managerial positions in staff divisions and business directorates within Rabobank Nederland. As Deputy Chief Economist, Groeneveld managed the Financial Sector Research division and the Knowledge and Information Center. Within the SME directorate, he was responsible for the Trade, Manufacturing and Service business division as well as manager of International Desks, which service retail clients of local Rabobanks across the world. Before joining the Rabobank Group, Groeneveld worked as a senior policy advisor and manager at the Dutch Central Bank in the monetary and supervisory departments, respectively. He holds a PhD from Maastricht University in financial and banking economics and has published in academic and policy journals. He is a board member of the Royal Society for Economic Affairs, a member of the Think Tank of the European Association of Cooperative Banks, a member of the Scientific Committee of EURICSE, and a lecturer on financial institutions and monetary theory at Radboud University Nijmegen.

Lakshmi Kumar is Associate Professor and Program Director at the Institute for Financial Management and Research (IFMR) in Chennai. She received a doctorate in economics from IIT Madras after graduating in mathematics and completing postgraduate studies in econometrics at the University of Madras. She has over twenty years of experience in research and teaching. Prior to joining IFMR, Kumar worked in the Madras Chamber of Commerce and Industry, taught economics in graduate programmes at Rizvi College and Sophia College in Mumbai, and conducted research at the SP Jain Institute of Management, Mumbai. She presently teaches macroeconomics, managerial economics, international business and microfinance. Her area of research lies in development, focusing particularly on development banking, financial inclusion, microfinance and poverty reduction. She works on several sponsored projects and publishes papers in peer-reviewed international journals.

Antonio Lopes is Professor of Economics at the Department of Political Science of the Second University of Naples and teaches economics at the Department of Law of LUISS University in Rome. A graduate of the University of Naples, he holds an MPh from New York University. His main research interests lie in the fields of development economics, banking systems analysis and monetary policy. He is the author of several publications on the Italian banking system and on development policies in southern Italy.

Kurt von Mettenheim is Professor in the Social and Legal Sciences Department and Graduate Programs of the Escola de Administração de Empresas de São Paulo, Fundação Getulio Vargas (FGV-EAESP). He was a university lecturer in Brazilian studies at the University of Oxford and taught at Columbia University, the University of Pittsburgh and the universities of São Paulo and Brasilia. He is the author of *Federal Banking in Brazil* (London: Pickering & Chatto, 2010) and *The Brazilian Voter* (Pittsburgh, PA: University of Pittsburgh Press, 1995), co-editor of *Government Banking: New Perspectives on Sustainable Development and Social Inclusion from Europe and South America* (São Paulo: Konrad Adenauer Foundation Press, 2008), and author of other publications on comparative politics and banking.

Alfredo Schclarek is Assistant Professor of Macroeconomics at the National University of Córdoba, Argentina, Assistant Researcher at the National Scientific and Technical Research Council (CONICET) and Academic Director of the Center for Participatory Research in Economic and Social Policies (CIPPES) in Argentina. He received his PhD, Masters and Bachelor degrees in economics from Lund University, Sweden, with further studies in Argentina, Canada and Sweden. He worked at the European Central Bank in Germany, the United Nations in Denmark and the National Agency for Investment Development in Argentina. Awards include the 'Ten Outstanding Young Persons of the Year 2007' prize from the Cordoba Stock Exchange and the Economic Research Annual Award in 2007 for Young Professionals from the Central Bank of Argentina. He has published and presented papers on banking and finance in international journals and associations, including a publication in the *Journal of Financial Stability* and presentation at the Central Bank of Brazil.

Reinhard H. Schmidt, an economist by training, holds the Chair for International Banking and Finance at Goethe University Frankfurt since 1991. Before that, he was a Professor of Finance at the universities of Göttingen and Trier in Germany and a visiting scholar at the Stanford Graduate School of Business. He has been a visiting professor at Georgetown University in Washington, DC, various universities in Paris, Bocconi University in Milan and the Wharton School in Philadelphia. His research and teaching cover topics in financial theory, financial management and international banking. His recent work focuses on comparative financial systems and finance and banking in developing and transition countries. Professor Schmidt has published twenty-three scholarly books and about 140 academic articles in German and international journals and books and numerous articles in newspapers, and he is a frequent commentator on German and international radio and TV stations. He is a founding member of the European Shadow Financial Regulatory Committee and was the dean of his school and the chairman of the supervisory board of an investment company that invests in microfinance institutions.

Ulrich Schüwer is Assistant Professor in the Chair of International Banking and Finance at the Goethe University House of Finance in Frankfurt. His research focuses on financial intermediation and behavioural financial theory. Recent papers include 'How Do Banks React to Increased Credit Risks? Evidence from Hurricane Katrina', an American Economic Association annual meeting paper, and 'Add-on Pricing, Consumer Myopia and Regulatory Intervention', an American Economic Association annual meeting paper and CEPR Discussion Paper no. DP8636. He holds an MSc in operations research from North Carolina State University, a Diplom-Kaufmann in business from RWTH Aachen University and a doctoral degree in finance from Goethe University Frankfurt. Schüwer has five years of working experience with Citigroup Global Markets in Frankfurt.

LIST OF FIGURES AND TABLES

INTRODUCTION

Olivier Butzbach and Kurt von Mettenheim

Back from the Dead: Alternative Banks in the Shifting World of Banking

More than six years after the beginning of the subprime mortgage credit crisis in the United States, many banks and banking systems are still either ailing or slowly recovering. Dozens of large banks failed at the height of the crisis, mostly in the United States and in Europe. Surviving banks had to merge or, in some cases, radically change strategies – although sceptics might point out that the perilous practices widely assumed to be at the root of the crisis (massive securitization, increased reliance of retail banks on wholesale funds, single-minded pursuit of higher yields, high bonuses) are now (in 2013) back in favour in the industry. At the same time, governments have had to step back into banking after years (if not decades) of apparent lack of interest. In particular, in 2008, during the acute phase of the banking crisis, many governments across the world had to rescue individual banks or, in some cases, finance an emergency bailout programme (such as in the case of the United States and Ireland, and, more recently, of Spain). Moreover, in order to avoid an outright collapse of the financial sector through the demise of 'too big to fail' banks, governments also forced ailing banks to merge (such as in the case of the Bank of America's takeover of Merrill Lynch) or simply national-ized them (the Anglo Irish Bank in 2009) or took over a significant share of their equity (Northern Rock and the Royal Bank of Scotland in 2008–9).

Furthermore, faced with evident regulatory failures and the profoundly dis-torted mix of constraints and incentives made visible by the crisis, governments also moved to revamp banking regulation. Indeed, the latter has since 2008 undergone (apparently) significant changes, both across countries and at the international level. In the United States, the Dodd–Frank Wall Street Reform and Consumer Protection Act, signed into law by US President Barak Obama in June 2010, represents the first large-scale banking regulatory reform since the 1930s. The Dodd–Frank Act touches on various aspects of bank regulation seen as profoundly flawed: in particular, it has changed the banking regulatory architecture, strengthening inter-agency coordination and instituting new agencies, such as the Financial Stability Oversight Council, in charge of assessing and monitoring systemic risk in banking. The Dodd–Frank Act is also known for including a somewhat watered-down version of the so-called 'Volcker rule', which imposes a low ceiling on the equity bank holding companies may hold in hedge funds or private equity firms. Other countries have also adopted reforms: in the United Kingdom, following recommendations by the Vickers Commission, a Banking Reform Bill is now discussed in Parliament; in France, in July 2013 the National Assembly passed an apparently ambitious banking reform as well. Both bills make explicit reference to the US Dodd–Frank Act; both bills re-institute a form of separation between investment banking and retail banking activities (called 'ring-fencing' in the British context).

These regulatory reforms have come together with a rethinking of traditional ('mainstream') theories in the field of finance and banking, starting with the efficient capital market hypothesis, already seriously challenged from various fronts in the years prior to the crisis. More importantly for the purpose of the present volume, there has been, since the 2007–8 crisis, an important academic and policy-oriented discussion on the nature and role banks do, can and should play within modern financial systems. In the immediate aftermath of the crisis, several scholars voiced their support for a 'return' to 'narrow banking'.[1]

However, these important developments, on the policy or the academic side, suffer from at least one very serious shortcoming: by focusing on either investment banks or large private commercial banks, most policymakers, scholars and observers of the banking industry have so far failed to see that banking does not come in one guise only; and, before considering how to reform joint-stock banks, they ought to take stock of the experience of banks that are neither run for profit nor dedicated exclusively to maximize the utility of their shareholders. Finally, they should realize that if such banks can survive and, indeed, flourish in a world dominated by for-profit banks and financial markets, their theories should be reconsidered; and banking regulatory reforms should incorporate the lessons learned from the operation, success and survival of these alternative forms of banks.

We call here 'alternative banks' all those banking organizations that are not run to maximize profit, are not required to satisfy shareholders, and have, as a result, developed over time a business model that is at the antipodes of the model embraced by most for-profit, shareholder-oriented retail banks in past decades around the world. We call these banks 'alternative' because they do, indeed, represent an existing and sustainable alternative to the 'mainstream' way of banking – a way that stands at the heart of policymakers' attention, of current regulatory efforts and of scholarly analyses. This term has the merit of underlining the fact that there are other banking models out there that one ought to analyse before trying to reinvent the wheel. However, the term has serious limitations as well.

The term 'alternative bank' is limited, first because it may create confusion as to both the origins and the actual behaviour of these banks. Indeed, speaking of 'alternative banks' might indicate that these institutions developed historically as responses or reactions to a prevailing mainstream banking business model. This is simply not the case: as Chapter 1 amply shows, many of the banks we call 'alternative' (cooperative banks, thrifts, mutual savings banks, etc.) were created in the nineteenth century, far before most of the joint-stock retail banks with which they now compete. Second, the term 'alternative' might mislead readers into thinking that these banks behave oddly – a bunch of hippies in a world dominated by business suits. When our friend (and contributor to this volume) Reinhard Schmidt 'tested' this term with an audience of German cooperative bank managers, the reaction was very cold – 'it makes us look like heroin addicts!', said one. Indeed, many 'alternative banks' base their reputation on their conservative behaviour – alternative banks are usually less diversified, they concentrate their assets in a limited series of core financial products (mortgage loans, loans to small- and medium-sized businesses, government securities), and they rely less on wholesale banking than their for-profit competitors. More importantly perhaps, they usually have longer-term horizons than private banks.

A perhaps more serious limitation lies in our attempt to characterize, with one single term, a very heterogeneous crowd. Our rough definition of alternative banks includes small, mutual banks with a limited range of products: small cooperative banks, small mutual savings banks, thrifts, credit unions, building societies (for instance, British building societies, German and Italian cooperative banks, US thrifts). Although a superficial observer might group those intermediaries together with microfinance institutions – something the editors of this book have experienced in at least one instance – these small mutual banks are often tied together in closely knit networks that play a key role in the performance of these banks, as will be argued in Chapter 4. In addition, our definition covers large, member-owned banking entities: mostly regional or cooperative groups, such as the Spanish Cajas, the Banche Popolari in Italy, the Crédit Agricole in France, Rabobank in the Netherlands. Finally, we also include, in our list, non-mutual but public banking entities – large state-owned banks, in other words, which have been completely ignored by the mainstream banking literature but for pointing out the 'anomaly' that they supposedly represent.[2]

These banks differ by size, corporate governance and ownership, and, very often, business model. What is the point, then, of grouping them under a very broad and, therefore, potentially meaningless umbrella? We do this for what appears (to us at least) to be one very good reason: these various types of banking organizations all share the characteristic of being very different from for-profit, commercial banks along the three dimensions mentioned above: their not-for-profit missions; their stakeholder-oriented governance; and their long-term horizons. A further common characteristic shared by alternative banks is that they have been shunned so far by many policymakers, commentators and most of the academic literature on banking.

To substantiate this claim, one may turn, on the academic side, to popular banking textbooks or handbooks, such as Matthews and Thompson[3] and the 2010 *Oxford Handbook of Banking*.[4] Specific reference to savings, cooperative or public banks in these works is scant. Matthews and Thomson ignore these banks completely. None of the thirty-six chapters of the 2010 *Handbook* deals explicitly or implicitly with the existence, specificities and organizational model of not-for-profit financial intermediaries or stakeholder-oriented banks. As a matter of fact, the terms 'savings banks' or 'mutual banks' do not appear in the *Handbook*'s index; 'cooperative banks' appears twice, in a chapter dedicated to Japan; 'development banks' once, under the heading 'Development Bank of Japan' in the same chapter; 'thrift institutions' twice, in a chapter dedicated to the US (alongside one mention of 'thrifts failures'); and 'state-owned commercial banks' four times in a chapter dedicated to transition countries. This ignorance of alternative banks, even in the post-crisis context (when, that is, the commercial bank business model has become heavily criticized), seems to us typical of the 'mainstream' literature on banks and banking. However, contemporary heterodox theories of banking share the same apparent lack of interest in alternative banks.[5]

Obviously (or maybe not so), economists *have* paid attention to non-profit financial intermediaries over time. One could cite the following (mostly) theoretical works on alternative banks: Akella and Greenbaum, 1988; Hansmann, 1988; Rasmussen, 1988; Kay, 1991; Mayers and Smith, 1994; Hansmann, 1996; Hart and Moore, 1998; Drake and Llewellyn, 2001; Gurtner et al., 2002; La Porta et al., 2002; Desrochers and Fischer, 2005; McGregor, 2005; McKillop, 2005; Cuevas and Fischer, 2007; Fonteyne, 2007; Hesse and Čihák, 2007; McKillop and Wilson, 2011; and Marsal, 2013 (for a review of the empirical literature on non-profit banks, see Chapter 2 in the present volume).[6] However, these studies, some of which are important and will be discussed in Chapter 4, deal with specific types of alternative banks (mutuals or savings banks or state-owned banks), and therefore do not provide the broader picture that led to the conception of the present volume; moreover, they mostly engage with the mainstream banking literature through a discussion of governance and ownership issues. Corporate governance is certainly central to any understanding of the peculiarities of alternative banks with respect to for-profit banks. But an exclusive focus on governance runs the risk of treating these peculiarities as issues mostly pertaining to theories of the firm, leaving the overall architecture of banking theory unaffected. This is why it is possible to argue that alternative banks have been ignored, overall, by the academic literature on banking theory in the past few decades.

Policy-wise, alternative banks have been largely left on the margins of post-crisis reforms. First, recent reforms have dismantled specific regulations dedicated to non-profit banks. In the United States, for instance, Title III of the Dodd–Frank Act terminated the Office of Thrift Supervision and transferred its powers to the Federal Deposit Insurance Corporation, the Office of the Comptroller and the Federal Reserve; similar plans underlie discussions around a 'banking union' in Europe. Whatever one may think of the effectiveness of specialized agencies such as the OTS to deal with systemic risk or even simply individual banking behaviour,[7] their dismantlement by lawmakers is a significant gesture towards the 'normalization' of alternative bank regulation along criteria designed for profit-maximizing private banks.

Second, new banking regulations reflect policymakers' apparent unawareness of the existence of alternatives to the for-profit banks they have in mind. For instance, section 616 of the Dodd–Frank Act requires bank holding companies to maintain 'counter-cyclical' capital levels, explaining how these counter-cyclical capital buffers should work. This is precisely one of the characteristics of mutual banks' business model; and yet it is not acknowledged in the bill.

To a large extent, then, the post-crisis reform environment perpetuates the beliefs and ideas about banking held pre-crisis; still, there are signs that policymakers might have grown more aware of the importance of alternative banks both as players in the financial industry and as role models for troubled banks. In the wake of the 2007–8 crisis, indeed, influential actors and observers of the banking industry (especially in the United Kingdom and continental Europe) have called for regulatory support to 'diversity' in banking.

The emerging academic and policy discussion on diversity develops three types of arguments. The first argument simply consists in acknowledging, on the one hand, the existing diversity of banking business models across and within national banking systems; and, on the other hand, the fact that these different business models are not equally performing in terms of efficiency, profitability and risk. Such an argument can be found in the empirical academic literature on 'alternative banks', which is reviewed in Chapter 2 of the present volume; it is also made in official government reports, such as the Liikanen Report commissioned by the European Commission and made public in October 2012.[8] In a recent paper, Michie and Oughton propose a classification of the various dimensions along which diversity can be measured – namely, ownership, competition, 'balance sheet resilience' and geographical spread.[9] Similarly, the Liikanen Report identifies six characteristics or attributes of banking diversity: size, ownership, capital and funding, 'activities' that are revealed by banks' balance sheet and income, corporate and legal structure, and geographical scope.[10]

The second argument is that diversity is valuable in itself, as a characteristic of the banking sector *as a whole*. In other words, a banking system composed of heterogeneous organizations does better at mitigating systemic risk than a homogeneous banking system, whatever the source of heterogeneity. This point is very similar to the view that homogeneous banking systems suffer from a 'too many to fail' problem, whereby an implicit guarantee by regulators 'induces banks to herd ex-ante in order to increase the likelihood of being bailed out' ex post.[11] More broadly, diversity in the banking system helps decrease systemic risk by decreasing the degree of similarity in bank portfolios. Indeed, the 2007–8 crisis was not caused by the fact that all banks specialized in the same asset class (say, mortgage assets) – rather, it was caused by the high level of correlation between banks' diversification strategies. As Andrew Haldane pointed out in a famous 2009 speech, individual diversification by banks might lead to a decrease of systemic diversity – and, simultaneously, an increase in systemic risk.[12] This argument lies at the core of the diversity literature, since it goes beyond the specific identity or type of organizational forms to plead for a more general form of diversity.

The third argument, developed, in part, by Michie, is that diversity is good for the functioning of the (banking) system in evolutionary terms – in other words, as Michie puts it: 'In a situation of uncertainty and unpredictability, we cannot know which model will prove to be superior in all possible future circumstances, so we ought to be rather cautious before destroying any successful model'.[13] This argument bears a strong resemblance to evolutionary analyses in economics and business, as Michie himself briefly acknowledges, and as will be discussed below.

Given its potential benefits, as mentioned above, diversity has become a policy goal for financial regulators. In the UK, for instance, the government recognized, in the wake of the crisis, 'the need to maintain diversity in the financial services sector (for example, by removing barriers to entry where possible, and ensuring that its rules do not disadvantage mutually owned financial institutions)'.[14] At the European Union level, the Liikanen Report, already mentioned, also devotes a full chapter to the 'necessary' diversity of the European banking industry.[15] In a recent paper, Michie has laid out a policy framework geared towards promoting diversity in the banking industry.[16] One way to increase diversity in banking, Michie and others have argued, consists in lowering barriers of entry for non-profit banks and financial organizations.

However, this growing awareness is yet to produce tangible results. And it occurs after a thirty-year-long process of transformation of the bank industry that has not been favourable to alternative banks, and has been characterized by bank privatizations (in the 1980s), credit market deregulation, market liberalization and increased competition – and in some cases, such as the UK Building Society Reform of 1986, outright assaults on the business model of alternative banks.[17] Yet in hindsight the growing emergence of a hostile environment in the 1980s and 1990s cannot be seen exclusively in a negative light. Indeed, a widespread expectation during this period was that over time, alternative banks would gradually disappear and their business models slowly converge towards the business model of for-profit banks. Yet, defying the odds, alternative banks have, through a variety of strategies, modernized and held their ground – maintaining or gaining market shares, especially in retail banking (deposits, savings accounts and lending to firms and households). This is a paradox. As Canning et al. put it, 'a central issue is why not-for-profit banks arise and survive in a world dominated by investor-owned banks, run for profit'.[18] Alternative banks have also outperformed private, for-profit banks in terms of profitability and efficiency. A growing empirical literature documents this superior performance in comparative perspective, building on, first, a tradition of studies in the structure-conduct-performance literature and, second, a more recent body of works on the links between ownership and performance in banking (for a review, see Berger et al.'s 2005 paper[19] and Chapter 2 in the present volume).

Therefore, the rebalancing of banking regulation, called for in the literature on diversity, does not mean bringing alternative banks back from the dead: many of them are still alive and kicking. Building on this observation, and on the timid but spreading rediscovery of the merits of alternative banks by scholars and policymakers, the present volume has three goals. First, it aims at offering a complete, if not exhaustive, view of what the empirical and theoretical banking literatures have to say about alternative banks – their nature, their history, their role in modern financial systems, their performance compared to their main competitors. This is the purpose of Part I. Second, this volume seeks to provide a broad overview of the very heterogeneous evolution of alternative banks across countries and regions, especially by bringing together European countries, the United States, and emerging economies where alternative banks often play a key role in the financial industry. The third and last goal of this book is to serve as a springboard for a debate, long overdue, on both the role alternative banks should play in modern financial systems geared towards stability and access, and the effects alternative banks might have on the way we think about banking – *tout court*.

Two final caveats. First, this volume is not a (extended) policy brief in favour of alternative banks: the balance of scholarly and policy attention was so tilted towards for-profit banks that we felt it necessary to pull it back towards alternative banks. But we do not hold the view that the banking industry should be made of state-owned banks or mutual banks only. For instance, in the first part of the book we seek to understand the foundations for alternative banks' competitive advantage: it does not mean that we think that alternative banks outperform their for-profit competitors always and anywhere; simply, we wish to shed light on the potential these banks have for 'performing' well – bank performance being here understood in a much broader way than a simple set of biased indicators, such as return on shareholders' equity.

Second, alternative banks not only vary in size, form, shape and performance; they also vary over time. What we have in mind is an ideal-type of alternative banks. There are many cases where historical developments undermine this ideal-type even as the organizations in question remain state-owned or mutual. As a matter of fact, alternative banks are almost always characterized by multiple tensions over their specific identity and the degree to which they should 'normalize', i.e. converge on the for-profit model. There is also a growing and very interesting literature that explores these tensions. Our effort, however, is located upstream: to understand these tensions, created to a large extent by past regulations, one needs to fully understand the richness and potential of the model.

The Book

The volume is organized in two parts. Part I, building on this Introduction, aims at putting alternative banks in a broader historical and theoretical context. In particular, in Chapter 1 Olivier Butzbach and Kurt von Mettenheim draw on a rich but fragmented literature to synthetically account for the origins and development of alternative banks – in particular in Europe, where, for instance, savings and cooperative banks emerged in the eighteenth and nineteenth centuries. Chapters 2, 3 and 4 offer complementary reviews of the modern and current literatures on alternative banks. More specifically, in Chapter 2 Butzbach and von Mettenheim review the growing empirical evidence on the surprisingly strong performance of alternative banks both prior to and after the 2007–8 crisis; in Chapter 4 the same authors try to explain this performance through a detailed analysis of the theoretical literature on banking. While the 'mainstream' banking economics literature has paid scarce attention to non-profit banking organizations, there is sufficient theoretical work in other areas of research to sketch a convincing theoretical account of the comparative advantages of alternative banks. In fact, as Butzbach and von Mettenheim argue in that chapter, the very anomaly constituted, in mainstream theorists' views, by the superior performance of alternative banks in many contexts should lead to a more radical rethinking of what banks (alternative and private) are about. In Chapter 3 Alfredo Schclarek complements this analysis with a detailed review of the literature on the counter-cyclical role played by alternative banks – especially in times of crisis. This argument, well established in a very recent stream of studies, also appears in several of the country studies in Part II of the volume.

Part II, indeed, groups together country or regional studies that focus on specific types of alternative banks. As emphasized in the present Introduction, no volume of this kind could be exhaustive, given the extraordinarily rich and heterogeneous nature of the alternative banking world. What we tried to do, however, in the spirit of this Introduction, was to offer as variegated as possible a picture of that world, both in terms of the banks studied (cooperative, savings, public) and in terms of regional coverage – most comparative studies we know being centred on Europe. Thus in Chapter 5 Hans Groeneveld provides a careful empirical analysis of the recent performance of European cooperative banking groups – an important introduction to Part II, since it underlines the importance of large alternative banks by contrast with the picture often held, at least in the Anglophone literature, of alternative banks as small, local credit institutions. In Chapter 6, in fact, Reinhard H. Schmidt, Dilek Bülbül and Ulrich Schüwer show how, in Germany, the 'three-pillar structure' composed of savings, cooperative and commercial banks, in place since the nineteenth century, is alive and well. Moreover, the solid performance of German cooperative and savings banks during the crisis lends support to the view that the diversity of banking business models should lie at the heart of current reassessments of the banking system. In Chapter 7 Luca Giordano and Antonio Lopes put cooperative banks in the broader and more complex context of a dual economy; in the case of Italy, indeed, the banking needs of the southern part of the country are different from those of the rest of the country and – the authors argue – better addressed by small cooperatives.

Chapters 8 and 9 explore alternative banks in contexts that seem a priori more hostile to them: the United Kingdom and the United States. In Chapter 8 Olivier Butzbach shows how British building societies, while having lost relevance due to a shift in the regulatory context in the 1980s, still do represent a sustainable alternative to for-profit commercial banks, especially in the post-crisis banking landscape. In Chapter 9 Kurt von Mettenheim shows how alternative banks in the United States have seen their once important positions in the credit system gradually weaken over the twentieth century.

Finally, Chapters 10 and 11 extend our coverage of alternative banks to emerging economies. In Chapter 10 Kurt von Mettenheim explores the variegated nature and role played by public banks in the BRIC countries – Brazil, Russia, India and China. He finds that by adapting to liberalization and repeatedly helping to adjust to emerging market crises during the 1990s and 2000s, government banks in those countries provided policy alternatives to adjust to the global crisis and accelerate social inclusion. In Chapter 11 Lakshmi Kumar discusses the performance of and the numerous challenges faced by Indian cooperative banks, emphasizing their strength in key areas of the country's economic and social fabric – rural areas – and their potential as a foundation of the Indian financial system in the years to come.

1 ALTERNATIVE BANKING HISTORY

Kurt von Mettenheim and Olivier Butzbach

Alternative banks with social missions were founded alongside private commercial and merchant banks very early in European history. Religious orders founded savings and pawn banks throughout Italy in the fourteenth and fifteenth centuries that were often consolidated into large institutions such as the Bank of Naples in 1463. Savings banks emerged throughout Northern Europe in the late eighteenth and early nineteenth centuries. Credit cooperative were founded to avert hunger after crop failures and crisis in the late 1840s. Development banks were founded across continental Europe during the nineteenth century to accelerate industrialization and finance infrastructure. Alternative banks rapidly attained large market shares and created unique organizational structures and governance traditions to manage risk and sustain profit while serving social, political and public policy missions. This chapter reviews the historical development of competitive advantage (stakeholder governance, two-tier organizational structures, long-term profit sustainability orientations, relationship banking, greater trust, lower cost of capital) to help explain how alternative banks, where they were not privatized or demutualized, modernized to maintain or expand market shares since the liberalization of banking in the 1990s and the financial crisis in 2008.

The structure of this chapter is as follows. First, antecedents to alternative banking are reviewed in ancient Roman financial statecraft, early Christian fund management, and social and pawn banking in medieval and early modern times. Second, we explore the early history of savings banks in two periods. The first is the consolidation of savings and pawn foundations of religious orders into the first savings banks such as the Monti di Pieta in Naples (1463) and, by grant from the republic of Siena, the Monte dei Paschi di Siena (1472). The second period is that of the founding of savings banks throughout Northern Europe in the late eighteenth and early nineteenth centuries. We then turn to the creation of credit cooperatives across Europe, beginning in responses to crop failures in 1845–6 and the 1848 economic crisis.

The fourth section examines the crowding out of savings banks and cooperative banks by postal banks that were created by central governments in the latter nineteenth century. Official postal savings banks grew rapidly through the use of postal branch office networks and served as a new channel for central government finance that bypassed parliaments. The final section reviews the emergence of development banks (special purpose banks) in France, Germany and other late developing nations as central agents for industrialization.

A historical perspective indicates how alternative banks developed specific organizational solutions to agency risks, transaction costs, liability risk and other matters at the core of banking. Savings banks emerged with strong roots in local communities, political movements and public agencies. Cooperative banks were created by the Raiffeisen and Schulze-Delitzsch social and religious movements. Savings banks and credit cooperatives thereby acquired powerful competitive advantages in terms of retail networks and relational banking in local communities. Independent local savings banks and cooperative banks then created a second tier of shared joint operations for giro payments and other wholesale banking services to reduce costs, achieve economies of scale and manage risks.[1] The social missions of savings banks and cooperative banks also sustained socially oriented corporate cultures and long-term profit sustainability orientations that helped to manage risks and avert losses in capital markets.

The lean organizational structure of development banks created by continental European governments provided a different competitive advantage. Without expensive branch office networks or large staff and operational costs, and with cheap access to official savings or other capital at low or zero cost, special purpose banks were able to direct credit to strategic economic sectors at below market rates, a powerful comparative advantage for continental European policymakers and governments.[2] Special purpose banks reduced the cost of policies for governments and helped alleviate fiscal constraints.

Four groups of theories about alternative banking history inform this chapter. The first is social economy. For theories of social economy, savings banks and cooperative banks were founded to help poor farmers and urban residents not served by private and commercial banks. Special purpose banks were founded as agents of national or regional development and financiers of public policy. Alternative banks therefore differ fundamentally from joint-stock private banks. The missions, governance and performance of alternative banks are not designed to maximize profits. They are designed to assist those excluded from banking. From the perspective of social economy, savings banks and cooperative banks should therefore be evaluated by the degree to which they help excluded groups accumulate savings and obtain credit, finance and banking services. Special purpose banks should be evaluated by how they contribute to development.

In terms of history, theories of social banking mirror Polanyi's focus on social reactions of self-defence against free markets.[3] Polanyi describes how British policies in the 1830s (enclosures, the poor law and free banking) overturned traditional institutions to transform land, labour and money into commodities for free exchange. His argument about social reactions of self-defence in the latter nineteenth century is of special interest. Polanyi describes how agricultural tariffs, labour unions and central banks were social reactions of self-defence against the imposition of markets in the late nineteenth century, especially after the 1873 depression. Polanyi did not refer to alternative banks. However, savings banks and cooperative banks also were social reactions of self-defence against markets, albeit earlier than the late nineteenth century. The dates differ. However, Polanyi's argument about social economy holds. Savings banks and cooperative banks were founded as reactions of social self-defence in the late eighteenth and early nineteenth centuries.

The second theory about alternative banks is that of political capture. Savings banks and cooperative banks were founded with social missions. However, once these institutions obtained substantial market shares of banking, their liabilities and assets, policies and investment capacity attracted the attention of monarchs and politicians. Italian savings and pawn banks were used in the eighteenth century to finance war and defeat revolutions. Postal banks were used in the 1890s and 1900s to finance imperialism and war. Savings banks and cooperative banks helped mobilize savings to purchase government bonds and finance World Wars I and II. In the 1920s and 1930s, fascist and falangist movements and governments took over cooperative banks and savings banks. Political capture haunts the history of alternative banks. However, the worst abuses occurred because of nationalism, xenophobia, fascism and war rather than democracy.

A third group of theories about alternative banks comes from banking theory proper. Banking theory clarifies how alternative banks must perform adequately as banks to realize their social and public policy missions. Banking theory often provides powerful micro-explanations for why alternative banks succeed or fail. Fundamentals from banking theory about asset and liability management, corporate governance, balance sheet mismatch, credit portfolios and liquidity risk therefore inform this chapter. Further concepts about agency costs, transaction costs and bank governance also help describe why alternative banks, as banks, have often proved superior to private commercial and investment banks.

Fourth, emphasis on the institutional foundations of competitive advantage in comparative political economy extends the analysis beyond banks to describe how broader social, political and public policy settings are critical for alternative banks. To date, most research in this approach of new institutionalism has focused on firms, not banks. Nonetheless, concepts and theories about institutional foundations and firms help explain how savings banks, cooperative banks and special purpose banks have realized competitive advantages over private banks. Because of the greater trust of clients, consumers and depositors, alternative banks are able to manage liability risk and avert runs on deposits better than private banks. Because of their presence in social and political networks and government policymaking, alternative banks retain powerful competitive advantages in relational and retail banking. The small central offices of special purpose banks provide cost advantages over private banks with large bureaucracies and branch office networks. And while savings banks and cooperative banks remain independent local and regional banks, they reduce costs, achieve scale and improve control of risks and management by sharing wholesale operations.

Four theories about alternative banking help explain the diverse and complex phenomena encountered in the histories of these institutions. However, before turning to savings banks, cooperative banks and special purpose banks, a look back at antecedents of social and public banking is in order.

Credit and Banking in Ancient Greece and Rome

A brief consideration of banking and credit in ancient Greece and Rome clarifies the classical references for the social missions and structures of alternative banks that emerged in the late medieval and early modern periods. Classical studies also focus almost exclusively on private banking. Nonetheless, evidence of the *social and political* character of banking and credit appears in primary and secondary sources on ancient Rome and the early Christian church.[4] Observations from Plutarch and Tertullian on financial statecraft, and Sallust and Livy on the abolition of debt bondage, suggest that the economics of banking and credit relations were understood by the classics.[5] However, credit, banking and finance were also considered as political and social phenomena and objects of financial statecraft. Early Christians also ran savings and pawn banks far earlier than standard histories of banking suggest. Alternative banking can thus trace traditions, policies and practices back to Roman financial statecraft and early Christian charity and savings banks.

Evidence is tangential from ancient Greece. Indeed, for Plato,[6] credit in the sense of formal agreements to transfer property rights for money or goods was abhorrent because it implied a lack of trust. Hesiod refers to loans of seeds and implements by peasants,[7] while Theophratus describes lending of small sums and household objects by city dwellers.[8] Demosthenes mentions borrowing by citizens to cope with bad times and crises. Aristophenes[9] and Plutarch[10] refer to substantial cash loans between the wealthy to support elite lifestyles. Standard accounts of ancient economic history suggested that banking was unimportant in ancient Greece and Athens.[11] However, recent research has reversed this view to suggest that *private* banking was indeed central for commerce and trade. Remarkably, Cohen justifies this focus by stating that private banks were not 'merely pawnbrokers'.[12] This begs the question of how pawnbrokers (a precursor of alternative banking) were, in fact, organized in ancient times.

In a broader sense, debt is central to classic and contemporary accounts of change in ancient society. From the Solonic crisis in Athens through late antiquity, creditors and debtors were often critical social groups that decided the fate of sieges and/or revolutions. Few events are cited more often in Athenian history than Solon's abolition of debt peonage and imprisonment. The Roman *Lex Petelia de Nexis* (326 BC) also prohibited imprisonment for debt. The debts of elites in ancient Rome are also widely cited as causes of crises and conspiracies. The debt crisis of 49 BC on the eve of civil war and the Catiline revolution-conspiracy are perhaps the most important examples. Debates about abusive interest rates also pervade Roman sources.

The political and social economy of debt was also central to classical policy. Accounts of Roman financial statecraft describe imperial management of debts and interest payments as matters of politics and social economy. For example, Plutarch praises Lucullus for policies adopted in near Asian cities that radically intervened to 'haircut' accumulated debts.[13] In ancient Rome, unless controlled, interest rates and debts may alter the legitimacy of imperial governance and the social fabric of cities. Imperial financial statecraft is thereby reference and antecedent for alternative banking and money management, a tradition that balances understanding of money and markets with understanding of political imperatives and social context. However, the most important antecedent of alternative banking in ancient societies is the emergence of savings banks as part of charitable organizations in the early Christian church.

Christian Charity and Savings Banks in the Early Church

Roots of alternative banking can be found in the practices of savings, charity and fund management in the early church. For Christians, the accumulation of treasuries was not a matter of imperial financial statecraft but instead a question of charity. Tertullian describes church finance as follows:

> Though we have our treasure-chest, it is not made up of purchase money, as if our religion had its price. On the regular day in the month, or when one prefers, each one makes a small donation; but only if it be his pleasure, and only if he be able; for no one is compelled, but gives voluntarily. These gifts are, as it were, piety's deposit fund. For they are taken thence and spent, not on feasts and drinking-bouts, and thankless eating-houses, but to support and bury poor people, to supply the wants of boys and girls destitute of means and parents, and of old persons confined to the house, likewise the shipwrecked, and if there happen to be any in the mines, or banished to the islands, or shut up in the prisons for nothing but their fidelity to the cause of God's Church, they become the nurslings of their confession.[14]

The accumulation of funds by early Christian church groups had a social role.[15] Evidence is short from ancient Greece and Rome about the social and political realities of banking, savings and finance. However, historical records of the early church suggest that banking was part of the social mission of the church from very early on.[16] Later, evidence improves to clarify how social banking remained part of medieval and early modern Europe.

Medieval Origins of Alternative Banking

The organization of pawn banks and savings banks by religious orders coincides with the emergence of commercial and merchant banking in Europe.[17] In 1463 the Bank of Naples was created through consolidation of eight pawn and savings institutions run separately by religious orders.[18] In 1472 the magistrates of Siena formalized rural statutes and credit relations as the Monte di Pietà savings and pawn bank. Pawn and savings banks emerged throughout Italy during the fifteenth and sixteenth centuries. Local public authorities created pawnbrokers in 1402 in Velletri and 1428 in Arcevia, followed by *forty* such institutions in central Italy and 'Bologna 1473; Savona 1479; Milan and Genoa 1483; etc. and south (Lecce 1520, Naples 1539, Caserta 1548, etc.)'.[19] At first, most *monte di pietà* accepted money deposits without paying interest. And as philanthropic institutions, early savings and pawn banks received endowments from charitable contributions and indulgences.[20] Restrictions also applied to loans such as local residence, pawn deposits as collateral at 9 per cent interest per year (in the case of Savona in accord with Franciscan order recommendations, despite canon law) and sale of pawned goods at public auction in case on non-payment. Zalin reports that the Monte de Pietà of Padua provided non-interest loans under 30 soldi, but charged 5 per cent for loans above this amount.[21] In 1515 Pope Leo X permitted interest charges to cover costs of savings and pawn banks and promoted the creation of these institutions in Italy and beyond to compete with moneylenders.

Savings and pawn banks emerged across medieval Italy as the consolidation or expansion of charitable institutions of the church. Recent research dates the development of *monte di pietà* during the fifteenth and sixteenth centuries alongside the development of merchant banking and commercial banking in Italy – well before the emergence of modern banking in Northern Europe.[22] The *monte di pietà* were encouraged by the church, despite concerns about usury, because the endowments and savings held by these institutions sustained operations and provided viable alternatives to moneylenders, often Jewish, that dominated pawn services and savings and credit in medieval Italy. By the seventeenth and eighteenth centuries, *monte di pietà* had accumulated significant capital reserves and large deposit bases and became important sources for mortgage lending and public finance. For example, the Bank of Naples became the primary source for lending to elites and to the King of Naples for the defeat of revolts during the eighteenth century, most markedly the 1799 revolution.[23]

Savings Banks

The second period in the development of alternative banking begins with the founding of savings banks in the late eighteenth and early nineteenth centuries across Northern Europe. Savings banks were created by local public agencies and social and religious movements.[24] Savings banks left a written record of founding ideas, social missions, organizational strategies, balance sheets and the social composition of clients. These institutions grew to obtain large market shares of banking in many European countries during the nineteenth century and remain central to social and political economy thereafter.

Monte di pietà in southern Europe inspired Huges Delestre to propose a French *mont de piété* in 1611.[25] Similar plans in England also failed to materialize. Instead, the first savings bank in Northern Europe was founded in Brunswick (1765), while Hamburg created an administrative savings bank in 1778.

Table 1.1: Founding dates of European savings banks.

1765: Brunswick, Germany	1812: Scwyz, Aarau and Neuchatel, Switzerland
1778: Hamburg, Germany	1816: Kilkenny, Ireland; Karlsruhe, Sleswick and Baden, Germany; Philadelphia, USA
1786: Oldenburg, Germany; Bern, Switzerland	1817: Haarlem, Netherlands; Gliiksburg and Lubeck, Germany
1789: Geneva, Switzerland	1818: Paris, France; Berlin, Stuttgart, Brieg and Apenrade, Germany
1796: Kiel, Germany	1819: Vienna, Austria
1801: Tottenham, Scotland; Göttingen and Altona, Germany	1820–1: Goteborg and Stockholm, Sweden
1805: Zurich, Switzerland	1820: Llubljana, Slovenia
1806: Lauf, Switzerland	1822-3: Pádua and Milan, Italy
1809: Basel, Switzerland	1825: Tournai, Belgium
1810: Ruthwell, Scotland	1838: Madrid, Spain
1810: Holsteinborg, Denmark	1844: Lisbon, Portugal
1811: St Gallen, Switzerland	1853: Luxembourg

Source: J. Mura (ed.), *History of European Savings Banks* (Stuttgart: Sparkassenverlag, 1996).

Table 1.1 indicates how savings banks quickly spread throughout Northern Europe after 1800. The first savings banks were often philanthropic entities or benevolent associations and linked to Protestant or Catholic churches. Later, savings banks tended to be created within municipal administrative entities or as municipal corporations backed by legal guarantee of operations. District savings banks (*Kassen der Kreiskommunalverbande*) were created first in Prussia and then throughout German states by district associations that pooled guarantees from local governments.

During the nineteenth century, savings banks accumulated savings, credit portfolios and reserves to become central players in banking throughout German states.[26] Table 1.2 reports the evolution of *Sparkasse* savings banks in German states and cities. From 1839 to 1913, the increase from 85 to 1,765 *Sparkasse* savings banks, with over 14 million savings accounts holding over 13 billion marks, indicates how local and regional savings banks emerged to become one of three pillars of the banking system in Germany.[27]

Table 1.2: Evolution of German savings banks, 1839–1913.

Year	Banks	Offices	Accounts	Per 100 residents	Balance*	Avg. balance	Balance per cap. pop.
1839	85				18		1.24
1845	157				38		2.37
1850	234		278,147		54	195.4	3.29
1855	323		423,542		97	228.7	5.60
1865	517		919,513		268	291.3	13.80
1875	1,005		2,209,101	8.6	1,112	503.4	43.20
1885	1,318	1,485	4,209,453	14.8	2,261	537.1	79.50
1895	1,493	2,448	6,876,664	21.5	4,345	631.9	136.30
1900	1,490	2,828	8,670,709	25.1	5,746	662.6	166.40
1910	1,711	4,619	12,900,304	32.1	11,107	860.1	276.20
1913	1,765	5,268	14,417,642	34.2	13,111	909.4	311.40

* Balance = million marks, avg. and per cap. pop. balance = marks.

Source: H. E. Büshegen, *Zeitgeschichtliche Problemfeder des Bankwesens de Bundesrepublik Deutschland* (Frankfurt: M. Knapp, 1983), p. 199.

Sparkasse savings banks were designed with social missions and mandates to contribute to the improvement of lower and middle classes. Credit was to be directed to the same classes that deposited savings.[28] Legal mandates reaffirmed the social mission of savings banks throughout the nineteenth century. However, two developments cast doubts about the ability of savings banks to fulfil social mandates. First, the influx of large deposits was seen as usurpation of these institutions by middle and upper classes and capitalists in search of safe, often guaranteed deposits. Second, the investments of *Sparkasse* savings banks appear to have often strayed beyond lending to the lower and middle classes, becoming important sources for small and medium businesses and government bonds and public finance.

Early in the twentieth century, debate ensued about whether savings banks had strayed from their social missions to become deposit banks for the middle class and capitalists.[29] Evidence turned on the evolution of the average value of savings deposits over time. In 1908 Seidel calculated the increase of the average value of deposits at *Sparkasse* savings banks from 195.4 to 909.4 marks in the period 1850–1913 to see if this increase can be explained by compound interest over time or, instead, by an increase in the values deposited.[30] For Seidel, 909.4 marks remained just *below* the 925.82 marks that would have accumulated exclusively from compound interest of 2.5 per cent per year from 1850 to 1913. Moreover, if, on average, depositors were to deposit an additional 20 marks of savings per year 1851–1913, this would bring the average balance of savings accounts to 3,916.3 marks, well above the 909.4 mark average reported in 1913. Seidel concludes that *Sparkasse* savings banks continued to serve workers, farmers and the urban poor rather than being dominated by larger depositors from the middle and upper middle classes or capitalists. Chapter 6 traces the evolution of German *Sparkasse* savings banks and discusses these institutions' role as one of the three pillars in German banking today.

Cooperative Banks

Credit cooperatives were created by Raiffeisen and Schulze-Delitzsch social movements in German provinces to support rural workers in the wake of crop failures and potato blight in 1846–7 and economic crisis in the following years.[31] Table 1.3 reports the evolution and basic business model of credit cooperatives in Germany from 1860 to 1920. The increase in the number of cooperatives (133–1245), members (31,603–746,058) and accumulation of assets (66 million–1.7 trillion marks in 1915) and credit (61 million–1.2 trillion marks in 1915) as well as savings deposits, interbank deposits and member balances and reserves suggest the traditional composition of alternative bank balance sheets and the basic functions of deposits and loans and the gradual accumulation of reserves and balances due members. The data also suggests how a large number of local credit cooperatives first emerged as simple retail deposit-taking and loan-making institutions. For example, interbank lending appears only in 1870.

Table 1.3: Evolution of German credit cooperatives, 1860–1920, in million marks.

Year	Number	Members	Assets	Credit	Savings deposits	Inter-bank deposits	Member balance	Reserves
1860	133	31,603			7		1	0
1865	498	169,595	66	61	53		13	1
1870	740	314,656	187	166	131	7	40	4
1875	815	418,251	432	390	317	13	84	8
1880	905	460,656	493	438	353	11	102	16
1885	896	458,080	544	467	390	12	108	22
1890	1,072	518,003	620	538	438	16	117	28
1895	1,068	525,748	666	569	454	13	126	38

Year	Number	Members	Assets	Credit	Savings deposits	Inter-bank deposits	Member balance	Reserves
1900	870	511,061	806	672	586	24	133	45
1905	921	539,993	1,109	899	836	23	166	66
1910	939	600,387	1,477	1,202	1,084	31	216	94
1915	941	601,395	1,754	1,212	1,319	23	231	121
1920	1,245	746,058	7,158	4,026	6,480		391	164

Source: Deutsche Bundesbank, *Deutsches Geld- und Bankwesen in Zahlen 1876–1975* (Frankfurt: Deutsche Bundesbank, 1976), pp. 344–5.

The growth of local credit cooperatives with traditional deposit-taking loan-making balance sheets provided the basis for subsequent creation of wholesale giro operations shared by cooperatives, a development that would remain a profound competitive advantage of cooperative networks. Unlike private banks forced to maintain both retail and wholesale networks, local and regional credit cooperatives in Germany shared the cost and reaped the benefits of central giro and other wholesale activities in specially created institutions with stakeholder governance structures and the corporate cultures of alternative banking. The single Prussian central cooperative bank served to centralize giro transactions, currency exchange, securities, inter-bank credit and other instruments across credit cooperatives in Germany, reaching over a billion marks on balance sheets by 1920. A full forty-six other central banking operations were created by networks of credit cooperatives in other German provinces, summing up to 472 million marks on balance sheets by 1920.

Data collected by the Bundesbank from 1876 to 1976 and additional sources going further back in time indicate the evolution of alternative banking business models. These models provide sound references for sustainable social banking relevant today. Although at odds with concepts from market-based banking and private, shareholder-oriented corporate governance principles based on shareholders and separation of management from ownership, the evolution of basic categories of social banking reveal simple, stable and viable strategies of social banking that retain solid deposit bases (that reduce liquidity risk and funding costs) and *shared* wholesale operations that reduce costs for independent local and regional savings banks and cooperative banks. Shared second-tier operations provide economies of scale and reduce costs while retaining local relational banking and institutional foundations of competitive advantage in social and political networks.

Official Postal Savings Banks

Savings banks and cooperative banks were founded by local public authorities and social and religious movements. Once established, the funds of these institutions attracted attention from central governments that created official postal savings banks to compete with regional and local alternative banks. In 1840 this already struck Alexis de Tocqueville as a dangerous development:

> In some countries these benevolent associations [savings banks] are still completely distinct from the state; but in almost all they manifestly tend to identify themselves with the government; and in some of them the government has superseded them, taking upon itself the enormous task of centralizing in one place, and putting out at interest on its own responsibility, the daily savings of many millions of the working classes. Thus the State draws to itself the wealth of the rich by loans, and has the poor man's mite at its disposal in the savings banks.[32]

The trajectories of savings banks, cooperative banks and postal savings banks and different national experiences will require further research. However, a review of the secondary literature and data collected by the US National Monetary Commission in 1910 permits comparison of alternative bank change in major European countries and colonies before 1913.[33] We infer the following:

1. Official postal banks tended to crowd out previous bottom-up cooperatives and regional and/or local savings banks by offering higher interest rates on savings deposits.
2. Deposits of alternative banks, but especially postal banks, became a source of public and war finance.
3. National experiences differed. In Britain, France and Italy, official postal savings banks appear to have crowded out local savings banks. However, the Prussian Savings Bank Association vetoed creation of a similar national postal bank.

The value of deposits and the number of depositors in postal savings banks in European countries and colonies from 1862 to 1909 suggest the importance of these institutions. The first postal savings bank was founded in the UK in 1862. By 1908 deposits reached over US$781 million equivalent and the number of accounts over 11 million (see Table 1.4). Postal savings banks were also founded in Belgium (1870), Japan (1875), Italy (1876), the Netherlands (1881), France (1882), Austria (1883), Sweden (1884) and Hungary (1886), as well as in the colonies: Australia (1863), Canada (1868), New Zealand (1867), New South Wales (1871), British India (1876), Ceylon (1885) and the Philippines (1906).

Table 1.4 reports the number of branch offices, the number of depositors and the value of deposits at the first year of recorded operations and in 1909 for ten European countries and five British colonies. Further analysis will be required. However, the substantial increases universally recorded suggest that central governments may have crowded out local savings banks and cooperative banks. The large number of branch offices also suggests the institutional breadth and reach of postal savings bank points of sale. In the UK, postal savings bank offices reached over 15,000 by 1907, with other European governments recording similar branch office networks in per capita terms.

Table 1.4: Postal savings banks in ten countries and five colonies, 1862–1909.

Country, founding date	Year	Branch offices	Depositors	Deposits (US$)
UK, 1862	1862	2,535	178,495	8,264,392
	1908	15,239	11,018,251	781,794,533
Russia, 1889	1893	2,626	240,000	14,471,500
	1907	4,471	1,788,990	128,873,169
Italy, 1876	1876	1,989	57,354	471,577
	1908	8,735	4,981,920	290,808,886
Belgium, 1870	1870		4,416	171,985
	1908		2,200,541	141,711,824
Netherlands, 1881	1881	909	22,831	345,166
	1910	1,463	1,462,615	64,490,082
Japan, 1875	1875		1,843	7,582
	1909		8,815,436	53,070,016
Austria, 1883	1883	3,219	352,886	1,624,707
	1908	6,614	2,106,539	46,009,897
France, 1872	1882	6,024	211,580	9,187,116
	1908	7,938	5,291,673	296,964,867
Hungary, 1886	1886	2,000	85,517	572,683
	1908	4,425	684,299	18,803,991
Sweden, 1884	1884	1,575	79,513	221,808
	1908	3,180	560,270	12,441,249
Canada, 1868	1868	81	2,102	204,588
	1909	1,102	155,895	45,190,484
New Zealand, 1867	1867	46	2,156	346,485
	1909	563	359,714	61,561,123
New South Wales, 1871	1871	53	952	69,236
	1909	603	334,381	64,684,625
Australia, 1863	1863	10	1,379	12,103
	1910	142	77,165	16,498,126
Ceylon, 1885	1885	49	2,193	9,835
	1909	160	79,704	794,135

Source: National Monetary Commission, 'Notes on the Postal Savings-Bank Systems of the Leading Countries' (Washington, DC: Government Printing Office, 1910), pp. 34–51.

While postal savings banks were created by central governments well after the establishment of local savings banks and local cooperative banks, they nonetheless grew rapidly by offering higher interest rates on savings through their large retail networks in postal offices. In the UK, the number of accounts in postal office savings banks increased to over 11 million, while the number of accounts at traditional trustee savings banks remained below 2 million from 1880 to 1908. The value held in savings banks mirrored this crowding out, with postal office savings accounts surpassing 200 million pounds sterling while savings deposits hovered around 50 million pounds sterling 1880–1909.

In France a similar process occurred of crowding out ordinary savings banks (*caisses d'épargne ordinaires*) by a new network of national savings banks (*caisses d'épargne nationales*).[34] Founded in 1872, French national savings banks grew, by 1908, to 7,938 branch offices, 5.29 million passbook savings accounts and US$296.9 million equivalent in deposits. In comparison, ordinary local and regional savings banks retained just 2,000 outlets and below 1 million passbook savings accounts.[35] Comparing deposits also confirms the crowding out of ordinary savings banks by the new national network of savings banks. Deposits held at regional and local *caisses d'épargne ordinaires* reached 2 million francs in 1883, but declined thereafter to under 500,000 francs for most of the period to 1906. In comparison, deposits placed in passbooks at the central Caisse d'épargne nationale increased 1870–8 to over 1 billion francs, then peaked in 1884 at over 2 billion francs.

The French postal savings bank soon became critical for central government finance. Funds from the *caisses d'épargne nationales* reached 50 per cent of all French government receipts by 1882, peaking at 94 per cent of government receipts in 1899. The French national government postal savings bank confirms the UK experience of providing substantial resources for central governments purchase of bonds and securities, in this case Crédit Foncier bonds and deposits from savings accounts held at the Bank of France and Treasury.

Chapter 6 in this volume explores the different trajectory of alternative banks in German states. The crowding out of cooperative banks and local savings banks appears to have occurred, but on a lower scale because the Prussian savings bank association vetoed legislation to create an official postal savings bank in 1885 and 1905. However, the creation of imperial Prussian federal cooperatives for agriculture in 1892 appears to have crowded out local and Schulze-Delitzsch cooperatives in a manner similar to the experiences of the UK and France.[36] By 1906 members in official credit cooperatives surpassed 1 million, while the number of members in Schulze-Delitzsch credit cooperatives remained below 600,000. However, the value of deposits held by Schulze-Delitzsch credit cooperatives grew to over 180 million marks by 1906, far more than the 20 million marks held in official cooperatives, with similar trends for credit provided by these institutions.

In general, postal savings banks offered higher interest rates than other alternative banks to attract funds and held government bonds that the market refused. The British postal office savings bank thereby soon ate up capital reserves and produced losses. This attracted significant attention from the press and Parliament, especially after deficits were reported in 1900.[37] Postal savings bank losses were explained by members of a Parliamentary Commission and observers as a mismatch of returns from investments in government bonds (imposed on the bank by Prime Ministers without parliamentary approval). Moreover, removal of a cap on the size of deposits in 1893 produced an influx of large deposits that increased liquidity risk. According to the 1858 Select Committee on Securities: 'It thus appears that large financial operations have been carried on by means of the capital of savings banks, which was at the command of the Exchequer, in purchasing, selling and varying securities'.[38] Gladstone clarified the consequences:

> This deficiency (the postal bank deficit), in truth, is a concealed portion of the National Debt, of which the House takes no cognizance in the course of its ordinary proceedings, and it is never brought before it as a portion of the national obligations.[39]

Balance sheets further deteriorated when government bonds paid less. Benchmark UK consol bonds had for some time paid 3 per cent interest. However, during the 1880s they declined to 2.5 per cent, the same interest rate paid on savings deposits by the postal savings bank.

For Prime Minister William Gladstone, the creation of the UK postal savings bank was designed to increase the power of finance ministers in money markets:

> It was necessary to provide for the savings of people with safety, cheapness and convenience ... Behind this I had an object of first rate importance which has been attained, to provide the Minister of Finance with a strong financial arm, and to secure his independence of the City by giving him a large and certain command of money.[40]

The large deposits of the postal savings bank were critical for the government to reduce the interest rates paid by government bonds. However, this left a vast sum of non-liquid, non-marketable bonds in the portfolio of the post bank. And interest rates on bonds were not sufficient to meet obligation to savings depositors. The UK postal savings bank thereby reported losses of 11 million pounds sterling in 1902.

A debate ensued in Parliament that remains relevant today. For Lord Monteagle, Chancellor of the Exchequer in 1835–9 and author of the 1858 Select Committee Report on Savings Banks, the savings bank model is flawed because deposits flow into the bank during good times (when asset prices are high) but flow out during bad times (forcing the bank to liquidate assets when prices are low). Seidel differs about savings banks in business cycles:

A close scrutiny of the oscillation of deposits reveals the fact that there is always a counterbalance between the large and small deposits. At times of economic prosperity wages rise, and small deposits are predominant, since the large capitalists then find investments in commerce and industry more remunerative. Contrariwise, economic depression brings large idle funds into the savings banks and checks the small savings.[41]

This cuts to the question of counter-cyclical lending that is reviewed in Chapter 3. Recent econometric evidence suggests that Seidel may have been correct: alternative banks appear to be counter-cyclical in comparison to the pro-cyclical behaviour of private banks.

In sum, savings banks and cooperative banks were created by local governments and movements to address the social question. After they grew to substantial market shares during the nineteenth century, central governments tapped into popular savings through postal savings banks. The variety of national experiences with these three types of alternative banks will require further research. However, evidence of crowding out local savings banks and cooperative banks by central government postal banks appears to confirm the warning of Tocqueville cited above.

Special Purpose Banks

Special purpose or development banks describe a variety of institutions that financed infrastructure and industrialization across continental Europe, Asia, Latin America and other developing nations.[42] Governments created special purpose banks to provide finance and credit on terms beyond the reach of private banks or markets, reversing the causal direction later asserted by theories of financial repression.[43] It is because private banks avoided long-term investments in infrastructure that continental European governments founded development banks in the nineteenth century.[44] The Crédit Mobilier in France soon became the model abroad and a shareholder in other development banks as its ability to finance railroads became acknowledged.[45] In turn, development banks in Europe became models for institutions such as the Industrial Bank of Japan and Industrial Bank of India.[46] Development banks continued to respond to the challenges of the twentieth century. They were founded after World War I to provide cash, subsidized loans and guarantee of private bank bonds for industrial reconstruction.[47] After World War II the Kreditanstalt für Wiederaufbau (Reconstruction Credit Agency, KfW) and Japan Development Bank were created to channel Allied funds for reconstruction. Newly independent countries in Africa and Asia also created development banks after World War II to channel World Bank loans and foreign aid.[48] German and Japanese development banks continued to adopt new policies and strategies as development challenges evolved. In the twenty-first century, old concepts of development have been replaced by new theories of environmental sustainability and community development. And while development banks were seen as restricted to continental Europe, the UK green investment bank was capitalized with 3 billion pounds sterling to operate as a special purpose bank. The chapter on BRICs in this volume also suggests the critical role of development banks in shaping the widely noted levels of growth in these countries and their importance in providing counter-cyclical credit since the crisis hit these economies in 2008.

Like most matters of banking and finance, development banks have their critics. Cummings-Woo summarizes three problems with development banks.[49] First, development banks tend to leverage large industrial groups with bank credit. This leads firms to avert going public through issues of equities. Second, the massive scale of political and economic interests associated with development banks often increases moral hazard and requires costly bailouts. Development banks can protect outmoded industry, impede innovation and sustain bad equilibrium. Large-scale development projects are also notorious for their impact on the environment. Finally, development banks may unfairly transfer the cost of risk either through inflationary finance that monetizes industrial losses or through government infusions of equity that hide losses in government accounts.

Development banks therefore inspire diametrically opposed and essentially contested views of government intervention, banks and markets, and differences between old and new theories of development. For critics, development banks reproduce financial repression, favour rent seeking and unfairly subsidize industry. Their centralized technocratic decisions tend to remain beyond public scrutiny and may have profound environmental impacts. Development banking also presents difficulties for international trade negotiations. Unfortunately, despite their large size and importance in advanced and developing countries, development and special purpose banks have nonetheless failed to attract in-depth case studies and independent academic research. Notwithstanding the need for further research, the financial statements of special purpose banks suggest the competitive advantages of these institutions over private banks. The lean central offices of special purpose banks and their access to capital at low cost (through official deposits or capitalization or issue of bonds guaranteed by governments) combine to produce operational costs at or below half the levels reported by benchmark private banks. The chapters in Part II of the present volume explore this competitive advantage of development banks in advanced and developing countries.

Conclusion

This chapter has reviewed primary and secondary materials on the history of savings banks, cooperative banks and special purpose banks to clarify how alternative banks acquired institutional foundations of competitive advantage over private banks. The four theories about alternative banking presented at the outset of this chapter – social economy, political capture, banking theory and the new institutionalism in comparative political economy – all provide explanations of phenomena encountered in the history of alternative banks. Savings banks and cooperative banks remit to traditions of social economy that we trace back to ancient societies and medieval Europe to inform founding missions in the late eighteenth and early nineteenth centuries. These traditions of social banking are especially important for reassessing banking in the twenty-first century, given the disregard of alternative banks by Marxists and liberals alike for much of the twentieth century. Although we have not fully reviewed the place of savings banks, cooperative banks and special purpose banks in the democracies of Europe and developing countries, a historical perspective suggests that theories of political capture should emphasize experiences of authoritarianism, nationalism and imperialism and consider that transparency and accountability under democratization may decrease political capture.

Banking theory presents perhaps the most important perspective to be brought to studies of alternative banking. While alternative banks and banking sectors are often large enough to influence the meso and macro levels of regional and national trajectories, the micro focus of banking theory and the clarity brought to analysis of bank balance sheets and performance provide a rich series of concepts and measures for case studies and comparisons.

The new institutionalism in political economy provides similar opportunities for analysis of alternative banks, but captures more than concepts and theories from banking theory by placing alternative banks in a broader context of local, regional and national contexts of communities, societies, politics and public policy. Comparative political economy analysis of advanced economies seems particularly amiss in ignoring the importance of alternative banking sectors as a fundamental difference between liberal- and coordinated-market economies. While mutual savings banks, savings trusts and cooperative banks were largely replaced by private banking in the UK and US, alternative banks retain large market shares in coordinated market economies and in many developing countries, especially the largest ones.

These four theoretical approaches control for alternative explanations to reinforce the core arguments presented in this volume. The history of alternative banking reveals a wealth of evidence about how these institutions served as agents for social inclusion, acquired competitive advantages, and provided policy options for local, regional and national governments. Experiences of capture and mismanagement clarify these characteristics as social constructions subject to reversal rather than prove that privatization or demutualization is required.

2 THE COMPARATIVE PERFORMANCE OF ALTERNATIVE BANKS BEFORE THE 2007–8 CRISIS

Olivier Butzbach and Kurt von Mettenheim

Introduction

As seen in Chapter 1, the long and rich history of 'alternative banks' has not ended in the 1980s but has taken a different turn. Since the liberalization of banking across Europe, domestic regulators and alternative bank managers have pursued a wide variety of policies and strategies. Some public savings banks, notably in France, opted for conversion into cooperatives. In Sweden, Belgium, Italy and Spain, savings banks were privatized. However, in Italy shares were granted to savings bank foundations designed to reaffirm and separate the traditional social role of savings banks from banking operations. And Spanish *Cajas de Ahorro* retain significant social mandates and regional and local corporate governance while competing with each other and private banks across regions. In Portugal, Ireland and Greece, alternative banks were modernized only to confront severe downturns since the 2008 crisis. German savings and cooperative banks retained their legal forms (mostly independent local or regional public companies) to consolidate and deepen wholesale networks and associations. In the Netherlands the Rabobank cooperative bank group declined during the 1990s, only to recover large market shares and globalize after 2000. This wide variety of policies, reforms and alternative bank strategies amidst the convergence of bank regulations under the European Community, single currency and revolution in information and communication technologies provides an exceptional quasi-experimental opportunity for further research and comparison. However, one phenomenon stands out: instead of declining or being replaced by more efficient joint-stock private banks and market-centred finance, alternative banks have reaffirmed their traditional business models, corporate behaviour and values, and modernized to retain or expand market share. In the following sections, we take a closer look at the strategies developed by savings banks, cooperative banks and development banks in reaction to market-centred reforms of the last decades, before examining the existing empirical evidence on the comparative performance of alternative banks before the 2007–8 crisis. The final section examines the consequences of the crisis on alternative banks in Europe and North America.

Shifts in Strategies

Savings Banks

Unlike the fiasco of savings and loan bankruptcies in the US in the 1980s and 1990s, local, regional and national savings bank groups still remain at the centre of domestic banking systems across Europe. For Carnevali, savings banks are part of a 'European Advantage' over the US and other countries without such institutions.[1] Far from being destined to fail in the face of pressures from private and foreign banks, savings banks have instead reformed, modernized, consolidated and adopted new strategies to compete in more open European banking, credit and finance markets.[2] They have also largely avoided the perils of financial market bubbles and crises, especially in comparison to private commercial and investment banks. Considered individually, local and regional credit institutions are often very small. However, as a whole they add up to a large part of political economy in most advanced economies. And since opening banking to competition during the 1990s, savings banks have maintained or *increased* market shares across Europe. In 2007 savings banks in Spain, Germany, Sweden and Austria held respectively 39, 34.8, 22 and 16.9 per cent of total banking assets.[3] In Germany, assets of independent *Sparkasse* savings banks (including *Landesbanken*) totalled 2,364 billion euros in 2009 (35.5 per cent of total German banking assets), making it the third largest banking group in the world (behind BNP and RBS). *Sparkassen* also held 38.7 per cent of bank deposits and 28.1 per cent of loans to non-financial firms in 2009. In 2008 Spanish savings banks, *Cajas de Ahorro*, held 50 per cent of deposits and 46.9 per cent of loans in the country.

Savings banks also remain important institutions in developing and emerging countries. Savings banks were an invention of the European Enlightenment; they are also a legacy of European colonization. Savings banks were critical for state formation after independence throughout Asia, Africa and the Middle East.[4] They remain so in the twenty-first century. Given the modernization of banking through the adoption of information technology, electronic and mobile banking, the recognition of microcredit and finance in development, and the importance of access to finance and banking services to alleviate poverty and promote social inclusion, it follows that large savings banks may provide important policy alternatives for developing countries. In many developing and emerging countries, very large public savings banks (often postal savings banks) have realized competitive advantages and provided policy alternatives even – and perhaps most importantly – in weak and failed states for public management, social inclusion and reconstruction after war and natural disasters. That is the case, for instance, of Brazil's *Caixa Economica Federal*, the country's third largest bank.

Cooperative Banks

Since the liberalization of banking in Europe, cooperative banks have modernized as well. They have restructured, merged local and/or regional cooperatives to reap economies of scale,[5] and broadened 'second-tier' wholesale divisions and operational networks to better offer banking, insurance, and financial products and services to members and clients. Cooperative banks have thereby retained or expanded market shares while seeking to sustain their business models of membership governance, profit sustainability and social missions. In 2009 the cooperative bank market share of lending to small businesses in Italy, France, Germany and the Netherlands ranged between 25 and 45 per cent.[6] Market shares of ATMs reached over 50 per cent in France and Austria and over 35 per cent in Germany and the Netherlands.[7]

Cooperative banks have also pursued a variety of new business strategies, such as wholesale banking, geographic expansion (even abroad), sale of shares on capital markets to capitalize new business lines, pursuit of non-member clients, adoption of profit incentives beyond traditional membership dividends, relaxation of membership rights and responsibilities, more strategic staff training, and education programmes and corporate communication strategies taken from private banking. Cooperative banks have also converged towards private bank accounting and reporting requirements and standards. These experiments may weaken traditional principles and operations. Further research is needed on how modernization has affected the traditional structures and missions of cooperative banks. However, in comparison to private banks, cooperative banks tend to offer standardized products and services and lower interest rates consistent with their socially oriented business model. They also seek to manage portfolios, investments and local business operations according to social mandates. Time series from central banks in Germany, Italy and France suggest that cooperative banks have retained or expanded market shares since the liberalization of industry in the 1980s–1990s and transition toward Basel Accord capital risk guidelines and International Financial Reporting Standards in the 2000s.

For many cooperative banks, the 2000 downturn in financial markets was a turning point as clients returned to more secure deposit and savings accounts. For example, the number of members in the Netherlands Rabobank had declined by half from a peak of 1,000,000 in 1980 to near 500,000 by 2000. However, from 2000–10 Rabobank membership increased to over 1,600,000.

Booming capital markets during the mid-2000s once again pressured cooperative banks by attracting members and clients away to more lucrative accounts
and investment funds offered by commercial and investment banks. However,
once again the 2008 crisis reversed this trend and produced another return to
basic banking. Since the 2008 crisis, members and clients appear to favour the
security of traditional large-scale cooperative bank networks and their social
models and missions over the greater risks, abuses and losses faced by private
banks and market-centred products and services.

Cooperative banks thereby remain one of three pillars in many European
banking systems, retaining between one-third and half the market shares of
banking. Broader branch office networks and better information about local
contexts have placed cooperative banks in a favourable position. The corporate governance principles of 'one member one vote' and the participation of
members in strategy, control, supervision and decision-making also provide an
advantage for cooperative banks in terms of self-regulation and risk assessment.
These characteristics led the Oliver Wyman consulting group to describe cooperative banks as 'customer champions' able to compete with private and foreign
banks since the liberalization of European banking.[8]

According to the Oliver Wyman study, the boundaries between cooperative
banks and commercial competitors are blurring because of reduced local autonomy, decreased reliance on members and customers for capital, and increased
organizational complexity. Moreover, the fundamental differences of the cooperative bank business model remain 'prone to attack' from media, regulators and
competitors that share a bias towards the private joint-stock bank model. The
'one member one vote' principle of governance, business model of profit sustainability, more cautious capital reserve policies, risk-averse, lower return business
strategies and broader independent regional and local branch office networks
remain anomalies for paradigms and perspectives based on private banking and
financial markets. Cooperative banks therefore remain subject to criticism and
competitive pressures. However, the Oliver Wyman report concludes by suggesting that the unique tiered organizational structure, information advantages,
sustainable dividend policies and positive images of cooperative banks provide
considerable competitive advantages able to counter lower profit margins, heavy
capital base and anomaly status.

Alternative banks hold a key role in many national banking systems. Table 2.1
provides an overview of selected statistics of savings banks and cooperative banks
from international associations, giving an indication of how important these institutions are across world regions. The total assets of reporting member institutions
of the World Savings Bank Institute and International Cooperative Bank Association amounted to over €13.4 billion in 2009 (by comparison, in 2009 the world's
largest twenty commercial banks had €24.3 billion in total assets).

Table 2.1: Summary statistics on savings and cooperative banks as of 2009.

Region (number of countries)	Banks	Employees	Assets (in € million)	Deposits (in € million)	Loans (in € million)
Sub-Saharan Africa (13)	13	5,365	1,647	1,282	359
Middle East and North Africa (3)	n/a	n/a	17,040	13,324	2,956
Europe and Central Asia (22)	4,572	5,242,527	11,306,824	5,336,572	6,227,091
South Asia (1)	1	n/a	18,803	8,294	1,573
East Asia (8)	114	256,545	643,506	396,040	151,443
North America (2)	487	339,947	1,320,196	395,460	440,571
Central and South America (8)	21	82,060	110,757	63,137	35,889
TOTAL	5,208	5,926,444	13,418,772	6,214,109	6,859,882

Source: World Savings Banks Institute and European Association of Cooperative Banks.

The Comparative Performance of Alternative Banks

Defying expectations, alternative banks averted the potentially devastating impact of the wave of regulatory reform in the 1980s–1990s. Through a variety of strategies, alternative banks have modernized, held their ground, maintaining or gaining market shares, especially in retail banking (deposits, savings accounts and lending to firms and households). Alternative banks have also outperformed private, for-profit banks in terms of profitability and efficiency. A growing empirical literature documents this superior performance in comparative perspective (see Table 2.2 in the Appendix of this chapter for a review),[9] building on, first, a tradition of studies in the structure-conduct-performance literature and, second, a more recent body of works on the links between ownership and performance in banking.[10] Most of this literature deals with European and North American banks and is focused on savings and cooperative banks rather than development banks. As Cornett et al. argue,[11] there is virtually no study investigating the link between bank-level government ownership and bank performance.[12] Indeed, the seminal (but very questionable) studies by La Porta et al.[13] and Barth et al.[14] focus on countrywide data on government ownership and its impact on financial development and growth.

The empirical studies reviewed in the following sections help explain how, in the past three decades and especially just before and during the 2007–8 crisis, alternative banks outperformed their commercial peers in terms of cost-efficiency, profitability and stability.

Cost-Efficiency

Overall, cooperative and savings banks are found to be as or more cost-efficient than their commercial competitors. In one recent study, Ayadi et al. show that European savings banks are as cost-efficient as commercial banks,[15] while the situation is a bit less clear concerning European cooperative banks: Ayadi et al. find that while German cooperatives might be slightly less cost-efficient, French, Italian and Spanish cooperative banks are largely more cost-efficient than their commercial peers.[16] This result is in line with Iannotta et al.'s findings that across fifteen European countries (but with a small sample of 181 large banks), government-owned and cooperative banks are more cost-efficient.[17] Altunbaş et al. find slightly higher cost-efficiencies with savings and cooperative banks in a sample study of banks in fifteen European countries and the US between 1990 and 2000.[18] Savings and cooperative banks were found to be more cost-efficient than private banks in all but three countries. Country case studies, such as Altunbas et al. on Germany,[19] Giordano and Lopes on the Italian cooperative sector,[20] or Ceneboyan et al. on the United States' savings and loans sector,[21] produce similar results. An exception is the study by Mester, who found that, on the contrary, in a sample of more than a 1,000 US savings and loans surveyed in 1988, joint-stock savings and loans outperform their mutual peers in terms of cost-efficiency.[22]

Profitability

When looking at profitability, the balance of empirical evidence seems again to be tilting in favour of alternative banks. This seems a paradox, given the non-profit maximizing goals of alternative banks – which leads Berger et al. to formulate a 'clear caveat' to the results shown by a stream of studies on government-owned bank profitability, in that 'the measures of performance and economic consequences employed in these studies do not always correspond to the objectives of the state-owned banks'.[23] This caveat might be extended to studies on savings and cooperative banks' profitability, and should lead us to dismiss those studies that exclusively base their comparison on measures clearly predicated on joint-stock firms, not cooperative institutions (such as stock returns, used in Cole and Mehran, on a sample of US thrift institutions).[24]

Even with this caveat in mind, however, the evidence is, at best, mixed. In a recent study, Dietrich and Wanzenried find that Swiss government-owned banks performed better than privately owned commercial banks during the crisis (while their pre-crisis performance was at par).[25] Millon Cornett et al. present mixed evidence on the comparative performance of government banks. Studying a sample of East Asian banks from 1989 to 2004, the authors find that state-owned banks were less profitable, held less core capital, and had greater credit risk than privately owned banks prior to the 1997 crisis – but that government banks caught up to private bank levels of performance in the years after the crisis.[26] Micco et al. find that state-owned banks in developing countries are less profitable than private-owned banks,[27] while Bonin et al. show that there is no significant difference between state-owned and privately owned banks in Eastern European countries in terms of profit-efficiency.[28] An earlier study on European banks in the 1980s, by Molyneux and Thornton, showed that on average state-owned banks posted higher return on assets figures than privately owned banks.[29]

Similarly, the evidence on the profitability of cooperative and savings banks is mixed. In their European study, Ayadi et al. find that German and Spanish cooperative banks are more profitable (higher RoAs and RoEs) than commercial banks – but not other countries' cooperative banks.[30] In a small sample that excludes small cooperative and savings banks, Iannotta et al. find that government-owned banks and cooperative banks perform worse than private, commercial banks, both in terms of profitability and riskiness.[31] Altunbas et al. also find that European commercial banks are slightly more profitable than their non-profit peers.[32] These results are reversed in a series of country studies: Chakravarty and Williams on Germany, Crespi et al. on Spain, Altunbas et al. on Germany, Valneck on the British building society sector and Cebenoyan et al. on the United States all find non-profit banks to be more profitable than their for-profit counterparts.[33]

Risk

Alternative banks also seem to be less risky – i.e. their profitability tends to be much more stable over time than the volatile returns of private commercial and investment banks, which tend to be exposed to variations of market returns and asset pricing on markets. This is perhaps the field where empirical evidence is more univocal – with the notable exceptions of La Porta et al., Millon Cornett et al. and Iannotta et al. who all find government-owned banks (but not cooperative banks in the latter case) to be less stable.[34]

Indeed, most empirical studies find that cooperative and savings banks (i) have a higher earnings stability over time with respect to commercial banks, measured inter alia by the z-score;[35] (ii) are less likely to default;[36] and (iii) have a lower proportion of non-performing loans in their loan portfolio than commercial banks.[37] In addition, finally, Carbò Valverde et al. show that the presence of savings banks decreases overall risk in banking systems.[38]

Overall, therefore, there is solid empirical evidence showing that in many countries alternative banks are, on average, more cost-efficient, more profitable and less risky than their commercial peers. This suggests that alternative banks have realized competitive advantage over private banks. Chapter 4 presents a theoretical discussion aimed at understanding the competitive advantages of alternative banks. The country chapters, in the second part of this volume, also shed light on the post-crisis performance of alternative banks – in the absence of a systematic cross-country comparison covering the past few years.

Appendix

Table 2.2: Summary of the empirical literature on the comparative performance of alternative banks.

Study	Main focus	Countries covered	Period of observation	Units of observation	Method
Ayadi et al. (2010)	Cooperative and commercial banks	7 European countries	2000–8	Sample of banks (total n. of observations: 29,978)	Pooled OLS regression and a fixed-effect panel regression
Cornett et al. (2010)	State-owned and privately owned banks	16 East Asian countries	1989–2004	Sample of 456 banks (of which 142 government-owned)	T-test; pooled cross-sectional and time-series regressions with error terms clustered at the firm level
Ayadi et al. (2009)	Savings and commercial banks	5 European countries	1996–2006	Sample of banks (19,139 observations)	Stochastic frontier based on a translog cost function
Beck et al. (2009)	Savings and commercial banks	Germany	1995–2007	Sample of 3,810 banks	Regressions; panel logit model
Bongini and Ferri (2008)	Cooperative and commercial banks	Italy	1995–8	Sample of 211 banks	OLS regressions
Garcia-Marco and Robles-Fernandez (2008)	Savings and commercial banks	Spain	1993–2000	Sample of 127 banks (total n. of observations: 1,030)	Dynamic panel data

Table 2.2 (continued).

Independent variables	Dependent variables	Main findings	Data sources
Bank type	Measures of efficiency, profitability and risk: RoA, RoE, cost:income ratio, earnings stability, regional growth, market power	Cooperative banks more profitable and in many cases more cost-efficient, and more stable	Bankscope; national cooperative associations
Bank ownership	Several performance measures: RoA and a modified RoA (pre-tax cash flows/book-value total assets), capital ratios, NPLs	Compared to state-owned banks, privately owned banks are more profitable, better capitalized, and have lower percentages of non-performing loans	Bankscope; additional sources for ownership data
Bank type	Measures of efficiency, profitability and risk: RoA, RoE, cost:income ratio, earnings stability, regional growth, market power	No significant differences between savings and commercial banks in terms of efficiency and profitability. Slight advantages in terms of earnings stability	Bankscope; national savings banks associations
Bank type	Z-score, likelihood distress, non-performing loan ratio	Savings banks more stable than commercial banks	Deutsche Bundesbank
Bank type; governance (board stability) and income diversification	Profit volatility (standard deviation of RoA)	Cooperative banks show lower profit volatility than commercial banks	Bankscope
Bank type	Earnings stability (z-score) and solvency ratio	Spanish savings banks less risky than commercial banks	Savings Banks Association; Spanish Securities and Exchange Commission; Private Banking Association

Study	Main focus	Countries covered	Period of observation	Units of observation	Method
Cihak and Hesse (2007)	Cooperative and commercial banks	29 OECD countries	1994–2004	Sample of banks (16,577 observations)	Regression; panel model
Iannotta et al. (2007)	Mutual and government-owned and commercial banks	15 European countries	1999–2004	Sample of 181 large banks	OLS regression
Carbó Valverde et al. (2007)	Savings banks		1992–2001	Sample of 77 commercial and savings banks	
Chakravrty and Williams (2006)	Savings and commercial banks	Germany	1999	516 banks	Stochastic frontier
Crespi et al. (2004)	Savings banks	Spain	1986–2000	Sample of banks (total n. of observations: 2,105)	Multivariate regression
Altunbas et al. (2003)	Savings, cooperative and commercial banks	15 European countries and USA	1990–2000	Sample of banks (total n. of observations: 25,841)	Stochastic frontier and translog function
Carbó Valverde et al. (2002)	Savings banks	12 European countries	1989–96	Sample of banks (total n. of observations: 4,083)	Stochastic cost frontier
Salas and Saurina (2002)	Savings and commercial banks	Spain	1983–97	1,381 bank observations	Regression; panel data analysis
La Porta et al. (2002)	Government-owned banks	92 countries	1960–95	Country sample	OLS regressions

Independent variables	Dependent variables	Main findings	Data sources
Bank type	Earnings stability (z-score)	Cooperative banks are more stable than commercial ones	Bankscope
Bank ownership	Cost-efficiency, profitability, earnings stability (asset quality and z-score)	Cooperative and government-owned banks slightly more cost-efficient, less profitable than commercial banks; mutual banks less risky, government-owned banks riskier	Bankscope
Bank ownership	Operating profit-efficiency	Commercial banks less profit-efficient than non profit banks	Bankscope
Bank ownership and governance mechanisms	RoA	Savings banks more profitable than commercial banks	Savings Banks Association; Private Banks' Association
Bank ownership	Cost- and profit-efficiencies	Commercial banks less cost-efficient but more profit-efficient than savings and cooperatives	Bankscope
Bank size and country	Cost-efficiency	Smaller savings banks more efficient than large ones	Bankscope
Bank type	Risk (measured as the ratio of problem loans)	No significant difference between commercial and savings banks	Central Bank
Countrywide degree of government ownership of banks	Financial development and economic growth	Government ownership of banks slows down financial development and growth	Various: Bankers Almanac, Thomson Bank Directory, World Bank

Study	Main focus	Countries covered	Period of observation	Units of observation	Method
Altunbas et al. (2001)	Cooperative and Savings banks	Germany	1989–96	7,539 bank-level observations	Stochastic frontier
Valneck (1999)	Building societies and commercial banks	United Kingdom	1983–93	Sample of 17 building societies and 7 banks	Parametric models
Cole and Mehran (1998)	Thrift institutions	USA	1983–95	Sample of 94 institutions	
Esty (1997)	Savings and loans and commercial banks	USA	1982–8	Sample of 2,515 savings and loans	Parametric and non-parametric methods
Cebenoyan et al. (1993)	Savings and loans	Atlanta, GA, USA	1988	Sample of 559 savings and loans	Stochastic cost frontier
Mester (1993)	Savings and loans	USA	1991	Sample of 1,0571 savings and loans	Stochastic frontier; parametric cost function

Independent variables	Dependent variables	Main findings	Data sources
Bank ownership	Cost-efficiency	Slight cost and profit advantages for non-profit banks	Bankscope
Bank ownership type	RoA, adjusted RoA, other earnings measures	Mutual building societies outperform joint-stock retail banks	Bankscope
Ownership change	Stock performance (annual stock returns)	Demutualized thrifts perform better than thrifts	
Bank type	Risk taking	Stock thrifts show greater risk-taking than mutual thrifts	Federal Agency annual reports
Bank type			
Bank ownership	Cost-efficiency	Joint-stock savings and loans more efficient than mutual savings and loans	

3 THE COUNTER-CYCLICAL BEHAVIOUR OF PUBLIC AND PRIVATE BANKS: AN OVERVIEW OF THE LITERATURE

Alfredo Schclarek

Introduction

The literature on public banks is quite varied but can be broadly divided into three categories: a) research on the relationship of public banks and economic growth and development; b) research that compares the performance of public and private banks, in terms of profitability, efficiency, outreach, etc.; and c) studies that assess the lending behaviour of public banks through the business cycle or during crisis periods. In this chapter we propose an overview of the literature focusing on the third aspect, namely the counter-cyclical lending behaviour of public banks over the business cycle and/or in crisis times. This issue has come to attract more attention since the onset of the recent financial crisis and will probably receive even more attention once the difficulties in reigniting growth become more evident, especially in Europe. As is widely discussed currently, the austerity measures in Europe have proven to be contractionary and may probably lead in the future to a reconsideration of alternative non-orthodox policy measures to stimulate private and public investment, reduce unemployment and spur economic growth.

In what follows, we start by reviewing the empirical papers that study the lending behaviour of public banks over the business cycle. In the next section, we consider the literature that investigates the lending response of banks to an economic crisis. In the third section, we analyse the very scarce papers that incipiently look at possible explanations for the observed behaviour of public banks over the business cycle or during crisis periods. Finally, in the last section, we conclude and put forward some thoughts on this incipient literature.

The Lending Behaviour of Public Banks over the Business Cycle

Among the empirical papers that study the lending behaviour of public banks over the business cycle, one of the first papers that use individual bank-level data is Micco and Panizza.[1] They use Bankscope data for 119 countries for the period 1995–2002 and find that lending by public banks is less pro-cyclical than lending by domestic private banks, i.e. public banks may play a credit-smoothing role over the business cycle and be used in the transmission of monetary policy. Specifically, they find that both public and private banks are pro-cyclical in their lending but that public banks are significantly less pro-cyclical, i.e. during a recession public banks reduce lending less than private banks and in booms they increase lending less than private banks. Furthermore, when comparing developing and industrial countries, they find that banks in industrial countries are less pro-cyclical than banks in developing countries, but that public banks in developing countries are less pro-cyclical than public banks in industrial countries. In addition, they venture, without showing concluding empirical evidence, that this differential behaviour between public and private banks is due to an explicit objective to stabilize credit over the business cycle.

Another paper in this line of research is Bertay et al., which uses an international sample of 1,633 banks from 111 countries for the period 1999–2010 using Bankscope.[2] They find results in line with those of Micco and Panizza,[3] i.e. lending by public banks is less pro-cyclical than lending by private banks. In addition, they find that in countries with 'good governance', this lower pro-cyclicality is more important. Moreover, lending by public banks located in high-income countries is even counter-cyclical. This result is in contrast to what is found in Micco and Panizza,[4] putting in doubt the robustness of the argument that public banks behave differently in developing and industrial countries. Another interesting result by these authors is that among private banks, foreign-owned banks' lending is especially pro-cyclical.[5] They speculate that this pro-cyclical behaviour could be due to the fact that these banks have ready access to funding from their international parent firms to take advantage of local lending opportunities during economic upswings. However, as their empirical methodology does not distinguish between banks' lending behaviour in boom periods and in recessions, the highly pro-cyclical lending behaviour that they find may also be driven by banks' behaviour in recessions. In other words, it could be the result of a higher counter-cyclical risk aversion by foreign-owned banks that imply that in recessions these banks cut lending drastically and use their funds to stay liquid or lend abroad.[6]

Following this last line of thought, Duprey also analyses the cyclical lending behaviour of public banks,[7] but he distinguishes the asymmetric responses of bank lending along the business cycle, i.e. he differentiates between expansionary and recessionary phases. Using Bankscope data for 3,249 banks, of which

459 are public banks, from ninety-three countries over the 1990 and 2010 period, he finds similar results to those of Micco and Panizza and Bertay et al.[8] However, he also finds that periods of positive economic shocks feature pro-cyclical public bank lending, with public banks sometimes increasing faster their credit than private banks, while periods of negative shocks are associated with a-cyclical public bank lending. This result would seem to point to a stabilizing influence by public banks at a time of recessionary tendencies. In addition, he finds a positive relationship between economic development and public banks' ability to absorb shocks, i.e. public banks in more developed countries are more able to act in a stabilizing manner during a recession. This result is in line with Bertay et al.[9] and in contrast to Micco and Panizza.[10]

In addition, Foos uses a sample of 950 German banks over the period 1987–2005 to show that lending by saving banks is less sensitive to business cycle conditions than lending by either cooperative or commercial banks.[11]

The Lending Behaviour of Public Banks during Crisis Times

In addition to the papers that look at the business cycle properties of public bank lending, there are also papers concentrating not on the business cycle but specifically on crisis periods. One of those papers is the work of Brei and Schclarek, where the role of public bank lending in the event of systemic financial crises is studied from an empirical perspective.[12] They compare the lending responses across public and private banks to financial crises using balance sheet and income information for about 764 major banks from fifty countries during the period 1994–2009. Using panel regressions, they find empirical evidence that the growth rate of lending during normal times is positive and not significantly different between the average private bank and the average public bank. However, during financial crises, the growth rate of private bank lending decreases importantly, while that of public banks slightly increases or keeps constant depending on the econometric specification. These results indicate that private banks have a pro-cyclical behaviour during times of crisis, while public banks have a counter-cyclical or a-cyclical behaviour. These results are in line with the work of Bertay et al., who, in addition to looking at the business cycle response of public bank lending, also check what happens during crisis times.[13]

Furthermore, Cull and Martinez Peria use bank-level data from 2004 to 2009 and find that government-owned banks in Eastern Europe did not significantly differ from domestic private banks.[14] However, they find that foreign banks in Eastern Europe declined at a faster rate than that of their domestic private counterparts during the crisis. In the case of Latin America, they find that public bank lending outperformed that of domestic and foreign banks. However, De Haas et al. provide evidence on the behaviour of credit for a larger sample of Eastern European countries than that of Cull and Martinez Peria.[15] The authors find that for a sample of 1,294 banks in thirty Eastern European countries over the period 1999–2009, credit provided by foreign banks outgrew that of domestic (public and private) banks before the crisis and sharply decelerated in 2008. On the other hand, lending by government-owned banks and domestic private banks declined in 2009, but government-owned banks were less pro-cyclical than (domestic and foreign) private banks. In addition, Allen et al. use Bankscope data for 416 banks in eleven Eastern European countries for the period 1994–2010.[16] They find that foreign banks provided credit during domestic banking crises in host countries, while public banks contracted. In contrast, foreign-owned banks reduced their credit base during the global financial crisis, while public banks expanded.

In addition, the cross-country evidence is also complemented with some bank-level country case studies. For instance, Leony and Romeu show for Korea that the credit contraction during the crisis would have been deeper if public banks had not expanded their loan portfolios.[17] Coleman and Feler argue that localities in Brazil with a large share of government banks experienced a relative increase in lending following the onset of the 2008 financial crisis compared to areas with a small share of government banks.[18] These areas with a large share of government banks similarly experienced a relative increase of approximately two percentage points in employment. In addition, using data for 348 large Russian banks, Davydov studies the impact of public bank lending and risk-taking over the period 2005–11.[19] He finds that during the crisis of 2008–10, public banks increased their lending at the same time that they charged lower interest rates, in contrast to private domestic banks and foreign banks. Also, Önder and Özyildirim study the lending activities of Turkish public and private banks during the period 1992–2010.[20] Their results suggest that although public banks might issue loans for political reasons in election periods, they also seem to play an important role in offsetting the adverse effects of economic shocks, especially in developed provinces. Finally, Lin et al. study the experience of public bank lending in Japan during the 1990 crisis using a firm-year panel data set that spans the period 1977–96 for all publicly traded companies on the Tokyo Stock Exchange.[21] They find that public banks lending has a positive and significant effect on corporate investment during the crisis, for more credit-constrained firms and for firms with higher growth prospects. Thus public bank lending can enhance efficiency of the firm's investment by mitigating credit constraints.

The Reasons for the Lending Behaviour of Public Banks over the Business Cycle and/or during Crisis Times

Clearly, the empirical data reviewed above show ample evidence that private bank lending is pro-cyclical and that public bank lending is less pro-cyclical or even counter-cyclical. Thus the next question that arises naturally is why there is such a difference in the lending behaviour of private and public banks. For this question, the literature is scarcer and the evidence is still preliminary without any strong conclusions. In what follows, the existent empirical evidence is presented and then some theoretical papers are reviewed.

Regarding the reasons for the less pro-cyclical behaviour of public banks, Bertay et al. find that funding at public banks is less pro-cyclical than that of private banks.[22] More specifically, they find that non-deposit liabilities for public banks are less pro-cyclical than that of private banks. Moreover, they find some weak evidence that short-term funding is also less pro-cyclical for public banks. This evidence implies than in boom times private banks are more active in the short-term wholesale market, while public banks are more active in recessionary times. In addition, for the case of countries with high government effectiveness, they find that equity is pro-cyclical for private banks and counter-cyclical for public banks, implying that equity increases for public banks when most needed (recessions) while it falls for private banks.

In addition, Brei and Schclarek investigate the causes of the differential behaviour of public and private banks and test two alternative explanations.[23] The first is that public banks suffer less deposit withdrawals than private banks during crisis times. The other explanation is that public banks increase their capital more than private banks during a crisis. However, these two hypotheses are rejected by the data, finding no difference between private and public banks. Therefore, the authors speculate, without showing empirical results, that the reason for the difference between private and public banks is due to the higher willingness (or risk tolerance) of the latter to provide lending in an unstable crisis environment.

Finally, McCandless et al. investigate Argentina's experience with bank runs and try to explain the variation in deposits during the 2001 crisis.[24] Using monthly bank-level data, they find that bank fundamentals rather than self-fulfilling prophecy theory better explain the bank run. Furthermore, they show evidence that during the first months of the crisis, public banks suffered less deposits withdrawals than domestic and foreign private banks, but as the crisis deepened the difference was blurred. Considering that this crisis ended up being an extremely deep exchange-rate crisis, this evidence may be suggesting that at first, when the crisis erupted, depositors trusted public banks more, but when it became evident that this was a systemic bank run, the difference in trustworthiness disappeared.

In what follows, some theoretical articles are presented. The theoretical framework offered by Brei and Schclarek allows them to explore three tentative explanations for the behaviour of public and private banks in crisis times.[25] First, the objective of public banks, in contrast to private banks, is not only to minimize losses in the event of a financial crisis but also to promote the recovery of the whole economy. Second, public banks are more likely recapitalized in times of distress because their owner, the state, tends to have more resources than private shareholders. Finally, public banks tend to suffer less deposit withdrawals than private banks in a severe crisis because depositors perceive public banks as a safer alternative than private banks due to the implicit guarantee by the state.

In addition, Andries and Billon build a theoretical model where banks face a risk of failure in bad states of the economy, i.e. when productive firms suffer a low productivity state.[26] They show that public banks have a more stable deposit base owing to the provision of a better deposit guarantee. This enables public banks to insulate their lending in periods of financial instability and provide more stable lending than private banks. The better deposit guarantee by public banks is assumed exogenously and not derived endogenously.

Another theoretical paper that tries to explain the differential behaviour of public and private banks is Duprey.[27] He argues that public banks' long-term inefficiency generates a lower short-term lending cyclicality compared to private commercial banking. In his model, public banks specialize in lending to shirking entrepreneurs because they face higher monitoring costs than private banks, while on this segment, the private bank prefers to step back to preserve its profits. Thus in crisis times, when more productive projects have a lower profitability, private bank lending is pro-cyclical while public bank lending is less sensitive to productivity shock. It should be noted, however, that in this model the increased lending by public banks over private banks in crisis times is an inefficient consequence of their lower capacity to screen good projects, not an active and rational policy decision.

Conclusions

In this review we have analysed the lending behaviour of private and public banks along the business cycle and during crisis periods. Although most of the empirical publications are very recent, there seems to be a consensus that public banks act less pro-cyclical or even counter-cyclical in comparison to private banks. This evidence tentatively shows that public banks may be used to avoid the deepening of a financial crisis or its contagion to the real sector through a credit crunch and the increased risks and uncertainties that prevail in the economy. The evidence suggests, moreover, that public banks can be used complementarily with monetary and fiscal policies to implement a counter-cyclical macroeconomic policy to mitigate the business cycle during more normal times. These are two new roles that public banks may have that have not received enough or proper attention in the wider literature on public banks. Furthermore, although the empirical evidence reviewed in this chapter has not looked specifically at the issue, it can be ventured that public banks may also be used in a strategy to reignite growth and get out of stagnation and the unemployment trap after a crisis.[28]

What is lacking in this literature is a better understanding of the *reasons* for the different lending behaviours of public and private banks. Although we have reviewed some empirical and theoretical papers that try to put forward some explanations, more empirical and theoretical research is needed. Among the different explanations put forward, those with seemingly more promising explanatory power are that: a) public banks do not only aim at maximizing profits but can also have as an objective to avoid the deepening of the crisis or smoothing the business cycle; and b) the owner of public banks, the state, is probably in a better financial situation or is more willing than private bankers to recapitalize its banks in times of financial distress or increased uncertainty.

Following this line of thought, it is obvious that the counter-cyclical role of public banks during a crisis is only possible when these banks are relatively solvent and not undercapitalized. Furthermore, if the state is already in dire conditions or even bankrupt when the crisis erupts, or if the recession deepens before the counter-cyclical policies are put in place, it is probable that it will even be difficult of the state to react properly and recapitalize banks. Evidently these issues show the importance of well-managed public banks, which are very prudent in normal times. Another important aspect to take into account is that firms and entrepreneurs should be willing to take loans for their productive projects. If they are not willing to invest, maybe because there is too much uncertainty, there is not much that public banks can do to foster private investment, i.e. the supply of credit also needs to be met by a demand for it. If private firms are not willing to invest despite public banks' willingness to lend at favourable conditions, public banks may still have a role to play. In this case, and for there to be an increase in investment and stimulation to the aggregate demand, it is probably up to public enterprises or public infrastructure projects to lead the process. In this case, public banks may be used to finance this public investment.

Other issues that have yet not been clarified are: first, whether public banks lend at more favourable terms than private banks during crisis times, not only in terms of interest rates but also in terms of the maturity structure of loans; and second, whether there is any difference, in terms of lending behaviour, between various types of public banks, i.e. commercial public banks, savings banks, development banks, etc. Most of the surveyed literature does not distinguish between types of public bank and treat them all as the same. However, it is very probable that although all are public banks, they act and react in very different ways during a crisis or along the business cycle. Finally, another issue that deserves more attention is whether the relative size of these institutions matters.

On top of the individual characteristics of public banks, it is important also to analyse more systemic issues related to public bank participation in the financial system. In this sense, the importance of the role of public banks is dependent on the size of this sector relative to the whole financial system. If the public bank, or the network of public banks, is small in comparison to the whole banking system, its effectiveness is diminished. In contrast, if the public bank is large, there is a higher probability that the increased lending will have systemic effects. Furthermore, as the recent financial network literature stress, the network structure of the banking system should be carefully taken into account when trying to devise policies that enhance the resilience of the financial system. Thus, beyond the individual behaviour of public banks, what is needed is a better understanding of how the network structure of the banking sector and the relative importance (size), position and role of public banks in this network matters for the cyclical behaviour and the strength of the banking system.

4 EXPLAINING THE COMPETITIVE ADVANTAGE OF ALTERNATIVE BANKS: TOWARDS AN ALTERNATIVE BANKING THEORY?

Olivier Butzbach and Kurt von Mettenheim

Introduction

As mentioned in the Introduction to this volume, the surprising performance of alternative banks cannot be explained by a mainstream literature on banking mostly focused on for-profit commercial banks. There is, it is true, a sizeable body of works specifically dedicated to not-for-profit financial institutions, and in particular to the theoretical understanding of the comparative performance of such organizations. The present chapter builds on these studies to theoretically explain the foundations of alternative banks' competitive advantage, furthering the advances made by the empirical literature reviewed in Chapter 2. Some of these works were cited in the Introduction to the present volume.

However, most research on alternative banks focuses almost exclusively on governance and ownership issues, which, as will become clear here, are only part of the answer to the question raised above. As Rasmussen put it in an important work twenty-five years ago, 'the difference between mutual and stock banks lies in who controls the bank and receives the profits'.[1] A sizeable part of this chapter will therefore be dedicated to a discussion of such works. Still, it is important to look at modern theories of banking for theoretical indications, or sketches, that might be relevant to the question raised at the end of Chapter 2 – in other words, how can we theoretically account for the competitive advantage of alternative banks over time?

Modern theories of banking emerged, in the early 1960s, in reaction to the 'pure theory of fractional reserve banking', as Towey called the then-prevailing views among neoclassical economists.[2] This theory was mostly a theory of money – banks playing, in these views, the sideman to monetary authorities, a cog in the money multiplier. In addition, banks were seen as pure money-creating entities, with no other relevant contribution to the economy. Several authors took positions against those views in the early 1960s.[3] The 'new view' they were credited for putting forward had two key characteristics. First, it rejected what Tobin called the 'mystique' of money. From the borrowers' point of view, there is, Tobin argued, some degree of substitutability between financial assets (hence the rejection of money as 'special'). Secondly, Tobin and others argued that banks are firms with specific corporate goals. Again, in Tobin's terms, 'Bank-created "money" is a liability, which must be matched on the other side of the balance sheet. And banks, as businesses, must earn money from their middleman's role'.[4] Indeed, from this perspective, bank assets and liabilities are determined by bank managers' strategies to maximize returns from lending and interest rates on deposits;[5] and lending is determined by the marginal returns of assets over the cost of liabilities.[6]

It is important, at this stage, to bear in mind that the new view was first and foremost an attack on mainstream monetary theory. Tobin and Gurley and Shaw aimed to reinstate a more realistic view of banking *within monetary theory*, not to offer a better understanding of banks per se. The latter developed as a secondary argument, following two parallel theoretical tracks. First, while unequally rooted in the neoclassical tradition (Tobin was a Keynesian and his monetary theory was neo-Keynesian), the 'new view' of banking applied to banks and financial institutions the hypotheses and assumptions of neoclassical theories of the firm – utility maximization and the pursuance of self-interest as the defining characteristics of individual behaviour. Secondly, the new view and subsequent theories of banking aimed at explaining the existence and operations of banking firms on the basis of a correct understanding of their functions within a monetized economy's financial system. Tobin, of course, focused on the not strictly monetary role of banks: 'the essential function of financial intermediaries ... is to satisfy simultaneously the portfolio preferences of two types of individuals or firms'.[7]

This 'double-track' development of banking theory (mainstream firm theory on the one hand; focus on specific functions of banks on the other) underlies most of the literature since.[8] There is a widespread consensus, among financial economists, that banks are multifunctional firms. In particular, as Bhattacharya and Thakor point out,[9] banks fulfil two key functions within modern financial systems: on the one hand, they provide brokerage services; on the other, they produce qualitative asset transformation. A fundamental concept in modern intermediation theory, qualitative asset transformation, means, in a nutshell, that bank loans present different risk profiles than the liabilities issued by banks to make those loans.[10] Recent reviews of the literature on banking have put emphasis on contemporary trends in the behaviour of banks, i.e. the shift from a relational view of banking towards a transactional view[11] and the growing integration of banks and markets,[12] which do not fundamentally alter economists' focus on the functions mentioned above.

However, seeing continuity between the 'new view' of the 1960s and modern theories of banking should not obfuscate a key difference between the two generations of studies. This difference lies in the widespread acknowledgement, since the 1970s, of the existence of information asymmetries on financial markets. Indeed, as Boot put it, the theory of information asymmetries helps distinguish 'modern theories of financial intermediation from the earlier transaction costs-based theories',[13] while Bhattacharya and Thakor argue, reflecting widely shared views among economists, that 'intermediation is a response to the inability of market-mediated mechanisms to efficiently resolve informational problems' inherent to financial transactions.[14] The specificity of banks, in other words, lies in the type of contractual mechanism used to solve informational asymmetries. While Tobin's banks helped decrease transaction costs through the pooling of risk,[15] modern theories insist on the 'informational advantages' of banks (with respect to markets) in reducing credit rationing;[16] acting as delegated monitors, and therefore reducing the cost of monitoring borrowers incurred by lenders/depositors;[17] and undertaking relationship lending, which also helps decrease information asymmetries and their consequences on the credit relationship: adverse selection and moral hazard.[18]

However, these rich, successive developments in banking theory over the past few decades cannot dispel the notion that theories still suffer from ignoring the organizational aspects of banking and, therefore, rely on a default theory of the modern firm, mostly based on parallel developments in neoclassical theory (agency theory and property rights theory). The following sections will, therefore, draw on these various layers of banking theory to formulate the beginning of theoretical answers to the empirical question posed above. First, we focus on the governance, ownership and control of banks, drawing on agency theory, which is the usual toolkit for comparing different forms of banking organizations. This focus on the 'first track' of modern banking theory suggests that, overall, alternative banks may lower agency costs compared to joint-stock, for-profit banks. Second, we turn to theories of bank behaviour, drawing from the literature on information asymmetries (the 'second track' of contemporary banking theory). This demonstrates how alternative banks can benefit from better abilities at relationship lending while reaping the benefits of economies of scale, while having access to capital at a lower cost. Third, and finally, we tentatively sketch a new theory of alternative banking, building on promising yet mostly uncharted developments within modern banking theory, in particular the theory of inter-temporal risk smoothing, showing how alternative banks can benefit from their long history and solid reputation to outperform other types of banks. The main point made in this chapter is that the competitive advantage of alternative banks can be explained by several factors treated in the different layers of modern banking theory.

Alternative versus Joint-Stock Banks through the Eyes of Agency Theory

A key source of the competitive advantages of alternative banks can be found in their ability to mitigate potential agency conflicts to reduce agency costs. As mentioned above, mainstream theories of the firm form the explicit[19] or implicit underpinning of most of the 'new' theories of banking that have emerged since the 1960s. For instance, the intuition behind seeing banks as 'delegated monitors'[20] comes from the assumption that banks are able to reduce the cost of monitoring borrowers that investors face on credit markets. This is a typical agency cost in financial markets. The large body of comparative empirical works on bank ownership, which blossomed in the 1990s, provides the main arguments for the 'stakeholder-shareholder' bank debate, made extensive use of agency theory.[21] Indeed, the very choice of terms such as 'stakeholder-oriented' and 'shareholder-oriented'[22] to qualify, differentiate and compare different forms of banks exemplifies the primary role of governance and ownership issues in this literature. This concern is not questionable per se; what is debatable, instead, is both (i) the explicit or implicit adherence to mainstream neoclassical theories of the firm of most works discussing the relative advantages of public or mutual versus private ownership; and (ii) the implicit assumption that ownership and governance are the key characteristics that distinguish alternative banks from other banks, ignoring other factors of differentiation (which will be tackled in the third section of the present chapter). Regarding the first point, it might be useful to briefly summarize the basic tenets of agency theory as used in comparative theories of banking organizations.

Of course, thinking about non-joint-stock forms of economic organizations has evolved since the dismissal of mutual firms as more conducive to shirking by managers by Alchian and Demsetz in 1972.[23] However, the bases of agency theory and property rights theory (often associated in modern theories of the firm) were laid down in a select number of influential works in the early 1970s.[24] The whole edifice built on these foundations[25] shares the same basic premises, and in particular the assumption that certain organizational forms are more efficient than others in reducing transaction costs. Alchian and Demsetz saw the constitution of the modern firm (and especially the separation between ownership and control famously studied by Berle and Means[26]) as the solution to the problems of measurement of marginal productivity in team production.[27] Given the need to monitor team member behaviour, but the difficulties of assessing individual behaviour (given information asymmetries and cognitive limits) and choosing the right monitor (and monitoring the monitor), early theorists placed the emphasis on the bearer of residual risk, i.e. the residual claimant, a.k.a.

the stockholder.[28] Most of these authors theorized, on this basis, the superior efficiency of shareholder-based forms of governance; several studies, within this stream of research, have even predicted a convergence of all organizations, over time, towards this organizational form.[29]

Private ownership and shareholder-based governance are thus seen as better (more efficient) answers to the multiple agency problems that characterize modern firms (i.e. where ownership and control are separate). However, agency problems differ across governance and ownership structures. Building on Cuevas and Fischer,[30] Table 4.1 summarizes the likelihood and degree of agency costs across three bank ownership types (cooperative, public and private). This also clarifies how monitoring mechanisms differ across bank categories – even between the two broad categories we brought together under the larger umbrella of 'alternative banks': cooperative banks and public banks. Notwithstanding their differences, we suggest that in both categories overall agency costs are lower than those sustained in for-profit, shareholder-based banks.

Table 4.1: Agency conflicts across bank categories.

Agency conflict	Cooperative and mutual savings banks	Public savings banks and development banks	Joint-stock banks
Shareholders–managers	High and positively correlated with dilution of membership; can be mitigated though supervision and control by apex institutions in network	Absent	High and positively correlated with dilution of ownership; can be mitigated through contractual arrangements and pay-for-performance schemes
Non-owning stakeholders–managers	Low	High due to the higher autonomy of government-owned bank managers and weakness of control incentives inherent to public ownership (according to property rights theories)	Low
Investors–borrowers	Absent (internalized, see below)	Low, either because of relationship banking (small public savings banks) or because public investors are not as risk-averse as private investors.	High; moral hazard risk can be mitigated through collateral, selection and monitoring
Managers–borrowers	Low because of relationship banking and peer pressure	Same as above	Same as above

Agency conflict	Cooperative and mutual savings banks	Public savings banks and development banks	Joint-stock banks
Shareholders–depositors	Absent	Absent	High (main source of risk according to Cuevas and Fischer, 2006); asset substitution risk
Managers–depositors	Low and correlated with size of bank and distance with respect to depositors; cost can be mitigated by network monitoring	Absent	Same as above
Net borrowers–net lenders	High according to Cuevas and Fischer (2006)	Absent	Absent

Manager–Shareholder Agency Conflicts

A key agency conflict within firms arises between owners and managers. It is, in fact, the 'discovery' of this conflict by Berle and Means in their seminal work on the modern corporation[31] that gave rise to modern theories of the firm. The owner–management problem in firms originates in the separation between ownership and management, resulting in the ability of managers to engage into rent-seeking and expense-preference behaviours.[32] The more diffused the ownership, the easier it is for managers to pursue their own interests, and therefore the higher the agency costs. Indeed, monitoring and controlling managers can be very costly, as owners attempt to design incentives to ensure that managers act in their interest. Another source of managerial autonomy resides in the free cash flows generated by the firm: as the availability of free or uncommitted funds increases, managers will invest in unprofitable projects.[33] The three categories of banks distinguished here according to ownership (cooperative, public and private) each face different versions of the owner–manager agency conflict. However, we argue that agency costs are likely to be lower for both types of alternative banks in comparison to joint-stock banks. As Hansmann pointed out, the opportunism of managers in joint-stock firms might have been one factor that led to the rapid growth of mutual forms of banking organizations in the nineteenth-century United States.[34] Yet authors such as Rasmussen for mutual banks,[35] Mayers and Smith for mutual insurance firms,[36] and LaPorta et al. in their work on government banks[37] argue precisely the opposite.

The mainstream argument, as Ayadi et al. note,[38] runs as follows: (i) stakeholder governance-based banks have more autonomous managers than shareholder-based banks, so they yield higher agency costs; (ii) stakeholder-based banks cannot rely on market mechanisms to increase these agency costs; and (iii) stakeholder-based banks cannot reduce agency costs by resorting to those tools typically available to private, joint-stock companies, such as stock options and other schemes linking pay to performance.

The question of the higher or lower autonomy of managers at alternative banks is actually difficult to decipher. Diffuse ownership is an obvious source of managerial autonomy, and mutual banks have more diffuse ownership; yet no one can accumulate ownership shares like in joint-stock banks. As Rasmussen put it, 'the [mutual] manager is freed not by the absence of concentration, but by the absence of the threat of concentration'.[39] Public savings banks and development banks, on the other hand, usually have a smaller number of stakeholders with higher stakes in the bank – typically local or national governments. But an axiom of the property rights literature (which has inspired much of the work on agency conflicts) is that public ownership is much less apt than private ownership at creating incentives for the monitoring of agents – or, as Andrei Shleifer put it, 'private ownership is the crucial source of incentives to innovate and become efficient'.[40] In addition, public ownership might extend the owner–manager agency conflict to the citizen–manager (indirect) relationship. Shleifer talked about the 'grotesque failure' of state ownership, drawing on the supposed utility function of politicians – who seem to always want to maximize clientelism and personal income.[41] Such a distortion of the principal–agent relationship arises from the presumed weak and perverse incentives inherent in public ownership,[42] which concern public owners as well as regulators: Kane argued that 'short-horizoned authorities can allow banks to snatch wealth surreptitiously from taxpayers and simultaneously require loan officers to pass some or all of the wealth that is snatched to a politically designated set of favored borrowers'.[43] This is the essence of the neoclassical theory of corporate governance espoused in Shleifer[44] and Shleifer and Vishny[45] and the ownership rights literature. Authors such as Millon Cornett et al.,[46] for instance, explained their findings (that state-owned banks performed worse than private banks) by using Shleifer and Vishny[47] and Kane[48] and their emphasis on the perverse incentives of state bureaucrats running financial institutions. Dinç[49] and Micco et al.[50] also found that it is politics that influence state-owned banks and therefore bias lending policies. Regulators, added Barth et al., are no 'angels'.[51]

Cooperative and mutual savings banks do not have shareholders either. But they have owners: cooperative members. Cooperative membership relies on the principle of one member, one vote, regardless of the equity stake each member actually owns. So it is very likely that cooperative membership will be highly dispersed, which increases managerial autonomy. In fact, Cuevas and Fischer argued that expense preferences constitute the main source of failure for cooperative bank managers;[52] and the dilution of membership, they say, aggravates this problem. In addition to ownership diffusion, cooperative banks managers face multiple constituencies of stakeholders: members, workers, net borrowers, net savers, public authorities, etc.[53] However, Fama and Jensen argued that a board with outside directors may exercise a check on management even in non-profit firms.[54] A third and final source of potential conflicts between managers and owners (or other stakeholders) in cooperative and mutual savings banks lies in the weak incentives presumably inherent to non-private ownership forms (as mentioned above in the case of public banks). Cooperative members are not exactly similar to a private bank's shareholders: their degree of control is unrelated to their equity stakes, and they cannot sell their equity stakes in the market. This has a bearing on the nature of cooperative banks' equity as well: Fonteyne speaks of an 'intergenerational endowment'. In this view, managers of cooperative banks should be considered as 'custodians' of the endowment,[55] thus reducing member incentives to exert effective oversight over management, raising a series of governance problems.

So it is debatable whether or not alternative banks face lower or higher owner–manager agency conflicts than joint-stock banks – especially if one relaxes the key assumption driving the argument that shareholder-oriented banks face lower owner–manager problems, based on the assumption that private ownership offers the best incentives for controlling agents. However, the key issue here is the extent to which alternative banks are better able than joint-stock banks to lower this specific agency cost through monitoring, control and incentives. As said above, joint-stock, shareholder-oriented banks can rely on two key devices to lower agency costs: (i) an external one, market discipline; and (ii) an internal one, contracts that comprise a set of incentives aligning managers' interests to those of shareholders.

Market discipline consists in the possibility for shareholders to sell their shares on the market and/or to facilitate a buy-out that threatens managers' tenure within the firm.[56] The latter is also called 'takeover threat' and has informed a number of studies since its first conceptualization by Williamson in the 1960s.[57] In addition, in shareholder-oriented banks, value added is appropriated by external shareholders, who can therefore demand ever higher increases in dividends as a way to decrease the free cash flow problem.[58] This is the shareholder value maximization paradigm, which became dominant in corporate finance theory and practice in the 1980s and the 1990s.[59] Alternative banks cannot, by definition, rely on such market mechanisms to discipline managers from outside the banking firm. This absence of a 'market exit' mechanism lowers alternative banks' capacity to discipline managers.[60] However, Cen et al. have shown how takeover threats might actually be damaging to banking firms' standing with all stakeholders.[61] Second, alternative banks have their own external monitoring and controlling devices. Third, if public savings and development banks are seen as too politically influenced,[62] that means that governments and public stakeholders are able to actually exert a stronger control over bank managers than the one available to private shareholders. And we are back to the issue of government intervention in banking. One could underline at this point the specific nature of banks, and the relevance of moral hazard in banking, which makes government regulation desirable.[63] Fourth, another problem raised by Bhattacharya and Thakor is the lack of a secondary market for residual claims.[64] However, as Ayadi et al. argued,[65] building on Fama and Jensen,[66] the unique nature of cooperatives members' equity claims (they are redeemable on demand) makes exit a more powerful disciplinary device, especially given the absence of capital market options to substitute potentially withdrawing members. So, paradoxically, the absence of market exit makes cooperative exit more powerful as a disciplinary device.

Cooperative banks and savings banks can rely on another powerful external device for disciplining managers: networks. As mentioned in Chapter 1, most cooperative banks and savings banks have, over time, developed second-tier network organizations. These organizations provide back-office services and set up specialized subsidiaries offering complementary services to those available in local banks; in addition, they supply joint-liability and cross-guarantee schemes useful to ensure the overall stability of the network. More important here, however, is the monitoring and control functions fulfilled by second-tier network organizations. Indeed, historical evidence shows, for instance, how German cooperative banks developed regional institutions for the specific purpose of performing auditing and monitoring functions.[67] The apex institution in cooperative networks also exerts pressure on member banks regarding the use of free cash flows, either through redistribution to members or through the constitution of cross-guarantees. Network supervision also limits the ability of managers to appropriate endowments.[68] But networks do not only exert supervision of member banks' management: they also provide peer pressure, which is another key characteristic of cooperative bank governance seen as a very effective device for controlling and disciplining managers.[69] Finally, cooperative networks constitute joint-supply alliances that address the uncertainties in the procurement of inputs, another potential locus of agency conflicts.[70]

So alternative banks can rely on networks, a specific external control and monitoring device that may discipline managers as effectively as the market mechanism present in the shareholder governance of joint-stock banks. What about internal devices? In joint-stock companies, potential agency conflicts between owners and managers can be offset by private contractual devices. As the literature on corporate finance and agency theory has long argued, owner–manager conflicts can be reduced through a contractual realignment of interests – thus making managers behave as shareholders.[71] This realignment may be achieved through compensation schemes that link managers' pay to their performance and that give managers a vested interest in the performance of a firm's stock – for instance, through stock options. As Fonteyne and Cuevas and Fischer pointed out,[72] such devices are not available to cooperative (or public) banks. Rasmussen called 'perks' the 'difference between a mutual manager's compensation and his market wage'.[73] Since perks are capped and unrelated to individual managerial performance, mutual managers have weak incentives to increase risk and profits (interestingly, the two are unproblematically related in Rasmussen's work; this kind of amalgam might be harder to hold in the post-crisis world). Therefore, the argument goes, alternative banks lack a key tool to control agency conflicts. The assumed widespread use of perks in the mutual industry is also a key (negative) point for Fama and Jensen and Deshmukh et al.[74]

There is a very extensive literature on pay and performance, and on executive stock option plans and their usefulness as agency conflict-reducing devices.[75] Suffice to say here that the pre-2007 empirical literature was mixed, and that there was widespread scepticism as to whether stock options would actually work as incentives to maximize shareholder value.[76] But the 2007 crisis has shown that top bank managers with multimillion stock option plans were not those least willing to put their banks' survival at risk by pursuing risky high-yield strategies.[77] In fact, excessive executive pay at large joint-stock banks has become a key political issue in the aftermath of crisis. In fact, as Polo argued (before the crisis), executive stock option plans in banks might be counterproductive by increasing manager incentives to invest in risky assets.[78] With hindsight, one can dismiss the argument that the non-availability of these contractual devices impairs alternative bank capacity to address and reduce agency conflicts between owners and managers. In addition, these contractual devices are actually very costly: one might argue, therefore, that alternative banks are much better off not resorting to these instruments that have proved costly and ineffective.

A broader argument can be made here on the relevance and usefulness of agency theory to address problems of bank stability and survival in the long run. One of the problems of firms in the US, some observers have argued, is the implicit (or explicit) theories their corporate governance relies on: seen as bundles of contracts without any real existence outside of legal forms, their managers cannot have an interest in the firm's long-term well-being but only in the specific costs and benefits they find in their contracts.[79] But this brings us too far beyond current discussions in banking theory. Another very promising line of research, which is understudied, is the actual level of commitment of managers and employees in alternative banks. One could argue, indeed, that the broad social mandate of these banks may provide incentives to perform well. And loyal employees are mentioned by Fonteyne as an important source of competitive advantage for cooperative banks.[80] Finally, the agency costs of delegated management may be, as Hansmann argued, 'at best of secondary importance when determining which organizational forms are viable'.[81]

Other Agency Conflicts

A second agency problem, one between shareholders and debt holders (or bank depositors), is another potential conflict typical of financial intermediaries. This conflict has been framed in peculiar terms by the asset substitution effect theory, which hypothesizes that equity holders have a higher incentive to gain from risk-taking than debt holders, who bear most of the consequences of risk.[82] Alternative banks are clearly less prone to the asset substitution problem, having no shareholder in the case of public banks, and having owners with non-transferable equity stakes in the case of cooperatives.[83] This point was acknowledged by Rasmussen, who swiftly diminished its impact on his overall argument (i.e. that mutual banks are less efficient than stock banks) by bringing up the issue of the diversity of views among mutual bank depositors, whereby only 'independent' managers picked by stockholders could guarantee a 'cautious investment policy'.[84] Apart from the obvious contradictions with his previous arguments (i.e. that mutual managers are more risk-averse than their joint-stock counterparts), this assumption is self-defeating because it brings up another group, different from bondholders: stockholders, who obviously have their own interest and whose difference from bondholders (bank depositors) was the source of this agency conflict in the first place. Finally, the opposite (from the mainstream story about the relationship between managers and depositors) could be said: 'the managers of investor owned-firms are much more willing to speculate with their depositors' funds than are the managers of customer-owned and non-profit firms'.[85]

Another important agency conflict specific to financial intermediaries may arise between depositors and borrowers. As argued above, delegated monitoring aims precisely at explaining how banks form as coalitions of depositors wishing to reduce the cost of monitoring borrowers.[86] According to this theory, borrowers and depositors have fundamentally different interests: depositors tend to be risk-averse and have a high liquidity preference, while borrowers have a low liquidity preference and are risk-prone (this asymmetry between liquid liabilities and illiquid assets also lies at the root of the theory of banks as liquidity creators, which is discussed below in relation to risk-taking). Banks do not eliminate this agency conflict – they just reduce its costs with respect to direct finance. We argue here that alternative banks reduce this agency cost below levels sustained by commercial, privately owned banks. First, in the case of cooperative and mutual savings banks, their cooperative status bridges the gap between bank debtors (i.e. its depositors) and bank owners, aligning the latter's interests to the former's.[87] Indeed, cooperative bank members are simultaneously owners and depositors; and borrowers often have to be depositors and owners too. According to Cuevas and Fischer, cooperative banks may actually face a similar agency conflict, between *net* borrowers (i.e. cooperative members whose borrowing exceeds their deposit holdings) and *net* lenders (the opposite).[88] But this agency conflict, we argue, is much less salient than the one between depositors and borrowers that exists in joint-stock banks. First, net borrowers in a cooperative bank have a vested interest in the sustainability of their bank over time – not only because they are also the bank's owners (indeed, it could be demonstrated that some net borrowers would gain more from their refusal to pay back their loans than lose from the bank's failure, which looks like the problem afflicting common goods), but because most cooperative bank borrowing takes place over a long period of time – it is relation-based rather than transaction-based. Second, peer pressure is also exercised, both among cooperative bank members and in the local community.[89]

In public savings banks and development banks, investors differ from borrowers as in joint-stock banks. However, this agency conflict can be attenuated by the fact that public investors have (i) a different clientele and (ii) a different degree of risk-aversion than private investors. For instance, public savings banks and development banks are usually the biggest lenders to public administration and social housing programmes, which have lower incentives to behave in an opportunistic way, given their link to the bank's key stakeholders. In addition, public banks have an explicit mission to serve those clients that are either unbanked (lower-income households) or have more difficult access to capital markets or private banks (small- and medium-size enterprises). Those two categories of borrowers certainly present a higher riskiness than those usually served by for-profit banks and, therefore, higher monitoring costs – but the agency costs are lower.

Finally, agency conflicts may arise between depositors and bank management. In alternative banks, these conflicts may be dramatically reduced by the higher level of trust placed in these banks by the general public. As Bhattacharya and Thakor put it, 'what makes the mutual form the preferred structure is that it resolves the classic shareholder deposit conflict regarding the appropriate level of risk'.[90] This is especially true in times of crisis: in hard times state-owned banks are considered as 'safe and better banks'.[91] This higher level of trust has various sources: the long history of alternative banks; their local rooting; their stakeholder-based governance; and their non-profit maximizing objectives.

A related argument in favour of mutual banks raises other behavioural incentives faced by managers in mutual versus stock banks. In the former, managers may be more 'altruistic'. However, as Rasmussen emphasized, 'what is important in a savings bank is not so much altruism as stability and conservatism'; and 'an altruistic manager devoted to buying the best high-yield, high-risk securities is worse than a risk-averse scoundrel'.[92]

A further argument made by Rasmussen is that the less complex mix of products and services offered by a particular bank, the lower the chances of potential agency conflicts between managers, stockholders and bondholders. Given savings and cooperative banks' smaller average size and narrower range of products, agency conflicts may be tempered in those banks by their business model.

Overall, it seems that alternative banks are more able than joint-stock banks to reduce the potential agency conflicts arising between banks' multiple stakeholders, and this might be an important source of competitive advantage for alternative banks. It is ironic, therefore, that before the 2007–8 banking crisis some would point at cooperative banking and highlight the risks posed by their peculiar governance, in particular empire-building and appropriation risks,[93] which instead were found to be so pervasive among private banks.

Alternative Bank Ability to
Mitigate Information Asymmetries

Relationship Banking and Economies of Scale

As seen above, one of the potential agency conflicts that arise in banking is between banks and borrowers. In the presence of information asymmetries (which, again, are seen as pervasive in the banking literature), borrowers may be induced to behave in an opportunistic manner, causing moral hazard problems. Vice versa, information asymmetries could lead to adverse selection through, for instance, credit rationing by loan officers.[94]

One way to reduce such information asymmetries (and the inefficiencies they entail) is through relationship banking, which has been the subject of a considerable empirical and theoretical literature in the past two decades.[95] Boot defined relationship banking as 'the provision of financial services by a financial intermediary that: (i) invests in obtaining customer-specific information, often proprietary in nature, and (ii) evaluates the profitability of these investments through multiple interactions with some customers over time and or across products'.[96]

Relationship banking offers multiple advantages: it adds value by improving the exchange of information between banks and borrowers and by providing contractual improvements on the bank–borrower relationship;[97] it improves the availability of credit;[98] and it reduces collateral requirements and the costs of financial distress.[99] We argue here that alternative banks are uniquely positioned to reap advantages from relationship banking. First, cooperative banks and savings banks are much closer to their clients (depositors and borrowers) through either their small size and local rooting or their extensive branch network, or both. The soft information (as opposed to the hard information generated by standardized screening and monitoring procedures) gathered through proximity with customers is a key source of competitive advantage for alternative banks.[100] Carnevali also argued that local organizational networks and lending discretion (retained by savings banks) provide competitive advantage and help usher small and medium enterprises through economic downturns.[101] Some argued that extensive networks generate high fixed costs, and that their branch offices will lose relevance in the near future of banking.[102] We disagree; the persistent strategy of alternative banks to add rather than reduce bank branches is certainly consistent with the view that branch networks are a key investment to sustain competitive advantage. As a matter of fact, alternative banks continue to operate in segments of the banking market (such as lending in low-income areas) where information asymmetries are so high as to discourage joint-stock banks to operate there (see the discussion on Brazil in Chapter 10 of this volume). Interestingly, two very different types of alternative banks are likely to be found in such contexts: low-income credit unions[103] and public development banks.[104]

In addition to being close to their customers, alternative banks also elicit a higher level of trust, as mentioned above. Indeed, as Kay argued, 'the special value of mutuality rests on its capacity to establish and sustain relationship contract structures'.[105] As a result, they also have a comparative advantage in establishing trust.[106] Trust is also maintained through public and cooperative bank policies regarding the (re)distribution of value added. As Ayadi et al. show, in shareholder-oriented banks value added is appropriated by external shareholders, whereas in stakeholder banks it is redistributed to customers and members through lower-priced loans or higher interest paid on deposits.[107] Such redistribution also feeds into the inter-temporal risk-smoothing effect of alternative banks (see next section).

Finally, mutual bank members usually belong to an identifiable group circumscribed to a profession or geographical area;[108] they exhibit a higher degree of cohesion and homogeneity than private bank clients, which allows mutual banks to reduce the risks of adverse selection and moral hazard and mitigate counterparty risk,[109] even if some authors argued that such benefits are limited to small-scale banks specialized in less complex operations.[110]

The advantages of small size, local rooting and extensive branch networks might appear contradictory with achieving economies of scale in banking, especially among smaller banks.[111] Fonteyne argued that cooperative banks have lost most of their competitive advantages in overcoming opportunistic behaviour by borrowers (because of the increase in size and the growing distance between banks and their members, and because contracts have become more enforceable by commercial banks).[112] We disagree. As a matter of fact, cooperative and savings banks found, very early in their history, a solution to this supposed trade-off between relationship banking and economies of scale: two-tier structures. Such structures have been mentioned above as a solution to several agency problems in banking. They also offer a solution to the problem at hand. Networks encourage economies of scale and enhance bank funding opportunities.[113] Network integration (within a banking cooperative network) may also help reduce volatility of performance among cooperatives, providing joint-liability and/or cross-guarantees,[114] as will be discussed in the following sections. Importantly, two-tiered networks help banks reap economies of scale while avoiding the pitfalls of vertical integration: as Fama and Jensen argued, the expense preferences of managers increase with institutional size – but less so in networks.[115] Finally, networks expand the range of products and services offered by local banks, which tends to strengthen relationship banking.[116]

The only problem with two-tiered networks seems to be the 'appropriability hazard' –basically a free-rider problem that arises from new agency conflicts within the network.[117] This hazard may also be overcome through tighter network integration and peer pressure, as seen above.

As a conclusion, therefore, the two-tier structure of independent local and regional retail banking institutions and shared wholesale operations allows alternative banks to reap significant advantages in terms of economies of scale while retaining relationship banking networks.

Access to Capital at a Lower Cost

As argued in previous chapters, a key characteristic of alternative banks is their source of funding: essentially retained profits (for cooperative and private savings banks) and public endowments (for public savings banks and public development banks). In particular, as Fonteyne pointed out, cooperative banks only need to remunerate the part of their equity that is represented by member shares.[118] This allows them to mobilize and retain capital and reach comfortable levels of liquidity, high deposit:loan ratios and be net lenders on the interbank market. In fact, low pay-out ratios mean that cooperative banks (and, one may add, public savings and development banks) 'can enjoy rapid growth in their capital base and therefore fast organic growth'.[119] Altunbas et al. further argued that cooperative and public bank performance can be explained by lower funding costs associated with their specific deposit base and their reliance on 'less interest rate sensitive' retail customers.[120]

Indeed, although it can be harder for cooperative and mutual savings banks than joint-stock banks to raise external capital,[121] their long history and stable deposit base provide viable options. Entrenched retail market positions and loyal customers, cited by Fonteyne as sources of comparative advantage,[122] do explain alternative bank capacity to grow deposit bases. But this entrenchment also results from, and is strengthened by, the exceptional level of trust placed by customers in alternative banks.[123] As argued in Chapter 1, trust in alternative banks is the outcome of a long history of serving low-income households and local communities. This also means that alternative banks are less inclined to exploit information asymmetries favouring banks over borrowers or depositors.[124] Further, Giannola argues that the greater capital reserves accumulated by alternative banks give them a 'patrimonial advantage' during transition to Basel II and III Accords.[125] This is a promising line of research that has not, to our knowledge, been explored yet.

Fonteyne further argued that the cost of capital will lose relevance in the overall cost of providing retail financial services in the near future (and therefore a lower cost of capital will lose saliency as a source of competitive advantage).[126] But he wrote that argument before the 2007–8 crisis. With the hindsight of very costly recapitalization of most banks throughout the world, either as a regulatory requirement or as a prudential strategy, being able to access capital at a low cost should remain a fundamental source of competitive advantage in the banking industry. This, of course, runs contrary to the argument put forward by Rasmussen and others,[127] namely that mutual managers should not be expected to minimize costs – and that therefore the 'choice' of mutual banks must be based on depositors' confidence that mutual managers will pick a safer portfolio. This is where the peculiar 'historical embeddedness' of alternative banks' business models become important.

The History and Durability of Alternative Banks as a Key Source of Competitive Advantage

Both the fruits of relationship lending and the access to capital at a lower cost might actually be a curse to alternative banks. Hart and Moore thus argued that institutions maximizing consumer surplus (and not profit), such as cooperatives, will distribute this surplus to customers through price subsidies (interest rate subsidies in the case of cooperative financial institutions).[128] This may distort decisions and lead to inefficient outcomes. Canning et al., however, suggested that credit rationing might be a more optimal solution for distribution of consumer surpluses.[129] In discussing the optimizing decisions of not-for-profit financial institutions, the same authors mentioned the possibility that alternative banks might have an advantage in 'achieving economically efficient outcomes'. However, they attributed this to market failures and monopoly power in general.[130] Yet these arguments underestimate the dynamic outcomes of the particular business models of alternative banks, and their capacity to provide a more sustainable basis for credit relationships over time.

Alternative Bank Sustainable Business Models

A fourth source of competitive advantage, which allows alternative banks to be simultaneously more profitable and less risky, stems from their long-term-oriented, sustainable business models. Their models rely, in turn, on multiple elements. Alternative bank shareholder-oriented governance, non-profit missions, social mandates, and independent operations and branch office networks embedded in local communities create a unique set of incentives and constraints that shape alternative bank behaviour. Their 'entrenched' retail base and the high level of trust they elicit also support more sustainable business models.

The governance characteristics of alternative banks generate higher stability at board and managerial levels,[131] which entails longer-term strategies and higher stability of earnings. Alternative bank aversion to short-term profit maximization helps explain better long-term performance. According to Iannotta et al., the lower riskiness of alternative banks arises from a higher loan quality and higher degree of risk aversion.[132] Alternative banks also tend to maintain lower revenue diversification, which is another factor of stability.[133] In fact, lower revenue diversification 'more than offsets [alternative banks'] lower profitability and capitalization'.[134] In addition, increased stability lowers the cost of credit risk, which may be an important factor in the better cost-efficiency of alternative banks.[135]

Lower-income diversification is a crucial factor explaining alternative bank performance in terms of risk management. As mentioned in the introduction to this chapter, banks have, in recent decades, diversified away from traditional banking (collecting deposits and making loans) on both sides of the balance sheet. On the liability side, diversification and expansion have made private banks much more reliant on other funding sources. Mainstream banking theory suggested that 'deposit financing makes banks vulnerable to runs'.[136] However, the 2007–8 crisis surely suggests that wholesale funding on capital markets may increase instability.[137] Given these different views, further research comparing the liability risk of alternative banks and private banks is required.

On the asset side, banking theory also for a long time expected markets to reduce risk: 'both theory and evidence support the expectation that risks should be reduced rather than increased should banks be permitted to engage in securities, insurance and other services'.[138] This view has also lost credibility since the 2008 banking crisis. As De Jonghe showed in a study of a sample of European banks, 'the shift to non-traditional banking activities increases banks' tail betas and thus reduces banking system stability because interest income is less risky than all other revenue streams'.[139]

There is also evidence that increased reliance on fee-based income leads to higher revenue volatility – so that income diversification actually increases rather than decreases risk.[140] DeYoung and Roland, in particular, showed that for US commercial banks, an increase in product mix (i.e. bank movement towards non-interest-bearing activities) has led to higher revenue volatility, compensated for by higher levels of revenues (as a risk premium).[141] Recent empirical evidence for European small banks showed similar results, i.e. income diversification increases risk;[142] De Jonghe showed that for European listed banks, income diversification increases systemic bank risk measured as 'tail beta', that is the likelihood that extreme negative swings in bank stock will be linked to negative swings in bank indexes.[143] By contrast, Chiorazzo et al. found a positive relationship between increased reliance on non-interest income and risk-adjusted returns for small Italian banks.[144] Stiroh found that diversification to non-interest income is related to lower profits and higher risks in the US banking industry.[145]

Therefore, it can be argued that one of the reasons for greater stability and better overall performance of alternative banks is their lower revenue diversification, which is the direct outcome of their specific governance and business model and, perhaps, their smaller average size (except for development banks). This also explains why alternative banks resisted the 'originate-to-distribute' (OTD) model and retained traditional 'originate-to-hold' (OTH) models. The originate-to-distribute model creates serious pitfalls. Banks selling loans on the secondary market face issues of adverse selection and moral hazard.[146] Berndt and Gupta also showed that banks actively engaged in loan selling on secondary markets underperform their peers by about 9 per cent a year in terms of risk-adjusted abnormal returns. The authors concluded that the OTD model might not be socially desirable.[147] This result is hard to reconcile with standard theory that 'in equilibrium, banks with private information cannot systematically take advantage of outside investors'.[148] So stakeholder-based banks, which have a higher propensity to remain faithful to the OTH model, are likely to exhibit higher earnings stability as well.[149]

Alternative Banks are Better Equipped to Smooth Inter-temporal Risk

One key comparative advantage of banks with respect to capital markets, Allen and Gale argued, lies in their ability to smooth inter-temporal risk.[150] That is, banks are able to accumulate capital in good times and use it in bad times. As Ayadi et al. point out, 'Creating and unlocking reserves is a specific technique of risk management'.[151] This argument is an extension of the liquidity creation thesis,[152] according to which access to refinancing at low cost and the ability of banks to enforce repayment or liquidate bad loans are key determinants of bank ability to create liquidity. This is the theoretical basis for our claim that greater client confidence and trust in alternative banks provide a competitive advantage over private banks. While clients tend to withdraw deposits from private banks during banking crises, deposits often *increase* at alternative banks during crises. This reinforces the capacity of alternative banks to provide counter-cyclical lending.[153] In other words, alternative banks are ideally positioned to perform the inter-temporal risk-smoothing function.[154]

This ability of alternative banks can be explained by several factors. First, as emphasized above, alternative banks benefit from greater trust by their depositors, which is the outcome of their history, stable governance, social mandate and prudent behaviour. Second-tier organizations also strengthen trust, for instance through cross-guarantee schemes.[155] As a consequence, alternative banks are able to accumulate capital more quickly through their extensive retail deposit base – even in hard times. In a related argument, Berlin and Mester showed that rate-insensitive core deposits allow for inter-temporal smoothing in lending rates.[156]

Secondly, alternative bank capital is different from joint-stock bank equity, in that it does not belong to the 'current cohort of members'.[157] Indeed, it can be viewed as an 'owner-less intergenerational endowment that is available for use by current members, under the implicit or explicit understanding that they will grow it further and pass it on to the next generation of members'.[158] In addition, alternative banks are under no pressure to sell these resources on the market – precisely the kind of pressure that capital markets put on joint-stock banks,[159] in line with the free cash flow problem evoked earlier.

Third, inter-temporal risk-smoothing is also linked to relationship banking. As noted by Boot,[160] the durability of the bank–borrower relationship positively affects credit availability, especially for young firms or borrowers without credit history: indeed, the losses incurred by banks at the outset of banking relationships, which constitute a form of credit subsidy,[161] are recouped over time as the relationship unfolds, in terms of better soft information and trust.

Conclusion

Alternative banks have many potential sources of competitive advantage that can be understood by drawing on contemporary banking theory. In particular, mainstream views of the banking firm, based on agency theory and property rights theory, yield perhaps surprisingly favourable conclusions on the efficiency and governance of savings banks, cooperative banks and public banks. Second, the ways in which modern theories conceive information asymmetries in banking provide further grounds to explain how alternative banks may outperform for-profit competitors. Finally, less explored hypotheses about the way banks operate, and in particular their role in smoothing inter-temporal risk, also potentially favour alternative banks. This, we suggest, may provide solid grounds for a more ambitious theory of alternative banking, or rather of banking tout court: one founded on institutional rather than functional bases.

5 A QUALITATIVE AND STATISTICAL ANALYSIS OF EUROPEAN COOPERATIVE BANKING GROUPS

Hans Groeneveld

Introduction

The European banking sector is not homogeneous. Basically, one can distinguish between public banks, investor-owned banks and stakeholder-owned banks. The latter category comprises savings banks, credit unions, mutuals and cooperative banks. There are indications that these stakeholder-owned banks weathered the subsequent storms relatively well so far, without large-scale state support.[1] At the same time, as stated in Part I of this volume, these types of banks did not receive much attention before the financial crisis hit, and hence the question arose why these banks apparently have avoided great financial distress.

This chapter tackles this question for the largest category within the family of stakeholder value banks: European cooperative banking groups (henceforth ECBGs). Acknowledging the heterogeneity of ECBGs,[2] the possible connection between the common features and the relative performance of fifteen ECBGs over the latest business cycles is explored. Where appropriate, the text will be larded with concrete examples of individual ECBGs. More specifically, this chapter investigates whether long-standing assertions about the corporate governance and organizational features of stakeholder-owned banks are reflected in differences between performance indicators of ECBGs and all other banks in the time span 1997/2002–2011.

In this respect, this chapter complements existing but scarce academic studies and policy reports on financial cooperatives in various ways. Contrary to other studies, this chapter analyses the central issue in a concise historical perspective and in the context of organizational characteristics of ECBGs. Second, we examine fifteen ECBGs simultaneously over a similar and relatively long time span, which enables us to draw robust conclusions about the cooperative banking sector. Most recent works addressing this issue are case studies of – specific aspects of – individual ECBGs in different times of financial distress and/or over relatively short time spans,[3] which result in a diffuse picture without general conclusions. Third, we shall empirically validate qualitative postulations about ECBGs from previous publications.[4] Fourth, we not only investigate the relative performance of ECBGs in (recent) times of crisis, but our sample period also incorporates times of economic prosperity.

The chapter is structured as follows. The following section sketches the roots, organizational structure and evolution of ECBGs. We briefly describe how they eventually emerged from small local credit cooperatives more than a century ago.[5] This clarification provides useful starting points for understanding their recent performance. Subsequently, the reasons for the past disregard and recent appraisal of the – proclaimed social-economic and governance characteristics of the – cooperative banking model are discussed. We then formulate testable hypotheses, which are derived from the preceding sections, after which we highlight our newly constructed and more comprehensive database. The database covers a broad range of indicators for fifteen ECBGs in ten European countries and similar measures for entire banking systems of the countries in question. The sample period runs from 1997/2002 up to 2011. This sample period encompasses more than one business cycle. The final section contains the empirical results, which are explained in the context of considerations from previous sections. An important research question is whether the comparative performance of ECBGs differs between economically good and bad times and whether the results are in line with the proclaimed specific features and original cooperative characteristics.

The Transformation of Local Credit Cooperatives into ECBGs

The history and evolution of many ECBGs is extensively documented.[6] In short, most cooperative banks were established more than a century ago in response to the problems that small urban and rural businesses had in accessing financial services. These groups could only obtain loans at exorbitant interest rates from moneylenders.[7] From the very first credit cooperatives promoted by Schulze-Delitzsch (1808–83) and Raiffeisen (1818–88), they adopted an organizational model based on democratic governance and mutualism. Beginning in Germany, the cooperative banking concept gradually spread to the rest of the continent and to the Nordic countries. It was about offering opportunities for banking inclusion to large groups in society. In economic terms, credit cooperatives were established to correct market failures and to overcome the associated problems of asymmetric information in favour of borrowers. They could do so because member/consumers financed the institutions and were involved in the decision-making process.

Within small communities, relatively intimate knowledge of each other's credit and trustworthiness guaranteed that loans were only provided to borrowers who could be expected to repay them. Financial incentives for members to monitor each other and social networks among members (i.e. 'social capital'[8]) contributed significantly to the flourishing of cooperative banks.[9] Local credit cooperatives became widespread and were physically close to their members via dense local branch networks. In line with their objectives, credit cooperatives did not aim at maximizing short-term profits; but profits were necessary for further growth and were for the larger part retained and added to the capital base. This feature made them financially solid and well capitalized, with a low risk profile. Credit cooperatives also inherently strived for long-term relationships with their members, who were clients, owners and depositors at the same time.

Not all cooperative banks managed to survive the ravages of time. Quite a few cooperatively organized banks were unable to adapt to technological, social or competitive changes and consequently disappeared or now just live a marginal existence.[10] Many countries never had a cooperative banking sector of any significance because the cooperative ideas did not find fertile soil as a result of cultural factors. In other countries, cooperative banks chose to be acquired by other banks or have converted into investor-owned banks.[11]

Over time the cooperative banking model of the 'survivors' evolved and differentiated into a multiplicity of European institutions, with characteristics reflecting the needs of cooperative members on the one hand and the specificities of national legislative frameworks on the other.[12] The majority of local credit cooperatives developed via national (network) organizations into internationally active banking groups. These developments were partly prompted by regulatory requirements or the necessary realization of economies of scale and higher efficiency levels from a competitive point of view. Some ECBGs have sold a part of their business activities to investors or became partly listed, thus gradually transforming into a hybrid type of financial cooperative.[13] Hence the organizational structures are definitely not static, but are constantly evolving.[14]

Figure 5.1 presents the distribution of ECBGs included in this study according to asset size, from the smallest to the largest. The ratio of the largest (the French Crédit Agricole Group) to the smallest (the Portuguese Crédito Agricola Group) is 144, which shows the great disparity in sizes. ECBGs also vary in terms of their attitudes to membership and their interpretation of cooperative values. Some banks strive to make every customer a member, while others are not actively recruiting members.[15] Other striking differences include the extent of centralization and integration within the networks,[16] the size and focus of international activities, and the design of the cooperative governance with member authority.[17] In most cases, governance reform and competitive pressures have fostered an accentuated centralization of strategic and operating functions and processes. This has led to the establishment of so-called higher-tier networks, which still vary from loose associations to cohesive groups.[18] In a few cases, the central institution has an important supervisory role over its local bank members.[19]

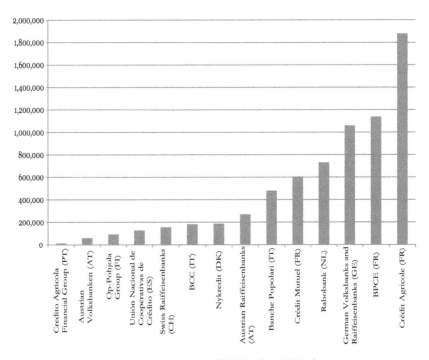

Figure 5.1: Asset size of ECBGs (in € billion).

Source: Data provided by ECBGs and pertain to 2011.

A general feature of ECBGs is the existence of some form of internal solvency and liquidity safety nets, except for the Italian *banche popolari*. These structures form the core of internal mutual support schemes in ECBGs. In essence, these schemes offer network resources to ensure the solvency and liquidity of the participating local or regional cooperative banks in a network organization. As such, these support schemes come on top of the coverage provided by the compulsory and supplementary deposit insurance schemes that are in place in individual countries. Most ECBGs have cross-guarantees that are commitments or obligations by participating entities to provide liquidity to a troubled local cooperative bank.[20] This makes them financially solid and contributes to relatively high ratings for ECBGs.[21] Due to all these factors, many outside observers find that cooperatives have relatively complex governance structures given their fragmentation of ownership (the 'one member one vote' principle), decision rights, mutual guarantees and multilevel boards.[22]

The Era of Underexposed and Fading Cooperative Banking Features

For a long time, the features and values of the cooperative banking model did not attract a lot of attention in articles, the press, reports and scholarly research for various reasons.[23] First, the original 'mission' of cooperative banks seems to have been largely completed and the original 'raisons d'être' of cooperative banks have become less valid; almost everyone in Western Europe has access to financial services today, and the need to promote financial inclusion is hardly present anymore. Moreover, the comparative disadvantages that non-cooperative banks faced in the past for servicing small farmers and small businesses have also largely disappeared. Legal frameworks now offer much stronger contract enforceability, and verifiable information about potential borrowers is generally available. In other words, the traditional differentiators of the former credit cooperatives have become less pronounced and less understood over time.

Another reason is that the transformation of local credit cooperatives into (inter)national network organizations (ECBGs) has resulted in varying degrees of hybridization with the 'capitalist' corporate model. Besides, the proclaimed multiple goals of ECBGs are generally more difficult to understand than the theoretically more easily interpretable goal of profit maximizing held by most listed banks. As pointed out by Ayadi et al.,[24] cooperative banks can be categorized as 'dual bottom line' institutions. They claim to fulfil other equally important objectives than mere shareholder value creation. This suggests that financial performance and economic efficiency are neither the only nor the ultimate standard of assessment for ECBGs. These aspects are indisputably important, but they are not sufficient to assess the contributions of cooperative banks to society and the economy.

As elaborated earlier, the rich diversity in existing governance and organizational structures and business models, the changing and varying degrees of member influence at the local and central level, the divergent functions of the central institutions and the different focal points in foreign activities also hinder straightforward evaluations of ECBGs. The European cooperative banking sector can be characterized as 'Commonality with Diversity'. Apart from this diversity, the limited attention for ECBGs was also due to perceived decreasing differences in employee behaviour, financial products, services, prices, operations and business lines compared to competitors.[25] ECBGs became visibly active in non-retail activities and expanded across domestic frontiers and evolved into large and complex business structures.

Moreover, the dominance of free-market thinking and the associated Anglo-Saxon model aimed at profit and shareholder value maximization did not encourage great interest in ECBGs. In this shareholder value era, some (subsidiaries of) ECBGs actually got partly listed[26] or adopted practices from banks with other organizational forms. Other ECBGs extensively debated whether or not to exchange the cooperative model for the shareholder value model,[27] because this was considered to be an appropriate way to attract external capital for faster growth.[28] Hence ECBGs themselves were also partly responsible for confusion and contempt of their cooperative business model. Besides, some ECBGs do not report reliable empirical data or longer and consistent time series for key cooperative and financial indicators, partly because they do not have the same extensive reporting requirements as listed banks. This aspect obviously hampers an objective evaluation of their business model and impedes empirical and scholarly research.

All these developments were not favourable to retaining a clearly visible cooperative identity, and the collaboration with or adoption of elements of non-cooperative enterprises have been sometimes viewed as a capitulation to capitalism. In fact, ECBGs were sometimes forced into a defensive position prior to the crisis as their cooperative business model was considered to be rather misty, outdated or even detrimental to the entire banking sector.[29] Cooperative institutions were not considered the most efficient, vibrant or innovative institutions for a long time. PA Consulting Group even accused cooperative banks for 'spoiling' the market conditions for other banks.[30] Others[31] underscored the sluggishness and lack of transparency of decision-making processes or exaggerated the principal–agent problem inside ECBGs on the basis of merely theoretical considerations.[32]

Assertions about ECBGs

The European Association of Cooperative Banks (EACB) and the International Cooperative Banking Association (ICBA) made efforts to emphasize the special nature of cooperative banks in various reports well before and during the crisis. One of the messages is that the customer has always been and is still at the core of their operations and, at a local level, members still have a say in the local member bank's policy.[33] It is also suggested that cooperative banks have an 'impact presence' on society and the entire banking market. Here, some qualitative publications refer to their contribution to economic growth, employment and the creation of more favourable interest rate conditions for customers.

Another claim is that the orientation of the domestic cooperative banking part inside ECBGs has remained relatively unaltered.[34] The first-level cooperative banks are still predominantly targeted towards retail banking and servicing the real economy, i.e. private individuals and SMEs, because effective member influence would force them into this direction. This would also translate into a lasting engagement with regional and local communities and the real economy, which would be visible in relatively dense branch networks, i.e. physical proximity to customers and members. It is also stated that proximity is further reinforced through the participation in numerous social networks and by actively supporting the local communities. Consequently, the well-known academic issue of asymmetrical information between the bank and the customer when providing loans could be less pronounced in cooperative banking. With their assumed strong local ties and networks, local banks are in theory better equipped to assess the creditworthiness and risks of customers at a local level. The danger of moral hazard and adverse selection would consequently be more limited. If that is true, it can be assumed that – alongside the asserted focus on customer value – this differentiator will be reflected, particularly in unfavourable times, in relatively higher lending to households and corporate customers.

Retail banking is mainly about relationship banking, which goes hand in hand with a long-term orientation.[35] This would imply that especially local cooperative banks within ECBGs do not aim at (short-term) profit from their operations, services and products for members and customers and themselves, but champion instead a 'dual bottom line' approach. They do seek profit, and they also strive for economic and social welfare in local communities. Consequently, their returns on equity or assets are expected to be more stable and lower. Their risk profile should be also comparatively moderate.

Despite all the changes in the financial structures and composition of their balance sheets, it is also assumed that ECBGs still add a considerable part of their net profits to their capital and reserves, which would lead to a solid capitalization and, consequently, relatively high ratings. These comparatively high ratings would also stem from existing legally binding cross-guarantees to connect different entities of the group as a risk management tool. Rating agencies tend to view this type of arrangement as less risky since the entire organization is viewed as a single consolidated risk unit.

Until the breakout of the credit crisis, many position papers and background documents extolling the virtues of cooperative banking had a predominantly qualitative character and lacked 'empirical' proof. It is undeniable, however, that cooperative banks stand out in terms of their history, structure, organizational form and original business objectives from other banks. But these aspects were often ill understood and misinterpreted, as elaborated in the previous section. The main observable differentiator of ECBGs is their specific corporate governance, and in particular the varying degree of member control. Member influence surely cannot rule out policy mistakes, but it can basically bridge the distance between executives and policymakers and the most important stakeholder, the customer. Theoretically, this intrinsic feature is *only* a precondition for ECBGs to be able to operate or position themselves differently in the market.

The Appraisal of Cooperative Banking Features

The crises of the past five years have changed opinions and views about cooperative banks for the better. Preliminary evidence indicated that the cooperative organizational form in general had performed significantly better than other organizational forms after the global financial crisis of 2007–8 and the following recession.[36] Policymakers, regulators and academics started to wonder whether these achievements could indeed be related to asserted specifics of the cooperative banking model. Furthermore, the interest in the cooperative business model was boosted by the United Nation, which declared 2012 as the International Year of Cooperatives.[37] In addition, international consultancy firms[38] and the *Economist*[39] started paying attention to the merits and characteristics of the cooperative business model.

The financial crisis cast doubt on the alleged shortcomings of the cooperative banking model and the perceived superiority of the shareholder value business model.[40] For a long time, comparisons of the pros and cons of corporate governance structures between cooperative banks and investor-owned banks were sometimes misleading as they were based on incorrect starting points. The issue is that it is not always clear on what basis the comparison was being made: (i) the ideal investor-owned bank, (ii) the ideal cooperative bank, (iii) the actual investor-owned bank, and (iv) the actual cooperative bank model. In other words, it is necessary to distinguish between how institutions behave in some abstract, theoretical or ideal state, and the way they operate in practice. The ideal investor-owned model has clear-cut principles defining objectives, accountability and control. Therefore the corporate governance of these banks was deemed to be superior to the observed cooperative model, where many theoretical flaws of any corporate governance were thought to apply in practice.[41]

However, recent experience unambiguously points to ill-functioning aspects of corporate governance arrangements in investor-owned banks: the actual investor-owned model is not ideal in practice.[42] At the same time, the theoretical shortcomings of corporate governance arrangements in cooperative banks were magnified and exaggerated for a long time.[43] For instance, it has often been – rightly – questioned whether cooperative banks really behave in the interests of their customers and members, particularly in light of their sometimes 'erratic' international strategies. Moreover, 'hard proof' for greater customer satisfaction and stronger customer advocacy at ECBGs compared to other banks is not readily available, though some surveys do hint at less loss of trust of customers in cooperative banks.[44] Be that as it may, one can assert equally well that the management of quite some investor-owned banks has visibly failed to operate in the interests of their shareholders by following strategies to maximize shareholder value, which caused huge losses and write-downs and necessitated large-scale government intervention in the last few years.[45] In conclusion, it is misleading to compare the actual behaviour of a cooperative bank model with some mythical, ideal form of investor-owned model. It must be acknowledged that in practice both forms operate imperfectly, and in the world of the second-best, no safe conclusions can be drawn regarding the superiority of one form over the other.

Another viewpoint regarding cooperative banking has also changed recently. It is increasingly acknowledged that cooperative banking is not synonymous to some kind of 'philanthropic' banking that mainly exists to achieve social objectives.[46] Cooperative banks simply need to have adequate and innovative products and services at fair prices and state-of-the-art distribution concepts. These are the basic conditions needed to survive and operate on banking markets and to be chosen by customers as their primary bank. Cooperative banks must be entrepreneurial, cost-effective, efficient and businesslike organizations. Otherwise, they will be unable to deliver customer value, to realize sufficient profits to ensure the continuity of their banking activities, and to cope with heavy and intensifying competition. The cooperative business model demands cost and revenue levels for banking activities that do not deviate substantially from the standards of the banking industry. Only if these business conditions are fulfilled can cooperative banks in principle use their corporate governance to position themselves and operate differently in the market, i.e. with a longer-term perspective focused on customer value, and pursue non-financial goals.[47]

Hypotheses

The aftertaste of recent academic and policy literatures on cooperative banks is that ECBGs still have internal characteristics and business orientations that can be traced back to the key features of the former credit cooperatives. In short, member ownership is believed to contribute to continuity and a cautious course of ECBGs via specific internal governance mechanisms. If true, these specifics will show up in a divergent performance of ECBGs compared to other banks. We shall test which proclaimed differentiators and assertions from previous sections are valid and visible throughout recent business cycles. From our understanding of cooperative banks' history and operations, we have inferred five main interrelated hypotheses.

Hypothesis 1: ECBGs Have a Strong Customer Focus and Client Proximity

The alleged engagement with local communities and the real economy as well as member influence should imply the existence of relatively dense branch networks. If ECBGs really put the customer interests first, are not risk-seekers or profit maximizers (with a view to obtaining excessive bonuses), this should also be visible in recent data, especially in times of crises. Indeed, many consumers lost confidence in their financial institutions and financial advisors and were not satisfied with their behaviour and performance in recent years. Moreover, the absence of explicit profit targets due to the proclaimed focus on customers' interests, member influence and the emphasis on retail banking is expected to show up in lower average returns on assets (and equity) than investor-owned banks.

Hypothesis 2: ECBGs Aim at Austerity and Efficiency in Operations

Austerity and efficiency in business operations were important characteristics of local credit cooperatives, which were set up with members' money. Since member ownership still exists, frugality and efficiency should ideally be virtues of present ECBGs as well. Among other things, this implies that the absence of a profit objective, or a lower profit requirement, may not lead to inefficient operations. With regards to income, inefficiency would mean that ECBGs set a suboptimal price and that efficiently operating competitors realize a concealed 'excess return', i.e. profit on top of the 'cooperative price'. Regarding costs, the stated focus on customer value cannot be an excuse for more relaxed cost control and inefficient operations. We shall test this hypothesis by comparing cost-income indicators of ECBGs with those of other banks. These ratios are assumed to be simple and quantifiable proxies for performance amidst austerity and comparative efficiency.

Hypothesis 3: ECBGs are Relatively Stable Institutions with a Focus on Retail Banking

Because of member ownership, ECBGs are believed to be mainly focused on retail, commercial and SME banking. Consequently, they would have a limited appetite for non-core add-ons and a bias towards serving and financing 'real economy' activities. This would be accompanied by a long-term view of relationships with local businesses and municipalities and an innate focus on customers. This area of banking is associated with relatively stable income streams across business cycles and a moderate risk profile. Hence ECBGs are assumed to be fairly stable organizations with moderate returns on assets/equity and a relatively large retail banking business.

Hypothesis 4: ECBGs are Well Capitalized and Have a Low Risk Profile

Independent governance with member influence and ownership and relatively limited access to third-party capital should also naturally lead to conservative behaviour. This could mean that ECBGs steered away from riskier activities and practices, for example operating at relatively high levels of tier 1 capital.[48] The higher capitalization should in turn result in lower returns on equity compared to banks with another business orientation.

Hypothesis 5: ECBGs Have a Positive Impact on their Broader Environment

It is hypothesized here that ECBGs have a positive impact on the macro and local levels, the banking market structure and banking conditions for customers. First, from an economic perspective, they create jobs, contribute to economic growth by granting loans and credits, and aim at a sustainable development of local communities. Second, they are assumed to stimulate stability, diversity and competition in banking. Third, the presence of ECBGs is believed to lead to better conditions for customers, e.g. higher interest rates on savings and lower interest rates on loans.

Sample Description

The main objective of this chapter is to test these hypotheses by investigating the performance of fifteen ECBGs vis-à-vis entire banking sectors in eleven countries over the last turbulent decade. These countries and some key characteristics of the included ECBGs are listed in Table 5.1 below.[49] Because of their specific nature, different reporting requirements and heterogeneity, it is inappropriate to use databases like Bankscope to collect data on cooperative banks. These databases contain inconsistencies and many caveats regarding cooperative banks. For some cooperative banks, consolidated data for the entire banking group are reported, whereas in other cases unconsolidated data for – small – individual local coopera- tive banks are given. If these differences are ignored, one easily arrives at misleading conclusions. Actually, data on individual local cooperative banks cannot be com- pared with those of other types of banks, which often pertain to consolidated group figures. Besides, individual cooperative banks usually obtain all kinds of support from a central institution (APEX), e.g. products, IT systems and HR services, to reach economies of scale inside the entire cooperative banking group.

For our empirical investigation, we combine several data sources. We use consolidated data for ECBGs which are composed by these groups themselves.[50] If possible and appropriate, we have corrected the figures for major breaks in the time series caused by sizeable mergers and/or acquisitions to be able to make sensible comparisons between ECBGs and entire banking sectors. In countries with more than one cooperative banking group, we have constructed aggregated indicators by using total assets of individual cooperative groups as weights.

Data on entire banking sectors in the countries under review are collected from national central banks or supervisory agencies as well as from the IMF and European Central Bank. The period of analysis is determined by the availabil- ity of good-quality data and spans either 1997–2011 or 2002–11. Both periods encompass years of strong economic growth and financial stability as well as years of economic slack and financial instability. This feature offers the oppor- tunity to test whether the asserted specifics of ECBGs really lead to different performances compared to those of entire banking systems in economically and financially prosperous and difficult times.

Empirical Analysis of ECBGs

Members

As stated before, ECBGs frequently publicly assert that they do not aim at maximizing profits but customer value.[51] Ideally, one would like to verify this assertion with direct insights and opinions from customers, i.e. 'hard data' or empirical evidence. Basically, it comes down to the perception of customers whether ECBGs banks 'walk their talk', or in other words, keep their promises and treat their customers fairly. Unfortunately, information about the perception and appreciation of customers of this proclaimed customer focus and the maximization of customer value is not available for many banks, including ECBGs. Indeed, some ECBGs perform customer satisfaction surveys on a regular basis, but they do not convey the results for competitive reasons. Besides, we feel that customer satisfaction measures do not expose the real issue in client relationships, which is about the level of emotional engagement of consumers with their bank and vice versa.

A more accurate indicator would be the level of 'customer advocacy', the perception by customers that their financial institution does what is right for their clients, not just what is right for the bottom line.[52] Trust and confidence are the key words in this respect. Some recent surveys and reports seem to suggest that cooperative banks have suffered less than other financial institutions from a loss of trust in recent years, but the empirical evidence remains flimsy.[53]

Hence we have to confine ourselves to indirect proxies for customer satisfaction and advocacy. We look at member:population ratios[54] and market shares that contain some implicit information about the attractiveness and popularity of ECBGs. Figure 5.2 shows the development of the number of members and member:population ratio of the included ECBGs in their domestic markets. Table 5.1 offers additional country insights. Strikingly, the number of members has increased every individual year, i.e. also in the era of underexposed cooperative banking features (see previous section). The total number of members rose from around 37 million in 1997 to approximately 52 million in 2011, which equals a growth of about 40 per cent. On average, the member base grew at an annual growth rate of almost 2.5 per cent since 1997. In relative terms, the average member:population ratio showed an upward trend; the ratio rose from 12.9 in 1997 to 16.9 in 2011. As Table 5.1 shows, every ECBG attracted more members, with the notable exception of Denmark.[55] The divergences in the level of this ratio can be explained by differences in the market position of individual ECBGs as well as variations in the attitude towards membership policy. The Dutch Rabobank witnessed by far the largest inflow of members (plus 250 per cent),[56] followed by considerable expansions in Switzerland, Spain and Finland.

Table 5.1: Branches and members in individual countries.

Countries	Branches (1997 = 100)				Member:population ratio			Number of members (1997 = 100)
	ECBGs		TBS*					
	2004	2011	2004	2011	1997	2004	2011	2011
Austria	73	73	129	135	29.8	28.2	28.7	102
Denmark	98	119	70	56	10.4	7.7	5.3	53
Finland	91	72	120	117	12.6	21.1	24.7	205
France	125	141	84	67	25.2	29.4	34.0	147
Germany	76	70	70	56	17.3	18.8	20.8	120
Italy	139	178	113	111	3.0	3.0	4.0	140
The Netherlands	71	48	50	38	3.4	8.9	11.1	355
Portugal	121	135	112	135	2.6	2.9	3.8	148
Spain	132	141	104	102	2.8	3.9	5.3	220
Switzerland	92	83	78	78	10.0	16.9	22.1	246
Total average	104	112	89	80	12.9	14.8	16.9	140

* Number of branches of all other banks, i.e. excluding branches of local cooperative banks.

Note: Data of French and total ECBG branch offices are adjusted for major breaks caused by the acquisition of Crédit Lyonnais by Crédit Agricole in 2006 and the merger of Groupe Banque Populaire and Groupe Caisse d'épargnes in 2009.

Source: ECBGs and the ECB.

Implicitly, the absolute and relative rises in membership point to an increasing popularity of the cooperative banking model. The underlying reasons for the absolute and relative surge in members are hard to isolate and will probably be of a financial and immaterial nature.[57] It merely indicates that ECBGs have succeeded in attracting new members with their products, advisory services, client approach, business models or other features. The increase also signals confidence of customers in ECBGs and corroborates tentative results of some fragmented surveys.[58] Indeed, clients would presumably not be very eager to become members if the level of trust and satisfaction were low.

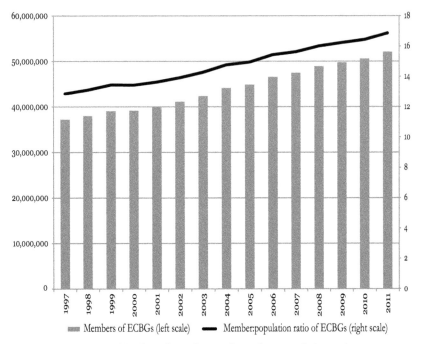

Members of ECBGs (left scale)   ▬ Member:population ratio of ECBGs (right scale)

Figure 5.2: Number of members and member:population ratio.

Source: National demographic statistics and ECBGs.

Domestic Loan and Deposit Market Shares

The increase in the number of members has translated into rising market shares in national retail banking markets. Since 1997 ECBGs succeeded in steadily and continuously increasing their domestic market shares in mortgages and consumer loans as well as in private savings throughout economic cycles. On average, both retail market shares rose by about 10 percentage points to 26 per cent in 2011. In the turbulent years of 2007–11, ECBGs also strengthened their domestic market positions, but the increase did not differ significantly from that in the other sub-periods. These rises imply shifts of many billions of euro in loans and deposits towards ECBGs. The annual increases were mostly caused by endogenous growth, though in some years acquisitions or mergers were also partly responsible for the rise in overall market shares.[59] The underlying data show that on balance no individual ECBG lost domestic market share over this period. Two-thirds of all ECBGs increased their market shares, whereas the market position of other ECBGs remained stable. Like the substantial increase in the number of members, rising market shares are just signs that customers felt relatively more attracted to ECBGs for a myriad of different reasons.

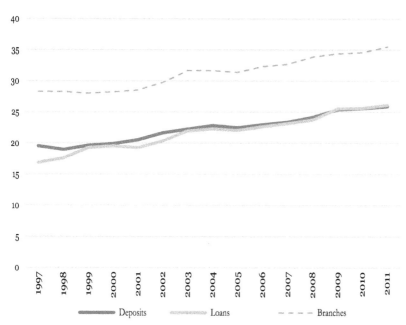

Figure 5.3: Average market share of deposits, loans and branches of ECBGs (as per cent).

Note: The unweighted market shares pertain to domestic loans to private households (mortgages and/or consumer loans) and domestic retail deposits of households. The market
share of branches is defined as the branches of the local cooperative banks as a percentage
of total bank offices.

Source: Calculations based on data from individual ECBGs and the ECB.

Total Loan and Deposit Growth

Total loan and deposit growth rates shed additional light on the performance
and specifics of ECBGs. Figure 5.4 and Table 5.2 provide visual and statistical
information about – the variance of – total (inter)national credit growth to the
non-financial private sector since 1997 for ECBGs (CG_{ECBG}) and entire banking sectors (CG_{TBS}). A couple of salient aspects stand out. CG_{ECBG} is fairly stable
and equals 8.3 per cent in every sub-period considered. CG_{ECBG} also surpassed
CG_{TBS} in every sub-period. Hence ECBGs are more stable loan providers to the
real economy than all other banks. The standard deviation of CG_{TBS} is generally
much higher, as Table 5.2 demonstrates.

Table 5.2: Average loan and deposit growth and loan:deposit ratio.

Period	Loan growth (standard deviation)		Deposit growth (standard deviation)		Loan:deposit ratio	
	ECBGs	TBS	ECBGs	TBS	ECBGs	TBS
1997–2004	8.3* (2.6)	5.8 (2.6)	5.7* (2.4†)	4.0 (2.9)	0.92*	1.31
2005–11	8.3* (1.8*)	4.7 (5.3)	6.1* (1.4*)	8.1 (6.1)	1.11†	1.18
1997–2011	8.3* (3.4*)	5.3 (4.0)	5.9 (1.9*)	6.1 (5.0)	1.01*	1.25

Note: Time series are adjusted for major breaks caused by mergers and acquisitions. 'ECBGs' stands for European cooperative banking groups and 'TBS' stands for total banking sectors. Fifteen ECBGs from ten countries are included in the sample. An asterisk (*) and a dagger (†) denote that the variable for European cooperative banking groups is statistically different from that for total banking sectors at the 1% and 5% significance levels, respectively.

Source: Own calculations based on figures from ECBGs, the ECB and national statistics.

Figure 5.4 shows a considerable deceleration of CG_{TBS} compared to CG_{ECBG} after 2006, and this even dropped below zero in 2009 and 2011. CG_{ECBG} also slowed down remarkably, but ECBGs were still in a position to expand their credit portfolios in the sub-period 2005–11 characterized by economically difficult times. This can presumably be largely ascribed to a relatively good capitalization of ECBGs (see section below), which allowed them to meet the credit demand of their customers for a longer period of time. Indeed, not few other banks needed state support to survive and consequently had much less room to grant loans in their deleveraging process. Hence loan data illustrate the relatively close ties of ECBGs to the real economy as well as their focus on retail lending. They also seem to behave in a counter-cyclical way (in line with what is argued by Schclarek in Chapter 3 of the present volume).

Regarding deposit growth, one can also observe some striking developments over the last decade. Like credit growth, deposit growth at ECBGs (DG_{ECBG}) shows a smooth development compared to that at all other banks (DG_{TBS}). ECBGs experienced a fairly stable growth of an important funding source (deposits); the variance of DG_{ECBG} was significantly lower than the variance of DG_{TBS}. The large swings in DG_{TBS} are remarkable. First, we can witness a sharp acceleration of DG_{TBS} from around 4 per cent in 2005 to about 10 per cent in 2006–8. During this period, investor-owned banks presumably needed funding for the strong expansion of their loan portfolios as well as for other investments with higher returns, which appeared to be relatively risky afterwards. Immediately after the initial credit crisis broke out, DG_{TBS} decelerated sharply, which continued in the subsequent years when a deep economic recession and banking crisis in Europe unfolded.

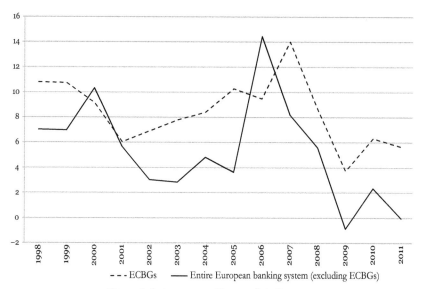

Figure 5.4: Average credit growth in Europe.

Note: The data refer to all (inter)national credits and loans to the non-financial private sector of ECBGs and all other banks.

Source: ECBGs, the ECB and national statistics.

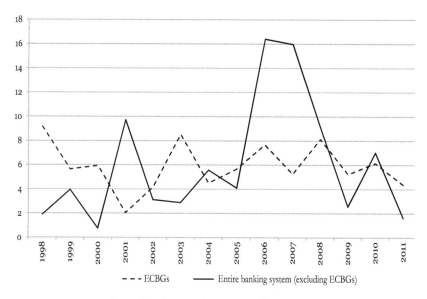

Figure 5.5: Average deposit growth in Europe.

Note: The data refer to all (inter)national credits and loans to the non-financial private sector of ECBGs and all other banks.

Source: ECBGs, the ECB and national statistics.

These observations hint at diverging loan and deposit growth rates between ECBGs and TBS in different economic environments. To check this empirically, we have performed correlation tests between $(CG_{ECBG} - CG_{TBS})$ and $(DG_{ECBG} - DG_{TBS})$ on the one hand and average economic growth on the other over the period 1997–2011. Figure 5.6 shows the resulting scatter diagram and an estimated regression line. Indeed, both $(CG_{ECBG} - CG_{TBS})$ and $(DG_{ECBG} - DG_{TBS})$ are significantly negatively related to economic growth, with correlation coefficients of –0.35 and –0.25, respectively. In a favourable economic climate, non-cooperative banks grant relatively more loans and obtain comparatively more savings and deposits from households and enterprises. In times of moderate economic growth, ECBGs attract relatively more savings and deposits and provide proportionally more loans than all other banks. This negative correlation could stem from the fact that uncertainty about the health of other banks in troubled times provokes customers to choose the – perceived and acknowledged – more financially solid ECBGs. ECBGs appear to fulfil a more stable role in the financial intermediation process. Put differently, customers tend to select banks with a higher risk profile and a more generous credit policy in a booming economy. These findings point to a safe haven effect and a risk-averse attitude of ECBGs.

Dividing total loans by total deposits yields so-called loan:deposit ratios (LDRs). These ratios indicate the extent to which banks depend on capital market funding. Over the entire time span and first sub-period, LDR_{ECBG} was significantly lower than LDR_{TBS}. ECBGs are on average less dependent on volatile and uncertain external funding than TBS. However, in the turbulent second sub-period, a remarkable convergence between both LDRs occurred; LDR_{ECBG} increased, whereas LDR_{TBS} came down. Yet the difference remained significant at the 5 per cent confidence level in 2005–11. When the crisis hit, the high LDR_{TBS} proved to be unsustainable and necessitated large-scale government intervention and a subsequent cutback in credit growth on behalf of private banks in Europe.[60] LDRs are yet another expression of the different nature of ECBGs with their predominant focus on retail banking.

Proximity and Dense Branch Networks

Financial cooperatives have historically maintained extensive branch networks to support strong links to their members and communities. Although ECBGs underscore the urgency to focus on efficiency improvements in their networks as a result of mobile banking, contactless payments and integrated cash management, they still operate with relatively dense networks. The average market share for branch offices of ECBGs even shows an upward trend since 1997. It is approximately 10 percentage points higher than that for loans and deposits. This fact supports Hypothesis 1 that ECBGs usually have relatively dense branch networks in their home markets. On balance, the number of branches of ECBGs increased from around 54,000 in 1997 to more than 60,000 in 2011, whereas total bank branches decreased from 191,000 to 170,000 over this period. As a result, ECBGs have strengthened their local presence.

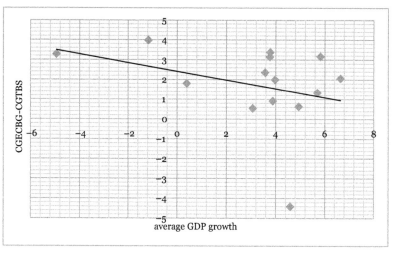

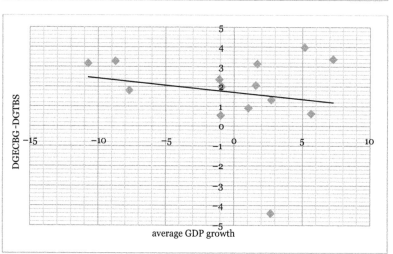

Figure 5.6: Correlation between differences in credit and deposit growth rates and average economic growth, 1997–2011.

Client proximity has been considered as a key driver of cooperative bank success in maintaining customer loyalty and understanding local customer dynamics and risk profiles.[61] However, the pace of technological change is accelerating, and new models for customer interaction with banks outside the traditional branch model are gaining momentum. Moreover, investor-owned banks have increased their focus on their retail clients over the last years as part of their deposit-gathering strategy, thus narrowing some of the differentiation from cooperative banks. Though on average ECBGs remain committed to supporting wide branch networks as a key part of their financial services industry infrastructure, they are also heavily investing in new online and e-mobile payment channels.

As a further example of the heterogeneity of ECBGs, Table 5.1 contains branch data for both ECBGs and national banking sectors. The table reveals that the market share increase was predominantly due to the expansion of branch office networks of ECBGs in Italy, Spain, France, Portugal and Denmark, respectively. Particularly, Italian ECBGs have considerably expanded their networks. The rise in branch market share is also due to the fact that ECBGs have slimmed down the number of branch offices to a somewhat lesser extent than their competitors in Switzerland, Germany and the Netherlands, respectively. Here, the strong consolidation in both the Netherlands and Germany catches the eye. On the other hand, Austrian and Finnish ECBGs lost branch market share because they closed down branches, whereas all other banks actually opened new bank offices. The divergent distribution network policies of ECBGs and different developments in the density of a country's branch networks again mirror diversity in cooperative banking as well as differences in market and competitive conditions in their home markets.

Capitalization

Figure 5.7 shows the average tier-1 ratio for ECBGs (tier-1_{ECBG}) and national banking sectors. This ratio reflects the amount of equity relative to the risk-weighted assets of ECBGs and national banking sectors. One can conclude that ECBGs maintain a comparatively high level of capital, e.g. the risk profile of ECBGs is more conservative than that of all other banks. There are a number of explanations for this.[62] First, high capitalization is connected with the strong focus of ECBGs on retail operations, for which relatively high capital requirements prevail. Second, ECBGs add a major portion of their profit to the capital reserves each year.[63] In effect, they build the core of their equity base the hard way: through increasing retained earnings. Third, solid capitalization is simply necessary for ECBGs with a view to continuity. ECBGs have less additional options to raise capital – after sizeable losses – than investor-owned banks, as most of them cannot issue shares.[64] Besides, this fact could mitigate the risk appetite of executives, because they know that capital cannot be easily replenished after incurring considerable losses.

Figure 5.7 shows that ECBGs entered the crisis period starting in 2007 with a relatively strong capitalization and even strengthened their capital position up to 2010 independently. In 2008 and 2009, not few private banks improved their battered capital positions with government aid or acquired fresh capital. In 2011, tier-1$_{ECBG}$ declined somewhat, whereas tier-1$_{TBS}$ continued to improve slightly. This development is again a reflection of the strong focus of ECBGs on serving the real economy. At that time, many European countries just had gone through a major recession or even re-entered a new one following the credit crisis. Given the emphasis on retail banking, the rising number of failures in the SME sector hit cooperative banks relatively hard.

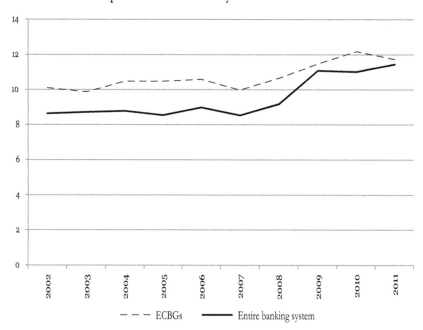

Figure 5.7: Tier 1 ratio.

Source: ECBGs, the ECB, the IMF and national supervisory agencies.

Efficiency

If the claims regarding the business orientation and principles of ECBGs are true, the benchmarking of expenses and revenues of ECBGs against banking sector standards is somewhat misleading. Be that as it may, it is a fact that ECBGs face competition from other banks with less emphasis on profit maximization due to public and political pressure. Hence ECBGs must build scale and operate efficiently to withstand competition. Figure 5.8 displays cost:income ratios for ECBGs (CI$_{ECBG}$) and entire banking sectors (CI$_{TBS}$) in individual countries. Over different sub-periods, CI ratios of individual ECBGs do not deviate significantly from CI ratios of entire banking sectors. This is in line with other preliminary and less comprehensive studies.[65] Moreover, the higher costs of relatively extensive branch networks of ECBGs were more than offset by higher revenues. This outcome suggests that they use their assets and capital base in an efficient way.

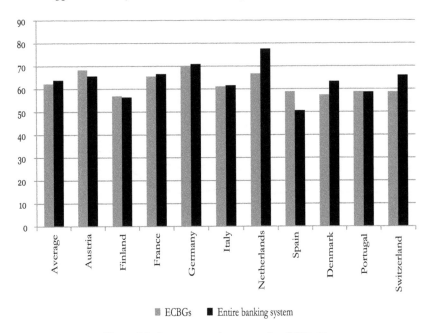

ECBGs   Entire banking system

Figure 5.8: Average cost:income ratios, 2002–11.

Source: ECBGs, the ECB and national supervisory authorities.

Stability

We measure the stability of ECBGs and entire banking systems by using the Z-score. The Z-score is a widely used measure of a bank's distance to default[66] that is monotonically associated with the bank's probability of failure (thus bank risk is defined as the inverse of the Z-score). This variable is defined as:

$$Z\text{-}score_i = (RoA_i + E_i/A_i) / \sigma(RoA_i)$$

where:

RoA is the Return on Assets

E/A stands for equity capital over total assets

σ(RoA) is the standard deviation (volatility) of RoA calculated as a four-year rolling time window[67]

and i denotes European cooperative banking groups (ECBGs) or total banking systems (TBS).

A higher Z-score implies a lower probability of insolvency. Figure 5.9 shows that the average Z-score for ECBGs (Z_{ECBG}) has always been much higher than that of total banking sectors (Z_{TBS}). This finding is in line with the few earlier studies.[68] Formal tests confirm that Z_{ECBG} is significantly higher than Z_{TBS} at the 1 per cent confidence level over the entire time period as well in two sub-periods (Table 5.3). One can also observe that the stability of ECBGs was negatively impacted by the financial turbulences after 2007. Z_{ECBG} dropped from almost 120 in 2007 to less than 60 in 2008, but remained well above Z_{TBS}. Entire banking systems were fairly unstable with a Z_{TBS} of less than 20 in 2008–9. During these years, quite some investor-owned banks had to be supported with state aid or were nationalized to maintain financial stability and confidence among the public.[69] In 2010 and 2011, national banking systems showed a fragile recovery with a slight improvement in Z_{TBS}. This picture does not hold for ECBGs. After reaching its low in 2009, Z_{ECBG} exhibited a strong recovery in the last two years, which points to resilience of ECBGs.

Table 5.3: Components of Z-scores in three sub-periods, unweighted averages.

	Z-score		Equity: assets ratio (in percentage points)		Return on assets (in percentage points)		Standard deviation of RoA	
	ECBGs	TBS	ECBGs	TBS	ECBGs	TBS	ECBGs	TBS
2002–6	91.7*	64.6	6.33*	5.88	0.54	0.58	0.10*	0.14
2007–11	62.8*	28.2	6.44*	5.18	0.35*	0.25	0.20*	0.29
2002–11	77.2*	46.4	6.39*	5.53	0.44	0.42	0.15*	0.22

Note: 'ECBGs' stands for European cooperative banking groups and 'TBS' stands for total banking sectors. An asterisk (*) denotes that the variable for European cooperative banking groups is statistically different from that for total banking sectors at the 1% significance level.

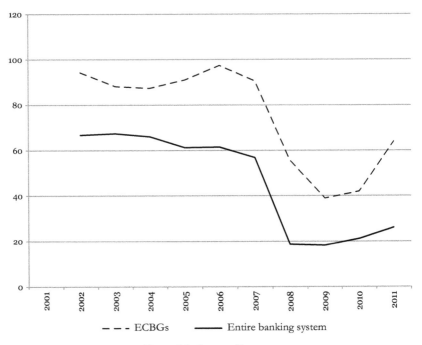

Figure 5.9: Average Z-scores.

Note: The chart displays the average Z-scores of fifteen ECBGs in ten countries and the
    Z-scores of the entire banking sector in these countries.

Source: Calculations based on data from ECBGs, the ECB, the IMF and national supervisory
    authorities.

Looking at the three components of the Z-score, we find that the first component, the ratio of equity/total assets (E/A), is systematically higher at ECBGs (E/
A_{ECBG}; see Figure 5.10 and Table 5.3). This supports Hypothesis 4 that ECBGs
maintain larger capital buffers on average. E/A_{ECBG} remained fairly stable up to
2007, but dropped in 2008. This decline stayed well behind the decrease of E/
A_{TBS}, which already began in 2005. Anyway, ECBGs banks entered the crisis
with larger buffers, which calls for the qualification that in good times, high
buffers are viewed as 'non-productive' as voiced by some earlier critical analyses of ECBGs.[70] On the contrary, the clockwork has swung to the other side.
Improving the resilience of financial institutions by raising capital (and liquidity) requirements is one of the key reforms that followed the financial crisis.
Some improvement in E/A_{TBS} occurred in 2009, partly due to capital injections
by national governments and deleveraging by many banks. This rise did not inau-
gurate a clear trend reversal, as E/A_{TBS} dropped again below 5 per cent in 2011.

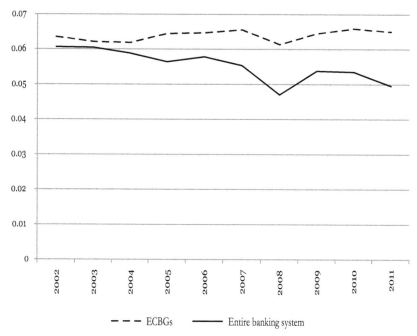

Figure 5.10: Average equity:assets ratio.

Note: the chart displays the average E/A ratio of fifteen ECBGs in ten countries and the average E/A ratio of the entire banking sector in these countries.

Source: Calculations based on data from ECBGs, the ECB, the IMF and national supervisory authorities.

The second component of Z_{ECBG}, the return on assets (RoA_{ECBG}), is a widely used proxy for profitability. Earlier assertions fuel the expectation that ECBGs have below-average profitability, as they target customer value maximization instead of profit maximization and operate with higher levels of equity. Our calculations show that RoA_{ECBG} is not statistically different from the return on assets of total banking systems (RoA_{TBS}) over the whole period and in 2002–6 (see Figure 5.11). This picture changes in the time span 2007–11, when the average RoA_{ECBG} was significantly higher than RoA_{TBS}. ECBGs were obviously affected by the subsequent crises, but RoA_{ECBG} fell less sharply than RoA_{TBS}.[71]

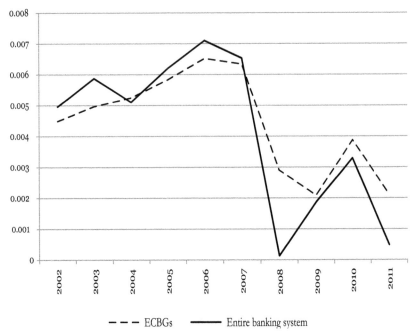

- - - ECBGs   —— Entire banking system

Figure 5.11: Average return on assets.

Note: The chart displays the average RoA of fifteen ECBGs in ten countries and the RoA of the entire banking sector in these countries.

Source: Calculations based on data from ECBGs, the ECB, the IMF and national supervisory authorities.

On the face of it, this finding does not seem to be in line with Hypothesis 1 that ECBGs would have a lower RoA due to their lower profit requirements stemming from their member influence and focus on retail banking. However, this finding can be plausibly explained by the fact that ECBGs were to a lesser extent involved in riskier wholesale operations, and expanded their credit portfolios rather moderately in the years before the crisis. Hence ECBGs experienced fairly limited losses and write-downs. Groeneveld[72] estimates that the share of ECBGs in total losses and write-downs of all European banks during the first years of the crises was around 8 per cent, which is much smaller than their overall market share.[73] In other words, the divergent development of RoA_{ECBG} and RoA_{TBS} confirms Hypothesis 3. It should be stressed that the general situation in banking remains rather troublesome, as illustrated by the sharp drop in RoA in 2011. It is generally expected that profitability in banking will definitely not return to the levels prevailing before 2007. There is general agreement that the situation in banking was not sustainable at that time. Moreover, due to their close ties with the real economy, ECBGs probably suffer more from economic slack in local economies and declining industries in the regions where they operate.

The third component of the Z-score, the volatility of returns, is significantly lower at ECBGs in all sub-periods, again in line with Hypothesis 3. This can be largely explained by the relatively extensive retail operations of cooperative banks, which on the whole generate more stable profits. However, we have to stress that the standard deviation almost doubled in the second time span at ECBGs as well as in total banking systems.

Conclusions

This chapter has aimed to contribute to a balanced view of ECBGs by describing their historical characteristics and investigating empirically to what extent their recent performance is connected with their proclaimed specific and historical features. In this respect, this study is one of the first of this kind providing statistically based evidence on the relationship between the characteristics of cooperative banks and their performance in good and bad economic times over the past fifteen years. This chapter stresses that cooperative banking is not better or worse than other banking models and not a panacea for post-crisis banking in general. It can only be considered as a viable and parallel alternative to investor-owned banks that have been in the spotlight for most of the time in recent decades.

The main message is that the overall performance of ECBGs can still be largely explained by their original features and roots. These characteristics are still present in the ECBGs that emerged from local credit cooperatives established more than a century ago. Using a new comprehensive database, we find that this conclusion holds in recent times of economic distress as well as in times of prosperity. This also implies that we must reconsider earlier studies and reports about the impact of the characteristics and business orientation on the financial performance of ECBGs in economic recessions and financial crises. The specific ownership structure at the local level still appears to result in a focus on retail banking,[74] moderate risk appetite, stable operations and solid capitalization for ECBGs. Indisputably, the economic and financial performance of ECBGs has deviated from that of all other banks in different phases of the latest business cycles.

From different angles, we find statistical support for most of the formulated hypotheses that were derived from unverified or poorly substantiated statements and rather partial analyses with deficient data material in previous policy documents and research papers. Table 5.4 (in the Appendix) summarizes the various sub-hypotheses and spells out whether they can be accepted or must be rejected on the basis of our empirical analysis. It should be noted that the postulations are stated in relative terms, i.e. ECBGs are compared to all other banks in the countries under review.

From a policy point of view, our findings suggest that it is important to acknowledge the relationship between the specific governance and ownership structure of ECBGs and their relative stability and performance.[75] This result has important implications for academics and policymakers alike, since it indicates that ignoring this ownership structure can lead to erroneous banking regulations that may eventually undermine the positive impact of the specific governance on ECBGs' stability and hence the stability of entire national financial systems.

As final remarks, we have to make some qualifications. First, the performance and stability of ECBGs have been assessed in relative terms, i.e. vis-à-vis other banks. In absolute terms, the performance and stability of all ECBGs have deteriorated in recent years. The subsequent crises had a negative impact on ECBGs, proving that they are not immune to economic and financial shocks. Nowadays, ECBGs are confronted with increased volatility in results, a surging number of bankruptcies of – local – SME firms, a damaged reputation of the entire banking industry, and an explosion of regulatory and compliance measures and costs. At the same time, access to external funding and accumulation of capital via retained profits have become more difficult. ECBGs cannot hide from cost reductions and efficiency improvements to remain competitive, financially solid and hence viable. In addition, they face an important internal challenge. ECBGs have to safeguard or improve internal governance structures to enable members to preserve the cooperative nature of their local banks and to determine the strategic course of the entire organization. In short, it will always remain an open question whether ECBGs will manage other future economic and financial crises equally well or will succeed in keeping their overall course and operations closely aligned with member interests in the future.

We also surmise that this chapter has touched upon many issues that deserve further research and elaboration. By refining the data set, cross-section analyses – over different sub-periods – can be conducted to examine whether the performance and stability differ between small and large ECBGs. It would also be illuminating to study developments in their international activities, which generally appear to be riskier than their traditional cooperative banking role.[76] Another important issue concerns the funding of ECBGs.[77] While these organizations have traditionally relied on retained earnings and member financing, they are now operating in a very different environment, like all other banks. For ECBGs, accessing new sources of funding is paramount. Differences in membership policies, the effectiveness and functioning of their governance, and the role and functions of central institutions are also topics for further exploration. In this respect, it would be helpful to set up a consistent international database with qualitative and quantitative information on ECBGs to stimulate academic research and to raise the understanding among policymakers, regulators and the general public about financial cooperatives. Last but not least, a European-wide survey among many bank customers to measure the level of customer satisfaction, value and advocacy is needed to test one of the most important yet unverifiable claims by ECBGs – that they have always put customers' interests first.

Appendix

Table 5.4: Assessment of formulated (sub-)hypotheses about ECBGs, 1997–2011.

Hypothesis	Assessment	Explanation	Empirical evidence
Customer focus, customer interests first, long-term relationships Presence value	Undecided	Absolute and relative increases in members and rising domestic loan and deposit market shares are not 'hard' empirical proof that ECBGs have a strong customer orientation. However, loan growth of ECBGs is less cyclical than that of all other banks. Besides, deposit growth is higher in economically difficult times, pointing to some safe haven effects. It is unknown whether the level of customer satisfaction and/or advocacy at ECBGs differs significantly from that of other banks.	None or implicit at best (rising domestic market shares and numbers of members)
1. Impact on macro and local economy	Trivial	This assertion is awkward. Every bank creates jobs and contributes to economic growth due to its intermediary role. It is impossible to investigate whether ECBGs perform better in this respect.	No adequate data or indicators available
2. Impact on banking market structures	Partly investigated and accepted	It is difficult to demonstrate a noticeable causal relationship between ECBGs and structural characteristics of banking markets. Such a causality is hard to demonstrate empirically, because it also works the other way around: the market environment influences cooperative banks. However, ECBGs do contribute to the stability of national banking systems and diversity in banking and have a focus on retail banking and serving the real economy. It has not been investigated how ECBGs influence the overall competitive environment in banking.	Z-scores point to positive impact on stability and diversity Impact on competitive conditions not investigated
3. Impact on banking conditions for customers	Not investigated	The impact of ECBGs on – the quality of – products and services, distribution methods, innovation and price conditions in banking is not investigated (and would be very difficult).	No adequate data or indicators available
'Dual bottom line' approach	Not investigated	Cooperative local banks within ECBGs are also believed to aim at contributing to a sustainable development of local communities of their members and to be engaged in many local networks. This statement is very difficult to substantiate with empirical data.	No adequate data or indicators available

Hypothesis	Assessment	Explanation	Empirical evidence
Physical proximity	Accepted	ECBGs have relatively dense branch networks in the domestic cooperative banking part.	Market share for branches
Austerity and efficiency in operations	Accepted	Over the entire period, ECBGs have operated with similar efficiency ratios as other banks (despite relatively expensive distribution methods in accordance with their historical roots). ECBGs were even significantly more efficient in the period 2008–11, where many other banks witnessed a larger drop in (volatile) revenues and a greater surge in (funding) costs following the initial credit crisis.	Cost:income ratios
Focus on retail banking and the real economy	Accepted	ECBGs are more stable loan providers to the real economy. They had a better loan:deposit ratio before the crisis hit. In 2010 and 2011 the impact of the economic recession is visible in declining profits (due to rising bankruptcies of SMEs).	Loan and deposit growth and loan:deposit ratio
Moderate/lower returns on assets and equity	Rejected	Despite the absence of profit targets, RoA/RoE$_{ECBG}$ is similar to RoA/RoE$_{TBS}$ in 2002–11, and even significantly higher in 2005–11. This is partly due to relatively large losses and write-downs at other banks.	RoA and RoE
Stable organizations	Accepted	Z$_{ECBG}$ is significantly higher than Z$_{TBS}$. The volatility of RoA$_{ECBG}$ and RoE$_{ECBG}$ is consistently lower. ECBGs have a lower risk appetite in booming times and less risk aversion in bad times. Deposit growth (DG$_{ECBG}$) exhibits a more stable pattern.	Z-scores, RoA and RoE, loan and deposit growth
High capitalization	Accepted	Most capital has been build up via retained earnings. Tier 1$_{ECBG}$ and E/A$_{ECBG}$ consistently surpass Tier 1$_{TBS}$ and E/A$_{TBS}$.	Tier 1 and E/A ratios
Moderate risk profile	Accepted	Focus is on retail banking which is a less risky activity. Besides, ECBGs did not need large-scale state support in recent years.	Loan:deposit ratio
Low cost of capital	Not investigated	The high capitalization and the high deposit base could make it cheaper for ECBGs to obtain external funding.	Information not readily available
High ratings	Not investigated	Some ECBGs are not supervised on a consolidated basis. Hence, no overall ratings exist for these ECBGs.	No overall ratings exist for many ECBGs

6 THE PERSISTENCE OF THE THREE-PILLAR BANKING SYSTEM IN GERMANY

Reinhard H. Schmidt, Dilek Bülbül and Ulrich Schüwer

Introduction

Historically, the banking systems of most European countries were largely similar. They were all 'three-pillar systems' comprising three important and largely distinct groups of banks. In this kind of system, the first pillar is that of the private banks – some large and some small, and some with and some without a branch network. The second pillar is that of a country's savings banks, consisting of local savings banks, central financial institutions and a host of other affiliated financial and non-financial institutions. Cooperative or mutual banks and their affiliated institutions constitute the third pillar. Thus almost by the definition of a three-pillar-system, savings banks and cooperative banks, the main topic of the present volume on 'alternative banks', have played an important role in the financial systems of almost all European countries until quite recently.

The wave of financial deregulation, liberalization and privatization in the late twentieth century has changed the role and the institutional forms of these two groups of 'alternative banks' in many European countries and thereby also altered the overall structure of their national banking systems. The general political tendency of the past years was to regard savings banks and cooperative banks as somewhat old-fashioned and inefficient, and to advocate and implement policies that correspond to this view. In some European countries, savings and cooperative banks have completely disappeared as specific groups of financial institutions, while in some others, they have changed so much that it suggests asking whether there is still today any substantial difference between these banks and conventional national and international commercial banks in the legal form of a corporation and with the set of objectives that private banks typically have. Thus the three-pillar structure of the banking systems of several European countries has also given way to simpler structures in which shareholder-owned banks clearly dominate. Germany is almost unique in Europe because it has maintained its three-pillar system, and because German savings banks and cooperative banks are still today similar to how these financial institutions were structured twenty-five years ago in most European countries.

However, under the influence of the financial crisis, the former critical view of savings and cooperative banks – and, more generally, of alternative banks in the sense of banks that are not owned by private persons or organizations and have a strict, one-sided profit orientation[1] – might give way to a more friendly assessment. After all, many big private banks had incurred so much risk that policymakers and regulators have adopted a sceptical view of their merits and are now trying to find ways of limiting their riskiness. This reassessment may also carry over to the assessment of three-pillar banking systems.

Apart from the important role that savings banks and cooperative or mutual banks still today play in several banking systems in Europe and other parts of the world, studying a specific three-pillar system and the nature of savings and cooperative banks as vital parts of this system is particularly interesting because of their unconventional organizational design, which sets them apart from private banks that operate solely in the interests of their shareholders. This is why the present chapter places special emphasis on the aspect of the institutional design of these types of 'alternative banks'.

The aims of this chapter are to characterize the German banking system as a three-pillar system, to analyse the former and the current roles of savings banks and cooperative banks as essential elements of this system, to provide a brief account of the recent changes, and also to speculate about the future prospects of these two groups of 'alternative banks'. These aims determine the structure of the chapter. In the next section, we characterize the German banking system in its entirety, focusing on its three-pillar structure. The following section looks more specifically at savings and cooperative banks in Germany and their development over time. We then very briefly discuss developments in other European countries. Finally, the chapter concludes with a plea for maintaining the three-pillar system and the diversity of institutional forms of banks, and explains why we regard it as important to safeguard the strengths of those types of banks that do not conform to the model of a large shareholder-oriented corporate bank.

The Structure of the German Banking System

The 'Three-Pillar System' as the Specific Feature of the German Banking System

By international standards, the most important and most remarkable feature of the German banking system is that it is – still today – a 'three-pillar system'. As the term suggests, one can say that the entire edifice of German banking rests on three pillars. In less poetic terms: there are three parts of the banking system and correspondingly three important groups – or types – of banks that differ considerably in terms of their institutional structures and that also compete fiercely for market share.

Pillar 1 comprises private credit institutions.[2] They are private in terms of their legal forms as well as their ownership structures. Since private banks mainly have private owners, it can be assumed that they are also clearly profit-oriented, at least more so than banks belonging to the two other groups. The broad class of private credit institutions is quite heterogeneous. It comprises several subgroups. One of them is the so-called 'big banks', which maintain large branch networks and offer all kinds of banking services to a wide spectrum of clients in Germany and worldwide.[3] Then there are a considerable number of smaller banks called 'regional banks and other commercial banks'. They are more specialized in some respect. Some are truly regional banks, others focus on certain industries as their main clientele, and others offer only a narrow range of services. This subgroup also includes private banking houses in the sense of banks with a limited group of owners or partners. These private banking houses have a great tradition and considerable reputation, but their role and number have decreased substantially over time. Finally, there is the subgroup of foreign banks that are subsidiaries of larger banks from other countries. One could also consider banks that specialize in investment banking services as a separate group, but this would create too much overlap, since in Germany investment banking services are offered by almost all banks and especially by the 'big banks'.

Because of their different business models, it is not easy to properly measure the size of banks and to compare banks by size. Nevertheless, a widely used measure of size is total bank assets. According to this metric, the first pillar makes up about 40 per cent of the entire banking system; two-thirds of this total are contributed by the 'big banks' and one-third by the smaller regional and other credit institutions and smaller subsidiaries of foreign banks.

Pillar 2 is that of the savings bank group. Its total assets are about the same as those of the private credit institutions. It also consists of two parts, that of the local savings banks and that of the regional banks called *Landesbanken*. With very few exceptions, the (local) savings banks are public banks in the sense that they are governed by a public law regime and therefore, strictly speaking, do not have owners. Instead of owners, they have what could be called sponsoring or supporting and governing institutions, the so-called '*Träger*'. These are typically municipalities, i.e. towns or counties or comparable public bodies, and these 'quasi-owners' have certain rights as well as obligations with respect to 'their' savings banks. However, the rights are weaker than the full property rights of the owners of a private bank. Every savings bank is a separate legal entity, and each one of them is a full-fledged small or mid-sized bank. Over the past thirty years, the number of savings banks has continuously declined due to a process of mergers within the group. At year-end 2012, 423 savings banks operated in Germany.

The second component is the so-called '*Landesbanken*', a term that is literally translated as 'state banks'. Some of them have the legal form of a corporation and some are public law institutions. Owners and shareholders or, as the case may be, sponsoring institutions are one or several federal states, in which a regional bank is domiciled and mainly operates, and local savings banks of the respective region. The fractions of shares and voting rights held by the federal states and by the savings banks differ from case to case.

The traditional functions of a *Landesbank* have been to serve as the main relationship bank (*Hausbank*) of the respective state or states, to act as clearing banks for the local savings banks in their catchment area, and to provide those services to clients for which the local savings banks would be too small. This includes granting or co-financing larger loans to local clients, various kinds of investment banking services and international banking operations that would overstretch the capacity of a local savings bank. However, their functions have changed over the years. During the 1990s the *Landesbanken* evolved into large banks operating nationwide and internationally. They competed vigorously with the big private commercial banks and also in some cases with the savings banks that they were formerly expected to merely support. Following several episodes of severe financial problems over the last decades, several *Landesbanken* were consolidated, such that there are now eight independent institutions left.

In terms of aggregated total assets, the savings bank group is about as large as that of the private credit institutions, and the respective total assets of the local savings banks and the *Landesbanken* are of almost equal size. However, when one tries to compare savings banks with *Landesbanken*, it is immediately obvious how imperfect total asset is as a size measure, since *Landesbanken* have (almost) no branches and only serve much fewer clients.

Pillar 3 is the group of cooperative banks. In terms of the number of independent institutions, it is larger than the other two groups or pillars, whereas in terms of total assets it is smaller, about half the size of the other groups. The cooperative banking group can also be subdivided into two parts: one of them includes the local cooperative banks, and the other includes the two central financial institutions.

The local cooperative banks are rather small regionally or even merely locally focused banks. Also in the group of cooperative banks, a drastic process of concentration based on mergers within the group has occurred over time. About fifty years ago, there were still 8,000 independent local cooperative banks; now their number has declined to slightly more than 1,000. Correspondingly, the size of the individual cooperative banks has increased greatly, and in fact most of them are now large enough to survive economically and thus able to combine their traditional strengths, namely their strong local roots and their proximity to clients, with sufficient economic power to withstand the competitive pressure emanating from the savings banks and the 'big banks'.

A process of concentration has also affected the central financial institutions that belong to the cooperative banking group. As of today, there are only two of them left. One of them, and by far the smaller one, is Westdeutsche Zentralgenossenschafts-AG (WGZ), the central institutions of the cooperative banks in

North Rhine-Westphalia, the Rhineland, and the other one is DZ-Bank AG, the central institution serving all other German cooperative banks. The numerous central banks that had once existed have been absorbed by what is now DZ-Bank AG. Both WGZ-Bank and DZ-Bank are corporations owned by their affiliated local cooperative banks, and their function largely resembles that to which the *Landesbanken* of the savings bank group had once been restricted.

Strictly speaking, talking about merely three pillars of German banking is not correct because there is also a fourth group called 'other banks'. Among them are mortgage banks, building and loan associations and the so-called 'special purpose banks', which include promotional banks (*Förderbanken*). The largest promotional bank is KfW Banking Group, a wholly government-owned bank and currently Germany's second largest bank in terms of total assets. Some of the special purpose banks are public institutions and some are private institutions. Taken together, they are such a heterogeneous group that it would not make much sense to call them a fourth pillar. In what follows, we therefore do not take them into account.

The Market Situation of the Three Pillars

An overview on the development of the three pillars of the German banking system from 2000 to 2012 is provided in the following tables. Table 6.1 shows the numbers of institutions and branches (percentage figures in brackets are calculated based on the number of institutions and branches of all German banks, respectively).[4]

Table 6.1: Number of banks and branches by banking groups in 2000 and 2012.

| | Institutions | | | | Branches | | | |
| | 2000 | | 2012 | | 2000 | | 2012 | |
	number	%	number	%	number	%	number	%
Private commercial banks	294	10.7	390	19.7	6,520	15.1	9,610	26.5
Big banks	4	0.1	4	0.2	2,873	6.6	7,041	19.4
Regional banks and others	200	7.3	209	10.6	3,567	8.2	2,444	6.7
Branches of foreign banks	90	3.3	177	9.0	80	0.2	125	0.3
Savings banks group	575	21.0	432	21.9	17,530	40.5	13,094	36.1
Savings banks	562	20.5	423	21.4	16,892	39.0	12,643	34.9
Landesbanken and DekaBank	13	0.5	9	0.5	638	1.5	451	1.2
Cooperative banks group	1,796	65.5	1,106	56.0	15,357	35.5	11,789	32.5
Cooperative banks	1,792	64.4	1,104	55.9	15,332	35.4	11,778	32.5
Central institutions	4	0.1	2	0.1	25	0.1	11	0.0
Other banks	75	2.7	48	2.4	3,887	9.0	1,746	4.8
ALL BANKS	2,740	100	1,976	100	43,294	100	36,239	100

Source: Based on Deutsche Bundesbank, Monthly balance sheet statistics 2013, at http://www.bundesbank.de/Navigation/EN/Statistics/statistics.html [accessed 1 August 2013]. Note that as of 2004, big banks include Postbank AG with its many branches.

Table 6.2 contains information on the group's market shares with respect to total assets, loans to non-banks and deposits and borrowing from non-banks for the years 2000 and 2012.

Table 6.2: Market share by banking groups in 2000 and 2012.

	Total assets		Loans to non-banks		Deposits and borrowing from non-banks	
	2000	2012	2000	2012	2000	2012
Private commercial banks	28%	39%	26%	27%	26%	36%
Big banks	16%	25%	15%	13%	14%	17%
Regional banks and others	10%	10%	10%	13%	12%	16%
Branches of foreign banks	2%	4%	1%	1%	0%	3%
Savings banks group	35%	28%	35%	36%	39%	34%
Savings banks	16%	13%	19%	21%	26%	24%
Landesbanken and DekaBank	20%	15%	16%	15%	13%	11%
Cooperative banks group	12%	12%	12%	15%	18%	17%
Cooperative banks	9%	9%	11%	13%	17%	16%
Central institutions	4%	3%	2%	2%	1%	1%
Other banks	24%	20%	26%	22%	17%	12%
ALL BANKS (in € billion)	6,148	8,315	3,479	3,949	2,261	3,328

Source: Based on Deutsche Bundesbank, Monthly balance sheet statistics 2013.

Ten Special Features of the German Banking System

The foregoing brief characterization of the three main banking groups and the relationships between them serves as a basis for discussing what might be the most important features of the German banking system and what makes it special in comparison to the banking systems of other countries. In this subsection we describe ten of these special features.

The *first special feature* follows immediately from the three-pillar structure: only a fraction of all German banks, which does not even make up half of total bank assets, consists of private banks that are exclusively profit-oriented. Public banks, and thus in particular those that belong to the savings bank group, have a 'promotional mandate', that is, they are expected to conduct their business in a way that supports the local economy or, as in the case of the KfW Banking Group, the national economy in Germany and in other countries as well. Naturally, this mandate limits the banks' profit orientation. In the case of cooperative banks, the dominant objective is also not to maximize bank profitability, but rather to support their members' own business activities. And at least a few years ago, the situation was not completely dissimilar for shareholder-owned banks, since it was not really clear how strong their profit orientation really was or even is today. This held particularly for the large private German banks, since in the past the incentive systems for top managers were geared more towards strengthening their personal influences in the German economy and to increase the role and size of their banks than towards maximizing profits for their shareholders.

Thus one can say that some time ago profit orientation was in general not strong in German banking. However, the more important competition is and possibly also the more pressure is exerted by the capital markets, the more banks, including those with a dual objective,[5] have to aspire to a sound profit that at least assures their survival as institutions. This general rule also applies to the German banking market, which had become more competitive when the big German banks decided to enter the retail market in the 1960s and then, twenty years later, had to react to the pressure that came from the intrusion of foreign investment banks into their traditional turf, the market for corporate clients. Nevertheless, even today the overall level of profit orientation in German banking is presumably less pronounced than in banking systems in which almost all banks are exclusively dependent on the interests of their shareholders in maximum profits and shareholder values.

One positive consequence of this limited profit orientation is probably the *second special feature* of German banking: its stability. For many years, the German banking system has been more stable than that of almost all other countries. Before the financial crisis started in 2007, Germany was almost unique among the industrialized countries in that it had not experienced a major banking crisis after World War II. Moreover, the way in which bank–client relations used to be structured and the dominant mode of firm financing had the consequence that elements of instability which may have affected the banks were passed on to the real economy to a lesser extent than in countries with a different overall structure of their financial systems. Even the rapid recovery of the German economy after 2009 may be a consequence of this lasting property of the German banking system.

The *third special feature* of the German banking system concerns the level of competition. This feature is also closely related to the three-pillar system. Still today, the local savings and cooperative banks adhere to the so-called 'regional principle'. This principle means that local banks that belong to the same network of banks are not expected to compete with each other. For savings banks, the scope of their activities is essentially restricted to the area for which its sponsoring or supporting and governing public body is responsible. A similar principle applies to local cooperative banks. Of course this is just a principle, and as such it is not really strictly observed everywhere and at any time. Even among the group of large private banks, one could in the past identify many elements of common interest and a spirit of cooperating rather than competing.[6] While intra-pillar competition used to be, and to a high degree still is, limited, inter-pillar competition has always been fierce. Measured on an aggregate level, the level of competition in banking is high in Germany.[7] This is good for bank clients because a high level of competition tends to lower the prices for banking services, but it also has the consequence of keeping bank revenues low.

This leads directly to the *fourth special feature*: the level of bank profitability appears to be low by international standards. Critics of the German banking system argue that low profitability is not primarily a consequence of a high level of competition but rather of the presumed fact that the dominant players in retail banking, the savings and cooperative banks, are not subject to the same return requirements as the private banks.[8]

The *fifth special feature*, which is again closely related to the three-pillar system, is the apparently relatively low level of bank concentration in Germany. If one counts the individual savings and cooperative banks as individual institutions, as is certainly correct from a legal perspective, bank concentration is much lower in Germany than in almost any other comparable country. This holds irrespective of how bank concentration is measured. However, if one considers all savings banks and all cooperative banks, respectively, as being merely parts of one coherent but highly decentralized group, a view which is more appropriate from an industrial economics perspective, then the level of bank concentration in Germany is more or less in line with that of other countries.

The large number of banking institutions, the – at least formerly – lower overall level of profit orientation and the fierce inter-pillar competition for retail banking clients may have led to the *sixth special feature* of German banking: for many years, the number of banking outlets was relatively high by international standards. However, with the ongoing process of within-group concentration and the increasing pressure to maintain profitability by reducing costs, this feature has by now lost its significance. The number of bank branches per 1,000 inhabitants has fallen significantly since 1980 and has now reached a level that is lower than the average in large EU countries.[9]

The *seventh special feature* is that almost all German banks are universal banks. Most medium-sized and larger banks offer services that one can classify as commercial and investment banking services in the traditional sense of these terms that were introduced by the American banking legislation of the 1930s. The predominance of the universal banking model is based on traditional German banking law, and it conforms to the tradition of the German banks themselves and to the experience and expectation of clients to obtain all kinds of banking services from their preferred bank. That the banks have adjusted to this expectation of their clients has led to a relatively high level of bank loyalty on the part of bank customers.

Close relationships between banks and their clients also used to prevail in the market for corporate banking services, and this is the *eighth special feature* of German banking: the phenomenon of close relationship banking, the so-called 'Hausbank' relationship. However, this is a controversial issue. Some observers argue that the *Hausbank* relationship has always been merely a myth that bankers liked to entertain because it was good for their public image, while others argue that close relationships between a corporate client and his *Hausbank* used to exist but may no longer prevail.[10]

A typical *Hausbank* relationship manifests itself in the – presumed – fact that one among the banks with which a corporation works has a special status of being the firm's main relationship bank – and that this fact is known to the other banks and also to a certain degree respected by them. The *Hausbank* obtains and processes considerably more information on the client firm than the other banks, and in return it has a certain responsibility for the financial health of the firm. Its privileged access to non-public information enables the *Hausbank* to assess a client's creditworthiness better than other banks and support it even in a situation in which other banks might be tempted to reduce their credit exposures. Being the main relationship bank of firms and acting accordingly permits

German banks to stabilize the business of their clients even if other banks start to have doubts and reduce their credit exposure.

Formerly, *Hausbank* relationships were mainly observable in the interaction between large exchange-listed corporations and the large private German banks. Observable indicators of an existing *Hausbank* relationship were, for instance, that a banker chaired the supervisory board of the client corporation or that the bank held a substantial block of shares. These kinds of institutionally manifested bank relationships hardly exist anymore today. However, in slightly different forms and with different players on both sides, *Hausbank* relationships seem to still exist and to be important in Germany. Today, many large and medium-sized firms that belong to the so-called '*Mittelstand*' have a main relationship bank, which is now more often a savings bank or a cooperative bank than a large private bank.

The *ninth special feature* of German banking is the traditional low level of foreign bank presence in Germany. In view of the peculiarities of German banking described so far, it is not surprising that foreign banks were, and still are, reluctant to enter the German banking market in other roles than that of niche players. It is probably true that gaining a viable position in the German banking market is indeed difficult. Therefore the only possible entry route has been that of buying a German bank, which happened a number of times in the last decade. The most important case is the acquisition of the large Bavarian bank Hypo-Vereinsbank (HVB) by the Italian banking group UniCredit in 2005. However, even this case may not be a reason to negate the ongoing low level of foreign bank presence in Germany, since buying HVB may in the first place have been a way for UniCredit to get access to the attractive banking markets of the transition countries of Central and Eastern Europe. The acquisition of HVB may have served this purpose because a few years earlier HVB had acquired the Austrian bank Bank Austria, which had already built up a large network of subsidiaries in the East.

The *tenth special feature* of German banking that we want to present here is that with very few exceptions German banks are still primarily financial intermediaries, that is, their main business consists in taking deposits from non-banks and granting loans to non-banks. The extent to which banks are intermediaries can be measured using so-called 'intermediation ratios'. A high intermediation ratio of banks means that a large part of household savings is channelled to investors via the banking sector. In the German financial system, the intermediation ratios of banks vis-à-vis households as depositors and vis-à-vis non-financial firms as borrowers was, and still is, very high by international standards.[11] If one looks at other countries, one can easily see that in many countries, especially those with a capital market-oriented financial system, intermediation ratios are surprisingly low. For instance, in the USA banks are not primarily financial intermediaries but rather 'gatekeepers' that help their clients find the way to the right kind of capital market, as researchers had already pointed out twenty years ago.[12]

If banks are mainly financial intermediaries, the bulk of their revenue derives from the interest margin, while investment banking fees are a more important source of revenue for the banks in those countries in which capital markets play a strong role. Assessing a high intermediation ratio of banks combined with a limited role of fee revenue in a given country is not straightforward. On the one hand, it shows that banks do perform the important function of channelling savings to investors. On the other, it suggests that many banks and their managers may not be able or willing to adapt to new developments of the capital market, to seize the opportunities that result from these developments, and to support the developments as much as it would seem possible. Both assessments apply in the case for German banks: they perform the traditional intermediary role of banks as financial intermediaries well, but they may also be somewhat inflexible and not sufficiently open to innovation. That this is the case may also be a consequence of the traditional three-pillar structure of the German banking system.

Savings Banks and Cooperative Banks in Germany

The Definition and the Nature of Savings Banks and Cooperative Banks

The discussion of the nature of savings banks and cooperative banks focuses on two aspects: their business models and their institutional features. Both banking groups share the regional focus of their business models; nevertheless, they traditionally have very different institutional features that, for each banking group, proved quite successful over the last two hundred years. Importantly, the banks' business models and their institutional features are interdependent and complementary to each other.[13] As the last decade documented and as will be elaborated further in this section, changes in banks' institutional features immediately affect their business models, and vice versa.

It is almost impossible to define the savings banks of the twenty-first century in a general and meaningful way that is applicable to every institution that goes under that name today. They are a very heterogeneous group. Even across countries in Europe, they have few common features, and the distinction between savings banks and other banks is becoming less and less clear.[14] There are now only two features that all savings banks in Europe have in common: (i) their focus on savings and savings mobilization, and (ii) their clear regional and even local focus.

Until about twenty-five years ago, these two features of the business model of most European savings banks were closely connected to five further institutional features. The most pre-eminent feature was[15] (iii) that of being 'public' banks, which were in a certain sense owned or sponsored and governed by some regional or local public body such as a city or a county or a region. As public banks, savings banks were (iv) organized under a public law regime. The next feature was (v) their dual objective: they were expected to support the local economy and the local people, and at the same time to operate according to common business rules and thus to be financially sustainable enterprises.

Another common feature was (vi) their adherence to the so-called 'regional principle' already explained above. As banks that adhere to the regional principle and are firmly rooted in the local economy do not compete with each other, the different savings banks in a country or region had reasons to consider each other more as peers and colleagues than as competitors. This is why it is easy and attractive for them to cooperate, and it leads to the final traditional feature of savings banks in Europe: they were (vii) part of dense and closely cooperating networks of legally independent institutions that constitute a special banking group.[16] These networks offer the opportunity to have a common appearance vis-à-vis clients and the general public, share information and, most importantly, 'outsource' certain functions in which economies of scale can be achieved to central institutions that are also part of the networks. Being part of such networks strengthens their competitive position within the respective national banking system considerably.

This list of seven features constitutes the 'prototype' of a savings bank. In the past, it was also valid as a description and allowed us to distinguish savings banks from other banks. However, as stated above, today not all national savings bank systems exhibit all of these features any more.[17] In some countries savings banks are no longer public and municipal institutions operating under a public law regime and are no longer part of dense networks of affiliated institutions. Therefore one must restrict oneself today to defining savings banks simply as savings-oriented locally focused financial institutions that are called savings banks according to tradition and/or national laws and regulations.

Most cooperative banks in Europe are still today in many respects similar to how savings banks used to be. They are regional banks; they adhere to the regional principle; they are parts of dense networks that foster within-group cooperation; and they also have a dual objective. In their case, the mandate is to support the economic undertakings of their clients and to be cost-covering and profitable businesses. The specific feature of any cooperative bank – and thus also a criterion of demarcation from other banks – is their legal structure. Although they have some features of corporations, cooperatives are organized almost like clubs. Therefore the owners and providers of equity are not called shareholders but members. Three principles shape the institutional structure of financial and other cooperatives. The 'principle of self-help' implies that they are self-governed private organizations. According to the 'principle of identity', members are their main clients and conversely many of their clients are also members. Then there is the 'democratic principle', which manifests itself in the rule that one member has only one vote in the annual general meetings, irrespective of how many shares he or she may hold.

Since cooperatives are structured like clubs, members cannot sell their shares if they want to exit. They can only hand them back to the cooperative and in return get back what they have once invested, plus their part of accumulated profits. This feature has both negative and positive implications. Owner-members' incentives to monitor the performance of the managers are weak due to the fact that they can hardly benefit from policies that would increase the value of their shares because they cannot sell their shares at a higher market price, and they cannot exert pressure on management due to the fact that they cannot accumulate a sufficient number of voting rights. As a consequence, the incentives of the managements to perform well and to increase the going-concern value of cooperative banks are also weak. Evidently, this constitutes a handicap for cooperative banks in their competition with other banks. At the same time, the 'democratic principle' and the limited incentives for management to make high profits imply that potentially powerful members cannot dominate a cooperative and make management exploit weaker members, for instance by paying low interest rates on deposits. For the same reason, the incentives to incur high risks as a means of achieving high profits are weak in a financial cooperative.[18]

Historical Developments

The establishment of savings and cooperative banks in Germany goes back to the nineteenth century. The first savings banks were created about 200 years ago. They were foundations established by well-intentioned citizens with the mission of encouraging and enabling people of a low social standing to set aside some savings for a rainy day, a wedding or some other purpose, or to prepare for retirement. Shortly afterwards municipal and public savings banks were created, and they soon became the dominant form. Over the years the number of savings banks increased continuously, associations of savings banks were created, and with the introduction of giro transactions in the early twentieth century, regional clearing banks, which are now called *Landesbanken*, were established to support the savings banks operating in a larger region that would correspond to what are now different federal states in Germany. Together with the local savings banks, the *Landesbanken* and the associations formed a dense network of institutions. Later, additional institutions for special purposes, such as building societies, were founded and added to the network. However, the local banks remained the heart and the basis of the group.

The cooperative banks in Germany date back to the middle of the nineteenth century. Two groups of cooperative banks emerged at that time. The founder of the first group was Friedrich Wilhelm Raiffeisen. He laid the foundations for what was to become an extensive network of rural cooperative banks in Germany, which provided the model for cooperative banks in other European countries and finally the entire world. The second important group of cooperative banks was founded in an eastern part of Germany. They adopted the common name of people's banks (*Volksbanken*). The founder of this group was Hermann Schulze-Delitzsch, a former public administrator and a politician.

Cooperative banking expanded as much as savings banks and soon covered all of Germany and also some neighbouring countries, and like the savings banks they established dense networks of associations, clearing banks and affiliated specialized service providers.

The German Banking Act of 1934 placed savings and cooperative banks under the same regulatory regime as all other banks. As a consequence, they became universal banks by law and in practice. For many decades, the two cooperative networks remained separate until they finally merged in 1972. As of then, cooperative banks may also conduct business with clients who are not members.

The German savings banks and cooperative banks have until today adhered to the regional principle described above. This has enabled them to cooperate within their groups and to benefit greatly from being organized as parts of networks of closely connected but legally independent institutions. Therefore they are in a position to offer a full range of services to their customers without having to produce all of these services themselves, which would be too costly or, because of the small size of the local institutions, simply not feasible. Over time, and especially in the thirty to forty years after World War II, both groups of regional banks underwent a process of professionalization and concentration and of deepening the cooperation in their respective networks. During these years, the savings and cooperative banks were the most successful groups in the German banking system; they gained market share, were quite profitable and stable, and enjoyed a good reputation with clients and in the general public. In the early post-war years, the German banking market had been rather segmented, allowing savings and cooperative banks to become the main providers of retail banking services to German households and SMEs. The big private banks only started to serve the general public in the mid-1960s. This put some pressure on savings and cooperative banks, but they remained strong contenders in the banking market.

In 2001 the German government agreed with the EU Commission to phase out the former public guarantees for local savings banks and *Landesbanken* by the year 2005. While this had serious consequences for the *Landesbanken*, the local savings banks were hardly affected by this change since, first, they are largely financed by retail deposits, and second, for decades the group's internal risk control proved successful such that there was not a single case in which the public guarantees had been invoked. Further, in contrast to the business model of *Landesbanken*, the model of the local savings banks has always been very safe, as their focus remained on their core business of operating locally and being mainly financial intermediaries and not asset traders.

The Structure of Banking Networks

The savings bank group is organized in a three-level network. Savings banks operate at the local level. At the end of 2012, there existed 423 savings banks. Regional financial institutions such as *Landesbanken*, building societies and insurance companies typically operate at the state level. Other institutions, like DekaBank or Deutsche Leasing, operate at the national level. This three-level structure of financial institutions is mirrored in the structure of associations, with the German Savings Banks Association (DSGV) at the top representing the savings banks group to policymakers, public authorities and the general public. This national association also plays a certain role in shaping the general policy of the group. However, it is important to note that the savings banks group is neither by law and statute nor de facto a hierarchical system with central power residing at the top.

As in the case of the savings banks, the local cooperative banks – 1,104 at year-end 2012 – are the basis and the heart of the cooperative banking network. In addition, this network includes two central financial institutions and a certain number of specialized service providers operating nationwide.[19] In contrast to the savings banks group, there are now only two central financial institutions for cooperative banks. The larger one of them, DZ-Bank, is not only the central bank for most local cooperative banks but at the same time also one of the largest commercial banks in Germany. It operates on the national level and also to a certain extent internationally. WGZ-Bank is the only regional central or clearing bank that still exists today; the others have been merged into DZ-Bank over time. Similar to the case of the savings banks group, there are regional associations of cooperative banks and one national association. The latter plays a role that closely resembles that of the DSGV.

German Savings Banks and Cooperative Banks before and during the Financial Crisis

Figure 6.1 provides performance indicators of German branch banking and allows for an assessment of the financial situation of those banks in the three pillars that have extended branch networks and are therefore to some extent comparable. The left panel of Figure 6.1 shows that the cost:income ratio is lower for savings banks and cooperative banks than for the large commercial banks. As shown in the middle panel, return on equity is on average higher and clearly more stable for savings banks and cooperative banks. Finally, the right panel shows that the interest margins for all banks have been steadily declining, but throughout the years the interest margins are higher for savings banks and cooperative banks than for big banks.[20]

Not only do standard performance indicators show that the local banks performed about as well and in general even better than the private big banks, but more elaborate ways of analysing and comparing performance also confirm this result for the years before the financial crisis began in 2007. For example, Altunbas et al. examine a sample of German banks between 1989 and 1996.[21] They find that public and mutual banks are not less efficient, but instead have slight cost and profit advantages over their private sector competitors. This may appear particularly surprising given that savings and cooperative banks pursue the dual objective of profit and benefit for their customers, an effect that cannot be included in standard performance measurements.[22]

Probably less surprising, but equally relevant, is the empirical evidence for Germany that savings banks and cooperative banks are on average less risky than privately owned commercial banks.[23] Note that some earlier cross-country studies find that publicly owned banks are more risky than privately owned banks,[24] or that a higher share of government ownership results in higher banking fragility.[25] These studies, however, focus on large publicly owned banks and therefore do not provide any contradicting evidence as regards the stability of locally oriented savings banks.

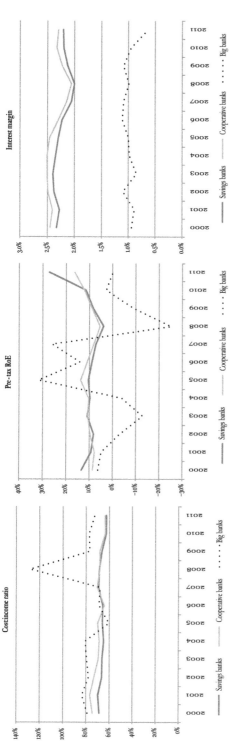

Figure 6.1: Performance indicators of German branch banking.

Note: i) Central institutions of cooperative banks and savings banks are not considered. ii) The cost:income ratio is defined as the ratio of general administrative spending to operating income. iii) Return on equity is defined as the ratio of pre-tax profit to equity. iv) Interest margin is defined as excess of interest received over interest paid.

Source: Data from Bundesbank.

Further, Behr et al.[26] find that the lending of German savings banks is less cyclical compared to that of the private banks and that German small and medium-sized enterprises that increase their borrowing from savings banks are less credit constrained, based on a sample for the period 1995–2007. Hence the high financial stability of German savings banks also benefits their clients.

In contrast to the 'big banks', some of which experienced large losses due to overly risky investments and off-balance sheet activities of a precarious nature in the years preceding the financial crisis, German local savings and cooperative banks weathered the storm largely unharmed. Almost all of them managed to remain stable and profitable during the crisis years.[27] This is foremost due to their traditional business model concentrating on the core business of banking and corresponds to their mission and tradition. The local banks benefited from their strong customer deposit-gathering ability and their established close relationships with their business clients. Moreover, their rather conservative business models prevented them from being involved in those lines of risky business that created great damage to several large private banks. Moreover, in contrast to other banks, the savings and cooperative banks have not curtailed lending in the crisis.

Nevertheless, like almost every financial group, the savings banks group as a whole was also affected by the financial crisis. Four *Landesbanken* (HSH Nord, BayernLB, SachsenLB and WestLB) suffered greatly, indirectly also causing large losses to local savings banks and other institutions in the banking group in their roles as co-owners, guarantors and business partners. This is one reason why some *Landesbanken* are currently undergoing major reforms (HSH Nordbank and BayernLB), were merged (SachsenLB with LBBW), were largely liquidated (WestLB), or are realigning their business models.

Being even less involved in structured finance and capital markets products than the savings banks, the cooperative banks have survived the financial crisis better than any other banking group in Germany, even though their central financial institution DZ-Bank also had some problems and needed help, which it got from other institutions belonging to the network. Very soon these problems were overcome, and DZ-Bank returned to profitability.

Summing up, one can say that the local savings and cooperative banks have been able to prosper over the years and at times – especially during the recent financial crisis – even outperformed the commercial and purely shareholder-oriented banks. Despite some problems of their central financial institutions, also during the financial crisis savings banks and cooperative banks have proved to be a stabilizing factor for the German financial system and economy, a factor that has strengthened the positions of these two groups of banks and thereby also stabilized the traditional three-pillar structure of the German banking system.

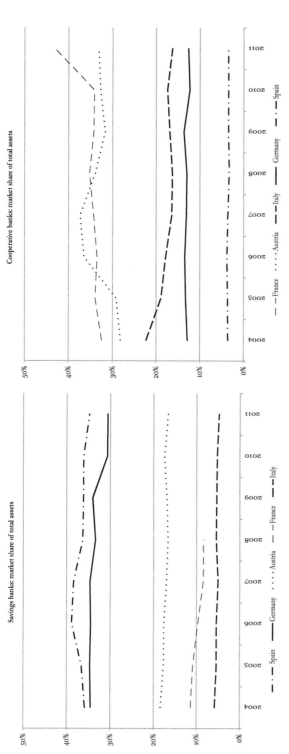

Figure 6.2: The role of savings banks and cooperative banks across Europe.

Source: Based on data from ESBG (2013), EACB (2013) and ECB (2013). Note that the figures for savings banks and cooperative banks include the respective central institutions. For savings banks and cooperative banks, we calculate the market share for each country as the total assets of the respective ESBG and EACB member organizations, respectively, divided by the total assets of all financial institutions in that country as reported by the ECB. Missing values for savings banks for the years 2006, 2009 and 2010 were interpolated.

A Brief European Comparison

The role of savings banks and cooperative banks varies significantly between European countries. This is related both to historic reasons and to developments over the last decades. Figure 6.2 presents the market share of total assets of savings banks and cooperative banks in terms of total assets in selected countries over the last years (including total assets of the respective central institutions). As illustrated in the left panel, until today savings banks play an important role particular in Spain and Germany, but not so anymore in several other countries. The right panel highlights the strong role of cooperative banks in France and Austria, and only a very limited role in other countries such as Spain. In some countries, such as Austria and Germany, both banking groups play an important role. In other countries, one of the two banking groups clearly dominates.

Until about twenty-five years ago, almost all European countries had the so-called 'three-pillar' banking system comprising private banks, (public) savings banks and (mutual) cooperative banks. Since that time, several European countries have implemented far-reaching changes in their banking systems, which have more than anything else affected the two 'pillars' of the savings and cooperative banks. The most important changes occurred in Austria, France, Italy and Spain. In a nutshell, the changes are as follows:[28]

- In Austria the three networks of formerly independent local savings and cooperative banks have been transformed in such a way that their respective central institutions have gained far-reaching power over the now de facto 'subordinated' local and regional institutions.
- In France savings banks have been converted into yet another group of cooperative banks and have been phased out as a special type of financial institution.
- In Italy savings banks were partially privatized, and several of them were integrated into large commercial banks like UniCredit and INTESA. Cooperative banks consolidated in a big way, and for both groups of banks, as much as for other Italian banks, the regional principle was abolished.
- In Spain the savings banks were privatized and the regional principle was abolished.

A few brief remarks on other European countries show that in some countries the changes have gone even further:

- In Belgium savings and cooperative banks have essentially disappeared.
- In Great Britain the former public savings bank (TSB) was sold to Lloyds Banking Group; several cooperative banks, the so-called 'building societies', were converted into corporations and some of them were sold to large private commercial banks. Most of the converted building societies or the private banks that had bought them ran into serious problems during the financial crisis.

- In the Netherlands savings banks have disappeared and the formerly independent cooperative banks have been amalgamated into one big national bank (Rabobank).
- In Sweden the former local savings banks have been converted into joint-stock corporations in the 1990s, and most of them were consolidated into a single national savings bank (Swedbank).

Only Germany stands out as the special case in which there was no substantial change during the last decades.[29] As far as their legal and institutional structures are concerned, the German savings and cooperative banks are today almost exactly as they had been fifty and even eighty years ago. Therefore they arguably still correspond best to what one might call their prototypes.

There have been several factors that drove the changes in Europe. Certainly, the political climate of the time and EU-wide harmonization were important. However, there was also the presumption that in their former set-up the regional banks were not competitive. To a certain extent this may have been true, and it may have been due to the fact that in most countries savings and cooperative banks had long been subject to different and more restrictive regulation than 'normal' banks, and/or to the small size of most local banks, and/or to their 'unconventional' institutional and governance features.

As one of the motives for initiating far-reaching reforms was the belief that the efficiency of local savings and cooperative banks is lower than that of other banks with comparably large branch networks, it is instructive to take a closer look at this aspect. As already discussed above, evidence from the German banking market does not support the belief that local savings banks and cooperative banks are less efficient. In two cross-country studies of regional banks in Europe for the period 2000 to 2008 and 1996 to 2006, Ayadi et al.[30] have investigated whether banking groups with different institutional features also differ in terms of efficiency. Like several earlier studies, these two studies did not find any systematic differences. The frequently used indicators of efficiency – return on assets, return on equity and cost:income ratio – are essentially the same for savings banks, cooperative banks and large private branch banks in almost all countries considered in the studies. More sophisticated econometric methods also failed to reveal any systematic differences. Of course, this could only be shown for countries in which savings and cooperative banks still existed during the years covered in the analyses, which were essentially the pre-crisis years.

As is well known, the former similarity concerning efficiency and stability across countries was not maintained during the financial crisis of 2007 to 2009 and the debt crisis that erupted in 2010. Most savings and cooperative banks fared relatively well in the crisis and better than most of their competitors from the ranks of large private banks, which is due to the facts that by virtue of their institutional design they have only limited incentives to take on greater risks, and that their strong local roots and their embeddedness into close networks also limited their possibilities to do so.

However, there are exceptions. The most important one is that of the Spanish savings banks. They were very seriously affected by the crises. For researchers who regard incentive systems and institutional design as important, their structural weakness does not really come as a surprise. Their current problems are most probably related to the fact that the *cajas* were transformed in an unbalanced way a few years before the crisis hit,[31] and the regional principle was abolished by law and statute as well as in practice. As a consequence, the *cajas* started to compete vigorously among themselves, putting pressure on their profitability. This could also explain why there is now hardly any cooperation between them, nor is there a network that could provide support and impose discipline on the individual *cajas*.

Conclusion and Outlook

Among other things, the financial crisis has led to a change in the prevailing political assessment of the various types of banks in Europe. Before the crisis, banks that did not conform to the 'model' of how a good modern bank should be structured and operate were considered old-fashioned and outdated. This assessment referred primarily to savings banks in so far as they were public banks. But at least indirectly cooperative banks were also under suspicion, since they are also not purely profit-oriented institutions and not large centrally coordinated and stock exchange-listed corporations. After the crisis, this attitude has changed. Banks with public ownership and member or client-based financial institutions have regained some recognition, because the vast majority of them had fared better than their larger, purely private competitors and also because they have held up their supply of loans to the economy at a time when big banks cut back lending. This reassessment bodes well for their future.[32]

One additional consideration points in the same direction. The financial crisis has generated the insight that in the area of banking there can be too much profit orientation, too much profit pressure emanating from the capital market on listed banks, and too much financial sophistication. Working together, these factors can lead to banks accepting and even generating too much risk for themselves as institutions and for society as a whole. Local and regional banks are less risky, and this contributes to the stability of entire financial systems. Their contribution to financial system stability seems to suggest that from an overall perspective they might simply be the better banks. However, such a claim would go much too far. But the converse is also not true. The 'modern' view that all financial systems should resemble as much as possible the model of a financial system in which capital markets are the most important force and in which 'good' banks are large, private, purely shareholder-oriented and exchange-listed corporations has been severely discredited by the experiences from the recent financial crisis. We simply do not know which type of banks and which structure of a financial system are better under different circumstances.

This agnostic position leads to the argument of diversity. In the life sciences, the value of diversity has been widely recognized in recent years, and there is a crucial underlining argument why biodiversity is so important: even the best experts do not know, and in fact cannot know, what the future challenges to human life and health and to the environment may be. There is the possibility that some specific species might in the future turn out to be extremely important, for example for curing a disease that may even not exist today. This is why protecting this species – and endangered species in general – is important: once they are extinct they cannot be revitalized even if they would be urgently needed.

Much the same applies to the types of banks and banking groups that are the topic of this article. As we simply do not know which type of banks is best if regarded in isolation and which mix of different types of banks within a financial system are best for the economy and for society at large, we regard it as very important to 'preserve' these types of banks and prevent them from being sidelined or even abolished. They are like an endangered species. If they cannot continue to exist and thrive today as what they are and cannot adapt to changing circumstances, the valuable knowledge and the social capital that they use and transfer to future generations might be lost forever. After all, these banks – and even more so the networks of such banks – are rather subtle organizations that have so far managed to cope quite well with the delicate tension between the business imperative of being successful enterprises and their social mandate to support their clients and members. If they disappeared, it would most likely be impossible to bring them back to life if later generations should come to the conclusion that it would be good to have strong and prospering banks that serve public or client interests more than, or at least as much as, the interests of shareholders. Once policymakers accept this argument and act accordingly, it would be a good basis for the future development of the banking systems in Europe and also offer good prospects for savings banks and cooperative banks.

Acknowledgements

The present chapter is a companion paper to D. Bülbül, R. H. Schmidt and U. Schüwer, 'Caisses d'épargne et banques cooperatives en Europe', *Revue d'Économie Financière*, 111 (2013), pp. 159–87. Significant overlaps exist between the two papers.

7 ALTERNATIVE BANKS IN A DUALISTIC ECONOMY: THE CASE OF ITALY BEFORE AND DURING THE EURO CRISIS

Luca Giordano and Antonio Lopes

Introduction

Between the early 1990s and 2005, the Italian banking system has experienced a profound transformation. The acceleration of European economic integration, culminating in the adoption of the euro, and the birth of a highly integrated European financial market have accentuated competitive pressures: Italian banks, which had been operating for a long time in a closed and protected market, suddenly faced a much more competitive market characterized by the widespread presence of large credit institutions.

These challenges have led successive governments to devise banking regulatory reforms and to choose new models of supervision. Thus Italian banking has gone from a closed system, in which access to the market and the range of services offered were subject to stringent administrative constraints, to one in which all obstacles to banking activities were removed, keeping only prudential controls in order to ensure stability.

A legitimate question would therefore be to ask whether, before the 2007–8 global financial crisis and the eurozone sovereign debt crisis but after the radical changes mentioned above, the Italian banking system was still able to meet the needs of an economic system characterized by a profound north–south dualism and dominated by small businesses dependent, almost exclusively, on bank credit for their funding.

Furthermore, it is interesting to see whether and to what extent non-profit banks, which in the Italian context are mainly small, local cooperative banks (*banche di credito cooperativo*) and medium to large-size cooperative banking groups (*banche popolari*), have behaved differently from joint-stock banks in the context of this transformation.

In this chapter we analyse the transformation of the Italian banking system – and alternative banks in particular – and its relationship with firms, with particular attention to the dualistic nature of the Italian economy. The chapter is organized as follows. In the next section we analyse the transformation of the Italian banking system and its ownership structure, while in the following section we assess the effects of changes in the banking system on the relationship between banks and firms in southern Italy. Then we consider the changes that have occurred in the distribution of bank branches in different areas of the country before the 2008 financial crisis, after which we provide an analysis of the lending strategies followed by banks before and after the unfolding of the crisis. We then focus on the deterioration of the relationship between banks and firms as a result of the crisis in the peripheral eurozone countries during 2010–11, after which we address the effects of the crisis on Italian banks and on the bank–firm relationship in southern Italy. In the final section, we offer concluding remarks.

Changes in the Ownership Structure of Italian Banks

From the early 1990s to 2005, the structure of the Italian banking system was profoundly transformed by a wave of mergers and acquisitions. These transactions were carried out primarily with the intention of reaping economies of scale and scope.[1] Generally, banking mergers and acquisitions were motivated by the desire to improve management efficiency and therefore profitability.[2]

To get a better idea of the scale of the phenomenon, one should consider that between 1990 and 2001 in Italy more than 552 aggregations involved banks controlling about 50 per cent total intermediated funds; the number of operating banks fell by 30 per cent, from 1,061 to 769. The intensity of the restructuring process in Italy can be highlighted through international comparisons: between 1996 and 2001 the share of bank mergers on the total number of operations was highest in Italy, where it reached 13.2 per cent, compared to 12.7 per cent in the United States, 10.3 per cent in Japan, 7.5 per cent in Germany, 6.2 in the UK and 6.1 per cent in France. In the following decade, the structure of the Italian banking system continued to show a clear trend towards consolidation that, although to a lesser extent, affected the entire European banking market; between 2001 and 2006 the number of banks in Italy dropped in a similar way to Spain, but much less than the European average and what was recorded in Germany, France and Great Britain.

Changes in the population of bank branches in Europe show a somewhat different picture: the increase in the number of branches registered in Italy during the years 2001–6 is second only to what occurred in Spain, but much higher than the European average and the French case, and in contrast with what occurred in Germany and Great Britain, where there was a significant reduction in branch numbers. As a result, Italian banks have now (in 2013) the highest number of branches after Spanish banks.

The rapid increase in the number of branches has further elevated the level of banking in relation to population density (55 branches per 100,000 inhabitants) that approximates now the European average (57 branches per 100,000 inhabitants) and is second among the major European markets, after Spain with almost twice the European average (99 branches per 100,000 inhabitants) in 2006. The relationship between gross domestic product (GDP) and the number of branches shows substantial convergence towards the European average, with 45.6 million euros against 46.4 for all EU countries.

However, the ratio between bank employees and total population is much smaller in Italy and Spain than in Germany and Great Britain. This raises the question of evaluating the economic dimension of Italian banks; in fact, at the end of 2006, the average size of Italian banks measured in terms of assets, although in line with the German banks, was still far from that of banks in Spain and France and, of course, Great Britain. In addition, during the period 2001–6 the relative size of Italian banks declined with respect to the European average. This implies that the productivity of Italian branches in terms of intermediated funds (total assets plus total loans) is on average lower than their European competitors, with the exception of Spain.

On the other hand, Spanish and Italian branches are 'lighter' in terms of employees per branch and in terms of loans per employee. In other words, the smaller average size of Italian banks reflects, beyond structural fragmentation, a more limited national banking market.

Banking System Consolidation and Regional Disparities

These transformations of the Italian banking system did not occur evenly from a territorial point of view but, on the contrary, have had serious repercussions especially on the ownership structure of southern Italian banks.

During the 1990s, in fact, the southern banking system, following a significant deterioration of the macroeconomic framework in that area, suffered a drastic decline. The number of banks operating in southern Italy dropped between 1990 and 2001 by 46 per cent, compared to a 20 per cent decrease in the centre-north. Consolidation has taken the form of a penetration of banks headquartered in the centre-north into southern markets.

Data reported by Bongini and Ferri[3] show that, at the end of 2004, out of thirty-seven banks (*banche popolari*, BPs, and joint-stock banks, JSBs) operating in the south, twenty-one belonged to banking groups with headquarters in the centre-north; as a result, the share of branches belonging to independent southern banks declined from 66 per cent in 1990 to 33 per cent in 2006.

As for the opening of new branches, we observe that the geographical distribution of branches has not changed substantially between 2001 and 2006: in essence, a growing share of bank branches are now located in the north-east and central Italy, at the expense of a corresponding drop in the north-west and the south.

Banking density is still uneven among the Italian regions. The branches:inhabitants ratio remains lower in the south compared to the rest of the country. This is due, in part, to the different economic weight of the regions.

This picture becomes more complex if we measure the loans:branch ratio and the deposits:branch ratio. Branches operating in Lombardy and Lazio intermediated a stock of loans and deposits well above the Italian average, while the southern regions show lower values.

In general, the greater spread of bank branches in the area can be interpreted as a symptom of a high customer focus and value of proximity. On the other hand, this may be partly offset by a parallel reduction of branch staff for reasons of cost containment. It is possible that the increase of the contact points with customers and the reduction in the number of employees may result in a worsening of service quality (in the sense of less customization) and be more functional to the sale of standardized financial products.

Therefore it is necessary to verify whether the growth in the number of branches and simultaneous average contraction in the number of employees have resulted in reducing staff either in branch offices or at headquarters. A first indication is provided by the change in the percentage of employees working at the counter out of total employees. The average figure for the banking system differs depending on the spatial extent of credit institutions.

The weight of employees working at the counter in Italian banks decreased in 2006 compared to 2001 in banks operating in larger markets, and increased in banks operating in smaller and local markets. This fact, in order to be properly interpreted, should be related to the development of the branch network in different types of banks. Comparing the number of employees working at the counter to the number of branches leads to a similar conclusion. Also in this case, banks operating in larger markets showed the most significant reduction, followed by regional banks. Only provincial and local banks, and cooperative banks (*banche di credito cooperativo*, BCCs), maintain a constant value for this ratio.[4]

In summary, the branch spatial distribution still reflects the country's dualistic economic and territorial structure in terms of wealth concentration, the presence of small local firms and population density. However, it seems that the north-east area has gained most new bank branches, while the southern regions still retain a relatively moderate degree of banking level. Empirical studies[5] show that that the impact of mergers and acquisitions on the degree of competition in the Italian banking system has been partly positive. Banks born out of mergers, while gaining market share, have not dramatically increased their market power, but have been following competitive strategies similar to those of other credit institutions.

However, this consolidation process is not immune from criticism. The above process in fact only partially led to an improvement of efficiency, both in terms of cost-efficiency – namely the ability to contain production costs and profit-efficiency – and in the ability to sell profitably one's output on the market.[6] Moreover, efficiency gains seem to have been distributed unevenly across bank sizes and across bank categories as well.

The Notable Performance of Cooperative Banks

Indeed, as Tables 7.1 and 7.2 indicate, BCCs show, on average, a positive cost-efficiency differential compared to JSBs and BPs. This gap between BCCs and JSBs, after a decrease between 1998 and 2000, remains pretty constant up to 2004 and then falls to some extent in the next two years, returning to growth over 2007 and 2008. The differential in favour of the BPs remains fairly stable until 2004, then declines over the next two years and then grows again in the years 2007–8.

Table 7.1: Cost-efficiency across Italian bank categories.

Year	All banks	Joint-stock banks (JSBs)	Popular banks (BPs)	Cooperative banks (BCCs)
1998	0.8238	0.6720	0.7235	0.8764
1999	0.8317	0.7283	0.7983	0.8643
2000	0.8511	0.7581	0.8287	0.8804
2001	0.8717	0.7564	0.8474	0.9083
2002	0.8802	0.7795	0.8504	0.9130
2003	0.8748	0.7674	0.8308	0.9112
2004	0.8813	0.7795	0.8455	0.9156
2005	0.8957	0.8164	0.8614	0.9213
2006	0.8880	0.8477	0.8558	0.9027
2007	0.9106	0.8587	0.8904	0.9286
2008	0.9110	0.8453	0.8954	0.9323

Source: L. Giordano and A. Lopes, 'Analysis of the Italian Banking System Efficiency: A Stochastic Frontier Approach', in A. G. S. Ventre, A. Maturo, S. Hoskova-Mayerova and J. Kacprzyk (eds), *Multicriteria and Multiagent Decision Making with Applications to Economic and Social Sciences* (Berlin and Heidelberg: Springer-Verlag, 2012), pp. 20–45.

Regarding profit-efficiency score dynamics as shown in Table 7.2, the differential in favour of BCCs has a tendency to rise continuously until 2007 and then declines in 2008; the gap in favour of the PBs, although fluctuating, has remained fairly stable until 2006, growing in 2007 and declining the following year.

Table 7.2: Profit-efficiency across Italian bank categories.

Year	All banks	Joint-stock banks (JSBs)	Popular banks (BPs)	Cooperative banks (BCCs)
1998	0.9053	0.8988	0.9359	0.9042
1999	0.9279	0.9079	0.9409	0.9326
2000	0.9216	0.9021	0.9325	0.9263
2001	0.9128	0.8916	0.9203	0.9185
2002	0.9107	0.8972	0.9225	0.9138
2003	0.9196	0.8916	0.9258	0.9278
2004	0.9226	0.8944	0.9245	0.9312
2005	0.9129	0.8768	0.8932	0.9249
2006	0.9024	0.8637	0.8859	0.9156
2007	0.8694	0.8175	0.8791	0.8854
2008	0.8271	0.8007	0.8346	0.8348

Source: Giordano and Lopes, 'Analysis of the Italian Banking System Efficiency'.

These results confirm that the Italian banking system is still characterized by a significant presence of cooperative banks whose performance stands out positively with respect to other bank types. In other words, the empirical evidence does not support the view that higher efficiency is associated with the joint-stock for-profit organization model, which was such a powerful assumption driving the consolidation of the Italian banking system.

Further empirical support for this hypothesis can be collected from other studies[7] in which traditional profitability ratios are calculated relative to the number of bank branches (see Table 7.3).

The total volume of net interest income divided by the total number of branches during the period 2001–5 has remained roughly constant in nominal terms (+0.9 per cent), which implies a decrease in real terms. The change in operating income is rather negative, even at current prices.

Table 7.3: Changes in Italian bank branch profitability and costs (in per cent), 2001–6.

	Net interest income	Operating income	Gross operating income	Total costs per branch	Net profits before tax	Borrowers per branch	Loans per branch
All banks	0.9	–3.9	–11.9	2.8	34.0	6.3	14.4
BCCs	5.5	7.0	4.8	8.2	61.1	–0.1	47.8
Other banks	0.7	–4.1	–12.2	2.8	32.7	7.1	13.2

Source: Data from S. Grimaldi, C. Guagliano and J. S. Lopez, 'L'evoluzione della struttura distributiva delle banche italiane dal 2001 al 2006', *Cooperazione di credito*, 195: 6 (2007), pp. 7–69.

Again, BCCs exhibit better performance compared to other bank types, with an average growth of net interest income of 5.5 per cent and operating income of 7 per cent. On the other hand, the overall costs broken down by bank window have remained very low in the system as a whole (+2.8 per cent from 2001 to 2005), especially because of the decrease in personnel costs (instead, operating costs, net of bank staff, grew by 6.4 per cent). Similarly, while borrowers per bank branch and loans per branch have grown in general, by 6.3 per cent and 14.4 per cent respectively, this increase in 'branch productivity' is particularly evident for BCC banks. As with profits, productivity has grown by 34 per cent for the entire system, with a much more significant growth of 61 per cent for BCCs.

This leads to an important observation: the growth in the number of bank branches in Italy, while having a moderate impact on costs, brought significant benefits for BCCs alone.

Two factors may explain this trend. One has to do with the time lag between corporate restructuring and its impact in terms of efficiency. Another is related to the different competitive strategies put in place: while big banks have mainly acquired already existing bank branches – following a strategy of market saturation – to prevent the entry of new competitors, BCCs adopted a different strategy, gaining position in the markets vacated by other lenders.

These results can be interpreted in light of the theoretical literature that highlights the comparative advantages of cooperative banks in an economic environment characterized by the widespread presence of small and medium-sized enterprises. In addition, it should be noted that the cooperative form tends to give stability to senior management, also because it limits exposure to the risks of takeover. The stability of top management can be good or bad: it is bad to the extent that it attenuates the market sanctions with respect to management inefficiencies; and it is good when, without prejudice to management efficiency, it helps articulate business strategies around long-term goals, thus promoting the accumulation of soft information about customers and, therefore, strengthening credit to small businesses.[8]

These results confirm that the Italian banking system, while having gone through radical transformation in the past two decades, remains characterized by the persistent presence of small, cooperative banks that stand out positively compared to the rest of the banking system.[9]

If we take into account the location of bank headquarters, Table 7.4 shows a widening gap in terms of cost-efficiency unfavourable to southern banks during 1998–9; then this trend stops and the gap decreases until 2002, but it widens again until 2006. In 2007 there is a reduction in the gap, which widens again in 2008. The gap in terms of cost-efficiency between southern banks and banks headquartered in central Italy fluctuates around zero until 2004 and then becomes increasingly unfavourable to the southern ones until 2006; in 2007 there is a gap reduction, which increases again in 2008. Overall, cost-efficiency score dynamics show a clear and permanent inferiority of the southern banks compared to those with headquarters in the rest of Italy.

Table 7.4: Cost-efficiency of Italian banks by headquarter location.

Year	All banks	North	Centre	South
1998	0.8238	0.8300	0.8043	0.8260
1999	0.8317	0.8442	0.8046	0.8230
2000	0.8511	0.8614	0.8325	0.8410
2001	0.8717	0.8761	0.8589	0.8721
2002	0.8802	0.8809	0.8758	0.8824
2003	0.8748	0.8790	0.8622	0.8756
2004	0.8813	0.8881	0.8697	0.8742
2005	0.8957	0.9031	0.8861	0.8842
2006	0.8880	0.9062	0.8699	0.8558
2007	0.9106	0.9191	0.8949	0.9028
2008	0.9110	0.9218	0.8933	0.8986

Source: Giordano and Lopes, 'Analysis of the Italian Banking System Efficiency'.

Regarding profit-efficiency scores also reported in Table 7.4, the unfavourable gap between southern and northern banks gradually decreases until 2000, then it tends to worsen until 2003; the gap decreases again in the following three years, and increases again in 2007, followed by a new reduction in 2008. What clearly appears is that the convergence between the performance of northern and southern banks was reached by means of a deterioration of the performance results of the former rather than an improvement of the latter.

The comparison between banks based in the south and those based in the centre is favourable to the former, although the gap has been characterized by large fluctuations; it was favourable until 2006, significantly deteriorated in 2007, and improved again in 2008.

We may conclude that the changes in ownership that have taken place after the late 1990s, which 'stabilized' and 'consolidated' southern banks, have obtained only a partial gap reduction in terms of cost-efficiency; in addition, we found a progressive alignment and convergent performance in terms of profit-efficiency even though this process was achieved at lower levels.

This empirical evidence allows us to state that the smaller banks organized as cooperatives may also play a significant role in the southern regions; but in these regions, this segment of the banking system has a limited relevance in terms of branches, on the one hand, and on the other, is largely controlled by banking groups headquartered in the north, which do not necessarily consider the southern credit market as a priority.

In other words, the disappearance of an autonomous southern banking system significantly impairs the prospects for development of production systems located in the weakest areas of the country.[10]

Bank Branch Network Transformations before the Crisis

Understanding the transformation of branch networks on the eve of the crisis is crucial for the definition of business development strategies of banks, especially the large ones.

At the end of 2001 there were seven banking groups in Italy with more than 1,000 branches, and fifteen with more than 500; five years later these groups had become, respectively, nine and sixteen. Banking concentration at branch level has changed little in five years: the top three banking groups have maintained in this period a 35 per cent share of all branches, while the top ten banking groups rose from 56.8 per cent in 2001 to 57.9 per cent at the end of 2006.

Practically almost all banking groups and banks have increased the number of branches, with the exception of Banca Intesa and Banca Antoniana Veneta among the big banks, and only eight small banks (with less than twenty branches). One may ask whether there is a relationship between the size of the network at the beginning of the period and subsequent changes; in other words, we can ask whether the initial size of the intermediaries has influenced their strategy of branch expansion.

In 2001 banks with more than 700 branches were those who reported a lower net increase in branches: the median growth in fact amounted to 3.9 per cent, versus 24 per cent of banks with branches between 100 and 700, and 27.6 per cent of banks with less than 100 branches.[11]

The dimensional change of a bank's branch network is the balance of dynamic processes that combine new openings, acquisitions, divestitures and closures of branches. It is therefore important to understand how banks have made use of these different options. In particular, the share of closures and disposals was more relevant for large banks. Large groups (with more than 700 branches) either expanded through acquisitions (rather than new openings) or achieved a moderate expansion through a combination of purchases and sales.

Medium-sized banks (between 100 and 700 branches) instead adopted two different approaches: some developed a growth strategy by resorting to acquisitions (BPI, Popolare di Vicenza, Cr Firenze, Carige Popolare di Milano); others preferred new openings (Banca Popolare di Sondrio, Banca Sella, CR Valtellina).

Another important aspect of bank strategies relative to the growth of their branch network is the choice between expanding into new territories or deepening their presence in areas already served. Large banks opted for the former, with, between 2001 and 2006, a very limited increase in the municipalities already served by each bank (5 per cent); for medium and small banks, by contrast, the increase was 31 per cent and 24 per cent, respectively. However, the branches:municipalities ratio shows a higher degree of territorial concentration for large banks (1.8 branches per municipality against 1.6 and 1.4 for medium and small banks).[12]

Table 7.5 shows that the share of large bank branches has grown in the north-west and in the south at the expense of branches of medium-sized banks. Small banks have increased their share in Sardinia and in Sicily and in the centre and the north-east, while BCCs have increased their share in northern and central Italy.

Table 7.5: Italian bank branch distribution, 2001–6.

Banks	2001					2006				
	South	Islands	North-west	North-east	Centre	South	Islands	North-west	North-east	Centre
Large	58.6	70.9	58.9	59.1	55.6	66.2	66.2	61.6	56.7	53.8
Medium	21.2	18.9	24.9	11.1	25.2	11.8	19.6	21.5	10.6	23.6
Small	11.8	4.4	8.1	11.7	9.9	12.7	76.0	7.5	13.4	11.9
BCCs	8.4	5.8	7.4	17.8	9.0	9.2	65.0	8.5	19.2	10.3
Foreign banks	0.0	0.0	0.7	0.2	0.4	0.1	0.0	0.8	0.2	0.4
All banks	100.0	100.0	100.0	100.0	100.0	100.0	100.0	100.0	100.0	100.0

Source: Data from Grimaldi, Guagliano and Lopez, 'L'evoluzione della struttura distributiva delle banche italiane dal 2001 al 2006'.

Taking into consideration the evolution of the presence of banking groups according the municipalities size in the period 2001–6 (see Table 7.6), large banks have increased their presence in the smaller municipalities (with less than 10,000 inhabitants) at the expense of medium and small ones, while they decreased in larger municipalities, where the smaller banks have increased their weight. BCCs have increased their presence in all municipalities, but in a more limited way than the larger ones. It would be interesting to investigate whether small banks have opened new branches especially where large banks did not open (or where they closed) them. These trends seem to indicate that small banks (in particular cooperative ones) have filled the spaces left by the larger banks, at least in several areas of the country.

Table 7.6: Italian bank window distribution by bank and municipality size (thousands of inhabitants).

	Branch distribution (%) by bank size and municipality size (thousands of inhabitants)						Percentage change 2001–6					
Banks	<10	10–25	25–50	50–100	100–250	Over 250	<10	10–25	25–50	50–100	100–250	Over 250
Large	51.6	57.9	61.7	59.4	65.7	70.2	3.1	1.2	−1.2	0.1	−3.0	−2.6
Medium	18.8	21.4	21.7	23.5	16.9	20.7	−3.3	−3.7	−3.2	−2.3	−1.8	−1.7
Small	10.6	9.6	9.5	11.3	11.9	5.6	−0.1	0.6	2.7	1.3	3.4	3.5
BCCs	18.9	11.0	7.0	5.6	5.2	1.7	1.6	1.8	1.7	1.1	1.6	0.5
Foreign banks	0.0	0.0	0.0	0.2	0.3	1.8	0.0	0.0	0.0	−0.1	−0.1	0.3

Source: Data from Grimaldi, Guagliano and Lopez, 'L'evoluzione della struttura distributiva delle banche italiane dal 2001 al 2006'.

Bank Lending Strategies and Small Firms before the Crisis

Ownership changes and transformations of the branch network have influenced the lending strategies of Italian banks, particularly with regard to the degree of decision-making autonomy of bank subsidiaries. A study conducted in 2006 by the Bank of Italy on a sample of banks shows interesting findings in this regard,[13] especially in light of the assumption that small banks should be better able to establish intense relationships with local firms.

The Bank of Italy analysis shows an expansion of the territory by small banks between 2000 and 2006; the distance between local branches and headquarters, in particular, has increased.

Moreover, the survey also shows that the complexity of banks' internal organization (and especially local, cooperative banks) has increased between 2003 and 2006; in particular, the degree of decision-making decentralization (i.e. the autonomy of the branch manager in the small businesses financing decisions) has increased – especially so in banks operating in north-eastern and central Italy, but less in southern banks (Table 7.7). A greater degree of decision-making decentralization increases the incentives for the branch manager to gather information on customers and reduces transmission costs, but it also increases the risk of opportunism. Possible tools for mitigating this risk could be the mobility of the managers in the area and a flexible remuneration linked to performance. In the three-year period there was, in fact, an increase in the branch managers' mobility (see column 4 of Table 7.7).

Table 7.7: Organizational variables of small and minor banks by geographical area.

Territorial areas	Distance centre/ periphery* 2000	2006	Decentralized decision- making (%)	Stay branch manager (%)	Average length of stay of the branch manager (months)	Delegating index (%)†	Incentives for managers of subsidiaries‡
Small banks	28	34	47.1	25.0	47	16.0	7.8
Southern Italy	47	61	39.4	16.6	42	18.2	6.2
North-west	34	40	46.5	25.9	40	16.6	9.9
North-east	19	25	48.3	28.0	57	12.3	6.9
Centre	21	23	50.0	24.0	45	18.7	5.9
Sample	42	47	49.5	25.0	45	14.7	8.8

*   Average distance between branches and head office (km).

†   Balance between the responses which indicated an increase of decentralized decision-making in the three years 2003–6 and those which indicated a decrease in relation to the total number of banks in the sample (%).

‡   Average impact (%) of incentives on the annual salary of a branch manager.

Source: Banca d'Italia, *L'Economia delle Regioni Italiane* (Rome: Banca d'Italia, 2007).

Additional data from the same source provides information about the degree of decision-making autonomy of branch managers concerning lending to small businesses. It shows that such autonomy is lower in southern bank branches.

Overall, these empirical findings suggest that the reorganization of the Italian banking system in recent years has given rise to very rigid and hierarchical banking organizations. The increasing reliance on standardized information-processing techniques (hard information) has widened the distance between bank decision-making centres and firms. At the same time, these new organizations are less well equipped to gather intangible (soft) information, which arises out of more intense relationships with customers and in less vertically integrated organizational structures. This reorganization of banks, moreover, has taken place in an economy characterized by the widespread presence of small and medium-sized enterprises, inherently opaque, which tend to produce more heterogeneous and intangible information than larger firms.

Therefore the changes in organization and structure in Italian banking are rightly perceived to exacerbate the issue of access to credit for small businesses, further undermining the prospects of growth of the production system in the weakest areas of the country, which are characterized by more vulnerable and opaque firms.[14]

Banks' Lending Strategies and Small Firms after the Crisis

The international financial crisis, which began with the bankruptcy of the US investment bank Lehman Brothers on 15 September 2008, had a major impact on the stability of the major US and European financial institutions and led to a sharp fall in the growth rates of world's leading economies.

It is now, however, five years later, that the impact of the crisis on the Italian financial system, hitherto quite limited, has become visible: concerns about the soundness of the intermediaries are now acute, leading to a sharp rise in risk premiums on inter-bank rates, already growing for over a year. The market capitalization of the major Italian banks collapsed in a few weeks during 2012 as a result of deep uncertainty about the quality of bank assets; major stock indices dropped, which made the issuance of securities more difficult and costly; finally, the supply of credit contracted sharply.

An event of this magnitude strongly influences bank behaviour concerning the definition of the criteria, terms and conditions for granting loans to businesses. How, then, have Italian banks behaved, especially given the fundamental changes in organization and structure that took place in the previous fifteen years, as documented above? Useful indications are provided by the findings of the quarterly survey conducted by the Bank of Italy on eight banking groups representing more than two-thirds of the Italian loan market.[15]

The first issue concerns the definition of the criteria for granting credit to businesses. These, in other words, are the criteria, not necessarily codified in writing, or other practices related to policies, which define the types of loan considered desirable or not, the priority in the granting of loans, and the guarantees considered acceptable or not. It is interesting to note a gradual tightening of credit standards applied by banks for lending, especially in the long term, which reached its maximum at the beginning of 2009.[16] According to the survey, the main factors behind that tightening were expectations regarding overall economic activity, and perceived risks on collateral, particularly for small firms with five or less employees.[17]

Turning to the terms and conditions applied to loan approval and the opening of new lines of credit, we observe that since January 2008 there has been a significant increase in the interest rates charged to riskier loans. Another aspect that characterizes the tightening of conditions applied by banks to businesses is the shrinking of the overall amount of disbursed loans.

The survey also analyses changes in the demand for loans: in this case we observe a significant drop in demand, especially from smaller firms, in the 2008–9 period. This contraction owes, essentially, to a reduction in investment in fixed capital, inventories and working capital; at the same time, short-term loans were partially replaced with long-term loans through debt-restructuring operations. In fact, borrowers have chosen to modify terms and conditions of loans to avoid insolvency, or to make debt more sustainable by postponing repayment deadlines or reducing its burden.

Bank–Firm Relationship Deterioration during the Eurozone Financial Crisis

In 2010, while the world economy was trying to recover from the real and financial consequences of the global crisis, a new outbreak occurred in the euro area. Troubles in Greece triggered a new escalation of risk perception by international investors, who now turned their critical attention to sovereign debt. Unable to place their securities on the market in May 2010, Greece had to resort to the European Union and International Monetary Fund for assistance. Over the following months, Ireland (November 2010) and Portugal (April 2011) required the same kind of help. The three countries faced different problems: competitiveness in Portugal, public finances and also competitiveness and external imbalance in Greece, a banking crisis in Ireland.

To avoid the possibility that tensions in sovereign debt markets, through their impact on the money markets and on bank lending, could jeopardize the smooth transmission of monetary policy, the European Central Bank (ECB) decided to refinance European banks with fixed-rate tenders satisfying fully the demand for credit; in addition, the ECB adopted a programme of purchases of government securities (securities markets programme, or SMP), although, given statutory constraints, that programme was limited.

These public interventions were not evaluated by financial operators as decisive because the very meaning and the internal coherence of the eurozone's construction were being challenged. The nature of this second phase of the crisis is different from the first one: at the root of the US and then global financial crisis in 2007–8 were excesses of monetary creation of uncontrolled financial innovation and an irrational faith in the self-regulating capacity of financial markets. At the root of the problems facing Europe today, there are serious institutional weaknesses: lack of fiscal coordination, constraints on the ECB, inadequate regulation and supervision of European financial markets, all of which weakens the eurozone.

Since the summer of 2011, signs of a slowdown in global growth, fears of repercussions on public finances and on the soundness of the banking sector, and uncertainties concerning the involvement of the private sector in the resolution of the debt crisis in Greece have increased tensions, which are now involving Italy and Spain as well.

Under the combined effect of rising public deficits due to bank bailouts and measures to support domestic demand and the deteriorating economic situation, public debt has soared in eurozone countries, creating doubts about the solvency of so-called peripheral countries. Public perception of a greater risk for government bonds issued by these countries was then compounded by the inadequacies of European institutions, mainly because of a lack of common fiscal policy and the inability of the ECB to guarantee the value of government bonds of countries in difficulty.

In early August 2012, the EBC Board of Directors finally announced the introduction of 'outright monetary transactions' (OMT), a plan to purchase government bond purchases on the secondary market without any quantitative restrictions. However, such interventions would be implemented by the ECB only at the request of countries in difficulty and subject to adoption by the latter of a 'memorandum' of measures of fiscal consolidation. Yet the announcement yielded immediate benefits: medium and long-term interest rates on bonds issued by peripheral countries sharply decreased. However, tensions remain due to the unwillingness of 'core' countries to adopt expansionary fiscal policies.

The inability of Europe to handle problems in the 'peripheral' countries has undermined market confidence, especially in Spain and Italy. The drop in value of sovereign bonds has had a negative impact on banks' capitalization given the latter's heavy exposure to the former. Thus governments have had to finance the recapitalization of their banking systems with additional burdens on public finances and a higher risk premium on government bonds. The sovereign debt crisis in the periphery is thus linked to the banking crisis in the whole euro area – a significant source of instability for the next few years.

Faced with this situation, European institutions have subordinated the financial assistance aimed at refinancing the public debt of the peripheral countries to the implementation of supply-side policies (i.e. market liberalization and privatizations) and restrictive fiscal policies (i.e. drastic cuts in public spending and tightening of the tax burden). The assumption behind those 'austerity' policies was that in this way peripheral countries could improve their competitiveness on international markets, increasing exports more than imports, thereby reducing current account imbalances, restoring their reliability on international financial markets, thereby reducing yields on government bonds and finally restarting economic growth. However, what has been happening in the eurozone in the past two years goes exactly in the opposite direction: austerity measures, causing a fall in domestic demand, tended to have a depressive effect on economic activity, resulting in a significant contraction of GDP.[18]

Not surprisingly, the peripheral countries have fallen into a vicious circle in which the worsening of the debt:GDP and deficit:GDP ratios imposes additional restrictive fiscal measures that determine even more substantial reductions in production and a further deterioration of those indicators. It is obvious that the simultaneous adoption of recessionary policies from countries that have a high degree of integration tends to amplify the depression.

It is at this stage that the international financial crisis, interacting with the banking system, reverberated negatively on businesses. Concerns about the soundness of banking systems are acute, leading to a sudden increase in risk premiums on inter-bank rates; market capitalization of the major Italian banks collapses as a result of deep uncertainty about the quality of bank assets in which government bonds of the peripheral countries are now included; in addition, the flow of credit to the economy shrinks and credit requirements become more stringent.

In the last few years we can observe an increased heterogeneity of monetary conditions in the euro area: the intensification of capital outflows from the countries most affected by the crisis and a clearer segmentation of bank deposits along national borders increase the risk of a crisis in banks' funding, giving rise to a strong restriction of credit to firms in peripheral countries, with serious consequences to their macroeconomic performance.

The case of Italy, from the point of view of bank corporate lending, confirms the existence of a strong dualism within the euro area: while Northern European countries (Austria, Belgium, Germany, Finland, France and the Netherlands) show a pretty stable trend in bank loans, peripheral countries (Portugal, Ireland, Greece and Spain) show a strongly negative trend.

ECB data[19] show that only 48 per cent of Italian firms, especially small and medium-sized enterprises, who made a request for a bank loan in the latter six months of 2012 saw their demand accepted – much worse than in France and Germany, where loan requests were granted in 80 per cent of cases. Among the major euro area countries, only Spanish SMEs are in a worse situation.

The deterioration in the macroeconomic environment negatively affects a firm's financial situation, leading to a progressive deterioration in the quality of bank credit. Banks respond, on the one hand, with ever more stringent non-performing loans (NPL) provisioning policies, at the request of the supervisory bodies, and, on the other, with tighter credit. Solvent but illiquid firms are thus taken into a vicious cycle that eventually increases NPL.

Figure 7.1 shows that Italy experienced a gradual contraction of business loans compared to the overall performance of the eurozone countries and, above all, Germany. Moreover, lending conditions diverge as well: Figure 7.2 shows the difference between the average interest rate on loans in Italy and Germany.

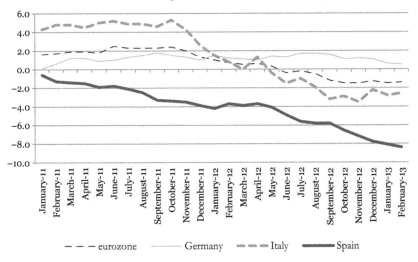

Figure 7.1: Annual growth rates of loans to firms in the eurozone.

Source: Data from ECB, *Survey on the Access to Finance of Small and Medium-Sized Enterprises (SAFE)* (Frankfurt: ECB, 2012).

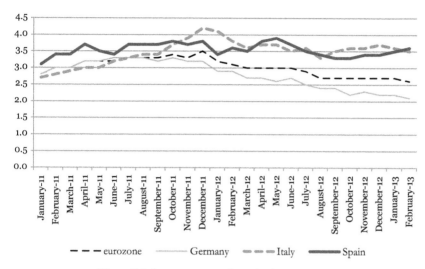

Figure 7.2: Interest rates on loans in the eurozone.

Source: Data from ECB, *SAFE*.

More information on the comparative behaviour of European banks can be obtained from a reordering of the ECB Bank Lending Survey. The data shows a moderate tightening of credit standards in 2010 in Italy, which remained stable in Germany and Europe, and a very sharp tightening of the criteria in the former during the second half of 2011. This tightening reflected the rise, in the same period, of the spread between the rate of return on Italian BTPs and German Bunds, from 301 basis points in July to 552 basis points in November. In the second half of 2012 we observe in Italy a relaxation of criteria for credit granting, while in Germany they remain unchanged. The beginning of 2013 sees the alignment of the Italian data to European ones, while in Germany we note a further slight easing of credit standards for approving loans to companies.

By analysing banks' assessment of the demand for loans, according to the ECB Survey, in contrast to the overall trend in the eurozone (and especially Germany), Italian banks have faced a significant decline in demand for credit from the beginning of 2012 onwards. This decline in loan applications is attributed by Italian bankers to the substantial halt of fixed capital accumulation by Italian firms. Finally, Italian firms were more likely than elsewhere to use credit with a view to restructure outstanding debts and reduce the probability of insolvency.

Italian Banks and the Crisis

In the aftermath of the global crisis and the midst of the eurozone one, Italian banks have experienced a decrease in net interest income, this being partly due to the rising costs of funding from customers because of tensions on both deposits and bond markets. In addition, interest earned on loans is more sensitive to low market rates (Euribor) than the interest paid on bank deposits. Finally, Italian banks were adversely affected by the reduction of interest-bearing assets with respect to interest-bearing liabilities, due to loan reduction.

This phenomenon contrasts with a significant improvement in operating income on financial instruments (securities, financial liabilities and derivatives) over the previous year. This positive result owes to gains realized through the repurchase/exchange of securities issued in recent years, made possible by the low prices of securities and the recovery of values for many financial assets in portfolios (bonds, shares, etc.).

Operating costs continued their downward trend due to the implementation of programmes to limit personnel (staff reductions, unions agreements) and administrative costs (organizational rationalization), with a consequent improvement in the cost:income ratio from 68.5 per cent to 63 per cent in the last year. However, NPL increase negatively affected gross operating profits.[20]

A worrying fact is the continuing reduction in credits to the corporate sector, especially for smaller firms. In this respect, Bank of Italy data show that the percentage of rationed firms is growing. Access to credit remains difficult for smaller companies, for which resorting to alternative sources of finance is also harder.[21] Restrictive credit policies also reflect bank financial conditions: in 2012 the growth of lending to businesses was positive for banks with best capital ratios and funding.

Regarding lending quality, Bank of Italy data also show that the new bad loans:total loans ratio was stable for family loans, whereas the ratio worsened for business loans, especially for firms in the construction sector. At the end of 2012, NPL accounted for 7.2 per cent of gross loans, while total deteriorated loans (NPL, doubtful, restructured or past due) represented 13.4 per cent.

In line with what was observed previously, smaller banks, especially small cooperative banks, show a lower incidence of deteriorated loans and a lower coverage rate, which indicates a greater propensity to finance small business compared to larger banks (see Table 7.8); in addition, smaller banks have a higher share of loans fully secured by real or personal collateral (50 per cent, compared to 33 per cent for the total system).[22]

Table 7.8: Italian bank lending according to quality and coverage ratios as of December 2012 (in per cent and in € million).

	Loans	Deteriorated loans	NPL
Top five banking groups			
% composition	100.0	14.0	7.7
Coverage ratio	6.3	41.1	56.1
Large banks			
% composition	100.0	11.5	6.1
Coverage ratio	4.7	36.7	52.2
Small banks			
% composition	100.0	14.4	7.4
Coverage ratio	5.9	37.8	56.0
Minor banks			
% composition	100.0	13.8	6.1
Coverage ratio	4.1	27.2	46.1
All banks			
% composition	100.0	13.4	7.2
Coverage ratio	5.7	38.8	54.6

Source: Banca d'Italia, *Rapporto sulla Stabilità Finanziaria* (Rome: Banca d'Italia, 2013).

With regard to funding, the latter has grown on average by 4.6 per cent in 2012, mainly thanks to ECB refinancing operations and, to a lesser extent, the good performance of domestic deposits. The increase of these components offsets the decline in bonds and deposits from non-residents; the average cost of raised funds collection has decreased, reaching 1.3 per cent, thanks both to the easing of tensions in sovereign debt markets and to the greater resort to refinancing by the ECB.

However, despite the expansion of assets readily convertible into cash and the solidity demonstrated so far by retail funding, the short-term liquidity position of Italian banks still remains quite vulnerable to a possible worsening of the sovereign debt crisis, and a consequent downgrading of government bonds and banks.

In relation to these issues and at the request of supervisory authorities,[23] in 2012 the largest listed banking groups have continued to improve their capital position, while the adequacy of the balance sheet was confirmed for small local banks, who have benefited from a more limited exposure to financial risks. The strengthening in capital adequacy ratios is mainly due to a decrease in risk-weighted assets. The reduction of risk-weighted assets has helped portfolios shift towards activities with a lower capital absorption: this has obvious negative consequences for credit to small businesses located in the weakest areas of the country.

At the end of 2012, the core tier 1 ratio of the first fourteen listed groups had reached, on average, 10.5 per cent versus 7.5 per cent in 2010. The core tier 1 ratio of banks has increased over the same period from 7.3 per cent to 9.3 per cent, while the tier 1 ratio of cooperative banks is now at 14.1 per cent. The capital of the latter category of banks remains large, although low profitability reduces their self-financing capacity. The data also confirms a higher level of capitalization for southern banks compared to centre-northern banks: 12.6 per cent versus 9 per cent.

At the same time, the slow alignment of Italian banks with the new capital requirements imposed by Basel 3 has continued; according to estimates by the Bank of Italy, the overall need for quality capital for banks would amount to €8.8 billion in 2012. This implies that compliance with the new capital requirements, especially for larger banks, can be achieved only by further reducing risk-weighted assets or otherwise rearranging the portfolio towards those activities with lower capital absorption; in any case, this would result in a further decrease of credit supply.

Bank–Firm Relationship Deterioration in Southern Italy

The critical issues in bank lending identified above are even more apparent in southern Italy. Over the past eleven years (2001–12), the south has suffered a 3.8 per cent decline in GDP, very far from the centre-north (+3.3 per cent), reflecting the continuing development gap between the two areas. The performance is still more dramatic if we observe only the crisis years: from 2008 to 2012 the south lost more than 10 per cent of its GDP, almost twice that of the centre-north (−5.8 per cent).[24] The worsening of the southern economy is more intense because of greater reliance on domestic demand, which was reduced significantly by the restrictive policies implemented to stabilize public finances in recent years.

This negative performance has also affected, to some extent, the demand for credit:[25] the reduction of loan applications to the largest banks was much more pronounced in the south than in the centre-north. At the same time, deposits collected in the south by large banks have grown much more than in the rest of the country – respectively, 27.7 per cent and 10.5 per cent. This data confirms the trend by which larger banks increase their deposit:loan ratio in the south.

A different picture emerges for smaller banks; if we consider the period 2008–11, the demand for credit has grown more in southern Italy than the rest of the country. As already noted, it is clear that small local banks pay more attention to businesses rooted in the south compared to larger banks.

It is interesting to note that both the expansion and the decline of loans occur in a more pronounced way in central and northern Italy than in the south. The less intense loan contraction observed in the southern regions is due to the presence of persistent and more selective criteria for assessing creditworthiness there. This allows banks operating in the south to reduce loans to a lesser extent to companies already selected, and much less frequently, than is the case in other areas of the country (however, the opportunity to expand credit in the south is much more limited than elsewhere).

When we consider firm size, a perhaps surprising finding is that companies who have suffered a more severe credit restriction between 2009 and 2011 were firms with at least twenty employees in northern and central Italy. In the south, the firms with fewer than twenty employees have recorded the greatest credit contraction; it is reasonable to conclude that the expansion of loans recorded in the south over the past two years is explained mainly by the larger firms, while small businesses still experience increasing difficulty in accessing credit.[26]

Another issue that is important to consider is the cost of credit: Svimez has calculated the interest rate gap by dividing the difference between the interest rate earned on short-term loans in the south and in the centre-north by the national level.[27] At the end of 2008 it was around 10 per cent, doubled at the first quarter of 2009, and reached a peak of 27 per cent at the end of 2010; afterwards the differential continued to average more than 20 per cent, before rising strongly in 2012 to almost 35 per cent.

These data confirm the increased risk associated with a more uncertain macroeconomic environment in southern Italy; it is also evident that the more permissive monetary policy practised by the ECB during these months has not translated into a reduction in interest rates charged by banks to businesses, since the latter have increasing risk coefficients that have, in fact, more than offset these reductions, especially in the weakest areas of the country.

The NPL quarterly growth rate provides a further indication of deterioration in the quality of bank portfolios. Svimez data provide a comparison of new NPL between the centre-north and the south: the smaller deterioration in the quality of loans to the south than in the rest of Italy could be due, at least in part, to the fact that southern firms have already been experiencing, for a long time, a more acute restriction in access to credit and higher bad loan levels by virtue of an exogenous environmental risk. Finally, between the end of 2010 and 2011, NPLs for smaller amounts have increased by less than what happened to those of a greater entity. Again it should be noted that the adoption of tighter criteria for smaller loans occurred over time with the adoption of more standardized procedures that clearly act more decisively on these size classes. A wider margin of discretion could still apply to larger loans; evidently the escalation of the crisis has increased the deterioration of loans belonging also to larger-size classes.[28]

Conclusion

At the beginning of the 1990s, the Italian banking system was characterized by predominantly public ownership, low concentration, little internationalization, capital inadequacy and modest income capacity. The last fifteen years have seen a significant restructuring process relative to all these aspects, which gradually improved many structural limitations. Nevertheless, the process towards a modernized system is still far from complete and is plagued by problematic elements that need further examination.

On the one hand, this process has not reduced the comparative superiority of cooperative and small banks in terms of cost- and profit-efficiency. Despite the fact that these banks hold a marginal share of the overall lending market (7 per cent), they have prospects for profitable expansion in the future. This is consistent with the hypothesis of an underlying demand for credit that does not meet with supply by larger banks but can be adequately met by smaller banks with decentralized structures (or rather, in the Italian case, by cooperative banks). The empirical results are in line with a substantial amount of evidence based on other credit systems (the United States and Germany), as seen in other chapters of this volume. In addition, Italian cooperative banks appear to invest more in intangible information (soft information), develop more intense customer relationships, and adopt a less vertical structure, characteristics that help us understand their comparative advantage, as argued in Chapter 4 of this book.

On the other hand, the process of consolidation of the Italian banking industry has encouraged the growth of medium-sized intermediaries and the adoption of rigid hierarchical models not favourable to credit access by small and medium-sized firms. In addition, economic and territorial dualism has been reinforced by the transformations of the Italian banking systems: the massive ownership changes following southern banks' acquisition by other financial intermediaries at the end of the 1990s have not achieved the expected outcome. Moreover, southern banks' poor asset quality (due to their external environment) adversely affects their cost- and profit-efficiency.

On top of these structural issues, the financial crisis in the eurozone, caused by doubts about the sustainability of sovereign debt in peripheral countries and aggravated by the weakness of the main European institutions, has motivated the adoption of austerity policies that have compromised the prospects for growth in Europe. In the absence of expansionary and coordinated policies at the European level, the likely situation of gradual disintegration of the euro area, with the deepening of the differences between 'central' and 'peripheral' countries, is envisaged.

Divergence tendencies within Europe also concern the banking system. The empirical evidence discussed here indicates a progressive separation between the Northern European core and the Mediterranean periphery in terms of the availability of credit to businesses, interest rates, the tightening of criteria for the assessment of creditworthiness, and the perception of economic risk by banks.

This scenario captures what is happening within the Italian economy: the fall in activity levels has led businesses to curb demand for loans (which is mainly limited to the restructuring of existing debt with the banking system); symmetrically, the worsening of their financial situation has caused a significant deterioration in credit quality. On the supply side, credit tightening has been uneven in the banking system because the reduction of loans granted by the top five banking groups was partially offset by the expansion of loans granted by small banks, but, unfortunately, in 2012 this second component has also undergone a significant slowdown. Therefore, one should insist on the significant role of small and cooperative banks in supporting the activities of smaller companies that continue to be a key pillar for the Italian economy. However, the reaction of the banking system is consistent with the application of ever more demanding criteria of capital adequacy, and with the increasingly more automatic setting of customers ratings that tend to penalize smaller companies and cast doubt on future economic growth.

These endemic problems of the Italian economy, then, tend to worsen in times of crisis such as now, resulting in deepening the problems of access to credit for smaller companies. Financial constraints become more stringent, especially for companies operating in territorial and institutional contexts that are more fragile and therefore exposed to greater systemic risks, such as in the case of southern Italy.

There is now ample evidence that within this scenario, the south, more than other areas of the Italy, has suffered the repercussions of the crisis on the productive system. The problems faced by southern firms in terms of access to credit are inevitably influenced by the role played by banking supervision in balancing the need of stability of the banking system with that of financing the economy. In a dualistic context like the Italian one, the pursuit of general goals (like banking system stability) translates into deeper asymmetries. From the banks' point of view, for a given capital, the deterioration of the rating necessarily determines a significant reduction in loans to customers in order to maintain adequate capital ratios. It follows that the deterioration in ratings, even in the presence of expansionary monetary policies such as those conducted by the ECB in the last two years that were perhaps intended to curb significantly the level of interest rates, can make substantially non-operational the 'credit channel' through the constraint posed by the 'balance sheet channel' of the banks.

Basel 2 criteria are particularly exposed to these eventualities because they only prescribe adequate provisions to cover expected losses. As a consequence, during phases of economic expansion (when a rise in lending lays the ground for the growth of bad loans once the economy changes course), expected losses are systematically underestimated compared to actual future results; in the absence of adequate provisions to cover this event, a bank's capital is highly susceptible to being inadequate.

Capital inadequacy becomes visible when the economy goes into recession; it follows that the associated depressive and restrictive effects of today's austerity policies are amplified exponentially by the persistence of a negative cycle, turning into stagnation and outright recession. Therefore current banking regulation, which sets progressive and increasingly stringent controls on capitalization, certainly does not help the real economy in a period of prolonged recession such as the one that the eurozone in general, and its peripheral countries in particular, are experiencing.

In conclusion, several warnings emerge concerning trends in the Italian banking system, and we must ask whether the significant structural changes that have taken place are sufficient to increase efficiency, or rather if the future scenario, which has become more critical after the global financial crisis, will not raise again, in a more dramatic way, the problem of availability of credit – or the problem, more generally, of the absence of a virtuous model of a bank–firm relationship able to operate as a factor for development in the Italian economy.

8 ALTERNATIVE BANKS ON THE MARGIN: THE CASE OF BUILDING SOCIETIES IN THE UNITED KINGDOM

Olivier Butzbach

Origins and Development of an Alternative Banking Model

The Origins

Although the purpose of the present chapter is to show how British building societies might constitute a viable alternative to the failed business model that was exposed in British banking post-2007, it would be a mistake to consider that this was always the case. Originally, building societies were not banks. They were financial institutions of another, specialized kind. They were a mix between a savings bank and a cooperative mortgage lender. It is only belatedly (in the third quarter of the twentieth century) that they were allowed to expand beyond mortgage lending and become more bank-like.

The history of building societies is not unknown to the economic historian.[1] As pointed out by Bellman, the history of building societies is longer than that of joint-stock banks – with the exception of the Bank of England.[2] The first building societies saw the light in the 1770s in Birmingham, a city of rapid economic development and accumulation of wealth. The first building society was founded in 1775 by the owner of an inn, Richard Ketley, and was aptly named the Ketley Building Society. It was founded on a very simple principle, which has stood at the core of building society business models ever since: every member would pay a monthly subscription to the society; the funds so collected would then be used to pay advances (loans) to members wishing to acquire property; the property would be used as collateral to the loans.

Housing was then, as it is perhaps now, a hotly debated social and political issue. Those who advocated the funding of housing by building societies did so on social and moral grounds. Their first concern was to ensure that working classes may have access to descent housing, especially in rapidly growing cities where 'the growth of habitations bears no proportion to the requirements of population'.[3] But the housing problem was not only a matter of quantity. Chambers pointed out how often the 'humbler classes' paid high rents for 'dwellings of a very insufficient kind'.[4] And these high rents and low-quality houses were not (only) the fault of landlords; they were equally the outcome of the 'little dependence to be placed on the rents being paid'. As the same author summarized,

> Among the various methods by which a person in comparatively humble circumstances may improve his condition, and rise in the social scale, is that of becoming, by a course of economic management and saving, the proprietor of a house, in which he and his family may dwell in respectability and comfort.[5]

Chambers further demonstrated the positive impact of building societies on housing by narrating with extraordinary detail his travels to Birmingham and Manchester, seeing as many as 4,000 or 5,000 dwellings (in his estimate).[6] As transpires from the above statement, however, a second concern was also prominent among early building societies supporters: that working classes may be encouraged to save (or, in Chambers's words, that they 'must feel themselves under a sort of compulsion, in order not only to begin, but to continue to save, and the money they invest must not be instantly recoverable as every whim or seeming necessity arises'). This concern was shared with the French, German and Italian philanthropists at the origin of the savings banks movement, who saw a categorical imperative in tightly integrating the working classes to capitalism through savings.[7] This view obviously reflected a widespread perception, on the part of members of the bourgeoisie, that working classes were to be re-educated away from a life of intemperance (one of the largest building societies in nineteenth-century London was called the London Temperance Society) and recklessness (epitomized by the abuse of alcohol): 'Never was there such an auxiliary to the cause of temperance as these land and building societies', writes Chambers.[8] At the same time, this integration was instrumental in cementing the values on which capitalist society had been built, and guaranteeing social order. As the prospectus for a Birmingham building society put it in mid-nineteenth-century words,

> The moral and social effects of such a society are not to be overlooked. The best security for a comfortable and contented people is the possession of property, in the acquisition of which this society will aid industrious and persevering persons. The directors feel confident, from past experience, that it will tend, as similar institutions have done, to cement that union of interest and good-feeling between the operative and the wealthier classes which has happily commenced; the effects of which must be *to render the rights of property more sacred*, by making them better understood, and to diffuse a kindlier feeling and better understanding throughout the population of this industrial locality.[9]

However, neither savings banks nor cooperative banks nor building societies were philanthropic enterprises. British authors were keen on drawing a distinction between the two. Chambers warned against the 'injuriously enervating effect' benevolent actions by philanthropists might have on the working classes by 'tak[ing] away all manly feeling and sense of independence from the objects of their solicitude'.[10] Building societies were not philanthropic enterprises in the sense that members themselves contributed to the funds they drew from to buy a house. They were much closer to self-help institutions. Building societies were not private enterprises either, since housing for the working classes was clearly not a private good – hence the 'desirability of some better arrangements than private enterprise has offered in habitations'.[11]

Within two decades of the creation of the Ketley Building Society, twenty-three further societies were established in Birmingham, and the 'building societies movement' started expanding in other areas of the country: a society was created in Leeds in 1785, in Manchester in 1792 and in London in 1795. Soon dozens of building societies were scattered across Britain. This rapid diffusion of building societies is very similar to the expansion of savings and cooperative banks in France, Germany and Italy at the same time. However, building societies differed from continental non-profit banks under a key aspect: members were treated as investors, not savers. Their contribution to the building societies funding was made through two channels: deposits and shares, the latter being the original and preferred form of funding for several decades. And shares were transferable, unlike savings, albeit to other members only.

At that point (the first half of the nineteenth century), most building societies were fixed-term: called 'terminating societies', they were meant to dissolve once all members had acquired a house. It is only in the late 1830s and 1840s that permanent societies appeared, soon outpacing and crowding out the terminating ones – although some of the latter kind survived up until the late twentieth century. This succession of organizational forms within the building societies movement was made possible by the first Building Society Act in 1836, which addressed the problem of lack of funds. Indeed, the new form allowed additional funding by savers not necessarily interested in buying houses. As Cook et al. pointed out, this enlargement of the investor base was achieved at the cost of a weakening of the 'bond' between savers and borrowers. But, the same authors argue (building on secondary sources), permanent building societies were a very effective organizational form.[12] By the end of the nineteenth century, building societies had grown to several hundreds. In 1877 an observer could start his pamphlet by writing: 'That building societies are amongst the most important financial institutions of the day is beyond doubt'.[13]

As Figure 8.1 shows, the number of building societies continuously increased during the nineteenth century, reaching a peak in the 1890s (almost 2,800 societies), and then declined throughout the twentieth century. This decline in number reflects an aggregation process, however, and not a decline in popularity: in fact, the number of members continuously increased from 1913 onwards, reaching a peak in 1988 (43 million members: more than two-thirds of the overall population!), followed by a steep decline in 1989 (with the demutualization of Abbey), and again in 1997 (with the larger societies choosing to opt out of the mutual sector).

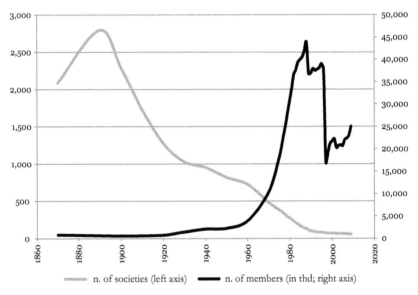

n. of societies (left axis)   n. of members (in thd; right axis)

Figure 8.1: Building societies and their members, 1870–2010.

Source: H. Bellman, 'Building Societies – Some Economic Aspects', *Economic Journal*, 43:169 (1933), pp. 1–39, and Building Societies Association.

Building societies' early success was so rapid that soon societies faced the problem of scarcity of borrowers – again, a classic problem among cooperative and savings banks during the nineteenth century. This problem was turned into a bonanza by governments eager to tap into these easily available savings, through the creation of national postal savings banks, trustee savings banks or other schemes (such as the centralization of savings by the State in France since the late nineteenth century).

An Alternative Business Model?

The original mission of building societies was stated clearly in a document accompanying the 1838 Building Society Act ('Instructions for the Establishment of Benefit Building Societies, with Rules and Forms of Mortgages, &c. Applicable Thereto'): building societies could be established 'for the purpose of raising by monthly or other subscriptions [by members] ... a stock or fund for the purpose of enabling each member thereof to receive out of the funds of such society the amount or value of his or her share or shares therein, to erect or purchase one or more dwelling house or dwelling houses ... to be secured by way of mortgage'. So building societies were specialized financial institutions dedicated to mortgage lending. However, as explained above, more than as a by-product, building societies were also savings institutions and in that respect very similar to other non-profit banks that developed in Great Britain and continental Europe during the nineteenth century.

This mission translated itself in a number of operational and organizational characteristics: (i) their specialization; (ii) their non-profit objective; (iii) their equal treatment of investors and borrowers; (iv) the high level of trust they elicited among the population; and (v) their governance, typical of cooperative firms. A first characteristic of building societies was their specialization in one segment of the credit market. As mentioned above, this specialization was very much a legacy of their origins and a cornerstone of their history; however, it was also maintained over time by the so-called 'straightjacket', i.e. the legislative limitation of building societies' corporate object (more on this below).

A second characteristic of building societies has been (to this day) their non-profit-maximizing objective. As stated in the 'Instructions' mentioned above, 'no member shall receive or be entitled to receive from the funds of such society any interest or dividend by way of annual or other periodical profit upon any shares in such society'. Societies would not seek to maximize profit, but they would earn profit – although in a sustainable way: the prospectus for a large society in the late nineteenth century explained that building societies earned profit through 'the constant return and re-investment of Funds, resulting from the system of monthly repayments, and not by charging an excessive rate to borrowers'.[14]

Reasonably low interest charged to borrowers and reasonably high interest paid to investors were and have been the key bases of building society business models. But these tenets leave room for interpretation. In a 1877 pamphlet, for instance, Platt argued that the interest paid to investors should be 'as high a rate of interest for his money, as the capitalist can get when investing on good mortgage security, which is as much as any reasonable investor has a right to expect',[15] while the society should 'offer the Borrower money at the same rate of interest at which it can be obtained on a private mortgage'.[16]

Platt was quick to observe the potential conflicts of interest between investors and borrowers, especially if and when profits are distributed among them. Such distributed profits would violate the spirit of the constitution of building societies, Platt observes, since

The sum so credited to an Investor as bonus, whilst it is to him actual net profit, being an augmentation of his interest without any corresponding payment, is to the borrower only a return of a portion of the interest he has already paid; and that he has actually paid, if not all, certainly by far the major part of the expenses and losses of the society, whilst the Investors have contributed little or nothing thereto.[17]

This is a remarkable early formulation of the investor–borrower tension mentioned by many authors as a key agency conflict within banks (and discussed in Chapter 4 of the present volume). As several contemporary authors suggest, the mutual form precisely offers a solution to this agency conflict: when cooperative members are both savers (or investors) *and* prospective borrowers, they should have converging interests.[18] In addition, investors participating in the profits generated by the society would be unlikely to ask for high interest and therefore drive the society to undertake riskier investment.[19]

However, again, the broad latitude of interpretation allowed by the loose characterization of building societies (and cooperative banks in general) policies towards investors (or deposit-takers) on the one hand, and borrowers on the other, has enabled different societies, over time, to embrace very different practices. This problem is discussed at length by Platt, who, quoting a motion written by a member of the London Temperance Society for the general meeting, noted that building societies 'become often mainly agencies for the investment of capital, rather than for enabling the industrious to provide dwelling for themselves'.[20] Platt took as an exemplary case the Leeds Building Society, where the same rate of interest (5 per cent) was applied to investors and borrowers, each contributing equally to the operational expenses of the society.

A fourth historical characteristic of building societies business models has been the high level of trust they enjoyed among the population: 'the society believed to be doing the safest business ... will eventually receive the largest amount of support'.[21] As Holmes pointed out about the Leeds Permanent Building Society, 'the people believe it so safe that abundance of money can be had at 4, and even at 3.5 per cent'.[22] At the same time, in the 1850s the same society introduced rules that allowed borrowers to interrupt payment of the principal in case they found themselves unable to pay – certainly a rule that would not be acceptable in a 'normal' bank. These two seemingly contradictory sides of the coin (low interest rate paid to depositors, flexible attitudes towards borrowers) can be explained by looking at sociological and psychological elements common to all cooperative financial institutions. At the same time, as Platt rightly pointed out, 'when the rate of interest is so much lower, the periodical repayments are necessarily much smaller, and the member's ability to keep up his payments is thereby proportionately increased'.[23]

Trust was also nurtured, according to certain accounts, by the emphasis on transparency of operations. For instance, Chambers pointed out, in 1863, how

'any member can at any reasonable time call at the office with a friend to compare the entries in his pass-book with the entries to his account in the ledger: A
finance committee checks the accounts monthly; and the books are periodically
audited along with vouchers by regular accountants'.[24] Transparency was actually an often discussed issue in the world of building societies, from the origins
right through the twentieth century. As Platt pointed out, 'one of the injustices
felt to exist was that an investing member never knew what his exact pecuniary
position was', while borrowers were frequently unaware of the rate of interest at
which the loan was to be granted.[25]

However, concerns with transparency could easily be overcome through the
guarantees produced by building societies' peculiar governance. The latter was
very similar to the governance of other mutual organizations throughout Europe,
and boiled down to the 'one member one vote' rule and the rapid turnover of
managers: directors ('officers') were elected for one-year mandates in a general
meeting where each member could have 'no more than one vote' ('Instructions',
mentioned above). It is ironic to consider that while in the nineteenth century a
rapid turnover of top management was seen as instrumental in abetting managerial discretion, in the early twenty-first century, low turnover of top management
is seen as a basis for cooperative banks' stability.[26]

Together with complex rules for winding up societies or transferring their
assets, the 'straightjacket' and the peculiar governance of building societies had the
effect 'to minimize internal divergencies of interest and to lock away the surplus or
residual from the organization's activities in such a way as to preclude predatory
strategies for gaining access to it by a particular generation of members'.[27]

These are the core characteristics of the building societies; they were put in
place in the nineteenth century and to a large extent have survived up to the
present day. It is important to consider, however, that they were not only bottom-up principles imposed by building societies members: those were principles
approved by, legitimized and somehow nurtured by lawmakers throughout the
nineteenth and twentieth centuries.

The Role of State Policies and Regulation

Building societies, very early in their history, elicited the interest of lawmakers
and regulators, to the point where the history of their rapid growth and development in the nineteenth and twentieth centuries would be misleading without a
careful analysis of political and regulatory developments. It is especially interesting to analyse the role of state policies in supporting cooperative banks in
Great Britain, often considered, in the comparative political economy literature,
to epitomize the 'liberal market economy' category.[28] This category is clearly not
that relevant in the present case. As Bellman put it in 1933, 'building societies,
being subject to a measure of government control, share with the limited range

of more or less kindred organizations the experience of having from early days induced reluctant governments to depart from the policy of laissez-faire'.[29]

The advent of permanent building societies coincided with the first legislative acts regulating the industry. First acknowledged by lawmakers under the 1834 Friendly Societies Act, building societies were the subject of a 'special statute' in 1836 – 6 & 7 William IV. Cap. 32. The 'Act for the Regulation of Benefit Building Societies' was passed in 1837. The 1836 Act delineated the main characteristics of building societies and the kinds of mortgages they could solicit. It formed a useful basis for the development of permanent building societies, the first of which was founded in 1845.

The Building Society Act of 1874 represented a major development in the relation between the state and building societies. First, the Act neatly defined the purpose of building societies: societies should be formed 'for making advances to members out of the funds of the society upon security of freehold, copyhold or leasehold estate, by way of mortgage'. Second, the Act went a step further than previous legislations in acknowledging the banking functions of building societies, in particular through the protection of depositors with a ceiling put on the volume of deposits a building society may receive (the ceiling was then set at two-thirds of outstanding mortgage assets). Third, the 1874 Act enhanced supervision of building societies by requiring their balance sheet and income statements to be sent each year to the Registrar's office.

A subsequent legislation, the Building Society Act of 1894, reinforced the supervision and control of building societies instituted in the 1874 Act by (i) giving the Registrar power to prescribe a form of annual statement, thus assuring uniformity in the information sent by societies; and (ii) imposing a 'very stringent audit of the societies' accounts',[30] with the auditors certifying the mortgage deeds for each single mortgaged property. This stringent regulation was clearly aimed at 'silver-lining' the original business model of building societies. As the Chief Registrar of Friendly Societies said in the early twentieth century about these successive pieces of legislation, 'the Building Societies Acts themselves provide such stringent restraints on the method of operation of the societies that good conduct is almost inevitable ... One great advantage of these restraints has been that building societies have hardly ever been used in our generation as instruments for exploiting the public'.[31]

The Borders brothers clearly disagreed with this statement when they initiated their protest against poor building quality and general misconduct by building societies in Coney Hall in 1937, first through nationally famous 'mortgage strikes' and then a failed legal dispute. Misbehaviour by building societies was the outcome of the inter-war housing crisis in the UK, and led to an amendment to the 1894 Act passed in 1939. A 1960 Act subsequently amended the original 1874 Act without changing its fundamental tenets.

Balancing this hands-on regulation and tight supervision by the government, building societies could benefit from a very favourable tax treatment applied to small deposits, enabling them to offer lower rates than joint-stock banks. Again, the 'straightjacket', combined with favourable taxation, was also a characteristic of cooperative and savings banks regulation in continental Europe from the late nineteenth to the late twentieth century – until the far-reaching changes operated in the 1980s.

The 1980s: A Radical Transformation

The Evolving Role of Building Societies within the British Banking Industry during the 1980s

During the 1980s, British building societies were faced with large-scale changes in their legal and regulatory environment, which fully took effect a decade later. These changes profoundly modified (i) the competitive and organizational environment in which they operated (and, as a consequence, the peculiar mix of external constraints and incentives associated with that environment); (ii) their corporate governance (and the mix of internal constraints and incentives associated with that governance); and (iii) their relationship with the state. Indeed, Marshall et al. argued that building societies were the single component of the financial services industry most affected by such regulatory changes.[32]

At the outset of the decade, building societies occupied a commanding position (near monopoly) on the mortgage credit market; they had a very extensive membership base and steady earnings; they suffered little competition. This solid position had been built in the post-war decades, and reflects a long and deep history of mono-product specialization. The Building Society Act of 1962, amending the 1874 and 1894 Acts, did little to change this, ensuring that most (75 per cent at least) of societies' funds went to finance property. In addition, competition between societies was restricted by a cartel arrangement, with 'recommended' interest rates (by the Building Societies Association, the trade association) being followed by all but a few societies. Building societies were seen by some as too sleepy, dominated by an 'accounting and legal mentality'.[33]

But changes in information and communication technology, along with growing competitive pressures from banks desirous to increase their market shares in the mortgage lending market, led to public discussions about the role of building societies – very similar to what happened at the same time with savings banks in France and Italy. As Gough put it, the main question was: where did building societies belong? The same author answered that societies would eventually have to choose whether they were cooperative or commercial banks.[34]

Another stream of discussion about building societies focused on the industry structure and the 'right size' of building societies. On the one hand, some authors (along with voices from the banking industry) argued that building societies on average were too small, that there were economies of scale and scope to be reaped. On the other hand, excessive market concentration and the existence of cartels became again a major source of concern to supply-side economists and policymakers, who promoted a liberalization agenda. It is undeniable that building societies were operating in a quite protected and concentrated market. But this was not new in the 1980s. The concentration of the industry has been a long-lasting feature of building societies since the beginning of the twentieth century: as far back as 1930, Bellman observed that over 75 per cent of societies had mortgage assets of less than £100,000, while 1 per cent of societies had mortgage assets exceeding £5,000,000.[35]

So were building societies too big? Too small? Too protected? Should the regulation of the industry change? The answers to these questions were not straightforward. Informed observers such as Llewellyn posited that there were joint-production economies in the building societies sector.[36] In a careful multi-product cost analysis, Hardwick found that there were diseconomies of scope in the industry – but there were economies of scale for all but the larger societies.[37] In other words, building societies were mostly too small, but did not gain from entering new markets.

But these discussions took off following specific policy measures adopted by the Conservative government in the 1980s – measures aimed at de-segmenting banking markets and liberalizing banking in general. In particular, exchange controls were lifted in 1979; in 1980 the Thatcher government eliminated the 'corset' (a Supplementary Special Deposit Scheme introduced to curb bank lending); in 1981 the reserve asset requirement (requiring banks to hold at least 12.5 per cent of their deposits in a specified range of liquid assets) was abolished. These changes enabled banks to start entering the mortgage market, creating a new and yet unknown competitive pressure for many building societies.

This new competitive pressure both prompted managerial reactions within the building society movement and reinforced the positions of a minority of building society managers who were asking for regulatory restrictions on assets and liabilities to be lifted to be able to compete with banks who had access to capital markets for their funding and were present in many segments of the credit markets. These reactions led to a 'contested struggle, in the process of which the movement fragmented'.[38] But the outcome of this fragmentation was to become evident only in the late 1990s. For now (the early 1980s), the building society cartel collapsed (1983), following the decision by the larger societies to set their own interest rates; and that same year, building societies obtained access to wholesale money markets for funding.

The 1986 Building Societies Act and its Consequences

Of course, the game changer in the 1980s was the regulatory reform that took place under the Building Society Act of 1986. The Act reversed the regulatory approach that had been followed continuously since the nineteenth century: first, building societies were allowed to diversify their offer of banking products and services: they were able to conduct foreign exchange transactions and offer insurance services and real estate advisory services. Second, building societies were allowed to operate in wholesale money markets up to a limit of 20 per cent of their total funds (later increased to 40 per cent). A subsequent review of the Act in 1987 (the 'Schedule Review') enabled building societies to buy life assurance companies, own up to 15 per cent of a general insurance company, and offer full fund management services and a wider range of banking services. Finally, the 1986 Act also allowed the conversion of building societies into public limited companies (plc) – and full-fledged banks.

Abbey National was the first building society to convert to bank status and become a plc in June 1989. The next societies to demutualize did so after a few years. But in the meantime, the 'contested struggle' continued, with top management at large building societies asking for regulatory changes, and in particular the end of 'fine-tuning regulation' that put them, as they argued, at a disadvantage when competing with banks – indeed, banking regulation gave banks freedom to define and choose the activities they wished to engage in, provided that they abide by the laws of the land; by contrast, building societies' operations were constrained by specific regulations. As further evidence to this imbalance, the announced takeover of the Cheltenham and Gloucester Building Society (the sixth biggest society by total assets) by Lloyds Bank in April 1994 triggered a series of protecting moves by top management, such as the merger between the Halifax and Leeds Permanent building societies (respectively first and fifth biggest societies) and their conversion to a bank in November 1994; the takeover of National and Provincial Building Society (the ninth biggest) by Abbey National announced in July 1995; the announcement of conversion to plc status by Woolwich (the third biggest society), Alliance and Leicester (the fourth biggest society) and Northern Rock (the tenth biggest society) in 1996. That same year Bristol and West (the twelfth biggest society) was taken over by the Bank of Ireland.

Finally, in March 1996 the Major government announced draft legislation (rushed into a law before the May 1997 elections) that enlarged the scope of building societies' reliance on wholesale markets to 50 per cent, and allowed societies to have up to 25 per cent of their lending outside the mortgage lending market. In 1997 the conversions announced in 1996 took effect; the fragmentation of the sector was complete. Table 8.1 summarizes the key steps in the absorption of large building societies into the banking sector.

Alternative Banking and Financial Crisis

Table 8.1: Conversion and subsequent changes to building societies' status in the 1990s.

Building society	Year of conversion	Subsequent moves	Recent changes
Abbey	1989	Taken over by Banco Santander in 1994	Rebranded to Santander in 2010
Cheltenham and Gloucester	1995	Taken over by Lloyds Bank in 1995	Exists as trading name of Lloyds Banking Group
Halifax	1997	Merger with Leeds; merged with Bank of Scotland to form HBOS in 2001	HBOS taken over by Lloyds Banking Group in January 2009
Leeds Permanent	1997	Merger with Halifax (see above)	Ceased to exist as a trading name
National and Provincial	1997	Taken over by Abbey National, part of Santander Group, in 1997	Ceased to exist as a trading name
Woolwich	1997	Taken over by Barclays Bank in 2000	Exists as trading name of Barclays
Alliance and Leicester	1997	Acquired by Santander Group in 2008	Rebranded as Santander in 2010
Northern Rock	1997	Nationalized in 2008	Split and sold to Virgin Money in 2011
Bristol and West	1997	Acquired by Bank of Ireland in 1997	Assets successively transferred to Britannia
Bradford and Bingley	2000	Part-nationalized in 2008; sold to Abbey (Santander Group)	Rebranded to Santander in 2010

However, the logical link between regulatory reforms and demutualization is not automatic. As Cook et al. put it, 'was the demise of the mutual savings and loan sector the inadvertent result of regulatory failure, or were more fundamental economic forces at work in the unraveling of the mutual form?'[39] This question is important since it has a bearing on our consideration of building societies as a sustainable alternative to joint-stock banks.[40]

Through a careful examination of the impact of the 1986 Act on constraints and incentives facing building societies stakeholders, Cook et al. concluded that, indeed, regulatory changes did undermine the bases of building societies' governance. They did so not through the (modest) expansion of building societies' scope (whose 'principal purpose' was still to fund advances for mortgages), but through a series of dispositions that altered 'the nature of property rights and so shifted the basis on which internal corporate governance was conducted'.[41] In particular, sections of the Act, as interpreted by the courts, made it possible for short-term owners of building societies to gain from the change in status (through the transfer of assets to a commercial company made possible by Section 97); and the alignment of interests between investors and borrowers was undermined, thus enhancing incentives for conversion.

The Broader Impact: Decreasing Diversity in the British Banking Sector

Although most observers have emphasized the significance of the 1986 Building Societies Act for building societies themselves[42] and for the banking system as a whole, at least one lone voice has expressed a sceptical view about such significance. In a 2005 article, Tayler indeed sustained that the radical transformation associated with the 1980s regulatory reforms was, mostly, a myth. On the contrary, he argued, drawing on aggregate balance sheet data for the sector, the core business of building societies was, by the early 2000s, left untouched by the changes, and several top managers at building societies, whom he interviewed, emphasized the stability of their business models.[43] On the one hand, Tayler's argument could fit our hypothesis of path persistence very well; on the other, however, Tayler fundamentally underestimates the degree of change and misunderstands its nature simply by choosing to focus his empirical research on an extremely narrow sample of mostly surviving building societies (with one out of five interviewees overall working at a demutualized building society). Yes, a few surviving building societies might still do what they did before; but the number and relative importance of surviving building societies has dramatically declined following the regulatory changes of the 1980s – and the demutualization of all large building societies during the 1990s.

Michie is among the few authors to have systematically studied this phenomenon. As he pointed out, the United Kingdom shows a dramatic lack of diversity in its financial sector – a phenomenon that has worsened, he argued, since the 1980s.[44] In particular, the British banking industry has a lower presence of mutual banks than any other European country; it has the highest proportion of shareholder-oriented banks; and it has less geographical dispersion than many other countries as well. As mentioned in a previous section, Michie and Oughton present a list of indicators to measure diversity in the financial services industry.[45] Their findings show a decrease in diversity for most indicators, measured on data from the past ten years. In particular, while funding models seem to have grown slightly more diverse, a combination of the loan:deposit ratio with a funding indicator shows that this is not the case.[46]

These solid findings do not completely contradict Tayler's early argument. Rather, they shed light on the two-pronged phenomenon that is at the heart of this chapter: on the one hand, the tightening selection environment that has characterized the British banking industry over the past thirty years, fundamentally averse to mutual building societies; on the other hand, the persistence of an alternative path represented by surviving building societies during the same period. The next section turns to the analysis of some secondary data on the issue.

The Persistent Mutual Path

Surviving Building Societies' Performance after the 1980s Regulatory Changes

There are not many studies looking at the performance of building societies post-1986.[47] A 1999 article by Valnek is one.[48] In that article, Valnek, contradicting older findings by Barnes,[49] found that over a ten-year period starting before the 1986 Building Societies Act and ending in 1993, mutual building societies outperformed joint-stock banks on the basis of several measures of performance. In particular, building societies, over the period, reported higher risk-adjusted returns on assets, higher operating income and higher net income than banks. The data, however, is now twenty years old, so does not tell us anything about more recent performance.

One available indicator for the most recent period is, instead, the market shares of banks and building societies on markets where they compete. Here, again, the performance of surviving building societies has been quite remarkable in the years following the 1986–97 changes in their environment. Table 8.2 shows a slight decline in mortgage loans balances outstanding in the years leading up to the 2007–8 crisis. However, in the wake of the crisis building societies have stabilized their market share at around 16 per cent of mortgages outstanding. Furthermore, Table 8.3 shows that in terms of gross lending, building societies have actually reached a peak of 21 per cent market share in 2012, a much higher number than in the previous decade.

Table 8.2: Building societies' market shares of the individual mortgage lending market.

At end of period:	£ million	% share	£ million	% share	£ million	% share	£ million	% share	£ million
	Building societies		Banks		Other specialist lenders		Others		Total
Dec 2002	123,638	18.3	467,601	18.3	81,834	18.3	2,099	18.3	675,172
Dec 2003	142,312	18.4	511,049	66.0	118,737	15.3	2,494	0.3	774,591
Dec 2004	160,116	18.2	543,063	61.9	171,805	19.6	2,502	0.3	877,486
Dec 2005	173,205	17.9	575,797	59.5	215,662	22.3	2,356	0.2	967,020
Dec 2006	189,686	17.6	605,793	56.2	280,825	26.0	2,454	0.2	1,078,758
Dec 2007	202,665	17.1	627,026	52.8	354,553	29.9	2,973	0.3	1,187,217
Dec 2008	208,345	17.0	586,771	47.8	426,221	34.8	4,942	0.4	1,226,279
Dec 2009	189,712	15.4	732,329	59.3	307,088	24.9	6,447	0.5	1,235,575
	Mutuals		Other banks		Other specialist lenders		Others		Total
Dec 2010	198,754	16.0	847,081	68.3	186,349	15.0	7,518	0.6	1,239,702
Dec 2011	196,988	15.8	860,262	69.0	181,079	14.5	7,917	0.6	1,246,246
Dec 2012	203,759	16.1	873,497	69.0	179,014	14.1	9,464	0.7	1,265,734
Apr 2013	206,345	16.3	870,063	68.8	177,664	14.1	10,108	0.8	1,264,180

Source: Building Societies Association.

Table 8.3: Building societies' market shares of the individual mortgage lending market (gross lending).

Period	£ million	% share	£ million	% share	£ million	% share	£ million	% share	£ million
	Building societies		Banks		Other specialist lenders		Others		Total
2002	34,992	18.3	162,422	18.3	22,078	18.3	1,242	18.3	220,737
2003	46,300	16.7	194,959	70.3	35,395	12.8	684	0.2	277,342
2004	46,862	16.1	202,755	69.6	41,433	14.2	195	0.1	291,249
2005	43,515	15.1	201,833	70.0	42,585	14.8	345	0.1	288,280
2006	52,591	15.2	234,391	67.9	57,861	16.8	513	0.1	345,355
2007	51,692	14.2	247,149	68.1	63,172	17.4	747	0.2	362,758
2008	37,483	14.8	192,941	76.0	21,411	8.4	2,187	0.9	254,022
2009	18,574	12.9	118,458	82.5	5,031	3.5	1,596	1.1	143,660
	Mutuals		Other banks		Other specialist lenders		Others		Total
2010	20,415	15.1	106,734	78.9	7,433	5	759	0.6	135,342
2011	23,603	16.7	105,882	74.9	10,670	7.6	1,134	0.8	141,290
2012	30,701	21.5	99,395	69.5	11,158	7.8	1,728	1.2	142,981
2013 YTD	10,958	23.8	30,637	66.5	3,686	8	764	1.7	46,046

Source: Building Societies Association.

However, while stable or increasing market shares might signal the persistence of a certain path, the very existence of a distinct path still needs to be proved. In other words, it is not sufficient for building societies to have survived as a distinct organizational form; for an organizational path to persist, the business model crystallized in that path still needs to be distinctive.

Building Societies Business Model: Untouched by the Crisis?

As Figure 8.2 shows, building societies' business model has been remarkably stable over the past two decades – with loans to the private sector, and in particular mortgage lending to households, constituting on average 77 per cent of total assets from September 1992 until December 2003, and 80 per cent on average from January 2004 until June 2008. It is only in the second half of 2008 that loans as a percentage of total assets started decreasing, not because of deleveraging on the part of building societies (as a matter of fact, the amount outstanding of loans continued to grow until December 2008), but simply because building societies grew their total assets at a quicker pace. At above 72 per cent in March 2009, loans still constituted the largest slice of building societies' total assets – much more so than for banks.

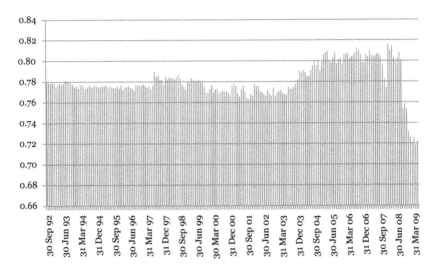

Figure 8.2: Loans to private sector as percentage of building societies' total assets.

Source: Data from the Bank of England.

As far as liabilities are concerned, here again one notes a remarkable stability in the relative weight of retail deposits and other liabilities. Throughout the 2000s, retail deposits have remained the main source of funding for most building societies, and wholesale liabilities (commercial paper, money market funding) have remained peripheral, as shown in Figure 8.3. On average, wholesale funding has represented 21 per cent of funding between April 1993 and August 1997; 21.4 per cent between September 1997 (after the exit of the largest building societies from the category) and December 2003; and 28 per cent from then until December 2007. The last four years before the crisis have seen an increase in the reliance on the wholesale credit markets for funding – but nothing of the sort experienced by 'wannabe banks' such as Northern Rock and Bradford and Bingley.[50] As Shin pointed out, Northern Rock mostly relied on wholesale money markets for its funding, and by the summer of 2007 retail deposits constituted only 23 per cent of its liabilities.[51] This unbalance paved the way for the bank's demise.

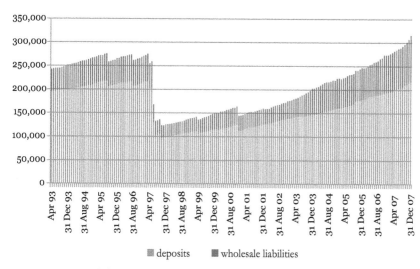

deposits ▪ wholesale liabilities

Figure 8.3: Breakdown of building societies' main sources of funding, 1993–2007.

Source: Data from the Bank of England.

Looking at both sides of the balance sheet helps us better understand (i) the specificity of building societies' business model (and its resilience over time) and (ii) the tragic fate of many demutualized building societies during the crisis. Indeed, the primary goal of those large building societies that chose to demutualize seems to have been expansion: increasing the size of operations, entering new markets, competing with large banks – the British banking system is peculiar in that it has exhibited a high level of bank concentration for a very long time, in contrast to both Germany and the United States. This seems to have been the main factor behind top management's support for demutualization. Support also came from members, who expected generous windfall from conversion: when Alliance and Leicester chose to float on the London Stock Exchange, along with Woolwich and Halifax, each member received a £5,000 windfall. Support also came from what Klemecki and Willmott called 'campaigners' – banks and financial institutions eager to take control of new assets; 'carpet-baggers' – speculators who invested in a society to be able to vote for conversion and then gain from windfall payments; and all kinds of interested intermediaries, such as lawyers, consulting firms and investment banks, bound to earn significant fees in the conversion process.[52]

Once demutualization was achieved, several growth options were considered and eventually adopted by top management at those 'wannabe banks'.[53] Some chose 'passive external growth' – they were bought by larger banking groups. Such was the case of Abbey National (Santander Group), Woolwich (Barclays) and Halifax (Bank of Scotland). Other preferred internal growth: this was the case of Alliance and Leicester, Northern Rock and Bradford and Bingley. The latter three did grow rapidly: Northern Rock, for instance, went from £17.4 billion of total assets in 1998 to £113.5 billion nine years later, a 552 per cent growth.[54]

A final consideration on the specific path created by building societies has to do with their risk profile, put to test during the aftermath of the 2007–8 crisis.

Building Societies: Counter-Cyclical?

As seen by Allen and Gale,[55] and emphasized in several theoretical works since then (including Chapter 3 in this volume), cooperative banks can fulfil an important role with regard to the inter-temporal smoothing of risk. This ability is directly linked to the specific characteristics of non-profit banks listed above, and in particular the high level of trust they entail – and therefore the higher stability of their deposit base, which allows them to provide credit in a counter-cyclical way. In other words, according to the theoretical arguments exposed above, building societies should exhibit counter-cyclical tendencies both on the asset and the liability side of the balance sheet.

This is exactly what happened during the 2007–8 crisis. While other banks suffered large, and in some cases massive, deposit withdrawals – Northern Rock is the obvious extreme case, although Shin is right to point out that the queues formed outside of Northern Rock were actually the consequence, and not the cause, of the bank's collapse[56] – building societies saw a rapid rise in deposits in 2007–8, only to find this trend reversed a year later, when the British banking sector exited the eye of the storm and, therefore, regained trust with customers (Figure 8.4). Building societies benefited from a flight to safety among British depositors.

On the asset side, did building societies play a counter-cyclical role? At first sight, they did not. Figure 8.5 shows, indeed, a slight decline in the amounts of loans outstanding between December 2007 and January 2008 (from £267 billion to £247 billion). However, this decrease is entirely due to a small statistical mismatch: as the Bank of England points out in a footnote to its statistical report on building societies, the statistical reporting on building societies was transferred from the Financial Services Authority to the Bank of England in January 2008, causing £19 billion to be shifted from loans to investment. What this means is that statistical changes notwithstanding, lending by building societies has continued unabated during the acute phase of the banking crisis, up until the second quarter of 2009.

One may of course discuss the extent of this counter-cyclical behaviour: building societies did decrease their lending in 2009, at a time when British GDP was declining. However, they maintained lending levels in the second half of 2007 and the whole of 2008, at a time when many banks were deleveraging and shrinking their balance sheets. So this continuity is, indeed, counter-cyclical.

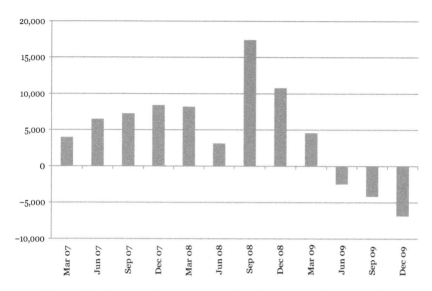

Figure 8.4: Changes in deposits at British building societies (in £ million).

Source: Data from the Bank of England.

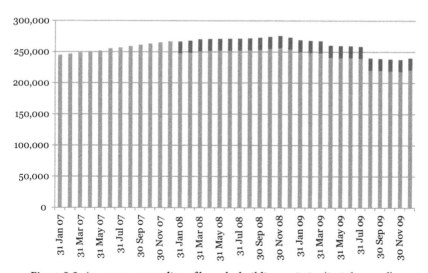

Figure 8.5: Amounts outstanding of loans by building societies (in £ thousand).

Source: Data from the Bank of England. Between January 2007 and January 2008 the Bank of England made small changes in accounting for outstanding amounts of loans by building societies. Thus from January 2008 onwards the black shaded areas of the bars represent what the amounts outstanding would have been, using the accounting methods in place until December 2007.

Furthermore, this continuity has been a long-term feature of building societies' operations. Using both data provided by the British Bankers' Association[57] and Bank of England data on building societies, Figure 8.6 shows how, during the late 1990s and throughout the 2000s, building societies were able to maintain a steadier growth rate in their lending to households than their commercial counterparts.

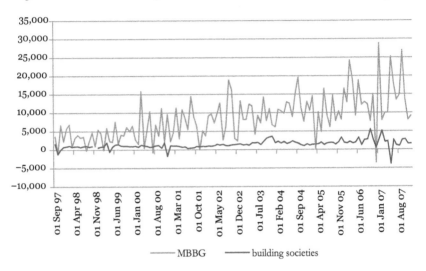

Figure 8.6: Monthly changes in total lending to private clients, by bank category (in £ million).

Source: Data from the Bank of England.

Beyond the amounts of lending building societies offer every year, another interesting indicator of a changed business model is the rate charged to customers. In an econometric study of the pricing behaviour of demutualized building societies in the late 1990s–early 2000s, Heffernan found that indeed, the former mutuals were consistently charging mortgage borrowers higher interest, paying lower interest to depositors and reacting more swiftly to changes in the market interest rate.[58] The latter is another aspect of the pro-cyclical behaviour of banks – and, by contrast, the counter-cyclical of mutuals, explored above.

This counter-cyclical behaviour also sheds light on an important part of the specificity of building societies: their lower riskiness with respect with banks. Doing safe business was both a constraint and a bonanza for building societies ever since their foundation in the nineteenth century. Then, one question raised by several observers was: how is it possible that financial institutions with a low interest margin can still be sounder than banks charging higher lending rates? The answer is simple, and it was formulated 135 years ago: *'the rate of interest determines largely the nature of the business the Society must undertake in order to do a safe business'.*[59] This is a very interesting statement in so far as it also encapsulates the risks borne by the opposite behaviour, which was experienced in the years preceding the financial crisis, when banks driven by the quest of high yields undertook investment in riskier securities. The soundness of building societies enabled them to maintain high reserve ratios throughout the twentieth century.[60]

Conclusion

The secondary evidence reviewed here is obviously not sufficient to respond to the somewhat ambitious research question raised at the outset of this chapter. Rather, the aim of the previous section was to show whether building societies did or did not, in front of adverse conditions, maintain a business model that was distinct from that of banks, and whether they did so successfully. This seems to be the case; in other words, building societies do seem to represent an alternative path for the British banking system.

This is, however, just a first, tentative step to address the issues raised in the first section of this chapter, i.e. understanding persistent organizational diversity within contemporary capitalism. To answer this broader question properly, one should buffer the conceptual framework proposed here; empirically question the diversity of building societies; and investigate the complex relationships between building societies as organizations, the building sector as structured, in part, by the Building Societies Association, and the whole banking industry, seen as both a population and a field.

9 THE UNITED STATES: ALTERNATIVE BANKING FROM MAINSTREAM TO THE MARGINS

Kurt von Mettenheim

Introduction

Banks in the market-centred financial system of the US remain, paradoxically, exception and paradigm. Like past cycles of financial speculation and crisis, bank changes in the US since the 1980s have marginalized alternative banks and traditional banking (that of accepting deposits and making loans). Instead, liberalization and deregulation have increased disintermediation. Private banks in the US tend to place household savings and pensions directly in a variety of products and services based on securities and derivatives. In historical perspective, the exceptional structure of US banking is 'largely due to a different political history'.[1] Alexander Hamilton looked to the Bank of England as a model. However, opposition from federalists and democrats led to 'bank war' and the veto of the Second Bank of the United States charter by President Jackson in 1832. Thereafter, 'aversion to powerful institutions of any kind',[2] especially big banks, is widely cited as causing financial instability through the early twentieth century.[3] Political events also reinforced capital market-based banking. Histories of US banking place the Civil War and World War I at the centre of explanations for the emergence of money centre banks and capital market deepening in New York.[4]

US banking history turns on crises caused by commercial banks and financial market bubbles (1837, 1857, 1873, 1884, 1893, 1907, 1929).[5] The Federal Reserve System (1913) and Glass–Steagall Act (1933) introduced deposit insurance, separated commercial banking from investment banking, and banned cross-state banking.[6] This ended banking crises and created a more stable system of local and state banks until deregulation in the 1970s released, once again, boom-and-bust cycles driven by banks and market-based banking.[7] Deregulation sought to reduce the large number of local banks to encourage competition and free market forces.[8] The ensuing changes have been widely debated.[9] This chapter focuses on the place of alternative banks in the exceptional trajectory of bank change in the US.

Alternative banks played important roles and grew to large market shares in several periods of American history. Soon after independence, mutual banks and savings banks began to mobilize the savings of workers, farmers and merchants.[10] These institutions grew steadily alongside notoriously unstable state- and national-licensed commercial banks to control half of savings deposits and like shares of credit markets until the end of the nineteenth century.[11] From 1911 to 1967, the postal savings system provided easy access to savings accounts and payment services through the branch offices (7,300 in 1935) of the US Postal Service. Credit unions were founded in the early twentieth century and continue, in the twenty-first century, to provide over 98 million Americans trusted service on cheaper terms than private banks on loans, credit cards, payments, finance and insurance. US community banks are privately owned and profit-oriented, but advocate local relationship banking and retain traditional business strategies of deposit-taking and loan-making that belie the concentration of the industry in a small number of 'too big to fail' banks too exposed to capital market risks.[12] Although they remain small, community finance companies also emerged since the 1970s alongside Community Reinvestment Act (CRA) mandates for US banks to lend to neighbourhoods previously redlined and subject to credit rationing.

US federal government-sponsored enterprises (GSEs) also remain critical agents for home mortgages, student loans and agricultural credit and finance. Most GSEs retain subsidies and guarantees from the US federal government and policy directives for corporate missions. The Federal National Mortgage Association (Fannie Mae), Federal Home Loan Mortgage Corporation (Freddie Mac) and Federal Agricultural Mortgage Corporation (Farmer Mac) were privatized. Fannie Mae and Freddie Mac went very wrong and required government takeover in 2008. The Federal Home Loan Bank System and the Farm Credit System were not privatized. Capitalized by the US federal government and run as cooperatives, they averted large losses as incurred by Fannie Mae and Freddie Mac after privatization. This chapter reviews these alternative banks in US history and, especially, since liberalization and the 2007 crisis.

Alternative Banks in US History

Parallel to the boom-and-bust cycles of commercial banks and financial markets in US history, mutual savings banks and cooperative banks averted asset bubbles and crises by retaining traditional deposit-taking and loan-making business models and focusing down-market on immigrants, workers, farmers and small businesses.[13] Mutual savings banks grew during the nineteenth century to peak in the 1890s at half of all US savings deposits and credit. The first mutual savings banks created in the 1810s were inspired by English savings banks. By 1820 mutual savings banks had won 9,000 depositors and $1.1 million in deposits; by 1850 depositors reached 251,000 and deposits $43.4 million. In 1910 depositors exceeded 7.4 million and deposits reached over $3.35 billion; in 1940, 14.5 million Americans held over $10.5 billion in savings deposits at mutual savings banks.[14]

From 1911 to 1940 mutual savings banks retained larger market shares of clients and consumer deposits than state-licensed commercial banks and near the share of national-licensed commercial banks (see Table 9.1). In 1911 depositors (7.7 million) and the value of deposits ($3.4 million) at mutual savings banks exceeded the $2.3 billion held by state-licensed commercial banks and $1.4 billion held by national-licensed commercial banks (2.3 million depositors). By 1940 mutual savings banks almost doubled the number of depositors to 14.5 million and increased deposits to $10.5 million. Deposits at state-licensed banks remained below this level, albeit increasing to $7.2 billion and 15.1 million depositors in 1940. Depositors at national-licensed banks increased to 16.1 million and deposits to $7.9 billion. US postal savings reached 2.8 million depositors and $1.3 billion by 1940.

Mutual savings banks and state- and national-licensed commercial banks thereby retained roughly equal market shares through 1940. Other assets and liabilities at state- and federal-licensed commercial banks *expanded geometrically* after 1911 until the 1929 Crash and Great Depression. Commercial banks pursued new business such as discounting, issue and trade of corporate and government securities, and inter-bank loans and acceptances. Mutual savings banks did not. In 1911 mutual savings banks held $3.4 million consumer deposits of $4.6 million total liabilities, increasing to $10.5 million deposits of $11.9 billion liabilities in 1940. In 1911, of $8.4 million in liabilities at state commercial banks, only $2.3 million were consumer deposits. In 1940 commercial bank liabilities increased to $36.8 billion, while consumer deposits remained at $7.9 million.

The asset creation of commercial banks that peaked in the 1920s thereby overshadowed mutual savings banks (See Table 9.1). The number of clients and the value of deposits at mutual savings banks remained proportional to levels at state- and national-licensed banks. However, the balance sheets of state-licensed commercial banks grew almost tenfold in 1905–25 (3.3–29.6 billion dollars) and over threefold in 1935–45 (22.4–70.5 billion dollars). The balance sheets of national-licensed commercial banks increased from 1.9 billion to 81.8 billion dollars in the period 1875–1945.

Table 9.1: Number and balance sheets of savings banks, licensed commercial banks and private banks, 1875–1945 (in $ million).

| | Mutual savings banks | | Commercial banks | | | |
| | | | State-licensed | | National-licensed | |
Year	Number	Balance sheet	Number	Balance sheet	Number	Balance sheet
1875	674	896.2	586	395.2	2,076	1,918.2
1885	646	1,203.0	1,015	801.9	2,689	2,421.8
1895	1,017	2,053.7	4,105	1,945.6	3,715	3,470.5
1905	1,287	3,868.2	1,237	3,368.2	5,668	7,327.8
1915	630	4,319.4	17,791	11,551.4	7,605	11,975.6
1925	611	7,913.0	19,635	29,637.9	8,072	24,350.8
1935	571	11,172.5	9,808	22,442.6	5,431	26,056.4
1945	534	16,987.1	9,003	70,555.2	5,021	81,794.8

Source: US Census Bureau, *Historical Statistics of the United States, 1789–1945* (Washington, DC: US Bureau of the Census, 1949), pp. 266, 271.

In sum, mutual savings banks retained traditional banking, while US commercial banks turned to discounting, trading of securities and inter-bank lending from 1875 to 1945. Understanding how these differences related to financial instability and the 1929 Crash, mobilization for war and modern American cultures of consumerism and credit remain beyond the scope of this chapter.[15] However, the data clearly suggest that alternative banking coexisted with commercial banking in the US through the late nineteenth and early twentieth centuries.

Trends after 1945 suggest further disintermediation. The credit market share of banks (chartered depository institutions) in the US declined from 62.2 to 25.1 per cent in the period 1945–2010, albeit in a market that increased from 225.9 billion to 37.1 *trillion* dollars. Since the 1970s a variety of entities have increased market shares, such as government-sponsored enterprises and related mortgage pools, life insurance companies, money market funds and mutual funds, asset-backed securities issuers, finance companies and private pension funds. These entities transformed individual savers into investors and brought financial markets into direct competition with banks.

Table 9.2: US credit market assets by type of financial institution, 1945–2010.

Year	1945	1955	1965	1975	1985	1995	2005	2010
US chartered depository institutions	62.2	56.9	58.2	57.7	46.7	29.1	26.1	25.1
Government-sponsored enterprises	0.9	1.3	2.2	4.5	4.6	5.6	8.3	17.0
Life insurance companies	18.2	20.8	16.9	11.8	10.3	11.7	9.0	8.5
Mutual funds	0.1	0.2	0.5	0.4	2.1	5.7	5.7	8.2
Monetary authority	10.8	6.3	5.0	4.7	3.0	2.8	2.4	6.1
ABS issuers	0.0	0.0	0.0	0.0	0.6	4.5	10.7	5.9
Money market mutual funds	0.0	0.0	0.0	0.1	2.8	4.0	4.4	4.4
Finance companies	1.6	4.4	5.2	4.8	5.6	4.8	5.7	3.9
Agency and GSE-backed mrg pools	0.0	0.0	0.1	1.4	5.9	11.6	11.6	3.1
Private pension funds	1.7	2.9	3.6	3.6	5.2	4.5	2.3	3.0
Other	4.5	7.3	8.4	11.0	13.3	15.8	13.8	14.8
Total per cent	100.0	100.0	100.0	100.0	100.0	100.0	100.0	100.0
Total billion dollars	225.9	387.7	817.2	1,989.2	6,287.5	13,595.5	30,636.6	37,152.6

Source: US Federal Reserve, *Flow of Funds Accounts of the United States* (Washington, DC: Federal Reserve, 2012).

This has widely been seen as a shift towards free markets. However, government-sponsored enterprises increased from 0.9 to 17.0 per cent of credit markets in the period 1945–2010. And government agency-backed mortgage pools reached 11.6 per cent before declining to 3.1 per cent in 2010. We turn to these alternative banking institutions.

Government-Sponsored Enterprises

Since the liberalization and deregulation of banking, seven US government-sponsored enterprises have played critical parts in the US economy. Two remain cooperative banks (the Federal Home Loan Bank System and the Farm Credit System), three are investor-owned (Fannie Mae, Freddie Mac and Farmer Mac), while the Financing Corporation and the Resolution Funding Corporation are temporary institutions designed to remove federal financial operations from government budgets. Privatization of the Student Loan Marketing Association (Sallie Mae) was completed in 2004, but excesses led the Obama administration to recast policy after the financial crisis.

Privatized government-sponsored enterprises became central agents responsible for the US housing bubble – the creation of obscure mortgage-based derivatives that caused panic on Wall Street in 2007 and widespread abuse of student loan programmes.[16] US government-sponsored enterprises that remained cooperatives (the farm credit system and federal home loan banks) fared better. Federal home loan banks were created in 1932 to help home owners by channelling funds through savings and loan associations, credit cooperatives and thrift savings banks. In 2012 over 7,700 financial institutions provided home loans as members (holders of non-tradable shares) of federal home loan banks. This structure has reduced the price of home mortgages. However, reforms shifted business away from alternative banks. In 1989 the Financial Institutions Reform, Recovery and Enforcement Act freed commercial banks (and credit unions) to become members of federal home loan banks. And since the crisis, outstanding mortgages through federal home loan banks fell from over a trillion dollars in 2008 to $415 billion in 2011. Moreover, almost 75 per cent of mortgages through federal home loan banks are made by commercial banks, with nine banks accounting for over 30 per cent of loans.[17] Since the crisis, the US government increased regulation of federal home loan banks while retaining their cooperative structure. However, the original design of channelling funds through alternative banks has been transformed into a brokerage system for large financial institutions.

Alternative US Agricultural Banking

Government banking and credit cooperatives also remain central for US agriculture. Early rural cooperatives in America were soon overshadowed by large-scale programmes of land grants epitomized by the 1862 Homestead Act. In 1916 the Federal Farm Loan Act created twelve Federal Land Banks that encouraged hundreds of National Farm Loan Associations to be formed, a structure modelled on German *Landschaft* credit cooperatives. The Agricultural Credits Act of 1923 created Federal Intermediate Credit Banks in each Land Bank district for short-term credit through cooperative associations for farm machinery and modernization. After half of farm associations failed in The Great Depression by 1933, Congress passed legislation to reschedule debts and provide emergency credit through new cooperatives. The Farm Credit Administration consolidated programmes and supervised *all* credit cooperatives in the US until creation of the FDIC in 1942. By 1968 government capital was repaid, and independent cooperative governance resumed.

The Farm Credit Act of 1971 liberalized lending and helped expand production until the second oil shock, rising interest rates and falling demand for US agricultural exports led to the collapse of farm prices. By 1985 bankruptcies produced farm credit losses over $2.7 billion. The Agricultural Credit Act of 1987 allocated $4.0 billion ($2.8 billion in Treasury-insured bonds) through a Financial Assistance Corporation and Farm Credit System Insurance Corporation. In the 1990s Farmer Mac created secondary markets for rural mortgages by purchasing and pooling loans and issue of guaranteed mortgage-backed securities. Farm credit association lending thereby remained a third of farm credit in the US.

Table 9.3: Farmer Mac and the farm credit system, 2007–12 (in $ billion).

	2007	2008	2009	2010	2011	2012
Farmer Mac						
Assets	4.97	5.10	6.13	9.48	11.88	12.62
Liabilities	4.75	4.94	5.79	9.00	11.33	12.03
Net worth/equity	0.22	0.01	0.19	0.47	0.55	0.59
Farm credit system						
Loans		161.4	164.8	175.3	174.6	191.9
Bonds and notes		179.7	178.3	189.5	186.8	200.3
Non-performing loans, %		1.50	2.14	1.93	1.72	1.36
Capital/assets, %		12.65	13.90	14.46	15.60	15.65
Return on assets, %		1.41	1.32	1.59	1.71	1.73
Return on equity, %		10.70	9.86	10.85	11.17	10.89
Net interest margin, %		2.41	2.65	2.82	2.86	2.87

Source: Farm Credit Administration, *Annual Report on the Farm Credit System* (Washington, DC: Farm Credit Administration, 2012), pp. 14, 42.

Since 2007 the farm credit system and Farmer Mac have averted crisis and grown by participating in dynamic commodity markets. Farmer Mac increased assets from $4.97 billion to $12.62 billion in the period 2007–12, and reversed a decline in net worth during 2008. In the period 2008–12 the farm credit system increased loans from $161.4 billion to $191.9 billion and the value of bonds and notes held from $179.7 billion to $200.3 billion. Alternative banking thereby remains central for US agriculture.

Credit Unions

Immigrant workers from Quebec created the first US credit union in Manchester, New Hampshire – La Caisse Populaire. Massachusetts state regulation of credit unions (1909) became a model for the 1934 Federal Credit Union Act, while the philanthropist Edward Filene promoted campaigns to create credit unions throughout the country. Low start-up costs and simple charters from states or from the federal government accelerated growth. By 1969, 23,866 credit unions were chartered in the US. In 1970 the National Credit Union Administration (NCUA) was created to supervise and regulate US credit unions, most notably introducing federal government-guaranteed deposit insurance under the National Credit Union Share Insurance Fund. Pressures from liberalization and crises reduced the number of credit unions to 7,380 by 2011. These alternative banks nonetheless retained over 98 million members and balance sheets over $900 billion in 2011.[18] US credit unions represent another example of growth based on traditional deposit-taking and loan-making banking and adjustment to disintermediation and liberalization.

US credit unions are non-profit cooperatives owned by members and exempt from income tax. Governance remains based on the 'one member one vote' principle regardless of amounts deposited. Boards require voluntary and elected service by those in the 'field of membership' as defined in charters. Credit unions grew along functional lines according to employment or associations. However, many credit unions have expanded operations to local communities and beyond since the 1970s. Long-term profit sustainability orientations are reinforced by the absence of external shareholders and distribution of net income either as dividends proportionally to members (based on deposits) or increasing net worth and reserves. The inability to capitalize by selling shares constrains growth. However, US credit unions also developed a second tier of wholesale operations similar to European savings banks and cooperative banks. Most US credit unions remain small but participate in central credit unions for wholesale banking services. This retains local or associational relationship banking while maximizing scale and scope in wholesale banking and capital market operations.[19]

US credit unions grew by providing inexpensive credit to members, specializing in personal credit, automobile loans, single-family residential mortgages after 1977 reforms, and credit cards and student loans. Since the 1970s liberalization and deregulation allowed US credit unions to expand services, increase business beyond members and functionally defined 'fields of service', and enter into mergers and acquisitions. Federal regulators created a Central Liquidity Facility as lender of last resort, and a deposit insurance fund was capitalized with 1 per cent of deposits at federally insured credit unions. Business lending is limited to 12.5 per cent of total credits. However, loans under $50,000 and certification as Community Development Financial Institutions for low-income credits win exemption.

Tax-free status provides a powerful competitive advantage for US credit unions. Other restrictions impede growth while the economic downturn and mortgage crises since 2008 have hit credit unions.[20] However, the aggregate performance of US credit unions from 1980 to 2012 nonetheless compares favourably with US commercial banks. Indicators of performance such as net income, late loans, net charge-offs, asset growth and loan growth for US credit unions and US commercial banks are reported in Table 9.4. In every category and for each decade, the average performance of credit unions surpasses the average performance of commercial banks, with the exception of equal net incomes during the 1990s and a 0.21 per cent higher net income average for the 2008. This is another paradox of alternative banking in the US. Despite indications of superior performance and retaining over 98 million members, credit unions retain much smaller market shares than private banks and financial institutions, albeit increasing from 6.5 to 8.1 per cent of the total assets of US credit institutions in the period 2007–12.

Table 9.4: Comparison of credit union and commercial bank performance, 1980–2012.

	Net income		Late loans*		Net chg offs		Asset growth		Loan growth	
	CUs	Banks	CUs	Banks	CUs	Banks	CUs	Banks	CUs	Banks
1980s	0.94	0.62	1.9	2.9			1.30	0.65	1.23	0.80
1990s	1.00	1.00	1.1	1.8	0.51	0.70	0.75	0.57	0.74	0.54
2000–12	0.75	0.96	1.0	2.3	0.68	1.17	0.72	0.68	0.63	0.56
2008–12	0.50	0.51	1.5	4.2	0.96	1.86	0.60	0.37	0.25	0.13
1980–2012	0.91	0.88	1.3	2.3	0.61	0.91	0.89	0.64	0.83	0.63

*   60 days late for credit unions and 90 days late for banks because of different reporting standards.

Source: Credit Union National Association Research and Statistics, at www.cuna.org/research [accessed 1 October 2013].

Alongside traditional credit unions in the US, Community Development Financial Institutions were created under 1993 legislation from President Bill Clinton based on proposals by Hyman Minsky and a special commission.[21] The number of Community Development Financial Institutions reached 971 in 1997 and remained at 962 in 2011 (certified by dedicated funds at Treasury). Lending increased under the Community Development Financial Initiative and Small Business Jobs Act of 2010. Bond guarantees expanded funds, while certification qualifies for a variety of lending and subsidies programmes by the federal and state government.

New Initiatives in Alternative Banking

Since 2007 new initiatives of alternative banking have emerged in the US. The state government-owned Bank of North Dakota has attracted attention for its ability to help the state avert crisis and economic downturn. Since 2010 the Public Bank Initiative has sought to promote the Bank of North Dakota as a model for other states and local communities in the US, providing assistance to campaigns in over twenty states and dozens of local campaigns to present legislation to create public banks. The Occupy Money Cooperative was incorporated in 2013 to launch a prepaid debit card, the Occupy Card, to address perhaps the major problem of financial exclusion in the US – the high cost of prepaid debit cards offered by private payment firms. The Obama administration has proposed an Infrastructure Development Bank as an alternative to traditional bond financing of local, state and federal infrastructure projects. Finally, the National Association of Letter Carriers called for a viability study of how the US Postal Service may expand payment service and provide banking services to counter the losses imposed on the service by mandatory pre-funding of future employee pension funds.

Conclusion

Alternative banking in the US differs from other countries because of the degree of disintermediation in the financial system and dominance of market-based banking. In the nineteenth century, commercial banks pursued discounting, trading of bonds and securities and inter-bank lending over traditional consumer deposits and lending. Mutual savings banks therefore retained leading market shares of consumer deposits through World War II, but lost market share of bank assets to commercial banks. This trend continued after 1945, especially after liberalization and deregulation began in the 1970s. Alternative banks have been relegated from the mainstream to the margins. In 2013 credit unions retained just over 8 per cent of the total assets of US credit institutions, and community banks 4 per cent, while other alternative banks and financial institutions remain in very small niches. Government-sponsored enterprises run as cooperatives do indeed retain large market shares of agricultural credit and finance and important shares of rural mortgages. Since the crisis that led to the widespread failure of savings banks in the late 1980s (many having already been transformed into commercial banks), the US banking system has remained largely reliant on one pillar, that of private banking. Consequently, in comparison to advanced economies that retain strong sectors of savings banks and cooperative banks as well as government special purpose banks, the US has suffered deeper financial crisis, worse financial exclusion and capital drain that have caused rapidly increasing inequality. At the margins, alternative banks in the US have been unable to reverse broader trends of inequality and financial exclusion caused by over-reliance on private commercial and investment banks as direct intermediaries between citizens and capital markets.

10 BRIC STATECRAFT AND GOVERNMENT BANKS

Kurt von Mettenheim

Introduction

Until 2008 developing countries systematically fared worse during financial crises. After Mexico declared a moratorium on foreign debt in 1982, most of Latin America remained mired in a lost decade. During the 1990s the global south and east experienced financial crises in a seemingly endless sequence: Mexico, 1994–5; Asia, 1997; Russia, 1998; Brazil, 1999; Argentina and Turkey, 2001; Brazil, 2002–3. In 2007 panic in US financial markets quickly spread around the globe, only to find that BRIC countries were better prepared to counter shocks and resume growth. This chapter explores our findings about Brazilian federal government banks (that, since liberalization, they have modernized and realized competitive advantages to provide critical policy alternatives, most notably against crisis and for social inclusion) compared to Russia, India and China.[1] Further research will be required; other factors mattered and barriers to competition remain, especially in Russia and China. However, evidence from monetary authorities and comparison of bank balance sheets suggest that BRIC government banks did indeed realize competitive advantages over private and foreign banks during the 2000s, just in time to provide counter-cyclical credit in 2008. And contrary to biases in microfinance studies against the public sector, BRIC government banks have helped accelerate financial inclusion through new policies and technologies.

These findings differ from views held by critics of government banks,[2] theories of financial repression,[3] the realist tradition of financial statecraft,[4] market-based banking theory[5] and the Washington Consensus[6] that expected privatizations and liberalization to reveal the greater efficiency of private banks and produce transitions to market-centred finance. Evidence from BRIC countries raises new questions about alternative banking, the political economy of *domestic* financial statecraft and public policies for social inclusion. By financial statecraft, we mean the formulation of policies for money, credit, banking and finance that shape basic relationships in state, society and markets.[7] Financial statecraft in the BRICs requires balancing political legitimacy and market confidence to allocate savings, increase capital mobility and shape growth to ensure social inclusion.[8] Like most approaches in the social sciences, financial statecraft cuts to essentially contested theories and concepts about state banks, money, finance, politics, bureaucracy, public policies and government intervention.[9]

Government banks are especially contested. Financial repression approaches and bank-centred finance strategies (like liberal and coordinated political economy approaches) often see the same phenomena from profoundly different perspectives.[10] Liberal market economies are driven by private joint-stock banks in equity markets, thrive on public information, and spurn coordination. BRIC countries (and coordinated market economies) are driven by (often government) bank lending and finance, thrive on limited sharing of firm strategy with these institutions, and spurn markets because of volatility, failures and cycles of financial instability.[11] From private and foreign bank perspectives, neo-institutionalism is largely protectionism, including many of the institutional foundations of competitive advantage retained by government banks, such as cheap access to capital and the low cost of operations of special purpose banks. Although many reformers see private investors as allies and the capitalization of government banks on markets as capable of increasing growth, for most BRIC policymakers and public bank managers, outright privatization of government banks would throw babies (cherished institutions of policy and political networks) out with the bathwater. In broader terms, market approaches insist that policies should allow free agents to 'get prices right', while bank-centred approaches argue that enough credit should be directed to accelerate innovation and/or social inclusion to 'get planning right'.[12]

These differences about government banking in the BRICs frame this chapter. The question of social inclusion may provide more grounds for agreement. Here we bring the Brazilian experience to the fore. Given the huge decline in the number of *bankless* Brazilians (those without bank accounts) from 80 to 50 per cent in the period 2000–10, the relation between financial statecraft and democratization is, in reality, a more positive sum than supposed by most scholars of banking and political economy. In contexts of inequality and financial exclusion, *positive sum* relations may obtain between social inclusion, good banking and more effective monetary policy. This implies that conceptions of fiscal constraints to change and central bank independence are dated in the BRICs context. Instead of seeking to ensure central bank independence from politics and social forces, or free markets and private banks through privatizations and deregulation, we found different experiences in Brazil. The deepening of credit markets and the improvement of central banking in Brazil have involved the realization of competitive advantage by large government banks, pursuit of downmarket business, and new public policies based on concepts of citizenship and basic income to reach the bankless and reverse poverty.

This requires rethinking constraints to change. Since the end of the electoral road to socialism exemplified by the military coup in Chile against President Allende on 11 September 1973, social scientists and policy communities largely concur that markets severely constrain social inclusion. For Gold et al., structural theories of the state replaced earlier instrumental and functional traditions of Marxism by better describing how markets constrain social policy and veto political change.[13] Since then, social scientists have remained structuralist in the sense of being fixated on fiscal control, emphasizing that markets cleared by individual investors require fiscal austerity and constrain change. The logic is zero-sum. Social policies are seen to pressure fiscal accounts and lead to either tax increases or adjustment policies that reduce the profits of firms and tax revenues of governments. This, in the worst cases, caused political economic crisis and the breakdown of democracy in developing countries. Similar forces in advanced economies led to stagflation in the 1970s and electoral turns to neoconservative governments and neoliberal policies in the 1980s that sought to downsize welfare states.

Theories of fiscal constraints are dated and, especially for the BRICS, incomplete because they ignore advances in monetary economics in the 1990s and the modernization of banks and central banking during the 2000s. Government bank modernization, new regulatory frameworks and better supervision of banks and markets provide a new setting for what we call *financial roads to social economies*. A fixation on fiscal constraints ignores new theories and concepts about the credit channel and interest rate channel and the modernization of public banks and central banking. BRIC countries have accumulated significant foreign reserves and sustained trade surpluses during years of economic growth. Moreover, in Brazil, transparent policy frameworks such as inflation targeting and flexible foreign exchange have been in place for over a decade. The primary constraints to change in the BRICs are not fiscal. Government bank modernization, the accumulation of immense foreign reserves and the liberalization of economies provide new channels for change.

And rather than culprits, government banks have provided critical policy alternatives. Government banks, as banks, multiply money. It follows that these institutions multiply public policy. Deposits in government banks are liabilities that free the lending of equal amounts. This multiplies money by two. Capitalization of government banks, whether on the stock market or through endowments from Treasury, covers the financial operations or credit *over tenfold* the amount placed as equity in the bank, assuming 8 per cent capital reserve requirements under Basel II and ignoring risk weighting. For governments facing hard budget constraints for fiscal shortfalls, government banks provide a very attractive alternative to simply spending public funds. The ability of government banks to counter crisis and provide policy options is more a question of banking and finance than a fiscal question. In comparative perspective, the capacity of government banks to multiply money is a profound advantage for policymakers and governments who retain government banks over those who do not. And it deserves repetition for clarity – the modernization of BRIC government banks has often involved *social banking*: new technologies such as electronic card payment channels have brought income grants and access to banking and public services in vast numbers in these large countries. In Brazil especially, a 'back to the future' modernization of government banks since liberalization of banking and basic income policies (albeit conditional) based on concepts of citizenship are big, largely untold stories that counter biases favouring non-governmental organizations, private banks and market-centred microfinance firms or funds.

Government Banks and Domestic Financial Statecraft

Our approach to government banks in the BRICS is not new. It remits to a long tradition in political economy that focuses on how politics and public policies shape markets.[14] As noted in Chapter 1 of this volume, Polanyi argued that laissez-faire policies in the nineteenth century generated movements of social self-defence in the form of organized labour, movements to address the social question and central banking.[15] Other policies such as tariffs, imperialism, subsidies to agriculture and industry and top-down social programmes also prevailed over liberalism and free markets, especially after the 1873 Depression. Two world wars and depression after the 1929 Crash meant that politics continued to determine economic policy in the early twentieth century. After 1945, Shonfield describes how continental Europeans reshaped state-owned enterprises left over after fascism and war in response to imperatives of recovery rather than by ideology or design.[16] Necessity and improvisation in post-war government banking thus place domestic statecrafting closer to Lindblom's 'muddling through' conception of administration than Marxist-Leninist or nationalist theories that saw large state banks as means to ideological ends.[17]

Recent research has returned to core ideas of statecrafting. For Kirschner, because the impact of different financial policies is often equal or unpredictable, politics rather than independent economic judgements explain policy choices and the shape of markets.[18] Hoffman traces how political ideas periodically recast US banking during critical junctures of change since independence.[19] Laurence, Toya and Amyx describe how politics drove 'big bang' financial reforms in Britain and Japan in the 1980s.[20] Over the last decades, economic statecraft became synonymous with imposing liberal reforms.[21] We report different developments in the BRICs: the realization of competitive advantages by government banks since liberalization and the importance of these large institutions for policy responses to crisis and prospects for social inclusion.

Why the BRICs Averted Crisis

Government banks are not the only story from the BRICs. Observers agree that BRIC countries averted crisis to the extent that their economic fundamentals were in order.[22] BRICs also were able to counter credit crunches to the extent that their banks had modernized in the sense of converging towards BIS Basel Accord capital requirements. This differs from the excessive leverage and errors of deregulation in the US and other advanced economies. Banking prudence in the BRICs is also a legacy of the financial crises that hit emerging markets during the 1990s and 2000s, experiences that left banks and bank supervisors in BRIC countries more conservative and insistent on safer levels of capital reserves and other traditional requirements. Finally, BRIC countries fared better in the face of crisis and downturn abroad after 2008 because of their large scale. Their closed economies were less exposed to crisis and recession abroad than smaller export-dependent economies. This provided policymakers in the larger BRIC economies options and often tipped the scales in favour of domestic investment and consumption, options of special importance given historical levels of poverty and skewed growth experienced in the BRICs over the last decades.

These broader explanations for why BRICS were able to adjust to crisis complement our core claims: that BRIC government banks i) realized competitive advantages over private and foreign banks during the 2000s, and ii) provided policy alternatives to adjust to the global crisis and accelerate social inclusion. Review of evidence from the BRICs follows.

Brazil

Since transition from military rule in 1985, the end of over a decade of monetary chaos and record inflation in 1994, and liberalization of banking in 1995, Brazilian federal government banks have used institutional foundations at the centre of political, social and economic networks to realize competitive advantages over private and foreign banks while providing policy alternatives to political and social forces. State-owned banks were widely denounced for crony credit under military rule (1964–85) and served as prized money machines that enabled oligarchs and politicians allied with the military regime to resist change and delay democracy (1985–94). Most state government banks were therefore privatized during the 1990s. However, in June 2001, federal government banks were capitalized by Treasury and challenged to reform to meet international regulations embodied in the 1988 Basel capital accord. Since 2001 the big three federal government banks, and two regional special purpose banks, have outpaced private and foreign banks in terms of credit and finance, most especially during crises in 2002–3 and 2008–9 by providing counter-cyclical credit and acquiring small and medium banks.

Table 10.1 compares credit from government, private and foreign banks as per cent of Brazilian GDP from 2001 to 2012. The Banco do Brasil, Caixa Econômica Federal (Federal Savings Bank, Caixa), Banco Nacional de Desenvolvimento Economico e Social (National Bank of Economic and Social Development, BNDES), Banco da Amazonia (Bank of Amazonia, BASA) and Banco do Nordeste do Brasil (Bank of Northeast Brazil, BNB) alongside remaining state government banks in Brazil increased credit from 8.9 to 25.5 per cent of GDP, well over private and foreign bank increases of 10.0–19.3 per cent and 6.9–8.7 per cent, respectively.

Table 10.1: Brazil: credit as per cent GDP by type of bank, 2001–12.

	Government	Private	Foreign	Total
2001	8.9	10.0	6.9	25.8
2002	9.8	9.7	6.5	26.0
2003	9.8	9.5	5.3	24.6
2004	9.9	10.2	5.6	25.7
2005	10.4	11.5	6.3	28.2
2006	11.3	12.8	6.8	30.9
2007	12.0	15.4	7.8	35.2
2008	14.7	17.3	8.5	40.5
2009	18.1	17.5	8.0	43.6
2010	18.9	18.4	7.9	45.2
2011	21.3	19.2	8.5	49.0
2012	25.5	19.3	8.7	53.5

Source: Central Bank of Brazil, SISBACEN, at www.bcb.gov.br [accessed 1 October 2013].

This aggregate data may conceal crony credit, bad loans or rolling over debts that, in the end, must be passed on to others through the fiscal or money supply. Further data from the Central Bank of Brazil control for these possibilities and expand comparison of government, private and foreign banks. Non-performing loans in Brazilian government banks fell *below* levels in private and foreign banks during 2004 and have remained so through 2012 (see Table 10.2). After transferring non-paying loans to an asset management entity in June 2001 (largely mortgages from the Banco Nacional de Habitação (National Housing Bank, BNH) dating from military rule), non-performing loans remained at 6.14 per cent in government banks (above 4.29 per cent in private and 3.42 per cent in foreign banks) at year-end 2001. However, by 2004 non-performing loans at government banks fell to 2.85 per cent of loans and have remained below that level through 2012. In comparison, non-performing loans peaked at private and foreign banks at 5.34 per cent and 5.59 per cent in 2012. Ten per cent of this difference may be due to rolling over agricultural finance by the Banco do Brasil, but this is just a small part of broader credit trends. No evidence has been reported in the financial press of other major experiences of rolling over loans to reduce non-performing loan levels at Brazilian government banks since 2008.

Table 10.2: Non-performing loans at banks in Brazil, 2000–12.

	Government	Private	Foreign
2000	10.15	3.99	3.84
2001	6.14	4.29	3.42
2002	3.97	4.62	3.27
2003	5.30	3.99	3.53
2004	2.85	3.86	2.34
2005	3.77	3.88	3.11
2006	2.84	4.44	3.64
2007	2.45	3.73	3.13
2008	2.07	3.89	3.53
2009	2.74	5.33	5.57
2010	2.05	3.95	4.11
2011	1.83	5.10	4.92
2012	1.82	5.34	5.59

Note: Non-performing loans = per cent of total loans > 120 days overdue.

Source: Central Bank of Brazil, SISBACEN.

Comparative studies during the 2000s confirm that, in general, Brazilian banks provide more expensive credit, produce higher returns and profits and retain higher levels of late and bad loans than peer countries.[23] Banks operating in Brazil also tend to retain higher administrative and personnel costs, not unexpected because of its large population and territory combined with shallow credit markets (25.8 per cent of GDP in 2000). Brazilian banks also remain more cautious, setting aside greater reserves and provisions against losses (above and beyond requirements to keep 45 per cent of deposits at the Central Bank of Brazil). Banks in Brazil thus incur higher operating costs and maintain higher reserves, provisions and capital against losses and risk, but nonetheless produce higher returns than peer country banking systems.

Again, previous crises reinforced these characteristics. In response to crises in Mexico (1994–5), Asia (1997) and Russia (1998), central bank interest rates were increased to over 42.0 per cent to discourage capital flight under the fixed exchange rate regime. In 1999 crisis forced the government to float the real and adopt policies that have remained in place ever since (flexible foreign exchange, inflation targeting and fiscal control). From 1994 to 2003 Brazilian banks weathered adjustment to five crises and two political transitions, first to full elections in 1994, then from reformist President Fernando Henrique Cardoso (1994–2003) to President Luiz Inácio Lula da Silva of the Partido dos Trabalhadores (Workers' Party, PT). After economic recovery during 2004, PT administrations under presidents Lula (2003–10) and Dilma Rousseff (2011–) used government banks to recover from crisis, then accelerate growth and social inclusion and, once again in 2008, counter the effects of crisis and economic downturn abroad. Policies have not undermined economic fundamentals, reversed reforms or eroded the institutional foundations of competitive advantage of Brazilian federal government banks.

Table 10.3 provides an overview of the top twenty-five banks in Brazil in March 2013. Three of the five largest banks in the country remain federal government banks. Their branch office networks, greater client confidence and ties to government ministries and agencies and political and social forces in all sectors of finance, banking and the economy have proved institutional foundations for the realization of competitive advantage since liberalization of the industry in the 1990s. This runs counter to contemporary banking theory and the widespread favour of private banks and market-based banking in social science research, think tanks, foundations, industry associations, lobbies and the media. The advances of Brazilian banks towards regulations in Basel Accords I, II and III, tighter central bank supervision, adoption of more transparent financial reporting standards, and the modernization of government banks under pressure from private and foreign banks combined to enable these institutions to weather the crisis that hit in 2008. A brief review of the big three federal government banks follows.

Table 10.3: Top twenty-five banks in Brazil, March 2013 (in US$ million).

Bank	Assets	Deposits	Net Worth	Tier 1	Staff	Offices	Basel
Banco do Brasil	551,699.0	232,766.0	31,000.1	36,384.9	128,811	5,392	16.6
Itau-Unibanco	479,132.7	121,856.1	41,257.2	40,179.0	119,381	3,871	18.9
Bradesco	384,161.3	102,680.0	34,575.3	33,659.2	98,880	4,696	15.6
Caixa Econômica Federal*	363,036.9	160,543.8	12,628.8	14,409.8	119,696	2,972	14.2
BNDES*	336,763.9	10,211.4	23,239.1	24,011.8	2,815	1	15.1
Santander	228,088.5	61,092.4	31,712.5	31,430.3	52,962	2,591	21.5
HSBC	70,453.1	25,823.2	5,006.2	4,956.0	29,714	869	13.0
SAFRA	61,866.7	5,215.7	3,534.4	3,516.5	5,882	106	14.1
Votorantim*	60,541.9	6,203.5	3,809.1	3,771.6	1,529	39	13.6
BTG Pactual	51,453.8	7,587.7	5,239.4	5,234.1	1,255	7	18.3
Citibank	31,050.6	7,516.7	3,854.8	3,838.8	6,174	128	14.2
Banrisul**	23,808.6	13,685.5	2,373.6	2,363.7	11,568	473	20.0
JP Morgan Chase	23,309.8	2,823.6	1,727.8	1,727.8	683	6	19.5
Credit Suisse	19,397.3	1,238.4	1,741.8	1,739.8	34	2	18.1
BNB**	16,083.2	4,973.3	1,235.3	0	10,368	217	16.3
Top 15 banks	2,700,848.0	764,218.1					
Other credit institutions	338,027.0	106,489.3					
Total credit institutions	3,038,875.3	870,707.4					

Note: * = federal bank. ** = state government bank.

Source: Central Bank of Brazil, SISBACEN.

The Banco do Brasil

Created in 1808 (to honour GB£1.4 billion of Portuguese debt to British banks), the Banco do Brasil financed the defeat of liberal, republican and regional forces to consolidate the anomaly of a new world monarchy. Since then, three different institutions with the Banco do Brasil name have remained the monetary authority, financial monolith and prized resource for politicians and public policy. National-developmentalist groups at the Banco do Brasil delayed creation of a central bank under democracy (1945–64), but ceded prerogatives in 1965 as part of reforms after the military coup and the condition of accord with the International Monetary Fund (IMF). Under military rule from 1964 to 1985, the bank managed state-led development by channelling unprecedented world liquidity and domestic forced savings to enterprises favoured by military presidents and ministers. Even after a second oil crisis (1979), interest rate shock (1980) and moratorium on foreign debt by Mexico (1982), the Banco do Brasil continued to multiply money and drive cycles of record inflation punctuated by price and wage freezes (1983–94).

Price stability and the return to democracy in 1994 reinforced attempts to reform the Banco do Brasil. Capitalization on Brazilian stock markets in 1996 was designed to transfer control of the bank to the private sector. However, because investors (amidst a banking crisis) failed to purchase stock, the federal government did and, as an unintended consequence, *increased* government ownership to over 73 per cent. Powerful lobbies and networks thereby retained control of the largest financial institution and bank in the country and governed the modernization of the Banco do Brasil during the 2000s. Upon taking office in 2003, President Lula retained the core reforms and policies of the Cardoso administration, such as liberalization, inflation targeting, fiscal reform and tight monetary policy. Economic recovery during 2004 led to what the Central Bank of Brazil describes as a period of organic growth at the bank. From 2004 to 2008 the Banco do Brasil led in deepening credit and capital markets. In 2008, when markets collapsed, credit became short and the economy stalled, the bank provided emergency loans and infusions of capital through stock purchases, and also acquired firms and banks, large and small, unable to weather the sharp downturn. Since 2008 the Banco do Brasil has used its networks across government, politics and society, and its other institutional foundations of competitive advantage as a bank, to remain the largest bank in Latin America, after briefly being displaced by the merger of Itau and Unibanco.

In Brazil, many capital market and financial operations involve networks centred in the Banco do Brasil, such as the PREVI pension fund (the Banco do Brasil employee pension fund – the largest in the country) and bank consortia often led by the Banco do Brasil investment banking division. Counter-cyclical lending and leadership in capital markets did not deteriorate Banco do Brasil balance sheets. From 2003 to 2012 the Banco do Brasil remained well within central bank and Basel Accord regulations. In 2002–3 reforms sought to reduce costs and improve ratings. Relations between the bank and President Lula therefore *reversed* past patterns. In the past, developmentalists at the Banco do Brasil largely ignored policies for tight money or austerity. In 2003 bank management refused President Lula's request to increase loans and reduce interest rates. President Lula respected the bank's independence amidst crisis. However, in similar conditions in 2009, he fired Banco do Brasil President Antonio Francisco de Lima Neto for refusing to expand counter-cyclical lending and finance.

Before 2008 Banco do Brasil balance sheets confirm a period of growth based on loans to the private sector, with deposits and shareholder equity increasing largely apace. In 2008 balance sheets changed, with capital injections from money market borrowing up R$49.2–R$91.4 billion, and liabilities with Treasury and the BNDES up R$14.3–R$22.4 billion. Assets also changed. Private sector lending increased in 2006–8 from R$117.8 billion to R$181.0 billion, reflecting acquisition of the São Paulo state government savings bank (Nossa Caixa). Inter-bank investments also increased in 2006–8 from R$17.5 billion to R$95.1 billion. Lending to the public sector increased in 2007–8 from R$2.4 billion to R$23.0 billion. And after the central bank reduced reserve requirements in 2008, the Banco do Brasil accessed R$12.2 billion of its customer's deposits to cover loans and investments.

The Banco do Brasil has therefore expanded its substantial market shares in virtually every aspect of banking in the country since crisis. At year-end 2008, the bank retained R$246.3 billion or 20.7 per cent of asset management funds, 28.0 and 24.6 per cent respectively of export and import foreign exchange markets, 23.2 per cent of the mutual fund market, over R$224.8 billion in loans (R$17.6 billion payroll loans, 22.4 per cent of the market), 59.8 per cent of loans in the rural credit system, and R$97.0 billion in loans to business. Total funding reached over R$362.6 billion. Banco do Brasil customers reached 47.9 million in 2008, while the bank retained 39,700 ATMs and 76.6 million bank cards (23.9 million credit cards and 52.7 million debit cards).

A stock offering in January 2008, granting of shares by VISA to the Banco do Brasil, and upgrading of the bank to investment grade BB– by Standard & Poor's in April 2008 suggest that market-oriented reforms at the bank continued during the Lula presidency, despite fears to the contrary among investors and the use of the bank for counter-cyclical policies. A lower income department was also created to acquire the failed Banco Popular do Brasil operations (not all government banks succeed) and improve correspondent banking and sustainability programmes. The Banco do Brasil also received permission to use savings accounts for home loans and compete on level ground with the Caixa. During 2008 the Banco do Brasil acquired three state government banks: the Banco do Piaui, the Banco de Santa Catarina (the thirty-third largest bank in Brazil, with US$3.0 billion assets at year-end 2007) and the São Paulo savings bank, Nossa Caixa (the twelfth largest bank in Brazil, with US$26.7 billion assets at year-end 2007). The

Banco do Brasil thereby grew amidst crisis while providing policy options to government and credit to help firms, families and domestic banks adjust.

In sum, the Banco do Brasil has emerged from capture under military rule since the liberalization of banking and return to democracy to remain the largest financial conglomerate in Brazil and South America. Until 1986 the bank retained unlimited access every Friday to funds at Treasury through a *conta movimento* (movement account). A sale of shares in 1996 failed to assert private sector control over the bank. In 2013 the federal government retains 65 per cent ownership after twice capitalizing the bank on the BOVESPA stock market during the 2000s. This appears similar to stock market capitalizations that grant minority stockholding to private investors in other BRIC government banks. Capitalization on markets does not mean convergence towards private control. The Banco do Brasil remains at the centre of networks across banking, financial markets, politics, social organizations and the business community. These institutional foundations, and others specific to banking such as greater client confidence and scale, can explain why the bank recorded profits equal to or greater than private and foreign banks during growth in the period 2004–8 and, since crisis, was able to provide counter-cyclical credit without deteriorating its balance sheet or macro fundamentals. More transparent financial reporting, advances in central bank supervision and greater scrutiny of press and opposition since the return to democracy suggest that the Banco do Brasil has averted problems expected by critics of government banks and, instead, served to promote growth and counter crisis.

Caixa Econômica Federal (Federal Savings Bank, Caixa)

Founded under monarchy in 1860, a single savings and pawn office in Rio de Janeiro grew despite banking crises, market crashes and regime changes (to oligarchic republic in 1889; national populism in 1930; and democracy in 1945–64) to become twenty-six independent regional savings banks. In a top-down, centre-out process, once Caixa branch offices accumulated sufficient reserves to cover operations, independent governance was granted. By guarantee of small deposits, independent regional savings banks led in downmarket savings, home mortgage lending and municipal finance. Until the military coup in 1964, Caixas remained members of international savings bank associations and sponsored the Brazilian society of *economiários* (savings economists) to host annual conventions to debate Caixa corporate strategy. The Caixa federal council also published a bi-monthly *Revista das Caixas Econômicas* (*Savings Banks Review*), which terminated after the military coup in 1964. In 1970 military rulers consolidated regional Caixas into a single corporation wholly owned by the federal government and run by three appointees of the military. Many political careers and machines were built under military rule by controlling Caixa lending and jobs.[24] And through the period of dual government (1982–5) and delayed transition to full elections (1985–94), administrative costs exploded and bad loans reached 40 per cent in areas of Caixa lending. However, instead of privatization, the reformist government of President Cardoso recapitalized the Caixa in 2001 to meet Basel Accord I requirements. Since then, reforms have attempted to modernize the Caixa amidst liberalization, legacies of military rule, delayed transition and new realities of coalition politics and capture amidst democracy.

Since 2001 the Caixa has continued to serve as the primary agent for federal government social policy and the lead in rebuilding home mortgage lending, with special charge for downmarket home loans, urban sanitation and development, simplified accounts for the bankless, and management of basic income and other social policy payments through a single 'citizenship card', an electronic payment card. Investment banking, management of third-party funds and new products and services increased profits while the Caixa promoted financial inclusion. The Caixa thus emerged from downsizing in the late 1990s to expand organically as a bank since 2001. Assets and deposits declined in the period 1997–2002 (during twofold foreign exchange devaluation) from US$99.9 billion to US$36.3 billion and from US$54.1 billion to US$21.6 billion, respectively. Employees (many redundant top staff posts) were also cut, from 99,866 to 94,194 in 1995–9, and branch offices were shut, declining from 2,316 to 1,803 in 1995–7 (see Table 10.4). During the 2000s standard indicators of bank performance suggest that internal reforms and institutional foundations of competitive advantage combined for the Caixa to consistently outperform private and foreign banks.

Table 10.4: Caixa structure and performance, 1995–2012.

	Assets	Profits	Deposits	Staff	Branches	Basel	FA/Equity
1995	82.6	67.2	50.3	99,866	2,316		
1996	90.7	235.1	51.5	99,343	2,105		
1997	99.9	87.5	54.1	96,300	1,803		
1998	94.8	169.3	49.9	94,859	1,819		
1999	68.4	157.1	34.4	94,194	1,919		
2000	64.4	136.2	32.2	104,253	1,921		
2001	43.6	−126.5	29.8	98,971	2,013	13.5	63.8
2002	36.3	146.2	21.6	106,548	2,147	14.6	53.7
2003	52.1	261.7	28.1	100,498	2,046	19.2	41.3
2004	55.6	299.9	34.5	100,164	2,135	20.2	36.1
2005	80.6	485.2	45.6	106,729	2,321	27.8	20.1
2006	98.1	487.4	56.7	104,934	2,428	25.2	19.7
2007	140.9	448.5	80.0	106,770	2,052	28.8	12.8
2008	126.6	573.5	70.8	104,000	2,069	20.6	11.9
2009	196.3	1,057.9	103.7	107,000	2,850	17.5	16.6
2010	240.9	1,258.3	129.1	107,731	2,209	15.4	17.16
2011	272.4	1,550.3	138.5	110,242	2,300	13.3	16.6
2012	343.9	1,575.6	156.1	117,184	2,868	13.0	12.6

Note: Assets and Deposits = US$ billion. Profits = US$ million. Basel = BIS Basel Accord index of capital reserve adequacy. FA/Equity = Fixed assets / Equity, a summary indicator of bank modernization.

Source: Central Bank of Brazil, 'Top 50 Banks', at http://www4.bcb.gov.br/top50/ingl/top50-i.asp [accessed 1 October 2013].

Unlike the high levels of bad loans reported during the adjustment to price stability after 1994, the banking crisis in 1996 (when the Caixa was used by the federal government to acquire failed private banks) and the financial crises (1994–5, 1997, 1998, 1999, 2001, 2003), non-performing loans at the Caixa fell after 2004 as growth and credit recovered: from 6.8 to 4.0 per cent in the period 2006–8 (6.2–5.9 per cent for consumer loans, 7.5–2.2 per cent for loans to business, and 3.1–1.7 per cent for home loans). Caixa credit risk matrices available in its Annual Reports confirm improvement through 2012 and reveal a greater transparency from new reporting and accounting standards. In 2001 central bank regulations dropped two categories of credit (i.e. good (< 90 days overdue) and bad (> 90 days overdue) in favour of international standards (AA to H) and required banks to make provision accordingly, from zero against AA loans to 100 per cent for loans classified as H (> 180 days non-payment).

The Caixa was captured under military rule. Opposition leaders struggled to unseat oligarchs and cronies ensconced in the savings bank throughout the 1990s and 2000s. Gradually, reforms recovered the dual role of the Caixa (as savings bank and agent for federal government policy) that provides institutional foundations of competitive advantage over private and foreign banks. Policies such as family grants and other social services (unemployment insurance, social security and payroll savings) have been widely credited with reducing notorious levels of inequality in Brazil since the return to democracy. The Caixa is paid to manage these social policies. This, in turn, helped the Caixa expand branch offices and innovate through bank correspondent institutions to reach over 10 million bankless Brazilians and provide basic income to over 48 million women with no other sources of income (12 million women and their children). Contrary to expectations about privatizations, market-based banking and critics of government banks, research on the Caixa suggests that a 'back to the future' modernization of social banking presents an alternative to private and foreign banks since liberalization, especially in terms of counter cyclical-lending and downmarket banking that combine with the provision of social services and basic income policies to the many bankless Brazilians.

Banco Nacional de Desenvolvimento Econômico e Social (National Bank for Economic and Social Development, BNDES)

The BNDES is a paradigmatic development bank. During the 1950s the BNDES directed credit to transportation, electric energy, infrastructure and steel. After the military coup in 1964, market-oriented reforms transformed the BNDES (contrary to the intent of the reformers) into the agent of state-led import substitution industrialization in the 1970s by channelling foreign finance and forced savings into capital goods, project lending and regional development. The BNDES shrank in the 1980s due to a dual fiscal and foreign debt crisis. In the 1990s the bank changed fundamentally to become the agent for privatization of state-owned enterprises. During the decade of emerging market financial crises (1994–2003), the BNDES remained the best and often only source of long-term finance in Brazil. Under the PT administrations of Lula and Rousseff, the BNDES grew through retained profits, capital injections from Treasury and management of forced savings funds to remain the fifth largest bank in the country, with over US$336.7 billion assets, US$10.2 billion deposits and 2,815 employees.

From 2004 to 2011 capital inflows and a booming Bovespa stock market reinforced the capacity of the BNDES to underwrite long-term investments and launch large Brazilian firms as multinational corporations. Since 2007 BNDES President Luciano Coutinho has pursued a full service approach, attempting to help small and medium firms; finance successful firms; participate in joint ventures and capital funds to modernize businesses; and place firms on the Bovespa exchange and help globalize the operations of select 'national champions'. In 2008, when the financial crisis stopped credit and caused a collapse of share prices and industrial production, the BNDES turned to counter-cyclical lending. Although the bank has received funds from Treasury, the primary source of BNDES funds remains the returns from credit and finance. President Coutinho claimed that returns provided over 77.4 per cent of funds in 2012, compared to 4 per cent from forced FAT savings deposits and 15.6 per cent in liabilities to Treasury.

The BNDES has realized powerful competitive advantages typical of a government special purpose bank (critics and private bank presidents have charged these as *unfair* advantages). Contrary to the extensive branch office networks of the Banco do Brasil (5,392), Itau (3,871), Bradesco (4,696) and Caixa (2,972), the BNDES retains a single corporate headquarters and three regional branch offices. Payroll costs from 2,815 BNDES employees provide another powerful competitive advantage, as the other top five banks retain employees as follows: Banco do Brasil (128,811), Itau (119,381), Bradesco (98,880) and Caixa (119,695). The BNDES thereby increased share of non-bank loans from R$8.0 billion (3.8 per cent) in 1995 to R$20.0 billion (14.1 per cent) during crisis in 2003 to remain at that market share through 2012. BNDES inter-bank lending has also increased. Since the Real Plan ended inertial inflation in 1994, the BNDES increased market share of inter-bank lending from 15.6 billion (32.4 per cent) in 1995 to 53.0 billion (49.3 per cent) in 2008 to avert crisis. Similar increases occurred in past crises: in 1999 and 2001 BNDES inter-bank lending reached 41.0 and 50.4 per cent of the total, respectively.

Because of its lean staff, low administrative costs and access to near zero cost of capital, BNDES long-term interest rates (6.25 per cent) remained substantially lower than other banks lending to business (18.1 per cent average for the top twenty-five banks in August 2013) and Selic benchmark overnight inter-bank interest rates (8.5 in mid-2013). Increased participation of the BNDES in capital markets has built new relationships and networks across government, the private sector, labour unions and the pension funds of government bank and enterprise employees. In 2007 BNDES stockholding reached across 261 firms and twenty-five mutual fund participations totalling over R$91.0 billion. The BNDES retains a broad portfolio and network that helps stabilize financial markets and leverage government development policies and the globalization of Brazilian firms.[25]

Comparison of BNDES with other development banks suggests its large scale (see Table 10.5). At year-end 2011 BNDES assets were over fourfold the assets reported by the Inter-American Development Bank (IADB), 1.2 times the total assets held by the World Bank, and just over half the assets of the China Development Bank (CDB). In 2011 BNDES credit (US$82.6 billion) reached almost tenfold IADB lending (US$8.4 billion) and fourfold World Bank lending (US$21.8 billion), while approaching levels of CDB lending (US$86.7 billion). BNDES net income, returns on assets and returns on equity also exceeded these three development banks. Despite its size, compared to other BRIC banks, the BNDES remains sorely understudied.

Table 10.5: BNDES and other development banks, 2011 (in US$ million).

	BNDES	IADB	World Bank	China DB
Total assets	369,720	89,432	312,848	774,180
Shareholder equity	36,102	19,794	38,697	60,953
Net income	5,345	20	930	5,618
Loan disbursement	82,676	8	21,839	87
Capitalization, %	9.76	22.10	12.30	7.90
RoA, %	1.65	0.02	0.30	0.80
RoE, %	23.10	0.10	2.40	9.50

Source: H. A. C. Pinto, 'Estruturação de Projetos no BNDES' (Rio de Janeiro: BNDES, 2012).

Further research is required. However, primary documents suggest that the BNDES was critical in providing counter-cyclical funds and has realized competitive advantages over private and foreign banks in the country. In his March 2009 testimony to Congress, BNDES President Coutinho argued that the bank would help reduce the cost and increase the supply of credit in Brazil. The BNDES has also used private equity finance and investment funds to counter the collapse of the stock market and the subsequent credit crunch. Since the crisis abroad in 2008, BNDES lending and finance increased from R$91 billion (2008) to R$136 billion (2009), R$168 billion (2010), R$139 billion (2011), reaching R$156 billion (2012). The bank also participated in overshooting deep-sea petroleum investments, whether by leveraging operations on capital markets or through the state-run oil giant Petrobras. BNDES also lent strategically since the crisis, to save auto and ethanol industries at home and globalize a select number of large Brazilian firms through acquisitions abroad in association with private equity firms.

In sum, the BNDES grew during four years of growth in the period 2004–7 and, having helped underwrite the stock market boom and capitalize Brazilian firms, the bank gained sufficient scale, scope and capital base to provide counter-cyclical credit after 2008. This runs counter to expectations about private banking. In 1995 BNDES credit and finance fell to 5.2 per cent of fixed capital formation. However, the bank grew to contribute 12.6 and 14.1 per cent of fixed capital formation in 2007–8. Market-oriented policies, joint ventures with mutual funds, investment funds and private equity firms, large blocks of shares in Brazilian firms, and massive amounts of credit and investment to the private sector at below-market but still profitable long-term interest rates suggest that the lean structure, large scale and wide scope of BNDES operations provide powerful competitive advantages over private and foreign banks.

Unfortunately, while development banks abroad have turned to green production, community development, and new technologies and industries, the BNDES has continued to pursue old developmentalism. The BNDES often sustains out-dated and polluting manufacturers and leads consortia for large-scale construction projects notorious for cost overruns and corruption, while inundating vast areas of the Amazon with massive hydroelectric dams too far from urban electricity markets. Abroad, development theory and special purpose banks have fundamentally changed to focus on development as freedom and sustainability, environmental and social. Meanwhile, the BNDES has remained a practitioner of old ideas about development.

Having reviewed findings about Brazil, in the following sections we briefly explore evidence from India, China and Russia about government banking.

India

In the 1990s India liberalized banking to free credit and private banks from the stranglehold of nationalized banks, the State Bank of India and associate banks, and other government agencies for savings and directed credit.[26] Since then, research has emphasized the greater efficiencies of private and foreign banks over government banks. However, given the large market shares of government banks and the pursuit of reforms at these very large institutions, descriptive evidence suggests that, like the Brazilian experience, Indian government banks have also used institutional foundations to realize competitive advantages over private and foreign banks. Indian government banks also appear to have been critical agents for counter-cyclical lending since the 2008 crisis. Moreover, these institutions, and the Reserve Bank of India, have explored how new banking technologies may be directed downmarket to the vast numbers of bankless Indian citizens.

Data from the Reserve Bank of India permit comparison of government, private and foreign banks from 1972 to 2008 in terms of market share and, after 2007, with more in-depth indicators of bank performance. Trends in both longer-term market share and comparison of banks 2007–12 suggest that our findings from Brazil are relevant: since the liberalization of banking in India, government banks have modernized and realized competitive advantages over private and foreign banks. They also proved critical for counter-cyclical credit and present new policy options for social inclusion.

Since liberalization, private commercial banks more than doubled market share from 7.9 per cent to 19.7 per cent of credit in India in the period 1996–2008 (see Table 10.6). In comparison, the State Bank of India and associate banks decreased market shares from 29.1 to 22.4 per cent of credit in the country in the same period. The market share of nationalized banks also declined slightly, from 51.1 to 48.8 per cent. However, both major categories of government banks slowed loss of market share after 2003, with nationalized banks recovering from 46.4 to 48.8 per cent in 2004–8. The broader trends of bank changes in India since liberalization do not suggest the displacement of government banks in favour of private banking. First, total credit increased from 25.4 million lakhs to 241.7 million in the period 1996–2008. Second, foreign banks and regional rural banks also lost market share (9.0–6.7 per cent and 2.9–2.4 per cent, respectively). The broader picture of bank change in India since liberalization thus suggests, from an overview of aggregate data, that government banks have maintained large market shares since liberalization and deepening of credit in the fourteen years to 2008.

Table 10.6: India: bank market share of credit by type of bank, 1996–2008.

Type of Bank	1996	1998	2000	2001	2002	2003	2004	2005	2006	2007	2008
State Bank of India & Ass.	29.1	28.6	27.6	26.8	25.0	24.1	23.7	23.1	23.1	23.0	22.4
Nationalized banks	51.1	48.7	48.7	48.6	47.3	46.8	46.4	47.8	47.9	47.6	48.8
Foreign banks	9.0	9.0	8.4	8.4	7.3	7.1	7.2	6.6	6.6	6.9	6.7
Regional rural banks	2.9	3.1	2.9	3.0	2.9	3.0	3.0	2.8	2.4	2.5	2.4
Other commercial banks	7.9	10.6	12.4	13.2	17.5	19.0	19.8	19.7	20.0	20.0	19.7
Total	100	100	100	100	100	100	100	100	100	100	100
Total lakhs, million	25.4	32.9	46.0	53.8	65.6	75.6	88.0	115.2	151.3	194.7	241.7

Source: Reserve Bank of India, historical statistics.

Further data from the Reserve Bank of India permit comparison of public and private banks since the financial crisis abroad. Table 10.7 clarifies how the very large scale of public banks in terms of branch offices and employees and more traditional interest earnings still contrast with private banking that retains smaller networks of branch offices. Private banks increased the number of branch offices from 8,325 to 13,408 and employees from 166,960 to 214,304 in the period 2007–12. However, from a larger base, public sector banks increased the number of branch offices from 55,103 to 69,498 and employees from 715,408 to 771,388 in the same period. Despite the larger scale of government banks, these institutions increased business per employee from 59.4 to 115.1 lakhs, *surpassing* the amount of business produced by private banks per employee (which increased from 71.5 to 99.9 lakhs). Profits per employee almost doubled for both groups of banks, with private banking recording substantially higher profits (1.6 versus 0.64 lakhs).

In sum, private banks in India record higher levels of efficiency and profits. However, government banks are not designed to maximize profits. Other data such as the increased generation of business per employee and other indications of the large institutional foundations of government banks in India suggest that systemic convergence towards private banking has not ensued and, since 2007, government banks have increased lending and investment while maintaining deposit bases largely proportional to private banks. Descriptive data from the Reserve Bank of India thus confirm the relevance of our findings from Brazil. An important dimension of recovery from the global financial crisis and downturn in the BRICs is the counter-cyclical lending policies and realization of competitive advantages of government banks. Instead of liberalization and privatizations producing transitions in BRIC countries towards capital market-centred financial systems and the predominance of private banking, government banks have realized competitive advantages over private and foreign banks while providing policy alternatives in the face of financial crisis and global economic slowdown.

Table 10.7: Comparing public and private banks in India, 2007–12.

	2007–8	2008–9	2009–10	2010–11	2011–12
Number of banks					
Public sector banks	28	27	27	26	26
Private sector banks	23	22	22	21	20
Number of branch offices					
Public sector banks	55,103	57,850	61,630	65,217	69,498
Private sector banks	8,325	9,241	10,452	12,031	13,408
Number of employees					
Public sector banks	715,408	731,524	739,646	755,102	771,388
Private sector banks	166,960	176,339	182,520	187,913	214,304
Business per employee					
Public sector banks	59.4	73.4	86.4	101.7	115.1
Private sector banks	71.5	74.4	79.7	95.8	99.9
Profits per employee					
Public sector banks	0.37	0.47	0.53	0.59	0.64
Private sector banks	0.57	0.62	0.72	0.94	1.06
Wages as % of total expenses					
Public sector banks	14.66	13.88	14.79	17.50	13.72
Private sector banks	10.35	10.83	12.73	14.53	12.29
Deposits*					
Public sector banks	24538676.8	31127471.0	36920194.3	43724486.7	50020134.2
Private sector banks	6750328.8	7363776.1	8228007.2	10027588.4	11745874.1
Investments*					
Public sector banks	7998413.5	10126657.9	12155981.2	13360763.7	15040764.8
Private sector banks	2785780.7	3065311.7	3541169.0	4220576.3	5259822.0
Credit*					
Public sector banks	17974007.8	22592117.4	27010186.7	33044329.1	38783124.7
Private sector banks	5184024.2	5753276.0	6324409.4	7975439.8	9664182.3
Interest income % total inc.					
Public sector banks	0.87	0.87	0.86	0.88	0.91
Private sector banks	0.83	0.83	0.80	0.82	0.85
Cost of funds					
Public sector banks	5.85	6.06	5.35	4.91	6.06
Private sector banks	6.15	6.27	4.83	4.60	5.84
Return on assets					
Public sector banks	0.998	1.025	0.970	0.959	0.883
Private sector banks	1.131	1.128	1.277	1.426	1.532
Basel index					
Public sector banks	12.52	13.49	13.27	13.08	13.23
Private sector banks	14.34	15.23	17.43	16.46	16.21
Net NPA ratio					
Public sector banks	0.99	0.94	1.10	1.09	1.53
Private sector banks	1.09	1.29	1.03	0.56	0.46

Note: * 000 lakhs (100,000,000 or 100 billion).

Source: Reserve Bank of India, historical statistics.

Financial inclusion has also become a primary policy goal at the Reserve Bank of India. The 2008 Report of the Committee on Financial Inclusion has been followed by sections of the Reserve Bank of India Annual Report reserved for the discussion of financial inclusion. And instead of focusing on liberalization and privatization to ensure the spread of banking products and services, alternative policies have been explored. One is of special note. The Committee on Financial Inclusion recommended the issue of identity cards as bankcards. This would profoundly change the landscape of banking in India, and has attracted attention from analysts at the Central Bank of Brazil charged with financial inclusion.

China

> Let me be frank. Our banks earn profit too easily. Why? Because a small number of large banks have a monopoly. To break the monopoly, we must allow private capital to flow into the financial sector.[27]

This quote from Wen Jiabao, premier of the Chinese State Council for ten years until March 2013, which appeared on the front page of the *Wall Street Journal*, indicates how reforms of banking and finance in China produced great expectations among foreign investors. Banking has played an important part of reforms that have produced unprecedented growth. However, past certainties about soft budgets under command economies,[28] the factional rivalries of transition[29] and the cost of shedding bad loans in the early 2000s[30] have given way to the realization of the political importance of government banks.[31] Although its single-party rule differs, aggregate data and secondary studies of banking and finance in China are consistent with our findings from Brazil. Since the opening of the industry to foreign investment and the capitalization of government banks on Chinese stock markets, banking in China appears *not* to be giving way to private and foreign banks or to a capital market-based financial system. Instead, the competitive advantages of Chinese government banks over private and foreign banks and their importance for state and communist party strategies as exemplified in five-year plans confirm the importance of statecrafting government banks in the BRICs. A review of bank changes in China helps clarify our findings from Brazil on the competitive advantages, policy roles and capacity for counter-cyclical credit of government banks.

Comparing the capitalization of banks with other financial institutions and markets in 1999–2010 in China suggests that banks and (because of their overwhelming market shares) particularly government banks remain central channels in the financial system. Table 10.8 reports the assets of banking institutions, insurance companies and securities companies alongside the value of bonds (government, financial and corporate) and stock market capitalization in 1999–2010. During this period of economic reform, bank assets increased from 137.0 to 241.6 per cent of GDP (recording declines only in 2003), while assets of insurance companies increased from 2.9 to 12.7 per cent, and securities companies peaked at 6.5 per cent of GDP in 2007 before declining to 4.9 per cent in 2010. Government bonds increased from 11.8 per cent of GDP to peak at 32.4 per cent in 2007, and remain at 28.1 per cent of GDP in 2010. Financial bonds increased from 7.2 to 15.0 per cent, and corporate bonds from 0.9 to 8.6 per cent of GDP. Finally, stock market capitalization increased from 29.5 per cent of GDP to reach 123.1 per cent in 2007, declining thereafter to 66.7 per cent by 2010. Previous declines in stock market capitalization include from 48.5 in 2000 to 17.5 per cent in 2005, suggesting that profound volatility has contributed to policy concerns about financial markets and market-based banking.

Table 10.8: Comparing banks and markets in China, 1999–2010 (per cent of GDP).

	Banks	Insurance firms	Securities firms	Government bonds	Finance	Corporate	Stock market capitalization
1999	137.0	2.9		11.8	7.2	0.9	29.5
2000	138.5	3.4		13.1	7.4	0.9	48.5
2001	145.4	4.2		14.2	7.8	0.9	39.7
2002	169.8	5.3		14.8	8.2	0.5	31.9
2003	179.7	6.7	3.6	18.0	8.7	0.7	31.3
2004	175.0	7.5	2.1	22.4	9.1	0.8	23.2
2005	175.2	8.3		27.3	10.8	1.7	17.5
2006	204.0	9.1		28.9	12.1	2.6	41.3
2007	179.6	10.9	6.5	32.4	12.7	3.0	123.1
2008	204.3	10.6	3.8	31.3	13.4	4.1	38.6
2009	237.8	11.9	6.0	29.3	15.1	7.1	71.6
2010	241.6	12.7	4.9	28.1	15.0	8.6	66.7

Source: World Bank, *China 2030: Building a Modern, Harmonious, and Creative Society* (Washington, DC: World Bank, 2013).

Second, comparison of the market shares of different types of credit institutions in China suggests that government-owned banks and cooperatives remain by far the largest players. Capitalization of government banks on the stock market (often by foreign banks and investors) and what appears to be a wide variety of hybrid combinations of bank ownership and governance are beyond the scope of this chapter.[32] However, the broader trend of shares in the threefold expanding market of bank assets in China (from 276.6 billion to 953.0 billion RMB in the period 2003–10) suggests that a variety of government banks and other non-joint-stock banks continue to be by far the major players in banking in China (see Table 10.9).

Table 10.9: China bank assets by type of bank, 2003–10 (per cent total).

Type of bank	2003	2004	2005	2006	2007	2008	2009	2010
Large state-owned banks	58.0	56.9	56.1	55.1	53.3	51.0	50.9	49.2
Policy banks	7.7	7.6	7.8	7.9	8.1	9.1	8.8	8.0
Joint-stock banks	10.7	11.5	11.9	12.4	13.8	14.1	15.0	15.6
City banks	5.3	5.4	5.4	5.9	6.4	6.6	7.2	8.2
Rural banks	0.1	0.2	0.8	1.2	1.2	1.5	2.4	2.9
Rural coops			0.7	1.1	1.2	1.6	1.6	1.6
Urban credit coops	0.5	0.6	0.5	0.4	0.3	0.1	0.0	0.0
Rural credit coops	9.6	9.7	8.4	7.9	8.3	8.4	7.0	6.7
NBFIs	3.3	2.8	2.7	2.4	1.9	1.9	2.0	2.2
Postal savings banks	3.3	3.4	3.7	3.7	3.4	3.6	3.4	3.7
Foreign banks	1.5	1.8	1.9	2.1	2.4	2.2	1.7	1.8
	100.0	100.0	100.0	100.0	100.0	100.0	100.0	100.0
RMB, 100 million	276,584	315,990	374,697	439,500	531,160	631,515	795,146	953,053

Note: 2007+ include assets abroad.

Source: China Banking Regulatory Commission, *Annual Report* (Beijing: China Banking Regulatory Commission, 2010), p. 154.

The big five government banks have been partly listed on stock markets. However, four retain large majority ownership of shares by the Bank of China, the Ministry of Finance and other state entities. In 2009 the Agricultural Bank of China (US$1.019 trillion assets) retained 83.1 per cent state ownership; the Bank of China (US$1.084 trillion assets) 67.5 per cent; the China Construction Bank (US$1.717 trillion) 57.0 per cent state ownership (and 10.9 per cent Bank of America shareholdings); and the Industrial and Commercial Bank of China (US$1.810 trillion) retained 70.7 per cent state ownership (and 4.9 per cent Goldman Sachs shareholdings).

The number of staff in each type of credit institution clarifies the larger scale of government policy banks and suggests the importance of new initiatives at the Postal Savings Bank (see Table 10.10). Of the almost 3 million staff employed in credit institutions in China in 2010, over 1.54 million worked in policy banks and over 550,00 employees worked in rural credit cooperatives. No information in English is available on the Postal Savings Bank website or from regulatory authorities in China. However, as a member of the World Savings Bank Institute (WSBI), the Chinese Postal Bank reported, for 2011, US$501.7 billion assets, 39,000 branch offices and 6 million customers. The second WSBI member from China, the Industrial and Commercial Bank of China, reported US$2.4 trillion in assets, 16,648 branch offices, 408,849 employees and over 286 million customers.[33] Case studies of such large banks are sorely needed.[34]

Table 10.10: China: number of staff and banks by type of credit institution, 2010.

Type of credit institution	Staff	Banks
Policy banks	1,545,050	5
Large commercial banks	59,503	3
Joint-stock commercial banks	237,158	12
City commercial banks	206,604	147
Rural credit cooperatives	550,859	2,646
Rural commercial banks	96,721	85
Rural cooperative banks	81,076	223
Finance cooperatives of enterprise groups	599	107
Trust companies	7,382	63
Financial leasing companies	1,235	17
Auto finance companies	2,391	13
Money brokerage firms	245	4
Consumer financial companies	254	4
New rural financial institutions and postal savings banks	15,282	396
Financial asset management companies	7,411	4
Foreign banks	36,017	40
Credit institutions total	2,990,716	3,769

Source: China Banking Regulatory Commission. *Annual Report*, p. 164.

Further research on the organizational structure and governance of the wide variety of banks and credit institutions in China is required. However, trends in the market shares of different credit institutions in 1999–2010 and data on the organizational structure of government banks and alternative banks in 2010 suggest that expectations of convergence towards private joint-stock ownership and market-based banking are overstated or amiss. Barriers to entry prevail and the lack of transparency under single-party control in China counsel caution regarding our comparisons. However, our findings from Brazil about institutional foundations of competitive advantage and the importance of government banking for public policies provide new research questions about the political economy of bank change in China.

Analysis of returns on equity reported by banks is also required because this indicator of performance appears inconsistent with broader trends of market share and size. Foreign banks produced much higher returns than all other types of banks from 2007 to 2010 (see Table 10.11). And while foreign banks increased their share of total bank assets in China from 1.5 to 2.4 per cent in the period 2003–7, their market share fell thereafter to below 1.8 per cent of bank assets in 2010. Because of their small market shares, foreign banks may perhaps best be seen as part of a new distribution of financial labour in the country. Government banks have clearly not been displaced by private and foreign banks, despite statements of reformers epitomized by the epigram to this section.

Table 10.11: Return on equity by type of bank in China, 2007–10.

Type of bank	2007	2008	2009	2010
Policy banks	7.3	16.6	11.5	10.5
Large commercial banks	6.4	5.5	5.5	5.6
Joint-stock commercial banks	6.0	5.2	6.1	6.0
City commercial banks	7.6	6.5	7.2	6.3
Rural commercial banks	7.7	7.3	7.5	7.2
Rural cooperative banks	7.5	6.3	6.3	6.2
Urban credit cooperatives	7.7	6.2	1.9	0.1
Rural credit cooperatives	9.7	10.1	10.3	12.0
Non-bank financial institutions	5.3	8.1	9.6	9.4
Foreign banks	19.3	11.9	26.0	23.8
New rural financial institutions and postal savings banks	18.5	34.0	10.3	6.2

Note: RoE = profit after tax of banking institutions 2007–10 as per cent of total owners' equity of banking institutions (2007–10).

Source: China Banking Regulatory Commission, *Annual Report*, pp. 156 and 158; banks in categories reported on p. 150.

A further similarity exists between Brazil and China: the need to write off bad loans early in the period of transition (despite differences in transitions). Chinese government banks transferred bad credits to asset management companies (AMCs) in 1999–2000 to liquidate non-paying loans from the big four government banks. The China Great Wall AMC received 345.8 billion yuan (24.6 per cent of Agricultural Bank of China loans) to recover 12.6 per cent of assets by 2006. The China Orient AMC received 267.4 billion yuan (20.4 per cent of Bank of China loans) to recover 27.2 per cent of assets by 2006. The China Cinda AMC received 373.0 billion yuan (21.7 per cent of China Construction Bank loans) to recover 34.5 per cent of assets by 2006. Finally, the China Huarong AMC received 407.7 billion yuan (17.9 per cent of Industrial and Commercial Bank of China loans) to recover 26.5 per cent of assets by 2006.[35] We return to the question of non-performing loans below.

Debates about government banks in China, even when critical, provide indications for description of their competitive advantages. Martin explains the competitive advantages of Chinese government banks in a report to the US Congress:

China's policy banks operate financially by either receiving a capital contribution from the central government or by issuing bonds to raise capital. Because the bonds are issued by a policy bank, they are presumed to be backed by the full faith and credit of the Chinese government, with little or no risk of non-payment. This allows the policy banks to raise capital at a reduced cost.[36]

While the US government has charged China with unfair competition, Martin suggests that government banks in China retain competitive advantages over private and foreign banks since the liberalization of the industry. Cheaper cost of capital and centrality in political networks and policymaking have proved barriers to entry that may or may not be considered unfair according to different theories of banking discussed in the introductions to this chapter and volume.

Four of the big five government banks were capitalized in record sales of shares on the stock market during the 2000s. However, the China Development Bank averted stock sales and pursued other strategies to compete directly with commercial banks:

> Over the last four years, CDB Chairman Chen Yuan ... has purposely forestalled CDB's equitization while at the same time expanding the bank's activities well beyond the policy role of financing China's major development projects ... CDB has become one of China's more dynamic banks, operating like commercial banks when it serves its purpose, and benefitting from its status as a policy bank when that is to its advantage.[37]

During the 2000s the CDB focused on large infrastructure projects (with large social and environmental impacts) such as the Three Gorges dam and high-speed rail network. In 2010 the CDB continued to focus on infrastructure, with 73.7 per cent of loans going to coal, electricity, oil, telecoms, transportation and public infrastructure. However, the CDB also created new business lines for local development and the globalization of Chinese firms as advocated in five-year plans. CDB credit for local public finance on collateral from local government investment corporations reached over a third of GDP in 2009.[38] Allen et al. confirm the centrality of the CDB for the rapid growth of local government bond issues and for shifting the economy away from industrial exports.[39] The CDB also promoted direct foreign investment and trade of Chinese firms in response to the 2002 CCP National Congress strategy of 'going out'. By 2009 over US$100.0 billion (17 per cent) of CDB outstanding loans were for projects overseas. The CDB has become an important agent for Chinese foreign policy and development projects.[40] The large scale and policy agility of the CDB belies expectations of change towards private bank-style governance.

The institutional foundations of competitive advantage retained by Chinese government banks and their insertion in networks of politics and policy making have brought charges of unfair competition. In 2011 the US government charged China with 200 unfair subsidies, many involving Chinese government banks. The US–China Economic and Security Review Commission reported to Congress in 2011: 'China's largest banks are state-owned and are required by the central government to make loans to state-owned companies at below market interest rates and, in some cases, to forgive those loans.'[41] However, Downs discounts the importance of direct subsidies and suggests instead that Chinese government banks may instead have realized competitive advantages over private and foreign banks primarily because of their access to cheap funds and ability to serve as agents of policy directives:

> The fact that CDB may be lending at interest rates lower than what a western bank might require does not mean that it acts simply as an agent of state policy with no regard to profit. Instead, CDB balances its commitment to profitability and its mandate to advance the policy priorities of the Chinese government. On a straight commercial basis, it may be rational for CDB to accept lower interest rates than western banks because CDB is backed by the Chinese government.[42]

Lardy and Martin also confirm the importance of government banks for policy, suggesting that Chinese state banks have shifted away from direct lending to large state enterprises to shape growth along lines set in five-year plans, that is to say towards private firms, family firms and small and medium enterprises.[43]

Since the onset of the global crisis in 2008, monetary authorities in China have sought to balance the supply of government bank credit necessary to counter crisis while averting higher inflation or over indebtedness. Increasing domestic production and consumption is of special priority in China. Meanwhile, Brazilian policymakers confront the inverse: the need to control consumer-led growth after policies that encouraged consumption helped avert crisis 2008–12 but increasingly face declining marginal effectiveness. In sum, recent studies of government banks in China and related charges of unfair competition suggest that these large institutions retain powerful competitive advantages and provide policy alternatives to central and local governments. Studies of Chinese politics also confirm the importance of government banks, ranking the political status of appointments to the big five banks equal to top ministerial posts.[44]

Shih has also traced Chinese political factions in financial flows and emphasized government banks as critical for careers and as policy instruments during the transition away from a command economy.[45] Again, the large write-offs of bad loans in the early 2000s and the situation of Chinese government banks in the 2010s appear similar to experiences in Brazil. Government banks were subject to widespread abuse during transitions in Brazil and China. However, once bad loans were transferred to asset management companies, more transparent accounting and more aggressive supervision of these institutions appear to have averted the recurrence of non-payment of loans at such a high level.[46]

Government banks in China present an anomaly for theories of transition from a command economy to a market economy and a financial system based on private banking and capital markets.[47] Expectations about bank change in China reinforce the focus on private banking and theories of liberalization and privatization that focus on the empowerment of reformers. In the past, crises were seen as opportunities to accelerate liberalization and privatizations.[48] We have reported different phenomena from Brazil and explored similarities in other BRICs. Aggregate data from Chinese bank regulators and secondary accounts that reassess Chinese government banks appear consistent with our findings from Brazil. Instead of wholesale privatizations and the adoption of market-based banking, Chinese government banks have used institutional foundations of competitive advantage to modernize, maintain market share and provide policy alternative to leaders of the state and communist party. Perhaps the latter is the most important difference. In Brazil, transition from military and oligarchic rule was critical for internal reform and modernization of government banks. In India, the amorphous federalism of its large and long-standing democracy may also prove consistent with the idea that greater transparency has been brought to state banks. However, single-party control and lack of financial press freedom in China counsel caution.

Aggregate data may well conceal other causes and processes. However, primary data and secondary accounts of Chinese government banks are consistent with our findings from Brazil: state banks have realized competitive advantages and maintained market shares since the 1990s while providing counter-cyclical credit to help adjust to crisis and redirect development after 2008. From the perspective of social banking, the China Postal Savings Bank is of particular interest, given its downmarket focus and 39,000 branch offices throughout the country. This institution presents profound opportunities, and risks, for policies in China similar to those reported from Brazil involving the federal government savings bank (Caixa).

Chinese government banks remain critical agents for strategies to redirect growth as set in the twelfth five-year plan for 2011–15. The tenth five-year plan (2000–5) focused on infrastructure construction, attraction of foreign investment and improving labour skills. The eleventh five-year plan (2006–10) raised concerns about sustainability of rapid growth, spreading improvements and balancing development across regions and social classes. The twelfth five-year plan (2011–15) calls for more inclusive growth and a variety of sectoral goals.

Chinese government banks remain critical agents for policy goals. These institutions are too big for bold claims. They make serve to siphon popular savings to large projects and party-state machines. However, our findings from Brazil provide hypotheses to explore anomalies about bank change in China for the Washington Consensus about privatizations and liberalization. Government banks in China remain commanding heights for financial statecraft. Although reformers and foreign investors retain great expectations about reforms, party elites and policymakers in China appear to value government banks as institutions able counter crisis and shape growth.

Russia: Political Realism and Transition Government Banking

The rush of 2003–8 increased the market share of foreign banks to 28.5% from 5.2%. However, '*the state-owned banks received enormous help from the federal budget in the days of the crisis, thereby strengthening their dominant position on the Russian financial market*,' says Sergey Aleksashenko, the former Deputy Chair of Russia's Central Bank, quotes Russia Profile. '*Today, one must not harbor any illusion of a fair competition with them: all the main cash flows in Russia are controlled by state-owned banks*.'[49]

Since 2008, political realism and central bank policies to counter crisis provided competitive advantage for Russian state banks to expand market share over private and, especially, foreign banks. Critics have denounced state interference in Russian banking, and the political climate has led foreign investment banks to leave the country.[50] The realities of politics in Russia are different than the experiences in the other BRICs. However, comparison of market shares and other data on state, private and foreign banks in the country are consistent with our findings in Brazil. Data from bank supervisors in Russia indicate that state banks in Russia performed above levels recorded by private and foreign banks since the onset of the global crisis in 2008. During the 1990s research on banking in Russia emphasized the inefficiencies of former Soviet state banks, liquidation of bad loans after transition and the promises of privatization.[51] However, by the late 2000s research on banking and political economy in Russia found confrontations between state elites and private firms, foreign and domestic, and the emergence of groups closely allied to government. In this context, primary and secondary evidence indicate that Russian state banks have used political realism and institutional foundations of competitive advantage to modernize, while providing counter-cyclical credit to reverse economic downturn and further expand market shares since crisis abroad hit the country in 2008.

Bank of Russia bank supervision reports indicate that state banks have expanded market share of assets and capital since crisis. Large private banks and foreign banks have lost market share of bank assets and bank capital in Russia. In comparison, state banks increased market share of bank assets 40.5–45.8 per cent and 47.1–47.6 per cent of capital (see Table 10.12).

Table 10.12: Russia: number of banks and market shares by type of bank, 2009–11.

Type of bank	Number of banks			% assets			% capital		
	2009	2010	2011	2009	2010	2011	2009	2010	2011
State	17	22	27	40.5	43.9	45.8	47.1	48.9	47.3
Foreign	101	106	108	18.7	18.3	18.0	17.2	16.9	19.1
Large private	136	139	131	34.6	33.3	30.5	27.6	28.7	26.9
Med-small Moscow	361	335	317	2.7	2.6	2.6	4.3	3.4	3.5
Med-small regional	443	412	372	2.8	2.8	2.7	3.6	3.1	2.9
Other credit institutions	50	51	57	0.7	0.4	0.4	0.1	0.2	0.3
Total	1,108	1,065	1,012	100	100	100	100	100	100

Source: Bank of Russia, 'Bank Supervision Report' (Moscow: Bank of Russia, 2011).

Additional data compiled by Raiffeisen Research confirms this trend (see Table 10.13). According to these calculations, state-owned banks in Russia increased market share of bank assets in the country 2008–12 from 44.0 to 53.0 per cent. This inverted previous trends, marked by the influx of foreign banks and foreign investment, and, despite crisis abroad, helped produced an increase in the total value of bank assets from 676.1 billion to 1.2 trillion euros.

Table 10.13: Russia: bank assets by type of bank, 2008–12.

	2008	2009	2010	2011	2012
Number of banks	1,108	1,058	1,012	978	956
Market share of state-owned banks, %	44.0	45.0	46.0	52.0	53.0
Market share of banks > 50% foreign-owned	17.3	18.3	18.0	16.9	17.8
Market share of 100% foreign-owned banks	10.9	9.0	8.6	8.3	7.9
Total assets, billion euros	676.1	678.3	838.2	998.9	1,238.7
Total assets, % GDP	67.9	75.8	73.0	74.6	79.4

Source: Raiffeisen Research, 'CEE Banking Report' (May 2013), p. 55.

Observers agree that state banks have used political and institutional foundations of competitive advantage. Differences arise about whether these advantages are fair. The Raiffeisen Bank research department describes the advantages of Russian state banks as follows:

> the enhanced credibility of the large state banks, an advantageous access to funding, their large size, extensive networks and the possibility to be price-setters on the domestic deposit and loan markets. All these factors supported the recent round of expansion of state-controlled banking groups. Sberbank, VTB, Gazprombank and the commercial banks within VEB group accounted for 53% of total banking assets as of end-2012. The increase of their market share by over 8 pp. over the past five years was a trend provoked by crisis events. State-controlled banks were the major rescuers of failed private banks, and the system's safe havens, which gained the population trust to a large extent. Their ability to get state funding to meet the respective depositors' claims and to provide help to distressed corporate borrowers supported their advantageous position in terms of funding and determined their new role in Russia's post-crisis financial system. Therefore, it comes as no surprise that the retail lending (or consumer lending) boom of the past two years was also pioneered by the state giants. They have enjoyed a matching deposit base already in place and were able to tap international debt market, placing over two thirds of Russian total banking debt volume in 2011 and 2012.[52]

This sequence is similar to experiences in Brazil, India and China, although the exit of foreign investment banks in the period 2010–12 seems unique to Russia. Large scale and credibility combined to avert runs on consumer deposits, increase public confidence and provide counter-cyclical credit. Preferential finance from the Bank of Russia reinforced the position of state banks. Russian state banks expanded market share since 2008 using competitive advantages and revenue growth to expand into retail banking and consumer finance. The context of transition in Russia also differs. During the 1990s Russian citizens developed unprecedented levels of distrust towards institutions in general, and especially banks.[53] In this respect, the recovery of confidence since the global crisis in 2008 is of special note. The increase of consumer and depositor confidence in banks in Russia amidst crisis indicates how government banks retain powerful competitive advantages over private and foreign banks in a critical area of banking – trust, confidence and liquidity risk.

Data on bank performance from Bank of Russia bank supervision reports confirm the realization of competitive advantages by state banks in Russia from 2008 to 2010 (see Table 10.14). Returns on assets and returns on equity at state banks exceed levels reported by other types of banks (with the exception of foreign banks in 2009).

Table 10.14: Russia: returns on assets and equity by type of bank, 2008–10.

	Return on assets			Return on equity		
	2008	2009	2010	2008	2009	2010
State banks	2.2	0.8	2.4	15.7	4.6	14.8
Foreign banks	1.8	1.1	2.1	14.6	8.3	14.5
Large private banks	1.3	0.3	1.1	10.6	2.8	8.4
Medium-small banks, Moscow	1.5	1.2	1.4	6.8	5.2	6.7
Medium-small regional banks	2.1	1.2	1.5	13.1	6.5	9.8

Source: Bank of Russia, 'Bank Supervision Report' (Moscow: Bank of Russia, 2009) and 'Bank Supervision Report' (Moscow: Bank of Russia, 2010).

In sum, realist politics and financial statecraft provided Russian state banks with a significant competitive advantage. Sperbank and Vneshtorgbank increased share of bank assets from 32 per cent in 2005 to over 50 per cent by 2011 through mergers and acquisitions and displacement of foreign banks. Adjustment policies provided further advantages. Data from the Bank of Russia suggest that monetary authorities released a series of counter-cyclical credit injections during 2008–9 to domestic banks. Although further research is required, our findings from Brazil would suggest that state banks received preference. However, the broader comparison holds. In Russia, state banks continue to perform at or ahead of levels reported by regional, private and foreign banks. The large market share and improved performance of state banks are therefore consistent with our findings from Brazil. Government banks in Russia appear to have modernized, realized competitive advantages and provided policy alternatives against crisis abroad to further expand market shares.

Conclusion

This chapter reports evidence about government bank modernization and financial statecraft in BRIC countries. BRIC government banks have contributed to the widely noted adjustment of these economies to global financial crisis and economic downturn. Contrary to the Washington Consensus that prevailed during much of the 1980s and 1990s (that privatization and liberalization, especially of banking, would free market forces and deepen domestic financial systems), a quite different process of bank change appears to have ensued, even after financial liberalization in the BRICs. Instead of being replaced by private banks, government banks remain central agents of domestic credit and growth. Moreover, liberalization and reforms appear to have encouraged the modernization of government banks during the 2000s 'just in time' to provide policy alternatives for adjustment to crisis.

These findings counter traditional foci on the private sector, individual entrepreneurship and ideals of free markets linked to the political and social advances recorded around the world in the last decades. We report an anomaly for theories of financial repression and the Washington Consensus. Abuse of government banks was indeed responsible for financial repression under military rule in Brazil, Soviet Russia and pre-transition China. These institutions reproduced underdevelopment and siphoned popular savings to state enterprises and political machines. Transition periods also shared large write-offs of bad loans from government banks. However, during the 2000s BRIC government banks seem to have had excesses comparable to those of private banks in the US that drove home mortgage bubbles and shadow banking in derivatives that ended in crisis. China may be the exception here. And since the liberalization of banking (we have not adequately discussed how much liberalization occurred in each country), government banks appear to have modernized to compete with private and foreign banks. Government banks have realized competitive advantages and provided policy alternatives. These two arguments help explain why BRIC countries have fared comparatively well in the face of financial crisis in core countries.

In Russia, political realism and central bank funds engineered recovery and scared several major foreign banks out of the market. In China, government banking attempts to recover from the bad loans and excesses of the 2000s and to help redirect credit and finance towards local public finance and domestic consumption and production. In India, the modernization of the nationalized banks and the State Bank of India amidst an amorphous federalism presents similarities to the challenges of government bank modernization amidst democratization in Brazil.

As members of the World Savings Bank Institute (a global association of savings banks), the Caixa in Brazil, the National Savings Institute and National Bank for Agriculture and Rural Development (NABARD) in India, and China's Postal Savings Bank also appear to be critical institutions that may provide access to very large numbers of previously unbanked citizens. Crony credit or abuse of these large institutions may also channel vast sums from the savings of those worst off into political machines or wasteful projects. However, instead of slating these institutions for privatization, we find that policymakers seek ideas from European savings bank traditions. This returns to traditional ideas of social banking and the history of savings banks and cooperative banks introduced in Chapters 1 and 2 of this volume. In this respect, the upmarket strategy into investment banking and international finance of the Russian Sberbank contrasts with downmarket strategies of large traditional government savings banks in Brazil, India and China.

During 2012 the financial press once again focused on bad loans in Chinese state banks. However, current estimates of 2–5 per cent bad loans in Chinese state banks pale in comparison to the US\$124.0 billion in bad loans shifted to asset management companies in the mid-2000s before capitalization of these institutions through sale of shares. Critics of state banking in Brazil also point to past levels of bad loans (reaching 30–40 per cent) because of capture during military government and the delay of democracy. However, the cost of capitalization and transfer of bad loans from Brazilian state banks remains below US\$30.0 billion. These numbers are small compared to Government Accountability Office (GAO) estimates of US\$12.0 trillion in emergency infusions by US monetary authorities to private banks and financial institutions in the period 2007–11.

These are anomalies for contemporary banking theory and neoliberal policy designs. However, they do not run counter to the orthodoxy in economics and traditional banking theory. Over the last decades, economic reforms (fiscal, financial, monetary and banking) have improved transparency and brought public policy and market expectations closer. However, expectations about deregulation and free market equilibria in banking and finance have come under scrutiny. This chapter finds evidence consistent with our findings in Brazil and the other BRICs: even after liberalization, an unexpected 'back to the future' modernization of big government banks has ensued – a process that presents both large risks and opportunities, given their imposing market shares and deeply embedded operations in state, society, politics and the economy.

Acknowledgements

Drafts of this chapter were presented at the workshop 'Financial Statecraft and Ascendant Powers: Latin America and Asia after the 2008–10 Global Financial Crisis' in the University of Southern California in April 2012, and at the meeting of the Association of BRICS Business Schools in November 2010 in the Xavier Institute, Bangalore, India. I thank C. Wise, L. Armijo, B. Cohen, V. Shih, M. Kravchenko, R. S. Deshpande, H. Lei, M. Chasomeris, C. P. Ravindranathan and M. A. del Tedesco Lins for their comments and suggestions.

11 COOPERATIVE BANKS IN INDIA: ALTERNATIVE BANKS IMPERVIOUS TO THE GLOBAL CRISIS?

Lakshmi Kumar

Introduction

Cooperative banks occupy a unique position in the rural credit delivery system of India, having long played a significant role in the provision of short- and long-term loans for agriculture and rural development. Although commercial banks (after their nationalization) and later the regional rural banks (RRBs) have entered rural areas, cooperative banks still continue to hold an important place in the rural credit scenario in India. The cooperative credit societies at the grass-roots level aim not only to cater to the credit needs of its members, but also to provide several credit-related services – such as the supply of inputs, the storage and marketing of products, and the supply of consumer goods, etc. – to farmers, whose basic need continued to be timely credit.

Keeping in view the importance of cooperative banks and credit societies in India, several committees have been set up by the Government of India to look into the efficiency of the sector, from the All India Rural Credit Survey Committee (created in 1954) to the latest high-profile Vaidyanathan Committee (2004) – all of which emphasized the important role cooperatives play in providing credit and related services to rural areas.[1] The process of economic reforms began in India during the 1990s, but cooperative banking, though an integral part of the country's financial system, was kept insulated from the effects of these reforms. Realizing that a healthy financial system is the prerequisite for the success of the globalization process, the Indian government initiated several steps to reform the financial system by appointing the Narasimham Committee (1991) and implementing its recommendations. But cooperative banking was left out of the gambit of this process. However, rules regarding financial discipline, such as the recommendations of the Basel Committee on Bank Supervision, prudential norms, non-performing asset (NPA) norms and capital adequacy norms were expected to be complied with by cooperative banks on par with commercial banks by 2007. Moreover, while attempts were made to reform the cooperative banking system through the appointment of dedicated government committees (the Kapoor Committee in 1999, the Vikhe Patil Committee in 2001 and the Vyas Committee in 2001), no serious effort was made to implement the recommendations of these committees.[2]

The rest of the chapter is ordered as follows: the next section presents the cooperative credit structure in India in order to put cooperative banks in context. We then introduce the history of cooperative banking and its different phases in India, after which we provide a brief literature review, with identification of the research problem. We then discuss the historical role of cooperative banks in India, while the following section focuses on the most recent period, i.e. from 2001 to 2010. Finally, we analyse the current challenges faced by Indian cooperative banks before providing our conclusions.

Structure of Cooperative Credit Institutions in India

The distinctive feature of the cooperative credit structure in India is its heterogeneity. The structure differs across rural and urban areas as well as across states and tenures of loans. Figure 11.1, which is taken from the Reserve Bank of India (RBI), depicts the structure of the cooperative banking sector. The urban areas are served by urban cooperative banks (UCBs), which are further subdivided into 'scheduled' and 'non-scheduled' UCBs. Scheduled UCBs form a small proportion of the total number of UCBs. The operations of both scheduled and non-scheduled UCBs are either limited to one state or stretch across states (multi-state). Most of the non-scheduled UCBs are primarily single-state UCBs with a single-tier structure.

Rural cooperative banks follow a three-tier federal structure, that is:

i.   a state cooperative bank at the apex level (i.e. state level);
ii. a central cooperative bank at the intermediate level (i.e. district cooperative banks at district level);
iii. primary cooperative credit societies at base level (i.e. village level).

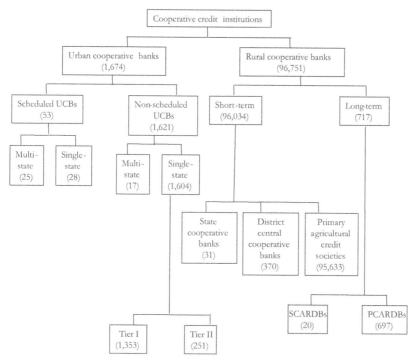

Figure 11.1: Structure of cooperative credit institutions in India, as of end-March 2010.

SCARDBs: State cooperative agriculture and rural development banks.
PCARDBs: Primary cooperative agriculture and rural development banks.

Note: i) Figures in parentheses indicate the number of institutions at end-March
2010 for UCBs and at end-March 2009 for rural cooperative credit institutions;
ii) for rural cooperatives, the number of banks refers to reporting banks.

A Brief History of Cooperative Banking in India

Europe is considered the cradle of cooperative movement in the world. It is interesting to note that the cooperative movement in Europe started as a response to various types of disadvantages and exploitation suffered by different sections of the society. In Britain, it was the post-Industrial Revolution scenario that propelled experimentations with the concepts of cooperation. Credit for starting the cooperative movement in Britain goes to Robert Owen, who involved workers in the reorganization of industries. Both Owen of Britain and Charles Fourier of France called for a new economic system based on cooperation and collective ownership. Elsewhere in Europe, the origins of cooperative credit systems are considered to have taken root in Germany. Once again it was famine, poverty, exploitation and indebtedness that fuelled the beginnings of cooperative movement there. Poorer farmers and labourers in Germany were heavily in debt and exploited by moneylenders. The situation was reportedly so dire that almost the entire farmland in Germany was encumbered with debt during the nineteenth century. The situation worsened even further due to famines. It is against this backdrop that F. W. Raiffeisen and F. H. Shulze-Delitzsch became pioneering personalities in the country's credit cooperative movement.

The cooperative movement in India also can be traced back to the problems faced by the rural society. During the late nineteenth century, large sections of farmers in India were under the clutches of moneylenders who charged usurious interest rates. Their acute poverty was thus worsened by indebtedness. The result was growing unrest among the farmers, which led to agrarian disturbances. India also faced a very large number of famines during this period. During the period 1858 to 1908, the country suffered twenty major famines, further aggravating the already precarious economic conditions of the poor farmers. Under these circumstances, several initiatives were taken by the government of the day. The Deccan agrarian struggle against the exploitation by moneylenders led to the enactment of the Taccavi legislation. The Northern India Taccavi Loan Act of 1875, the Land Improvement Loans Act of 1883 and the Agriculturist Loans Act of 1884 were enacted to mitigate the problems faced by farmers and to make credit at reasonable cost available to them. The cooperative movement itself in India can be divided into four phases as described below.

First Phase

The first phase (1900–30) witnessed the passage of the Cooperative Societies Act of 1904. In the twentieth century, the major cause of indebtedness and poverty among farmers was found to be the dependence of farmers on moneylenders for credit. At that time the cooperative movement had achieved great success in the Europe. Thus, in order to improve the conditions of rural India, the Cooperative Societies Act was passed. This marked the beginning of the cooperative movement in India. The cooperative movement gained popularity in 1919. The government set up various committees to follow up the functioning of these cooperatives.

Second Phase

The major development in the second phase (1931–50) is the role of the Reserve Bank of India. The main emphasis during this period was on setting up, strengthening and promoting financially viable cooperatives. The RBI also started providing credit facilities to the cooperatives for seasonal agricultural activities. But the government was not as active in promoting the cooperatives as it had been during the first phase. By 1945 the cooperative movement had slowed down, and many cooperative banks failed due to frozen assets and high overdue payments. The Cooperative Planning Commission identified the primary cooperatives to be the major reasons for failure.

Third Phase

The third phase (1951–90) corresponds to the period after independence, when the major area of focus was rapid and equitable development. Hence the rural cooperative societies were given importance. Another important development in this phase is that the government set up the National Bank for Agriculture and Rural Development (NABARD) for helping the rural cooperative institutions. As the government's financial involvement in cooperatives increased, its interference in all aspects of the functioning of cooperatives also increased. This interference often compelled cooperative institutions to compromise on the usual norms for creditworthiness, which ultimately began to affect the quality of the cooperatives' portfolios. The Agricultural Loan Waiver of 1989 and other political expedients greatly aggravated the already weak financial discipline of the cooperatives.

Fourth Phase

During the fourth phase (1990 and present), there has been an increasing awareness of the destructive effects of intrusive state patronage and politicization, and the consequent impairment of the role of cooperatives in general, and of credit cooperatives in particular, leading to a quest for reviving and revitalizing the cooperative movement. Many committees were set up to suggest cooperative reforms. But these suggestions were not properly implemented because of the state's unwillingness to share in costs and their reluctance to dilute their powers. New laws were formulated in eight states, and these laws enable the cooperatives to be democratic and self-reliant.

The Comparative Performance of the Indian Cooperative Banking System: A Brief Review of the Literature

Since the 1990s various studies were conducted and numerous suggestions were sought to bring effectiveness in the working and operations of cooperative banks in India. In particular, as mentioned above, various government committees have been set up, which came up with different ideas for reforming the cooperative credit system. The Narasimham Committee emphasized capital adequacy and liquidity;[3] the Padmanabhan Committee suggested CAMELS rating (in the form of ratios) to evaluate financial and operational efficiency;[4] the Tarapore Committee focused on non-performing assets and asset quality;[5] the Kannan Committee opined about working capital and lending methods; the Basel Committee (1998 and revised in 2001) recommended capital adequacy norms and risk management measures;[6] the Kapoor Committee recommended a credit delivery system and a credit guarantee;[7] and the Verma Committee recommended seven parameters (ratios) to judge financial performance.[8] Finally, several other committees were constituted by the RBI to bring reforms to the banking sector, putting much emphasis on the improvement of banks' financial health. Experts suggested various tools and techniques for effective analysis and interpretation of the financial and operational aspects of the financial institutions, specifically banks. These studies focus on the analysis of the financial viability and creditworthiness of moneylending institutions, with a view to predict corporate failures and incipient incidence of bankruptcy among these institutions.

In particular, in 2000 Bhaskaran and Praful[9] concluded that the recovery performance of cooperative credit institutions continued to be unsatisfactory, contributing to the growth of non-performing assets even after the introduction of prudential regulation. They suggested legislative and policy prescriptions to make cooperative credit institutions more efficient, productive and profitable organization in tune with competitive commercial banks. Jain[10] has done a comparative performance analysis of district central cooperative banks (DCCBs) of western India – namely Maharashtra, Gujarat and Rajasthan – and found that the DCCBs of Rajasthan performed better in profitability and liquidity in comparison to those of Gujarat and Maharashtra. Singh and Singh[11] studied the management of funds in the DCCBs of Punjab, with specific reference to the analysis of financial margin. They noted that a higher proportion of own funds and related recovery concerns had resulted in the increased margin of the DCCBs, and thus those banks had a larger provision for non-performing assets. More recently, Mavaluri, Boppana and Nagarjuna[12] have suggested that the performance of banks in general – in terms of profitability, productivity, asset quality and financial management – has become crucial to stabilize the economy. They found, in this regard, that public sector banks have so far been more efficient than other banks operating in India. Pal and Malik have investigated differences in the financial characteristics of seventy-four public, private and foreign banks in India in terms of profitability, liquidity, risk and efficiency.[13] They found that foreign banks are better performers in comparison to the other two categories of banks, both in general and in terms of the utilization of resources in particular. Campbell focused on the relationship between non-performing loans (NPLs) and bank failure and argued for an effective bank insolvency law for the prevention and control of NPLs for developing and transitional economies, since they have been suffering severe problems due to NPLs.[14] Singla, emphasizing financial management, has examined the financial position of sixteen banks by considering profitability, capital adequacy, debt equity and NPAs.[15] Dutta and Basak have suggested that cooperative banks should improve their recovery performance, adopt new systems of computerized monitoring of loans, implement proper prudential norms, and organize regular workshops to sustain themselves in a competitive banking environment.[16]

Without doubt, state interference in the cooperative banking sector has been total. The above literature, though scant, shows that all is not well with the sector in comparison to its counterparts, namely the public sector, the private sector or the foreign banks. However it would be worthwhile to re-examine under several parameters how well the cooperative banks have fared before, during and after the global financial crisis.

The Historical Role of Indian Cooperative Banks

The global economy, and the Indian economy in particular, have been going through a radical transformation in the past few years. The positive dimension of globalization includes liberal economic policies, reduction of excessive state intervention, and easy access to monetary capital and consequently new opportunities for economic participation. This is already evidenced in India in the form of increased economic growth and state withdrawal from many economic and social domains. On the other hand, there is apparently a misplaced perception developing in India that cooperatives may not be able to deliver in the context of globalized market conditions and the changes that are taking place as a result.

Under these circumstances, there is a need for the resurgence of cooperatives as important players. Cooperatives have a tremendous opportunity precisely because they have a special identity: they have both a social and an economic objective, they are community-based, they are people-oriented, and their network of linkages through the movement is almost impossible to replicate: 'In terms of the decent work paradigm ... cooperatives could lead the way by demonstrating what we really mean by freedom, equity, security and human dignity ... Thus cooperatives by being true to their basic principles provide locally-based answers to globalization'.[17] Therefore, contrary to the belief that globalization impedes the growth of cooperatives, one might argue that cooperatives are vital agencies for facing the challenges posed by globalization.

Cooperatives in India have mostly played the role of an agent of the government. They are seen to be the institutions that carry state programmes to people, and in turn they get state support. However, the very policies that have made the conventional role of the cooperatives redundant have also created new space for cooperatives to function. With a constitutional amendment likely to be passed soon and the state government bringing about required reforms in the Cooperative Acts, there would be ample scope for cooperatives to emerge as independent and self-reliant institutions for self-help and collective good. The new role of cooperatives emerges from this background. They are seen as alternative banks in the Indian context, making an important contribution at a very local level in terms of financial requirement, and they are also rather insulated from global risks, as seeking profits is not their only motive. The following discussion shows how cooperative banks are trying to seek a unique space for themselves, both in financial inclusions and in banking.

Occupying New Spaces

The globalization and liberalization of economic policies create new spaces in two forms. First, the government starts withdrawing from different domains thus far solely or generally occupied by them, creating vacant spaces, be it in manufacturing or in the services industry. Second, additional opportunities are continuously being created in newer areas under the new economic environment. Many of these domains are not regarded as being commercially attractive. However, they are very important for people and communities, and there is definitely a demand for these services. The challenge would be to make them commercially viable and profitable. Traditional social sectors, such as education, health, transportation, water supply, forest management and electricity, are some of the areas where 'cooperative solutions could be superior to either public or private approaches to utility management'.[18] In fact privatization efforts in India have already been made in this area. Cooperatives have been working in all these fields and have the potential to prove their strength, and in some cases have indeed proved to be effective alternatives to privatization. Furthermore, cooperatives are playing a major role in newer areas, such as precision farming, sun farming, water harvesting and microfinance. Other potential areas are information technology, communications, tourism and hospitality, etc., the demand for which is ever growing and which could provide alternative means of livelihood for cooperative members. Outsourcing of services would also be the practice as firms grow in size and specialization. Such outsourcing would expectedly lead to savings in transaction costs. Entering such services through the cooperative route could prove an attractive alternative employment-generating avenue.

The success of a cooperative bank has been only due to good governance and non-interference from the state government. All over the country cooperative banks collectively might look sick, but an individual analysis throws light on the fact that these banks have been able to break new ground, as discussed above, and are in a unique local position for financing the immediate needs of infrastructure and business. Hence their role in local development is very important.

Providing an Institutional Form for the Displaced

Globalization would also result in restructuring, leading to displacements due to exit policies, labour re-engineering, closure of less competitive units, adoption of new technologies and consequent downsizing, mergers, acquisitions, etc. including displacement from the agricultural sector. As pointed out earlier, displaced specialists could form cooperatives for providing essential specialized services that institutions would be increasingly outsourcing. The 2001 Census has clearly shown a sharp reduction in the population dependent on agriculture and an increase in the number of landless labourers. The alarming rate of unemployment among youth also continues in India. Collective endeavours through cooperatives of such marginalized sections of the people have worked, as many services would still be required by existing concerns, which may not wish to have such a service provider on their payroll.

Constructive Competitor

Cartels or predetermined market sharing by private enterprises can jeopardize free and fair trade. Cooperatives have, in this case, often played the role of the 'constructive competitor'. This could be either through a standalone cooperative or by entering into strategic partnership with the private sector in the form of cooperative–private sector collaborations. Cooperatives by their very presence have helped to maintain the balance in terms of price and quality in several regions. For this reason, several cooperatives have shown that full domination by the private corporate sector could eventually spell bad news to the consumers.

Safeguarding the Interests of Agriculture and Rural Areas

Agriculture will continue to be very important in terms of percentage share of population in India. The logic of agriculture would be applicable to almost the entire rural population too. Self-help initiatives by farmers in the areas of cultivation, marketing, accessing agricultural inputs, and finding jobs for landless labourers, displaced rural artisans, etc. continue to be a major role for the cooperative sector. No one else is equipped to handle this in India.

Facilitating Millennium Development Goals (MDGs)

The Government of India is committed to achieving the United Nations MDGs within a specified time frame. Yet in many of the specified areas, the country is clearly lagging behind. Rural health, and in particular maternal health, the fight against contagious diseases (through medical cooperatives), gender equity (through women's cooperatives), and poverty reduction (through agricultural and tribal cooperatives) are some of the crucial areas under MDGs where the cooperative sector is playing the lead role and where the private sector is failing.

Preserving the Cultural and Ethical Values of the Country

Cooperatives are the best channels to keep the spirit of collectivism and democracy afloat. The presence of a large network of social organizations, like cooperatives, would aid in the generation and utilization of social capital; and 'greater the social capital greater would be the possibility of development'.[19] Therefore cooperatives have an important role to play in the future for fostering collectivism and preserving the social capital base of the country.

It is thus clear that cooperatives have a significant role to play in the future setting of the Indian economy. In fact, they have a more important role to play in the future compared to their past role as agents of the state. It is only the presence of a strong and wide network of cooperatives that can make the process of globalization less painful and global integration smooth. It is the cooperatives again who are equipped to work as pressure groups to voice peoples' views in the market.

Analysis of Cooperative Banks in India, 2001–10

Profit/Loss of Cooperative Banks

Figure 11.2 clearly shows that the cooperative banks in India have collectively been profitable in the years 2001 to 2010. Because their mission was always social in nature, they have sought high profits while not taking high risks like commercial banks. As can been seen from the figure, cooperative banks' profits rose in the crisis year 2008, showing how they were insulated from the effects of the crisis and how they acted more as alternative banks than as purely for-profit institutions. Figure 11.3 shows, furthermore, how NPAs have been decreasing as a percentage of loans outstanding (as per Basel norms). This testifies that cooperative banks do adhere to sound banking principles while continuing to play an important role in fulfilling credit needs at the local level.

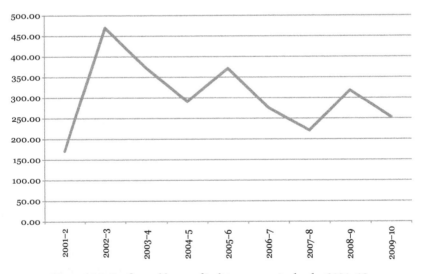

Figure 11.2: Profits and losses of Indian cooperative banks, 2001–10.

Source: Data from Reserve Bank of India.

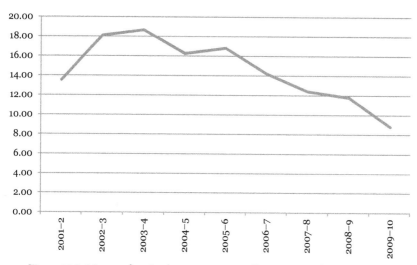

Figure 11.3: Non-performing loans as per cent of loans outstanding, 2001–10.

Source: Data from Reserve Bank of India.

Liabilities have been increasing at a steady state since 2001. A careful breakdown of its components reveals that no type of liability has increased significantly except for deposits, which rose by almost 30 per cent from 2008 onwards (see Table 11.1 in the Appendix). This could be explained by the rising importance of these local banks during times of crisis – an argument developed in Chapters 3 and 4 of the present volume.

Assets too have been increasing steadily, and a careful investigation of their breakdown reveals that most of the increase in funds since 2008 has not gone towards loans but instead towards investment, and in particular investment in government securities (see Table 11.2 in the Appendix). This shows that these banks have been very risk-averse and have no need to excessively diversify their loan portfolio. However, holding government securities is often compulsory. We argue here that this should end and that cooperative banks should be free to allocate more funds to lending for their growth.

Source of Capital

Figure 11.4 shows that the basic nature of the cooperative bank has been retained at all times in terms of the dominant source of capital. More than 50 per cent of cooperative banks' capital has come from cooperatives themselves, while other sources have been much less important. One of the reasons why the interference of the state governments can be very high in spite of its capital share being low is because of the individual affiliation to political parties being very strong in several states. This needs to be broken, as evidenced in several states where good governance has given rise to development and social inclusion.

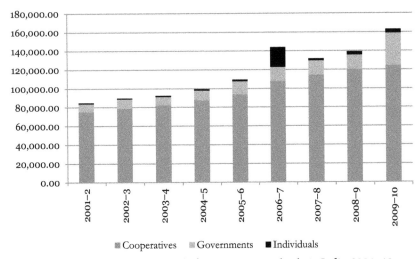

Figure 11.4: Paid-up share capital of state cooperative banks in India, 2001–10.

Source: Data from Reserve Bank of India.

Application of Funds

Figure 11.5 shows that cooperative banks, which have spearheaded the movement of short- and long-term lending in the agricultural sector in the first three phases of its development in India, are now moving towards lending in the non-agricultural sphere. This is a clear shift, and this jump happened in the year 2005–6, after which both short-term and long-term credit have been provided by these banks.

Membership

The total number of bank windows and branches has remained more or less stagnant, with very little growth in the past decade (see Table 11.3 in the Appendix). Similarly, the number of cooperative societies also grew rather slowly. However in the year 2009–10 a spike can be seen in the growth in individual and government membership, which has also contributed to the growth in total membership.

Cost Efficiency

Salaries have been increasing but other expenses have been decreasing, showing a certain amount of prudence in management in cooperative banks (see Table 11.4 in the Appendix). The total number of employees in the sector peaked in 2001–2, and cooperative banks have tried to be efficient by keeping its working capital as well its other expenses rather low.

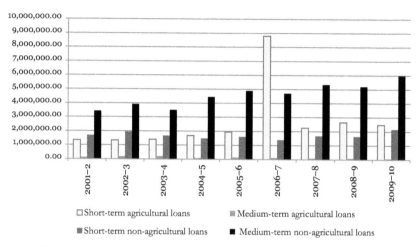

10,000,000.00
9,000,000.00
8,000,000.00
7,000,000.00
6,000,000.00
5,000,000.00
4,000,000.00
3,000,000.00
2,000,000.00
1,000,000.00
0.00

2001–2 2002–3 2003–4 2004–5 2005–6 2006–7 2007–8 2008–9 2009–10

☐ Short-term agricultural loans   ▦ Medium-term agricultural loans

▪ Short-term non-agricultural loans   ■ Medium-term non-agricultural loans

Figure 11.5: Agricultural and non-agricultural loans in India, 2001–10.

Source: Data from Reserve Bank of India.

Challenges Faced by Cooperative Banks in India

Membership

Theoretically and conceptually, a cooperative comes into being as the result of a common need between members. Ensuring 'active' member participation and enabling speedy exit of non-user members have remained a daunting task for cooperatives in India. Unfortunately, over the years we have come to a situation where either a large number of cooperatives are unable to cope with the needs of their members, or the members have in general become passive and apathetic and do not use the services offered. Quite a number of cooperatives have also become irrelevant to their members' needs. Poor member participation has also been due to the lack of effort to enhance member equity in cooperatives and the nea -absence of member communication and awareness-building efforts.

Governance

In an organizational context, governance refers to the institutional framework that defines the structure and relationships between stakeholders, their behaviour, interactions, rules of conduct, conflict resolution, and incentives and disincentives for behaviour. In cooperatives, governance issues primarily arise at the level of the board and its relationship with members, managers and the state. Sadly, the most important function of governance, which is that of aligning the tasks in tune with the basic objective with which a cooperative is organized, has received very little attention. The banks wherein governance has been given importance have done well in terms of profitability and responding to local needs, while those with state interference have floundered continuously.

Lack of Recognition of Cooperatives as Economic Institutions

A fundamental issue having substantial bearing on the governance of cooperative institutions is the lack of recognition of cooperatives as economic institutions meant to serve the needs of its members. The general perception has been that cooperatives are instruments of government meant for public good and therefore need to be supported by the government.

Design-Related Issues

The 'design' of a cooperative is an important factor in determining the manner in which it is governed, its success and its viability. While designing a cooperative enterprise, one needs to consider factors such as local sociopolitical conditions, local economy, leadership, structure, by-laws, norms and rules, critical links with federal and other organizations, macro policies, etc.

Most cooperatives in the country have come into being through a top-down approach or based on a blueprint model, and are a result of target-based programmes/actions taken by higher-tier organizations and state departments. Besides, there are numerous instances of suppression of local initiatives and ignoring the perceived needs of the members while structuring the cooperatives. Higher-tier cooperatives in most cases have hardly retained any cooperative character and operate like parasites, frequently with little or no member involvement.

Capital

Lack of capital, both equity and debt, are key constraints to the development and growth of cooperatives. In the case of value-added businesses, the problem is further compounded due to their high capital requirements. The need for equity in all forms of organization arises out of the requirement of containing the financial risk of debt within reasonable limits.

Conclusions

A cooperative bank by principle serves the needs of its members. Our analysis shows that in India during the period 2001–10, these banks have been profitable and not very risky. Having noted the challenges of the cooperative banks stemming from its capital, membership, design issues or governance, this chapter does clearly bring out the fact that these banks are very important local financial institutions. Their ability to process soft, local information is particularly crucial in India, where 'hard' information (such as credit history) about a vast majority of people is not readily available. In other words, the main way for banks to know about most clients in India is to access and process local knowledge, mostly captured through local presence, and small banks have proven to be much better at doing this. Big banks tend to skim the surface, while small banks can and usually do go deeper and provide services to many more. Complete financial inclusion means providing financial services at a high quality, so that people use the services actively. Quality can be understood in terms of the convenience, flexibility and reliability of these services, which are universal terms but must be defined locally. When cooperative banks are successful, this is due to understanding the local clients. This is their unique selling position and how they are alternative banks. In India they have recently diversified their lending outside of agriculture, a diversification that seems to be paying off. They do take risks, but these seem more calculated and better understood than those of commercial banks. Profit maximization has never been the goal. In India, if only the state interference disappears in these banks, they could perform much better than they are already doing.

Appendix

Table 11.1: Liabilities of Indian cooperative banks, 2000–10 (in crores).

Year	Capital	Reserves	Deposits	Borrowings	Other liabilities	Total liabilities
2000	636	4,266	29,557	10,859	2,260	47,578
2001	695	5,144	32,626	11,693	2,317	52,476
2002	844	5,879	36,190	11,672	2,903	57,488
2003	835	6,989	38,940	12,113	2,807	61,684
2004	1,032	8,068	47,405	14,228	3,624	74,357
2005	1,096	9,130	48,491	16,407	3,604	78,728
2006	1,115	9,433	45,403	16,988	3,542	76,481
2007	1,245	9,303	48,560	22,256	4,392	85,756
2008	1,468	9,250	52,973	22,164	4,296	90,151
2009	1,569	10,190	71,519	21,002	5,279	109,559
2010	1,636	10,382	83,034	23,639	6,272	124,963

Legend: Crore = ten million = 10^7. Lakh = one hundred thousand = 10^5.

Source: Reserve Bank of India.

Table 11.2: Assets of Indian cooperative banks, 2000–10 (in crores).

Year	Cash in hand and balances with banks	Investments	Loans and advances	Other assets	Accumulated losses	Total assets
2000	2,663	15,343	25,709	3,368	496	47,578
2001	2,313	16,156	29,861	3,653	493	52,476
2002	3,545	16,855	32,678	3,830	568	57,476
2003	3,868	18,662	34,509	4,029	342	61,410
2004	6,643	23,383	39,497	4,570	264	74,357
2005	7,301	24,687	41,894	4,573	273	78,728
2006	4,323	27,696	39,685	4,505	272	76,481
2007	9,290	24,140	47,354	4,583	389	85,756
2008	8,065	29,060	48,228	4,403	395	90,151
2009	7,874	48,087	48,370	4,771	457	109,559
2010	9,402	58,608	49,243	7,136	574	124,963

Source: Reserve Bank of India.

Table 11.3: Indian cooperative banks' membership details, 2001–10.

Year	Number of offices incl. head office	Membership Cooperative societies	Membership Individuals and government	Total membership
2001–2	899	17,029	100,514	117,543
2002–3	931	19,133	114,555	133,688
2003–4	929	17,288	133,687	150,975
2004–5	953	17,545	139,078	156,623
2005–6	962	20,103	133,594	153,697
2006–7	938	21,390	127,381	148,771
2007–8	994	19,414	181,354	200,768
2008–9	992	19,424	181,348	200,772
2009–10	1,015	19,732	311,076	330,808

Source: National Federation of State Cooperative Banks.

Table 11.4: Cost of management at Indian cooperative banks, 2001–10.

Year	Cost of management (CoM) (in lakhs) Salaries	Other expenses	Total	% of CoM to working capital	Total number of employees (in lakhs)	% of CoM per employee
2001–2	30,772	77,439	108,211	1.91	16,360	6.61
2002–3	32,034	93,563	125,597	2.07	15,793	7.95
2003–4	32,995	82,734	115,729	1.77	15,554	7.44
2004–5	36,841	73,674	110,515	1.56	15,288	7.23
2005–6	38,184	53,015	91,199	1.22	14,742	6.19
2006–7	41,226	26,203	67,429	0.81	14,748	4.57
2007–8	43,919	86,146	130,065	1.25	14,857	9.17
2008–9	46,580	84,577	131,157	1.24	14,635	8.96
2009–10	58,774	40,111	98,885	0.81	13,781	7.18

Source: National Federation of State Cooperative Banks Ltd.

CONCLUSION

Kurt von Mettenheim and Olivier Butzbach

The contributions to this volume identify anomalies about alternative banking for contemporary banking theory and counter expectations of convergence towards private market-based banking. In Europe, more than a decade after liberalization of the industry and thirteen years after monetary union, the realization of competitive advantages by alternative banks belies expectations of convergence towards joint-stock commercial and investment banking. In the BRICs and many developing countries, government banks have also realized competitive advantages over private and foreign banks (even after liberalization) to provide counter-cyclical credit and remain agents of public policy able to shape growth. Privatizations and liberalization were expected to replace traditional deposit-taking and loan-making banks and non-joint-stock forms of bank ownership and governance with more efficient private banks as financial intermediaries. The record explored herein suggests otherwise. Where alternative banks were not privatized or demutualized, a 'back to the future' modernization of these institutions ensued. This is true of savings banks and cooperative banks in Europe and abroad, especially in developing and emerging countries that retain large government banks with imposing market shares. European special purpose banks have also modernized to pursue new development strategies for the greening of industry, investing in communities and accelerating the use of new technologies.

This Conclusion explores the implications these findings for banking theory, comparative research in political economy and financial economics, and paradigms for bank regulation. For banking theory, the realization of competitive advantages by savings banks, cooperative banks and special purpose banks since liberalization amidst the radical changes in banking caused by new technologies suggests that a back-to-basics approach is in order. While the US has encouraged the consolidation of a select number of large investment banks that morphed into commercial banks, most other countries retain more traditional profiles of deposit-taking and loan-making banks and more alternative non-joint-stock banks such as savings banks, cooperative banks and special purpose banks. Contemporary banking theory therefore projects the US experience of disintermediation abroad and fails to account for the persistence of both traditional banking and alternative banks.

In 1998 White reviewed trends in banking theory to argue that past traditions of real bills had, in fact, given way to research that viewed banks as financial intermediaries.[1] Unfortunately, White left mutual savings banks aside as an anomaly. However, his general advice about research on banking remains valid. To build on the research reported in this volume, two strategies appear most promising. The first is to build on the considerable research available on cooperatives and non-joint-stock firms and new institutional economics. Alongside the bulk of research on private, market-based corporate governance, a significant literature during the 1990s and 2000s nonetheless continued to focus on non-joint-stock firms.[2] This literature accumulated considerable understanding of alternative traditions of governance and management and promises to clarify the institutional foundations of competitive advantage in alternative banking.[3] The broader contributions of new institutional economics about transaction costs, agency costs and theories of stakeholding governance also provide a rich series of theories and concepts that may explain the findings on alternative banking reported in this volume.

The second strategy for research on alternative banks is to pursue alternative theories of banking. Banks and banking theory have long been part of economics and quite independent from other social sciences. From this perspective, banks are and should remain independent from social and political pressures that produce bad equilibria. However, the increasing prevalence of banking and financial crises and their rising social costs suggest that banking theory needs to build bridges with the disciplines of political science and sociology. In this respect, evidence that relational banking, retail banking and social and political foundations of competitive advantage are at the heart of alternative banking promises to help overcome the separation of banking studies from the other social sciences. This second research strategy of pursuing alternative theories of banking implies reinserting banks in broader social contexts and institutions of politics and policymaking. This means posing questions about citizenship, equality, development as freedom, political capture, and how democratization and new public management may shape banking, public policy and growth.

This runs against a long tradition of economics that sees the emergence of private banking and credit as the essence of modernization and the separation of markets from society and politics as necessary for freedom and optimal equilibrium. However, the institutional diversity of alternative banking suggests that banking theory may also need to diversify. Contemporary banking theory retains core assumptions of economics: that markets imply an independent sphere of behaviour, and that freedom from government, social interests and political capture are needed to ensure optimal equilibrium and maximize welfare. Alternative banks and the 'back to the future' modernization of social banking and development banking imply movement in the opposite direction. Banking, from the perspectives of alternative banking, implies the embedding of credit and banking in social relations, politics and government policymaking. For cooperative banks, banking theory requires a sociological analysis of local credit relations, democratic governance and benefits accrued to members and local communities or functional groups served by cooperative banks. For local and regional savings banks, banking theory requires concepts and theories from political science, sociology and public policy for analysis of how these banks serve local and regional governments and communities. For special purpose banks, further concepts from political science and public administration are needed to evaluate how these banks may increase policy coordination, multiply money from limited budgets, and increase contractual control over policy implementation. All banks may share core characteristics. However, banking theory must accommodate the wide variety of banks and different types of banking, rather than assuming that all banks seek to maximize profit and shareholder returns or insisting that banks serve primarily as financial intermediaries.

The findings in this volume about alternative banks also challenge scholars of comparative political economy to improve understanding of banks and financial markets. Agreement is increasing that financialization may be the most important phenomena of political economy in the advanced economies. However, comparative research on advanced economies still tends to focus primarily on topics other than banking, such as labour relations, manufacturing, service industries, corporate governance, the impact of new technologies and other themes. Remarkably, the landmark volume by Hall and Soskice on varieties of capitalism, published in 2001, contained no chapter on banking and finance, despite recognition by the editors in the introduction to the volume that the sector is central for understanding both liberal market economies and coordinated market economies.[4] Our findings on alternative banking call for more considered comparison of banking in the two varieties of capitalism and beyond in comparative political economy. The much larger market share of cooperative banks, savings banks and special purpose banks in coordinated market economies than in liberal market economies indicates how important these differences are for debates about advanced economies in comparative political economy.[5]

Another implication of our findings on alternative banks for comparative political economy has to do with the welcome focus on firms and the micro or organizational level of analysis to emphasize institutional foundations of competitive advantage. Although this approach has been widely accepted in comparative political economy, we are unaware of studies that apply this approach to banks. As banking theory has long suggested, banks are a specific type of firm, with different balance sheets, revenue streams, governance traditions and accounting practices. Given the critical place of banks in economies, and our findings that many competitive advantages of alternative banks are indeed related to institutional characteristics, this area of research promises to improve understanding of alternative banks and, at the same time, improve understanding of advanced economies by placing the institutional foundations of banks at the centre of debates.

The implications of our findings about alternative banks for comparative financial economics are also considerable. Critics of government banking have prevailed for decades and continue to insist that privatization improves banking and releases market forces.[6] Finding that government banks have pursued internal reforms and responded to liberalization of banking to realize competitive advantages over private and foreign banks suggests that critics of government banks fail to capture the causal mechanisms of bank change and, specifically, government bank management and performance. Many assertions of critics about political capture, crony credit and inefficiencies in government banking are valid, especially in the past in developing countries under military rule, or single-party authoritarian governments, or imperfect democracies soon after transition from authoritarianism. However, the record of government bank change in BRICs and other developing countries, and the continued importance of government banks in advanced economies, suggest that positive concepts and theories about these institutions are needed. Critical theories of government banks cannot explain how these institutions may realize competitive advantages and improve public policymaking. In this sense, critics of government banks provide half of the theories and concepts we need: those able to explain mismanagement, abuse and capture. Comparative financial economics needs the other half: concepts and theories able to account for the competitive advantages and policy capacities of government banks reported in this volume.

Our findings about alternative banking also have implications for bank regulation and supervision. For decades, international institutions such as the International Monetary Fund and the Bank for International Settlements have retained biases favouring private banks and market-based banking. International regulatory frameworks and domestic central banks and monetary authorities have sought to encourage disintermediation as modernization in the belief that traditional deposit-taking and loan-making banking was less efficient that market-based banking. Since the 2008 crisis, different perspectives have emerged. Domestic monetary authorities are seeking to reform banking in a wide variety of new policies and strategies to avert further crises. Many new approaches return to the basics of banking. UK regulators have called for ring-fencing retail banking from market-based banking to protect depositors and local relational and retail banking from the financial risks associated with investment banking. Basel Accords have sought to increase capital reserve requirements to reduce the leverage of private banks and market-based banking. However, capture of Basel

II Accord rules by investment banks altered the definition of capital reserves to include the very financial products that the Accord sought to build capital reserves against.[7] In this respect, evidence presented in this volume about how alternative banks were able to avert the excessive leverage and risk taking by private banks that caused the financial crisis of 2008 is especially important for reconsideration of regulatory frameworks.

Alternative banking also presents opportunities for the broader reassessment of monetary theory and policy. Until the financial crisis of 2008, banks remained largely seen as neutral institutions in broader monetary dynamics. From the Miller–Modigliani theorem of 1958 through the growth models of Lucas, money creation was seen as exogenous.[8] This broader view is inconsistent with theories of banking that emphasize the multiplication of money through credit and finance. Banking has long been seen as a multiplier of money in two senses. First, banks multiply money twofold, when they loan money and register the loan as an asset on balance sheets while retaining the value of deposits on balance sheets as a liability that made it possible to extend credit. Second, banks multiply money up to tenfold in terms of equity capital or capital reserves. In this second sense, capitalization of equity or increases in capital reserves can cover up to tenfold their value in terms of finance or credit, according to Basel II capital accord requirements of 8 per cent reserves, ignoring risk weighting.

Moreover, advances in monetary theory and modernization of central banks and monetary authorities suggest that alternative banks face different regulatory contexts and constraints. Advances in monetary theory during the 1990s, exemplified by concepts such as the credit channel and interest rate channel, and the modernization of central banking during the 2000s with the adoption of new information and communication technologies to better supervise banks and markets, add up to suggest that alternative banking may provide new channels for social and political forces different from the hard fiscal constraints that have wracked economies since the 1970s. From this perspective, cooperative banks and savings banks provide new channels for change that may build capital in local communities and regions without pressuring fiscal accounts or inflation. Special purpose banks also provide important alternatives to governments under fiscal constraints because, as banks, these institutions may multiply and leverage budget allocations. The question of what governments and local cooperative banks and savings banks can do and cannot do is set not, most importantly, by fiscal constraints but by the place of these alternative banks in monetary flows and channels of credit and interest rates. For a world accustomed to fixating on fiscal constraints, advances in monetary economics and the modernization of monetary authorities provide important new channels for change largely unexplored by social scientists.

Our findings about alternative banking also have implications for heterodox approaches to money and banking. Post-Keynesian scholars also focus on the multiplication of money and bank balance sheets.[9] However, insistence that banks *first* sell loans to create assets only to later cover these operations with liabilities seems to elevate the abuses of profit-maximizing private banks that fail to control credit sales with standard or universal practices at all banks. This incurs the same risk as Minskyian critics of financial instability – that of asserting that the most problematic aspects of private banking are shared by all banks, including the banks under study in this volume. Although further analysis is required, alternative bank balance sheets, historically and today under the prudent policies of cooperative and savings bank management, suggest that deposits do indeed come first and lending comes second, after the accumulation of not only liabilities but also reserves sufficient to cover operations. This, of course, goes against core ideas about perfect and liquid markets that, supposedly, let banks manage risk in fundamentally different ways, but that cuts to the question of market-based banking that also is not shared by traditional alternative banks. In sum, Post-Keynesian analyses of sales strategies and excessive leverage (of credit over deposits) at private commercial and investment banks appear not to capture the behaviour of alternative banks that maintain prudent leverage and control sales divisions better than profit-maximizing private banks.

Minskyian approaches also risk reproducing their object of criticism, that is to say the excessive leverage of private banks in capital markets that drive cycles of financial instability. Theories and concepts from Minsky have proven very effective for analysis of increasing cycles of debt-driven growth and capital market crises in the US and beyond since the 1980s.[10] However, by defining banks and banking along lines of market-based banking, research in the Minskyian tradition risks reifying its very object of criticism. Two implications follow. First, for countries with important alternative banking sectors, whether cooperative banks, savings banks or government banks, Minskyian approaches are very effective at explaining how banks produce crisis. However, they fail to explain how traditional deposit-taking loan-making banks and, especially, alternative banks may serve to avert the excesses of market-centred banking and private banks and therefore ameliorate or eliminate Minskyian cycles altogether.

The second implication of Minskyian definitions of banking along the lines of market-centred banking and private banking is that realities in the US become an unexamined presupposition about banking abroad. To the extent that alternative banking continues to thrive abroad, Minskyian definitions of banks tend to project the US experience and overestimate the importance of market-based banking. Moreover, even in the US, traditional community banks, credit unions, mutual savings banks, the farm credit system and other government-sponsored financial enterprises sum to considerable market shares of banking in the country. In this respect, the 1992 proposal of Minsky et al. to create community development banks in the US stands out. Unless alternative banking is taken seriously, Minskyian approaches that focus on private banks and capital markets may overlook the importance of alternative banking and traditional banking. Minsky's view of community development banks provides an opportunity to reassess analyses of financial instability in a broader comparative perspective that includes a focus on alternative banking sectors.

This matters because alternative banks provide alternatives at central points of the Minskyian model of financial instability. Crises of confidence and market downturns break highly leveraged banks because they are exposed to market pricing and liquidity risk of liabilities. However, alternative banks tend to retain more conservative portfolios that are less subject to market downturns. A more traditional deposit base of liabilities and greater confidence of clients and depositors combine to make alternative banks less subject to liquidity risk. And where alternative banks retain large market shares, these micro or institutional characteristics provide buffers against meso or macro movements that may reduce economic downturns and make it possible for alternative banks to stay market crashes. Because alternative banks retain long-term profit sustainability orientations, unique cultures of management that remit to their social origins or public policy missions, they also tend to avert the excesses of marketing and sales that joint-stock banks and short-term profit maximization orientations produce. In sum, alternative banks tend to avert the creation of financial and credit bubbles during economic upswings and are able to provide counter-cyclical credit and finance to reinforce confidence and ameliorate the impact of market crashes and corrections. The concepts, methods and theories of Minskyian approaches to financial instability cycles provide opportunities for analysis of these claims.

The findings reported in this volume also call for the reassessment of bank change in Europe. This is an especially promising area, given that the wide variety of change since liberalization, monetary union and creation of a single banking market provide a quasi-experimental situation for case studies and comparisons. In Germany, all three traditional pillars of the banking system appear to have modernized. Savings banks in France consolidated from small local and regional banks into larger regional groups to modernize operations and sustain market share. Italian savings banks were privatized, but shares were used to endow savings bank foundations charged with continuing the traditional social policies of these institutions. Swedish savings banks were also privatized, but they appear to continue to pursue many of the social functions despite this change in corporate governance. Spanish savings banks notoriously pursued market-based banking strategies and helped drive the real estate bubble that burst after the crisis in 2008; this imposed losses on clients' savings and contributed to the economic downturn in the country. Austrian savings banks and cooperative banks also pursued expansion throughout Eastern and Central Europe in ways that appear to combine market-based banking and the more traditional profiles of these banking groups. In the Netherlands, the recovery of Rabobank from declines during the 1990s to rapid growth after the 2000 crisis has placed a cooperative bank at the centre of political economy and foreign business strategies in the country. European experiences with bank change since liberalization and monetary union provide examples of diverse strategies and patterns of change that will require case studies and comparative analyses.

In a broader sense, the reassessment of bank change will require that researchers overcome biases against alternative banks. This bias against alternative banks can be seen in works by Marxists and liberals since the nineteenth century. For many Marxists, savings banks and credit cooperatives remained utopian socialism that concealed capitalist realities from workers and kept them from the party fold. For example, Peabody cites the English socialist leader Bax:

> The socialists are radically at variance with thrift. A man who works at his trade more than his necessity compels him, or who accumulates more than he can enjoy, is not a hero but a fool from the socialist's point of view.[11]

This ignored the more positive views of cooperative movements held by Marx and Engels.[12] In 1906 the liberal economist Gide also criticized savings banks as, at best, preliminary piggy banks that, once they accumulate savings, should give way to more effective allocation of savings by private banks and financial markets. This perception among liberal economists of traditional banking at savings banks and cooperative banks (more accurately their retail networks, not their shared wholesale divisions and capital market operations) has pervaded research and policy in political economy through the latter twentieth and early twenty-first centuries.

The evidence about alternative banking reported in this volume presents important anomalies for theories of banking, political economy and financial economics. Since financial market liberalization in Europe and emerging countries, expectations about private banks and market-based banking have led research and policy to underestimate alternative banking. Instead of disappearing, however, either sooner through privatizations or later under the competitive pressures of private and foreign banks, alternative banks have drawn on institutional foundations of competitive advantage to retain or expand market shares in rapidly changing markets for credit, finance and related products and services. Contrary to expectations of many researchers, policymakers and international financial institutions, the twenty-first century has begun with a resurgence of cooperative banks, savings banks and special purpose banks.

NOTES

Butzbach and Mettenheim, 'Introduction'

1. G. Gorton, *Slapped by the Invisible Hand: The Panic of 2007* (Oxford: Oxford University Press, 2010); P. De Grauwe, 'Lessons from the Baking Crisis: A Return to Narrow Banking', *CESifo DICE Report*, 2 (2009), pp. 19–23.
2. See R. La Porta, F. Lopez-de-Silanes and A. Schleifer, 'Government Ownership of Banks', *Journal of Finance*, 57:1 (2002), pp. 265–301.
3. K. Matthews and J. Thompson, *The Economics of Banking*, 2nd edn (Chichester: John Wiley and Sons, 2008).
4. A. N. Berger, P. Molyneux and J. O. S. Wilson (eds), *The Oxford Handbook of Banking* (Oxford: Oxford University Press, 2010).
5. See, for instance, G. Bertocco, 'Are Banks Special? A Note on Tobin's Theory of Financial Intermediaries', Università dell'Insubria Working Paper, 2006/5 (2006); or E. Nasica, 'Rational and Innovative Behaviours at the Core of Financial Crises: Banking in Minsky's Theory', in D. B. Papadimitriou and L. R. Wray (eds), *The Elgar Companion to Hyman Minsky* (Cheltenham: Edward Elgar, 2010), pp. 100–16.
6. S. R. Akella and S. I. Greenbaum, 'Savings and Loans Ownership Structure and Expense Preference', *Journal of Banking and Finance*, 12 (1988), pp. 419–37; H. Hansmann, 'The Economic Role of Commercial Nonprofits: The Role of the US Savings Banks Industry', in H. Anheier and W. Seibel (eds), *The Third Sector: Comparative Studies of Nonprofit Organizations* (Berlin and New York: De Gruyter, 1988); E. Rasmussen, 'Stock Banks and Mutual Banks', *Journal of Law and Economics*, 31 (1988), pp. 395–422; J. Kay, 'The Economics of Mutuality', *Annals of Public and Cooperative Economics*, 62:3 (1991), pp. 309–18; D. Mayers and C. Smith, 'Managerial Discretion, Regulation and Stock Insurance Ownership Structure', *Journal of Risk and Insurance*, 61:4 (1994), pp. 638–55; H. Hansmann, *The Ownership of Enterprise* (Cambridge, MA: Harvard University Press, 1996); O. Hart and J. Moore, 'Cooperatives vs. Outside Ownership', NBER Working Paper, W6421 (1998); L. Drake and D. T. Llewellyn, 'The Economics of Mutuality: A Perspective on UK Building Societies', in J. Birchall (ed.), *The New Mutualism in Public Policy* (London: Routledge, 2001), pp. 14–40; E. Gurtner, M. Jaeger and J.-N. Ory, 'Le Statut de Coopérative Est-il Source d'Efficacité dans le Secteur Bancaire?', *Revue d'Économie Financière*, 67 (2002), pp. 133–63; La Porta, Lopez-de-Silanes and Schleifer, 'Government Ownership of Banks'; M. Desrochers and K. Fischer, 'The Power of Networks: Integration and Financial Cooperative Performance', *Annals of Public and Cooperative Economics*, 76:3 (2005), pp. 307–54; P. McGregor, 'Credit Unions and

the Supply of Insurance to Low Income Households', *Annals of Public and Cooperative Economics*, 76:3 (2005), pp. 355–74; D. G. McKillop, 'Financial Cooperatives: Structure, Conduct, Performance', *Annals of Public and Cooperative Economics*, 76:3 (2005), pp. 301–5; C. E. Cuevas and K. P. Fischer, 'Cooperative Financial Institutions. Issues in Governance, Supervision and Regulation', World Bank Working Paper, 82 (2006); W. Fonteyne, 'Cooperative Banks in Europe – Policy Issues', IMF Working Paper, WP/07/159 (2007); H. Hesse and M. Čihák, 'Cooperative Banks and Financial Stability', IMF Working Paper, WP/07/02 (2007); D. G. McKillop and J. O. S. Wilson, 'Credit Unions: A Theoretical and Empirical Overview', *Financial Markets, Institutions and Instruments*, 20:3 (2011), pp. 79–123; and C. Marsal, 'La Gouvernance Mutualiste Comme Levier de Contrôle: Le Cas d'une Banque', *Annals of Public and Cooperative Economics*, 84:1 (2013), pp. 83–101.

7. For a scathing account of how the OTS dealt with the downfall of Washington Mutual, see K. Grind, *The Lost Bank: The Story of Washington Mutual – the Biggest Bank Failure in American History* (New York: Simon & Schuster, 2012).

8. A. Liikanen, *High Level Expert Group on Reforming the Structure of the EU Banking Sector* (Brussels: European Commission, 2012).

9. J. Michie and C. Oughton, 'Measuring Diversity in Financial Services Markets: A Diversity Index', Centre for Financial and Management Studies Discussion Paper Series, 113 (2013).

10. Liikanen, *High Level Expert Group*.

11. V. V. Acharya and T. Yorulmazer, 'Too Many To Fail: An Analysis of Time-Inconsistency in Bank Closure Policies', *Journal of Financial Intermediation*, 16 (2007), pp. 1–31.

12. A. G. Haldane and R. M. May, 'Systemic Risk in Banking Ecosystems', *Nature*, 469:20 (2011), pp. 351–5. See also Liikanen, *High Level Expert Group*; and J. Michie, 'Promoting Corporate Diversity in the Financial Services Sector', *Policy Studies*, 32:4 (2011), pp. 309–23.

13. Michie, 'Promoting Corporate Diversity', p. 310.

14. HM Treasury, *A New Approach to Financial Regulation: Judgement, Focus and Stability* (London: TSO, 2010), p. 32.

15. Liikanen, *High Level Expert Group*, ch. 3.

16. Michie, 'Promoting Corporate Diversity'.

17. See J. Cook, S. Deakin and A. Hughes, 'Mutuality and Corporate Governance: The Evolution of Building Societies Following Deregulation', ESRC Centre for Business Research, University of Cambridge, Working Paper, 205 (2001).

18. D. Canning, C. W. Jefferson and J. E. Spencer, 'Optimal Credit Rationing in Not-For-Profit Financial Institutions', *International Economic Review*, 4:1 (2003), pp. 243–61, on p. 244.

19. A. N. Berger, G. R. G. Clarke, R. Cull, L. Klapper and G. F. Udell, 'Corporate Governance and Bank Performance: A Joint Analysis of the Static, Selection, and Dynamic Effects of Domestic, Foreign, and State Ownership', *Journal of Banking and Finance*, 29:8–9 (2005), pp. 2179–221.

1 Mettenheim and Butzbach, 'Alternative Banking History'

1. On the second tier of cooperative banks, see T. W. Guinnane, 'Delegated Monitors, Large and Small: Germany's Banking System, 1800–1914', *Journal of Economic Literature*, 40:1 (2002), pp. 73–124.

2.   B. Aghion, 'Development Banking', *Journal of Development Economics*, 58 (1999), pp. 83–100; W. Diamond, *Development Banks* (Baltimore, MD: Johns Hopkins University Press, 1957); J. Zysman, *Governments, Markets, and Growth: Financial Systems and Politics of Industrial Change* (Ithaca, NY: Cornell University Press, 1983).
3.   K. Polanyi, *The Great Transformation* (New York: Rinehart, 1944).
4.   R. Bogaert, *Les origines antiques de la banque de dépot* (Leyden: Sijthoff, 1966).
5.   P. C. Millett, *Lending and Borrowing in Ancient Athens* (Cambridge: Cambridge University Press, 1991); and J. Andreau, *La Vie financière dans le monde romain Les métiers de manieurs d'argent (IVe siècle av. J.-C.-IIIe siècle apr. J.-C.)* (Rome: École française de Rome, 1987).
6.   Plato, *Laws*, Book 8.
7.   Hesiod, *Opera et Dies* (*c.* 700 BC), paras 396, 453.
8.   Theophrastus, *The Characteres*, Book X.
9.   Aristophanes, *Nubes* (423 BC; rev. 419–426 BC).
10. Plutarch, *Morals*, trans. A. R. Shilleto (London: George Bell & Sons, 1898).
11. Classic studies cite M. I. Finley, *The Ancient Economy* (London: Chatto & Windus, 1973) as responsible for this underestimation of banking. For newer perspectives, see E. Cohen, *Athenian Economy and Society: A Banking Perspective* (Princeton, NJ: Princeton University Press, 1992).
12. See Cohen, *Athenian Economy*, p. 3, quoting M. I. Finley, *The Ancient Economy* (Berkeley, CA: University of California Press, 1973).
13. 'Lucullus now turned to the cities of Asia, in order that while he had leisure from military operations he might pay some attention to justice and the law, which the province had now felt want of for a long time, and the people had endured unspeakable and incredible calamities, being plundered and reduced to slavery by the Publicani and the money-lenders, so that individuals were compelled to sell their handsome sons and virgin daughters, and the cities to sell their sacred offerings, pictures and statues. The lot of the citizens was at last to be condemned to slavery themselves, but the sufferings which were still worse – the fixing of ropes, barriers and horses, and standing under the open sky, during the heat in the sun, and during the cold when they were forced into the mud or the ice; so that slavery was considered a relief from the burden of debt and a blessing.
     Such evils as these Lucullus discovered in the cities, and in a short time he relieved the sufferers from all of them. In the first place, he declared that the rate of interest should be reckoned at the hundredth part,* and no more; in the second, he cut off all the interest which exceeded the capital; thirdly, what was most important of all, he declared that the lender should receive the fourth part of the income of the debtor; but any lender who had tacked the interest to the principal was deprived of the whole: thus, in less than four years all the debts were paid, and their property was given back to them free from all encumbrance. Now the common debt originated in the twenty thousand talents which Sulla had laid on Asia as a contribution, and twice this amount was repaid to the lenders, though they had indeed now brought the debt up to the amount of one hundred and twenty thousand talents by means of the interest. The lenders, however, considered themselves very ill used, and they raised a great outcry against Lucullus at Rome, and they endeavoured to bribe some of the demagogues to attack him; for the lenders had great influence, and had among their debtors many of the men who were engaged in public life. But Lucullus gained the affection of the cities which had been favoured by him, and the other provinces also longed to see such a man over them, and felicitated those who had the good luck to have such a governor. *Note from editor: "This is the

Centesimae usurae of the Romans, which was at this time the usual rate. It was one per cent per month, or twelve per cent per annum. Caesar (Life of Caesar, c. 12) made a like settlement between debtor and creditor in Spain". Plutarch, *Lives*, trans. A. Stewart and G. Long (London: George Bell & Sons, 1899), p. 446.

14. Tertullian, *Apology*, trans. W. Reeve (London, 1709), at http://www.tertullian.org/articles/reeve_apology.htm [accessed 1 October 2013], 39, p. 110.

15. 'But though, in a short time, the disciples in general were left to depend on their own resources, the community continued to provide a fund for the help of the infirm and the destitute'. W. D. Killen, *The Ancient Church* (1859, Gutenberg Project), p. 52

16. W. D. Killen, *The Ancient Church* (New York, 1859), p. 347, reports on savings banks (italics added): 'Callistus, who was made bishop on the death of Zephyrinus, must have possessed a far more vigorous intellect than his predecessor ... He had been originally a slave, and he must have won the confidence of his wealthy Christian master Carpophores, for he had been entrusted by him *with the care of a savings bank*. The establishment became insolvent, in consequence, as Hippolytus alleges, of the mismanagement of its conductor; and many widows and others who had committed their money to his keeping, lost their deposits. When Carpophorus, by whom he was now suspected of embezzlement, determined to call him to account, Callistus fled to Portus – in the hope of escaping by sea to some other country. He was, however, overtaken, and, after an ineffectual attempt to drown himself, was arrested, and thrown into prison. His master, who was placable and kind-hearted, speedily consented to release him from confinement; but he was no sooner at large, than, under pretence of collecting debts due to the savings bank, he went into a Jewish synagogue during the time of public worship, and caused such disturbance that he was seized and dragged before the city prefect. The magistrate ordered him first to be scourged, and then to be transported to the mines of Sardinia. He does not appear to have remained long in exile; for, about this time, Marcia procured from the Emperor Commodus an order for the release of the Christians who had been banished to that unhealthy island; and Callistus, though not included in the act of grace, contrived to prevail upon the governor to set him at liberty along with the other prisoners. He now returned to Rome, where he appears to have acquired the reputation of a changed character'.

17. L. Palermo, *La banca e il credito nel Medioevo* (Milan: Bruno Mondadori, 2008); R. Lopez (ed.), *The Dawn of Medieval Banking* (Los Angeles, CA: Centre for Medieval and Renaissance Studies, 1979); D. Puncuh and G. Felloni (eds), *Banchi pubblici, banchi privati e monti di pietà nell'Europa preindustriale: Amministrazione, tecniche operative e ruoli economici* (Genoa: Società Ligure di Storia Patria, 1991); A. Usher, *The Early History of Deposit Banking in Mediterranean Europe* (Cambridge, MA: Harvard University Press, 1943).

18. F. Ammannati (ed.), *Religion and Religious Institutions in the European Economy, 1000–1800* (Florence: Firenze University Press, 2012); G. Caligaris, 'Evoluzione dei Monti di Pietà e politiche produttivistiche nel Regno di Sardegna in Età Moderna', in P. Avallone (ed.), *Il 'Povero' va in banca. I Monti di Pietà negli antichi stati italiani (secc. XV–XVIII)* (Naples: Edizioni scientifiche italiane, 2001), pp. 36–7; F. Landi, 'Clero regolare ed economia creditizia: il caso dei monaci della congregazione cassinese', in Puncuh and Felloni (eds), *Banchi pubblici, banchi privati e monti di pietà nell'Europa preindustriale*, pp. 703–32.

19. P. M. Piergiovanni, 'Artigiani, credito e Monti di Pietà: l'esempio di Savona alla fine del Quattrocento', in *Aspetti della vita economica medievale. Atti del convegno di Studi nel X Anniversario della morte di Federigo Melis* (Siena: Monte dei Paschi di Siena, 1985), p. 535.

20. F. G. James, 'Charity Endowments as Sources of Local Credit in Seventeenth- and Eighteenth-Century England', *Journal of Economic History*, 8 (1948), pp. 153–70, reports similar origins in England.

21. G. Zalin, 'Una provvida istituzione del secondo '400: il Monte di Pietà di Padova', *Studi trentini di scienze storiche*, 125 (1996), pp. 171–84.

22. J. Bergier, 'From the Fifteenth Century in Italy to the Sixteenth Century in Germany: A New Banking Concept', in Center for Medieval and Renaissance Studies, *The Dawn of Modern Banking* (Los Angeles, CA: UCLA Press, 1979), p. 105–29.

23. E. Simone, *Il Banco dela Pieta di Napoli, 1734–1806* (Naples: Arte Tipografica, 1987).

24. B. Vogler (ed.), *L'histoire des caisses d'épargne Européennes*, 5 edns (Paris: Les éditions de l'épargne, 1989–98); J. Mura (ed.), *History of European Savings Banks* (Stuttgart: Steiner Verlag, 1996).

25. H. Seidel, 'The German Savings Banks', *Zeitschrift für die gesamte Staatswissenschaft* (1908), pp. 58–107, reprinted in National Monetary Commission, 'Miscellaneous Articles on German Banking' (Washington, DC: Government Printing Office, 1910), pp. 341–403.

26. G. Ashauer, *Von der Ersparungscasse zur Sparkassen-Finanzgruppe: Die deutsche Sparkassenorganisation in Geschichte und Gegenwart* (Stuttgart: Deutscher Sparkassenverlag, 1991).

27. See Chapter 6.

28. Prussian regulations of savings banks in 1838 stated: 'It must be remembered that the institution is intended primarily for the needs of the poorer classes, in order to extend to them the opportunity for depositing small savings. Any deviation from this policy must be avoided; Seidel, 'The German Savings Banks', p. 350.

29. Seidel cites Rauchberg's 'The Savings Bank Question' (*Sparkassenfrage*) published in the *Oesterreich Rundschau* that posed the following questions: 'Were the savings banks really losing sight of their original aim? Was that aim to be impressed upon them only through state interference? Which was more expedient: To force them back into the old rut, or let them develop in their newly adopted course?' Seidel, 'The German Savings Banks', p. 68.

30. Seidel's calculations are part of the US National Monetary Commission Report available online from the St Louis Federal Reserve Bank.

31. H. Faust, *Geschichte der Genossenschaftsbewegung* (Frankfurt: Knapp, 1977).

32. A. Tocqueville, *Democracy in America*, Vol. 2, pp. 306–7; cited in R. D. Wadhwani, 'Institutional Foundations of Personal Finance: Innovation in US Savings Banks, 1880s–1920s', *Business History Review*, 85:3 (2011), pp. 499–528, on p. 507.

33. National Monetary Commission, 'Notes on the Postal Savings-Bank Systems of the Leading Countries' (Washington, DC: Government Printing Office, 1910).

34. C. Christen-Lécuyer, *Histoire sociale et culturelle des Caisses d'Epargne en France 1818–1881* (Paris: Economica, 2004); L. de Llamby, *Les métamorphoses de l'épargne* (Paris: Gallimard, 2003).

35. On passbook savings, see Caisse des dépôts et consignations, *Le Livret A: une histoire de l'épargne populaire* (Paris: Caisse des dépôts et consignations, La Documentation Française, 1999).

36. M. Blomer, *Die Entwicklung des Agrarkredits in der preussischen Provinz Westfalen im 19. Jahrhundert* (Frankfurt: Fritz Knapp Verlag, 1990); J. P. Thiolon, *Les Caisses d'Epargne* (Paris: Berger-Levrault, 1971).

37. A. Marks, *The Position of the Post Office Savings Bank* (London: Clement Wilson, 1905), p. 23.

38. Ibid., p. 36.

39. Ibid., p. 38.

40. E. J. Morley, *The Life of Gladstone*, 3 vols (Toronto: G. N. Morang, 1903), vol. 2, p. 52.

41. Seidel, 'The German Savings Banks', p. 354.
42. Aghion, 'Development Banking'; and M. Cummings-Woo (ed.), *The Developmentalist State* (Ann Arbor, MI: University of Michigan Press, 1999).
43. 'The existing commercial banks were unable to provide industry with long-term finance for two main reasons. First, they were unwilling to bear the inevitable risks associated with the financing of new enterprises. Second, they lacked the specialized skills required to deal with the higher risk long-term investments'; Aghion, 'Development Banking', p. 3.
44. R. Sylla, 'The Role of Banks', in R. Sylla and G. Toniolo (eds), *Patterns of European Industrialization in the 19th Century* (London: Routledge, 1991), pp. 45–63. Aghion notes: 'The oldest government-sponsored institution for industrial development is the Société Générale pour Favoriser I'Industrie Nationale which was created in the Netherlands in 1822. However, it was in France that some of the most significant developments in long-term state-sponsored finance occurred. In this respect, the creation in 1848–1852 of institutions such as the Crédit Foncier, the Comptoir d'Escompte and the Crédit Mobilier, was particularly important'; Aghion, 'Development Banking', p. 3.
45. On development banks in Europe, see C. Kindleberger, *A Financial History of Western Europe* (London: George Allen & Unwin, 1984); and R. E. Cameron, *Banking and Economic Development: Some Lessons of History* (New York: Oxford University Press, 1972). 'Of even greater importance than the outcome of the operations of the Crédit Mobilier were the intangible benefits such as the imitated skills of the engineers and technicians which it sent abroad, the efficiency of its administrators and the organizational banking techniques which were so widely copied'; R. E. Cameron, 'The Crédit Mobilier and the Economic Development of Europe', *Journal of Political Economy*, 61:6 (1953), pp. 461–88, on p. 486.
46. Diamond, *Development Banks*.
47. Aghion cites the Société Nationale de Crédit à I'Industrie (Belgium, 1919), Crédit National (France, 1919), National Bank (Poland, 1928), Industrial Mortgage Bank (Finland, 1928), Industrial Mortgage Institute (Hungary, 1928), Istituto Mobiliare Italiano (Italy, 1933) and Instituto per la Ricostruzione Industriale (Italy, 1933); Aghion, 'Development Banking'.
48. 'Probably the aggregate resources provided by the development banks have been small, but the fact that there were made available at particular times for strategically important enterprises and industries gave them a significance far greater than the amounts involved suggest'; Diamond, *Development Banks*, pp. 38–9.
49. Cummings-Woo (ed.), *The Developmental State*.

2 Butzbach and Mettenheim, 'The Comparative Performance of Alternative Banks before the 2007–8 Crisis'

1. F. Carnevali, *Europe's Advantage: Banks and Small Firms in Britain, France, Germany and Italy since 1918* (Oxford: Oxford University Press, 2005).
2. O. Butzbach, 'European Savings Banks and the Future of Public Banking in Advanced Economies: The Cases of France, Germany, Italy and Spain', *Public Banking Institute Journal*, 1:1 (2012), pp. 35–78.
3. According to data provided by the European Savings Banks Group (2009); total banking assets are from the ECB (2008).

4. On postal savings banks in Asia, see M. J. Sher and N. Yoshino (eds), *Small Savings Mobilization and Asian Economic Development: The Role of Postal Financial Services* (New York: M. E. Sharpe, 2004).
5. In Germany, for instance, the total number of cooperative banks dropped from more than 3,000 in 1980 to less than 900 in 2010.
6. According to the European Association of Cooperative Banks.
7. Ibid.
8. O. Wyman, *Co-operative Bank, Customer Champion* (London: Oliver Wyman Financial Services, 2008).
9. As Altunbas et al. argue, most of the empirical studies on banks' performance focused, until the early 2000s, on the private, commercial bank sector in the United States – while studies on the performance of savings banks or cooperative banks were until then mostly based on single countries and not, therefore, comparative; Y. Altunbas, S. Carbó Valverde and P. Molyneux, 'Ownership and Performance in European and US Banking – A Comparison of Commercial, Co-operative and Savings Banks', Fondacion de las Cajas de Ahorros Working Paper, 180/2003 (2003).
10. See, for a review, A. N. Berger, G. R. G. Clarke, R. Cull, L. Klapper and G. F. Udell, 'Corporate Governance and Bank Performance: A Joint Analysis of the Static, Selection, and Dynamic Effects of Domestic, Foreign, and State Ownership', *Journal of Banking and Finance*, 29:8–9 (2005), pp. 2179–221.
11. M. M. Cornett, L. Guo, S. Khaksari and H. Tehranian, 'The Impact of State Ownership on Performance Differences in Privately-Owned versus State-Owned Banks: An International Comparison', *Journal of Financial Intermediation*, 19 (2010), pp. 74–94.
12. However, Cornett et al. (see ibid.) do not distinguish between government-owned commercial banks and development banks – a distinction made instead in R. La Porta, F. Lopez-de-Silanes and A. Schleifer, 'Government Ownership of Banks', *Journal of Finance*, 57:1 (2002), pp. 265–301.
13. La Porta et al., 'Government Ownership of Banks'.
14. J. R. Barth, G. Caprio Jr and R. Levine, 'Banking Systems around the Globe: Do Regulation and Ownership Affect Performance and Stability?', *NBER Conference Report Series* (Chicago, IL: University of Chicago Press, 2001), pp. 31–88.
15. R. Ayadi, R. H. Schmidt and S. Carbò Verde, *Investigating Diversity in the Banking Sector in Europe: The Performance and Role of Savings Banks* (Brussels: Centre for European Policy Studies, 2009).
16. R. Ayadi, R. H. Schmidt, D. T. Llewellyn, E. Arbak and W. P. De Groen, *Investigating Diversity in the Banking Sector in Europe: Key Developments, Performance and Role of Cooperative Banks* (Brussels: Centre for European Policy Studies, 2010).
17. G. Iannotta, G. Nocera and A. Sironi, 'Ownership Structure, Risk and Performance in the European Banking Industry', *Journal of Banking and Finance*, 31 (2007), pp. 2127–49.
18. Altunbas et al., 'Ownership and Performance'.
19. Y. Altunbas, L. Evans and P. Molyneux, 'Ownership and Efficiency in Banking', *Journal of Money, Credit and Banking*, 33:4 (2001), pp. 926–54.
20. L. Giordano and A. Lopes, 'Bank Networks, Credit and Southern Italy's Productive System', *Rivista economica del Mezzogiorno*, 4 (2009), pp. 827–68.
21. A. S. Cebenoyan, E. S. Cooperman, C. A. Register and S. C. Hudgins, 'The Relative Efficiency of Stock versus Mutual S&Ls: A Stochastic Cost Frontier Approach', *Journal of Financial Services Research*, 7:2 (1993), pp. 151–70.

22. L. J. Mester, 'Efficiency in the Savings and Loan Industry', *Journal of Banking and Finance*, 17:2–3 (1993), pp. 267–86.
23. Berger et al., 'Corporate Governance'.
24. R. A. Cole and H. Mehran, 'The Effect of Changes in Ownership Structure on Performance: Evidence from the Thrift Industry', *Journal of Financial Economics*, 50 (1998), pp. 291–317.
25. A. Dietrich and G. Wanzenried, 'Determinants of Bank Profitability before and during the Crisis: Evidence from Switzerland', *Journal of International Financial Markets, Institutions and Money*, 21 (2011), pp. 307–27.
26. Cornett et al., 'The Impact of State Ownership'.
27. A. Micco, U. Panizza and M. Yañez, 'Bank Ownership and Perfomance: Does Politics Matter?', *Journal of Banking and Finance*, 31 (2007), pp. 219–41.
28. J. P. Bonin, I. Hasan and P. Wachtel, 'Bank Performance, Efficiency and Ownership in Transition Economies', *Journal of Banking and Finance*, 29:1 (2005), pp. 31–53.
29. P. Molyneux and J. Thornton, 'Determinants of European Bank Profitability: A Note', *Journal of Banking and Finance*, 16:6 (1992), pp. 1173–8.
30. Ayadi et al., *Investigating Diversity in ... Cooperative Banks*.
31. Iannotta et al., 'Ownership Structure'.
32. Altunbas et al., 'Ownership and Performance'.
33. S. P. Chakravarty and J. M. Williams, 'How Significant is the Alleged Unfair Advantage Enjoyed by State-Owned Banks in Germany?', *Cambridge Journal of Economics*, 30:2 (2006), pp. 219–26; R. Crespi, M. A. Garcia-Cestona and V. Salas, 'Governance Mechanisms in Spanish Banks: Does Ownership Matter?', *Journal of Banking and Finance*, 28:10 (2004), pp. 2311–30; Altunbas et al., 'Ownership and Efficiency'; T. Valnek, 'The Comparative Performance of Mutual Building Societies and Stock Retail Banks', *Journal of Banking and Finance*, 23:6 (1999), pp. 925–38; Cebenoyan et al., 'The Relative Efficiency of Stock versus Mutual S&Ls'.
34. La Porta et al., 'Government Ownership of Banks'; Cornett et al., 'The Impact of State Ownership'; Iannotta et al., 'Ownership Structure'.
35. Ayadi et al., *Investigating Diversity in ... Cooperative Banks*; Ayadi et al., *Investigating Diversity in ... Savings Banks*; T. H. L. Beck, O. G. de Jonghe and G. Schepens, 'Bank Competition and Stability: Cross-country Heterogeneity', Tilburg University, Centre for Economic Research Discussion Paper, 2012–85 (2012); P. A. Bongini and G. Ferri, 'Governance, Diversification and Performance: The Case of Italy's Banche Popolari', Milan Bicocca University, Department of Management and Business Administration, Working Paper Series, 02/2008 (2008); T. Garcia-Marco and M. D. Robles-Fernandez, 'Risk-taking Behaviour and Ownership in the Banking Industry: The Spanish Evidence', *Journal of Economics and Business*, 60:3 (2008), pp. 332–54; H. Hesse and M. Čihák, 'Cooperative Banks and Financial Stability', IMF Working Paper, WP/07/02 (2007); Iannotta et al., 'Ownership Structure'; V. Salas and J. Saurina, 'Credit Risk in Two Institutional Regimes: Spanish Commercial and Savings Banks', *Journal of Financial Services Research*, 22:3 (2002), pp. 203–24; B. C. Esty, 'A Case Study of Organizational Form and Risk Shifting in the Savings and Loan Industry', *Journal of Financial Economics*, 44:1 (1997), pp. 57–76.
36. Ayadi et al., *Investigating Diversity in ... Savings Banks*; Beck et al., 'Bank Competition and Stability'; Garcia-Marco and Robles-Fernandez, 'Risk-taking Behaviour'.
37. Beck et al., 'Bank Competition and Stability'; Salas and Saurina, 'Credit Risk'.
38. S. C. Valverde, E. Kane and F. Rodriguez, 'Evidence of Differences in the Effectiveness of Safety-Net Management of European Union Countries', *Journal of Financial Services Research*, 34 (2008), pp. 151–76.

3 Schclarek, 'The Counter-Cyclical Behaviour of Public and Private Banks: An Overview of the Literature'

1. A. Micco and U. Panizza, 'Bank Ownership and Lending Behavior', *Economics Letters*, 93 (2006), pp. 248–54.
2. A. C. Bertay, A. Demirgüç-Kunt and H. Huizinga, 'Bank Ownership and Credit over the Business Cycle: Is Lending by State Banks less Pro-Cyclical?', CEPR Discussion Paper, 9034 (2012).
3. Micco and Panizza, 'Bank Ownership and Lending Behavior'.
4. Ibid.
5. Rashid also find that foreign-owned bank lending is more volatile than domestic bank lending, without making a distinction between private and public banks; see H. Rashid, 'Credit to Private Sector, Interest Spread and Volatility in Credit-Flows: Do Bank Ownership and Deposits Matter?', United Nations DESA Working Paper, 105 (2011).
6. This argument implies that risk aversion is not a constant but a variable that varies with the business cycle. In boom times agents reduce their risk aversion as they are in euphoria, and in recessions they increase their risk aversion as they enter into panic. This argument follows the ideas of Minsky as expressed in H. P. Minsky, 'The Financial Instability Hypothesis', Jerome Levy Economics Institute Working Paper, 74 (1992).
7. T. Duprey, 'Bank Ownership and Credit Cycle: The Lower Sensitivity of Public Bank Lending to the Business Cycle', Banque de France Working Paper, 411 (2012).
8. Micco and Panizza, 'Bank Ownership and Lending Behavior'; Bertay et al., 'Bank Ownership'.
9. Bertay et al., 'Bank Ownership'.
10. Micco and Panizza, 'Bank Ownership and Lending Behavior'.
11. D. Foos, 'Lending Conditions, Macroeconomic Fluctuations, and the Impact of Bank Ownership', University of Mannheim, Department of Banking and Finance, manuscript (2009).
12. M. Brei and A. Schclarek, 'Public Bank Lending in Times of Crisis', *Journal of Financial Stability*, in press (2013).
13. Bertay et al., 'Bank Ownership'.
14. R. Cull and M. S. Martinez Peria, 'Bank Ownership and Lending Patterns during the 2008–2009 Financial Crisis. Evidence from Eastern Europe and Latin America', World Bank Policy Research Working Paper Series, 6195 (2012).
15. R. de Haas, Y. Korniyenko, E. Loukoianova and A. Pivovarsky, 'Foreign Banks and the Vienna Initiative: Turning Sinners into Saints?', IMF Working Paper, 12/117 (2012).
16. F. Allen, K. Jackowicz and O. Kowalewski, 'The Effects of Foreign and Government Ownership on Bank Lending Behavior during a Crisis in Central and Eastern Europe', Wharton Financial Institutions Center Working Paper, 13–25 (2013).
17. L. Leony and R. Romeu, 'A Model of Bank Lending in the Global Financial Crisis and the Case of Korea', *Journal of Asian Economies*, 22:4 (2011), pp. 322–34.
18. N. Coleman and L. Feler, 'Bank Ownership, Lending, and Local Economic Performance in the 2008 Financial Crisis' (unpublished working paper, 2012).
19. D. Davydov, 'Should Public Banks be Privatized? Evidence from the Financial Crisis' (unpublished working paper, 2013).
20. Z. Önder and S. Özyildirim, 'Role of Bank Credit on Local Growth: Do Politics and Crisis Matter?', *Journal of Financial Stability*, 9 (2013), pp. 13–25.
21. Y. Lin, A. Srinivasan and T. Yamada, 'The Bright Side of Lending by State Owned Banks: Evidence from Japan' (unpublished working paper, 2012).

22. Bertay et al., 'Bank Ownership'.
23. Brei and Schclarek, 'Public Bank Lending'.
24. G. McCandless, M. F. Gabrielli and M. J. Rouillet, 'Determining the Causes of Bank Runs in Argentina during the Crisis of 2001', *Revista de Analisis Economico*, 18:1 (2003), pp. 87–102.
25. M. Brei and A. Schclarek, 'A Theoretical Model of Bank Lending: Does Ownership Matter in Times of Crises?' (unpublished working paper, 2013).
26. N. Andries and S. Billon, 'The Effect of Bank Ownership and Deposit Insurance on Monetary Policy Transmission', *Journal of Banking and Finance*, 34 (2010), pp. 3050–4.
27. T. Duprey, 'Inefficient Public Banking and Heterogeneous Lending Cycle' (unpublished working paper, 2013).
28. Sanya and Mlachila analyse the post-crisis lending behaviour of banks in the Mercosur using both aggregate and bank-level data during the period 1990–2006; S. O. Sanya and M. Mlachila, 'Post-Crisis Bank Behavior: Lessons from Mercosur', IMF Working Paper, 10/1 (2010). They find insufficient lending and holding of high levels of excess liquidity, but they don't distinguish between public and private banks.

4 Butzbach and Mettenheim, 'Explaining the Competitive Advantage of Alternative Banks: Towards an Alternative Banking Theory?'

1. E. Rasmussen, 'Stock Banks and Mutual Banks', *Journal of Law and Economics*, 31 (1988), pp. 395–422, on p. 395.
2. R. E. Towey, 'Money Creation and the Theory of the Banking Firm', *Journal of Finance*, 29:1 (1974), pp. 57–72.
3. J. Gurley and E. Shaw, *Money in a Theory of Finance* (Washington, DC: Brookings Institute Press, 1960); J. Tobin, 'Commercial Banks as Creators of "Money"', in D. Carson (ed.), *Banking and Monetary Studies* (Homewood, IL: R. D. Irwin, 1963), pp. 408–19.
4. Tobin, 'Commercial Banks', p. 416.
5. J. Tobin, 'The Commercial Banking Firm: A Simple Model', *Scandinavian Journal of Economics*, 84:4 (1982), pp. 495–530; A. M. Santomero, 'Modeling the Banking Firm', *Journal of Money, Credit and Banking*, 16:4 (1984), pp. 576–602.
6. M. Klein, 'A Theory of the Banking Firm', *Journal of Money, Credit and Banking*, 3 (1971), pp. 205–18.
7. Tobin, 'Commercial Banks', p. 411.
8. As good illustrations of this trend, see E. F. Fama, 'Banking in the Theory of Finance', *Journal of Monetary Economics*, 6 (1980), pp. 39–57; D. W. Diamond and P. Dybvig, 'Bank Runs, Deposit Insurance and Liquidity', *Journal of Political Economy*, 91 (1983), pp. 401–19; E. Baltensperger, 'Alternative Approaches to the Theory of the Banking Firm', *Journal of Monetary Economics*, 6 (1980), pp. 1–37.
9. S. Bhattacharya and A. Thakor, 'Contemporary Banking Theory', *Journal of Financial Intermediation*, 3 (1993), pp. 2–50.
10. See D. W. Diamond and R. G. Rajan, 'Liquidity Risk, Liquidity Creation and Financial Fragility: A Theory of Banking', *Journal of Political Economy*, 109:2 (2001), pp. 287–327.
11. A. W. A. Boot and M. Marinč, 'The Evolving Landscape of Banking', *Industrial and Corporate Change*, 17:6 (2008), pp. 1173–203.

12. A. W. A. Boot and A. Thakor, 'The Accelerating Integration of Banks and Markets and its Implications for Regulation', in A. N. Berger, P. Molyneux and J. O. S. Wilson (eds), *The Oxford Handbook of Banking* (Oxford: Oxford University Press, 2010), pp. 58–89.

13. A. W. A. Boot, 'Relationship Banking: What Do We Know?', *Journal of Financial Intermediation*, 9 (2000), pp. 7–25, on p. 8.

14. Bhattacharya and Thakor, 'Contemporary Banking Theory', p. 14.

15. Tobin, 'Commercial Banks', and Tobin, 'The Commercial Banking Firm'.

16. J. Stiglitz and A. Weiss, 'Credit Rationing in Markets with Imperfect Information', *American Economic Review*, 7 (1981), pp. 353–76.

17. D. W. Diamond, 'Financial Intermediation and Delegated Monitoring', *Review of Economic Studies*, 51 (1984), pp. 728–62.

18. Boot, 'Relationship Banking'; M. Petersen and R. Rajan, 'The Benefits of Lending Relationships: Evidence From Small Business Data', *Journal of Finance*, 49 (1994), pp. 3–37.

19. See Fama, 'Banking'; and E. F. Fama, 'Agency Problems and the Theory of the Firm', *Journal of Political Economy*, 88:2 (1980), pp. 288–307.

20. Diamond, 'Financial Intermediation'.

21. For a review of the ownership and performance literature in banking, see Y. Altunbas, L. Evans and P. Molyneux, 'Ownership and Efficiency in Banking', *Journal of Money, Credit and Banking*, 33:4 (2001), pp. 926–54.

22. See G. Coco and G. Ferri, 'From Shareholders to Stakeholders Finance: A More Sustainable Lending Model', *International Journal of Sustainable Economy*, 2:3 (2010), pp. 352–64.

23. A. A. Alchian and H. Demsetz, 'Production, Information Costs, and Economic Organization', *American Economic Review*, 62:5 (1972), pp. 777–95.

24. See, in particular, ibid.; A. A. Alchian and H. Demsetz, 'The Property Rights Paradigm', *Journal of Economic History*, 33:1 (1973), pp. 16–27; M. C. Jensen and W. Meckling, 'Theory of the Firm: Managerial Behaviour, Agency Costs and Ownership Structure', *Journal of Financial Economics*, 3 (1976), pp. 305–24.

25. Fama, 'Agency Problems'; E. F. Fama and M. C. Jensen, 'Separation of Ownership and Control', *Journal of Law and Economics*, 26 (1983), pp. 301–25; E. F. Fama and M. C. Jensen, 'Agency Problems and Residual Claims', *Journal of Law and Economics*, 26 (1983), pp. 327–49; O. Hart and J. Moore, 'Property Rights and the Nature of the Firm', *Journal of Political Economy*, 98 (1990), pp. 1119–59.

26. A. A. Berle and G. C. Means, *The Modern Corporation and Private Property* (New Brunswick, NJ: Transaction Publishers, 1932).

27. Alchian and Demsetz, 'Production, Information Costs'; Alchian and Demsetz, 'The Property Rights Paradigm'.

28. Fama and Jensen, 'Separation of Ownership and Control'; Fama and Jensen, 'Agency Problems'.

29. In particular, R. La Porta, F. Lopez-de-Silanes and A. Schleifer, 'Government Ownership of Banks', *Journal of Finance*, 57:1 (2002), pp. 265–301; and H. Hansmann and R. Kraakman, 'The End of History for Corporate Law', Harvard Law School John M. Olin Center for Law, Economics and Business Discussion Paper Series, 280 (2000).

30. C. E. Cuevas and K. P. Fischer, 'Cooperative Financial Institutions. Issues in Governance, Supervision and Regulation', World Bank Working Paper, 82 (2006).

31. Berle and Means, *The Modern Corporation*.

32. Fama and Jensen, 'Agency Problems'; Hart and Moore, 'Property Rights'.

33. Jensen and Meckling, 'Theory of the Firm'.

34. H. Hansmann, *The Ownership of Enterprise* (Cambridge, MA: Harvard University Press, 1996).
35. Rasmussen, 'Stock Banks and Mutual Banks'.
36. D. Mayers and C. Smith, 'Managerial Discretion, Regulation and Stock Insurance Ownership Structure', *Journal of Risk and Insurance*, 61:4 (1994), pp. 638–55.
37. La Porta et al., 'Government Ownership of Banks'.
38. R. Ayadi, R. H. Schmidt, D. T. Llewellyn, E. Arbak and W. P. De Groen, *Investigating Diversity in the Banking Sector in Europe: Key Developments, Performance and Role of Cooperative Banks* (Brussels: Centre for European Policy Studies, 2010).
39. Rasmussen, 'Stock Banks and Mutual Banks', p. 397.
40. A. Shleifer, 'State versus Private Ownership', *Journal of Economic Perspectives*, 12:4 (1998), pp. 133–50, on p. 135.
41. Ibid.
42. See S. J. Grossman and O. D. Hart, 'Takeover Bids, the Free-Rider Problem, and the Theory of the Corporation', *Bell Journal of Economics,* 11:1 (1980), pp. 42–64; and Fama and Jensen, 'Agency Problems'.
43. E. J. Kane, 'Capital Movement, Banking Insolvency, and Silent Runs in the Asian Financial Crisis', *Pacific Basin Finance Journal*, 8 (2000), pp. 153–75, on p. 161.
44. Shleifer, 'State versus Private Ownership'.
45. A. Shleifer and R. W. Vishny, *The Grabbing Hand: Government Pathologies and their Cures* (Cambridge, MA: Harvard University Press, 1998); and A. Shleifer and R. W. Vishny, 'A Survey of Corporate Governance', *Journal of Finance*, 52 (1997), pp. 737–83.
46. M. M. Cornett, L. Guo, S. Khaksari and H. Tehranian, 'The Impact of State Ownership on Performance Differences in Privately-Owned versus State-Owned Banks: An International Comparison', *Journal of Financial Intermediation*, 19 (2010), pp. 74–94.
47. Shleifer and Vishny, 'A Survey of Corporate Governance'.
48. Kane, 'Capital Movement'.
49. S. I. Dinç, 'Politicians and Banks: Political Influences on Government-Owned Banks in Emerging Markets', *Journal of Financial Economics*, 77 (2005), pp. 453–79.
50. A. Micco, U. Panizza and M. Yañez, 'Bank Ownership and Perfomance: Does Politics Matter?', *Journal of Banking and Finance*, 31 (2007), pp. 219–41.
51. J. R. Barth, G. Caprio Jr and R. Levine, *Rethinking Bank Regulation: Till Angels Govern* (New York: Cambridge University Press, 2006).
52. Cuevas and Fischer, 'Cooperative Financial Institutions'.
53. Ibid.
54. Fama and Jensen, 'Separation of Ownership and Control'.
55. W. Fonteyne, 'Cooperative Banks in Europe – Policy Issues', IMF Working Paper, WP/07/159 (2007).
56. 'Market discipline' has also been long advocated by regulators in the 1990s. For instance, in the *Core Principles for Effective Banking Supervision* (Basel: Basel Committee on Banking Supervision, 1997), p. 8: 'Supervisors should encourage and pursue market discipline by encouraging good corporate governance and enhancing market transparency and surveillance'. In a similar vein are these enlightening comments made by a senior US monetary policymaker in the late 1990s: '*I also believe that we ought – where we can – to skip the middlemen and go right to our first line of defense: market discipline. By aligning market incentives with regulatory incentives, policies designed to harness market forces could complement bank supervision by encouraging banks to refrain from excessive risk-taking*'; 'Market Discipline as a Complement to Bank Supervision and Regulation', Remarks by

Governor L. H. Meyer before the Conference on Reforming Bank Capital Standards, Council on Foreign Relations, New York, 14 June 1999, at www.federalreserve.gov/boardDocs/Speeches/1999/19990614.htm [accessed 1 July 2013].

57. O. E. Williamson, *The Economics of Discretionary Behaviour* (New York: Prentice-Hall, 1964).
58. M. C. Jensen, 'Agency Costs of Free Cash Flow, Corporate Finance and Takeovers', *American Economic Review*, 76 (1986), pp. 323–47.
59. Hansmann and Kraakman, 'The End of History'.
60. Fonteyne, 'Cooperative Banks in Europe'.
61. L. Cen, S. Dasgupta and R. Sen, 'Discipline or Disruption? Stakeholder Relationships and the Effect of Takeover Threat', SSRN Working Paper (2011), at http://dx.doi.org/10.2139/ssrn.1540346 [accessed 4 July 2013].
62. Shleifer and Vishny, 'A Survey of Corporate Governance'; Dinç, 'Politicians and Banks'.
63. R. Levine, 'The Corporate Governance of Banks: A Concise Discussion of Concepts and Evidence', World Bank Policy Research Working Paper, 3404 (2004).
64. Bhattacharya and Thakor, 'Contemporary Banking Theory'.
65. Ayadi et al., *Investigating Diversity in … Cooperative Banks*.
66. Fama and Jensen, 'Separation of Ownership and Control'.
67. T. W. Guinnane, 'Cooperatives as Information Machines: German Rural Credit Cooperatives, 1883–1914', *Journal of Economic History*, 61:2 (2001), pp. 366–89. See also Chapter 6 in this volume.
68. Fonteyne, 'Cooperative Banks in Europe'.
69. Ibid.
70. M. Desrochers and K. Fischer, 'The Power of Networks: Integration and Financial Cooperative Performance', *Annals of Public and Cooperative Economics*, 76:3 (2005), pp. 307–54; Cuevas and Fischer, 'Cooperative Financial Institutions'.
71. M. C. Jensen and J. L. Zimmerman, 'Management Compensation and the Managerial Labour Market', *Journal of Accounting and Economics*, 7:1–3 (1985), pp. 3–9.
72. Fonteyne, 'Cooperative Banks in Europe'; Cuevas and Fischer, 'Cooperative Financial Institutions'.
73. Rasmussen, 'Stock Banks and Mutual Banks', p. 398.
74. Fama and Jensen, 'Agency Problems'; S. D. Deshmukh, S. I. Greenbaum and A. V. Thakor, 'Capital Accumulation and Deposit Pricing in Mutual Financial Institutions', *Journal of Financial Quantitative Analysis*, 17 (1982), pp. 503–32.
75. See, for a critical review, L. A. Bebchuk and J. Fried, 'Executive Compensation as an Agency Problem', *Journal of Economic Perspectives*, 17 (2003), pp. 71–92.
76. Ibid.
77. See A. R. Sorkin, *Too Big To Fail* (New York: Allen Lane, 2010).
78. A. Polo, 'The Corporate Governance of Banks: The State of the Debate', *MPRA Paper no. 2325* (2007); see also K. John and Y. Qian, 'Incentive Features in CEO Compensation in the Banking Industry', *FRBNY Economic Policy Review*, 9:1 (2003), pp. 109–21.
79. 'An integrated hierarchical reward structure ceased to regulate the pay of top executives, who embraced wholeheartedly the ideology of maximizing shareholder value as their boards bestowed on them ever more generous stock-option awards'; W. Lazonick, 'Innovative Business Models and Varieties of Capitalism: Financialization of the US Corporation', *Business History Review*, 84 (2010), pp. 675–702, on p. 684.
80. Fonteyne, 'Cooperative Banks in Europe'.
81. Hansmann, *The Ownership of Enterprise*, p. 4.

82. H. Leland, 'Agency Costs, Risk Management, and Capital Structure', *Journal of Finance*, 53 (1998), pp. 1213–43.
83. Ayadi et al., *Investigating Diversity in ... Cooperative Banks*; L. Drake and D. T. Llewellyn, 'The Economics of Mutuality: A Perspective on UK Building Societies', in J. Birchall (ed.), *The New Mutualism in Public Policy* (London: Routledge, 2001), pp. 14–40.
84. Rasmussen, 'Stock Banks and Mutual Banks'.
85. Hansmann, *The Ownership of Enterprise*, p. 263.
86. See Diamond, 'Financial Intermediation'.
87. T. Valnek, 'The Comparative Performance of Mutual Building Societies and Stock Retail Banks', *Journal of Banking and Finance*, 23:6 (1999), pp. 925–38.
88. Cuevas and Fischer, 'Cooperative Financial Institutions'.
89. See M. Ghatak, 'Screening by the Company You Keep: Joint Liability Lending and the Peer Selection Effect', *Economic Journal*, 110:465 (2000), pp. 601–31.
90. Bhattacharya and Thakor, 'Contemporary Banking Theory', p. 15.
91. A. Dietrich and G. Wanzenried, 'Determinants of Bank Profitability before and during the Crisis: Evidence from Switzerland', *Journal of International Financial Markets, Institutions and Money*, 21 (2011), pp. 307–27, on p. 321.
92. Rasmussen, 'Stock Banks and Mutual Banks', p. 407.
93. Fonteyne, 'Cooperative Banks in Europe'.
94. Stiglitz and Weiss, 'Credit Rationing'.
95. For a review, see Boot, 'Relationship Banking'.
96. Ibid., p. 10.
97. Ibid.
98. Petersen and Rajan, 'The Benefits of Lending Relationships'.
99. T. Hoshi, A. Kashyap and D. Scharfstein, 'The Role of Banks in Reducing the Costs of Financial Distress in Japan', *Journal of Financial Economics*, 27 (1990), pp. 67–88.
100. Ayadi et al., *Investigating Diversity in ... Cooperative Banks*; R. Ayadi, R. H. Schmidt and S. Carbò Verde, *Investigating Diversity in the Banking Sector in Europe: The Performance and Role of Savings Banks* (Brussels: Centre for European Policy Studies, 2009); Fonteyne, 'Cooperative Banks in Europe'; Cuevas and Fischer, 'Cooperative Financial Institutions'.
101. F. Carnevali, *Europe's Advantage: Banks and Small Firms in Britain, France, Germany and Italy since 1918* (Oxford: Oxford University Press, 2005).
102. Fonteyne, 'Cooperative Banks in Europe'.
103. P. McGregor, 'Credit Unions and the Supply of Insurance to Low Income Households', *Annals of Public and Cooperative Economics*, 76:3 (2005), pp. 355–74; D. G. McKillop and J. O. S. Wilson, 'Credit Unions: A Theoretical and Empirical Overview', *Financial Markets, Institutions and Instruments*, 20:3 (2011), pp. 79–123.
104. K. von Mettenheim and L. Gonzalez, *Government Ownership of Banks Revisited* (São Paulo: FGV-EAESP, 2007).
105. J. Kay, 'The Economics of Mutuality', *Annals of Public and Cooperative Economics*, 62:3 (1991), pp. 309–18.
106. J. Kay, 'The Mutual Interest in Building Trust Still Remains', *Financial Times*, 26 April 2006, at http://www.ft.com/intl/cms/s/0/57a7fa94-d3b7-11da-b2f3-0000779e2340.html#axzz2j3WE1gUY [accessed 21 June 2013].
107. Ayadi et al., *Investigating Diversity in ... Cooperative Banks*.
108. Hansmann, *The Ownership of Enterprise*.
109. Hart and Moore, 'Property Rights'.

110. S. R. Akella and S. I. Greenbaum, 'Savings and Loans Ownership Structure and Expense Preference', *Journal of Banking and Finance*, 12 (1988), pp. 419–37; Rasmussen, 'Stock Banks and Mutual Banks'; M. Berlin and L. J. Mester, 'On the Profitability and Cost of Relationship Lending', *Journal of Banking and Finance*, 22:6–8 (1998), pp. 873–97.

111. A. N. Berger, G. R. G. Clarke, R. Cull, L. Klapper and G. F. Udell, 'Corporate Governance and Bank Performance: A Joint Analysis of the Static, Selection, and Dynamic Effects of Domestic, Foreign, and State Ownership', *Journal of Banking and Finance*, 29:8–9 (2005), pp. 2179–221.

112. Fonteyne, 'Cooperative Banks in Europe'.

113. Ayadi et al., *Investigating Diversity in ... Cooperative Banks*; Cuevas and Fischer, 'Cooperative Financial Institutions'.

114. Cuevas and Fischer, 'Cooperative Financial Institutions'.

115. Fama and Jensen, 'Separation of Ownership and Control'.

116. Boot, 'Relationship Banking'; H. Degryse and P. Van Cayseele, 'Relationship Lending within a Bank Based System: Evidence from European Small Business Data', *Journal of Financial Intermediation*, 9 (2000), pp. 90–109.

117. Ayadi et al., *Investigating Diversity in ... Cooperative Banks*; Desrochers and Fischer, 'The Power of Networks'.

118. Fonteyne, 'Cooperative Banks in Europe'.

119. Ibid., p. 47.

120. Altunbas et al., 'Ownership and Efficiency'.

121. One should, however, make an important caveat here: in several countries over the past decade or so, large savings and cooperative banks have been able and willing to list specialized subsidiaries and funding instruments (with a varying degree of success: see the fate of Natixis in France as an edifying example).

122. Fonteyne, 'Cooperative Banks in Europe'. The same author warns that this characteristic could actually turn into a liability, as it makes cooperative banks more dependent on a specific category of customers.

123. Kay, 'The Economics of Mutuality'.

124. Fonteyne, 'Cooperative Banks in Europe'.

125. A. Giannola, 'Origins and Evolution of Credit', in A. Giannola and G. D'Angelo (eds), *Financing Enterprises* (Naples: Liguori Editore, 2009), pp. 13–44.

126. Fonteyne, 'Cooperative Banks in Europe'.

127. See Rasmussen, 'Stock Banks and Mutual Banks'.

128. O. Hart and J. Moore, 'Cooperatives vs. Outside Ownership', NBER Working Paper, W6421 (1998).

129. D. Canning, C. W. Jefferson and J. E. Spencer, 'Optimal Credit Rationing in Not-For-Profit Financial Institutions', *International Economic Review*, 4:1 (2003), pp. 243–61.

130. Ibid.

131. P. A. Bongini and G. Ferri, 'Governance, Diversification and Performance: The Case of Italy's Banche Popolari', Milan Bicocca University, Department of Management and Business Administration, Working Paper Series, 02/2008 (2008).

132. G. Iannotta, G. Nocera and A. Sironi, 'Ownership Structure, Risk and Performance in the European Banking Industry', *Journal of Banking and Finance*, 31 (2007), pp. 2127–49.

133. L. Giordano and A. Lopes, 'Bank Networks, Credit and Southern Italy's Productive System', *Rivista economica del Mezzogiorno*, 4 (2009), pp. 827–68.

134. H. Hesse and M. Čihák, 'Cooperative Banks and Financial Stability', IMF Working Paper, WP/07/02 (2007).

135. As is shown in the case of French cooperative banks by E. Gurtner, M. Jaeger and J.-N. Ory, 'Le Statut de Coopérative Est-il Source d'Efficacité dans le Secteur Bancaire?', *Revue d'Économie Financière*, 67 (2002), pp. 133–63.
136. Bhattacharya and Thakor, 'Contemporary Banking Theory'.
137. R. Huang and L. Ratnovksi, 'The Dark Side of Bank Wholesale Funding', *Journal of Financial Intermediation*, 20 (2011), pp. 248–63.
138. G. J. Benston, 'Universal Banking', *Journal of Economic Perspectives*, 8:3 (1994), pp. 121–43.
139. O. de Jonghe, 'Back to the Basics in Banking? A Micro-Analysis of Banking Stability', *Journal of Financial Intermediation*, 19 (2010), pp. 387–417.
140. R. DeYoung and K. P. Roland, 'Product Mix and Earning Volatility at Commercial Banks: Evidence from a Degree of Total Leverage Model', *Journal of Financial Intermediation*, 10 (2001), pp. 54–84; K. J. Stiroh, 'Diversification and Banking: Is Noninterest Income the Answer?', *Journal of Money, Credit, and Banking*, 36:5 (2004), pp. 853–82; de Jonghe, 'Back to the Basics'.
141. DeYoung and Roland, 'Product Mix'.
142. S. Mercieca, K. Schaeck and S. Wolfe, 'Small Banks in Europe: Benefits from Diversification?', *Journal of Banking and Finance*, 31 (2007), pp. 1975–98.
143. De Jonghe, 'Back to the Basics'.
144. V. Chiorazzo, C. Milani and F. Salvini, 'Income Diversification and Bank Performance: Evidence from Italian Banks', *Journal of Financial Services Research*, 33 (2008), pp. 181–203.
145. Stiroh, 'Diversification and Banking'.
146. A. Berndt and A. Gupta, 'Moral Hazard and Adverse Selection in the Originate-to-Distribute Model of Bank Credit', *Journal of Monetary Economics*, 56:5 (2009), pp. 725–43.
147. Ibid.
148. G. Duffee, 'Moral Hazard and Adverse Selection in the Originate-to-Distribute Model of Bank Credit. A Discussion', *Journal of Monetary Economics*, 56:5 (2009), pp. 744–7.
149. Coco and Ferri, 'From Shareholders to Stakeholders Finance'.
150. F. Allen and D. Gale, 'Financial Markets, Intermediaries, and Intertemporal Smoothing', *Journal of Political Economy*, 105:3 (1997), pp. 523–46.
151. Ayadi et al., *Investigating Diversity in ... Cooperative Banks*, p. 108.
152. Diamond and Rajan, 'Liquidity Risk, Liquidity Creation and Financial Fragility'; D. W. Diamond and R. G. Rajan, 'A Theory of Bank Capital', *Journal of Finance*, 55:6 (2000), pp. 2431–65.
153. However, as one of the contributors to this volume, A. Schclarek, has pointed out, the counter-cyclicality of alternative banks might be more visible in certain phases of business cycles. See his contribution to this volume (Chapter 3) for a much more detailed and exhaustive treatment of this issue.
154. Ayadi et al., *Investigating Diversity in ...Cooperative Banks*.
155. Coco and Ferri, 'From Shareholders to Stakeholders Finance'.
156. Berlin and Mester, 'On the Profitability and Cost of Relationship Lending'.
157. Ayadi et al., *Investigating Diversity in ...Cooperative Banks*.
158. Fonteyne, 'Cooperative Banks in Europe', p. 4.
159. Allen and Gale, 'Financial Markets'.
160. Boot, 'Relationship Banking'.
161. Petersen and Rajan, 'The Benefits of Lending Relationships'.

5 Groeneveld, 'A Qualitative and Statistical Analysis of European Cooperative Banking Groups'

1. EACB, *European Cooperative Banks in the Financial and Economic Turmoil: First Assessments*, Research Paper (Brussels: EACB, 2010); J. Birchall, *Resilience in a Downturn: The Power of Financial Cooperatives* (Geneva: International Labour Office, 2013).
2. R. Ayadi, R. H. Schmidt, D. T. Llewellyn, E. Arbak and W. P. De Groen, *Investigating Diversity in the Banking Sector in Europe: Key Developments, Performance and Role of Cooperative Banks* (Brussels: Centre for European Policy Studies, 2010).
3. M. Stefancic and N. Kathiziotis, 'An Evaluation of Italian Banks in the Period of Financial Distress', *International Business & Economics Research Journal*, 10:10 (2011), pp. 103–13; J. Mooij and W. W. Boonstra (eds), *Raiffeisen's Footprint: The Cooperative Way of Banking* (Amsterdam: VU University Press, 2012); A. Bley, 'Lending Stabilizer – German Cooperative Banks during the Financial Crisis', paper presented at the Conference on 'Cooperative Responses to Global Challenges', Berlin, Germany, 21–3 March 2012.
4. EACB, *Cooperative Banks in Europe: Values and Practices to Promote Development* (Brussels: EACB, 2005).
5. See Chapter 1 of the present volume for a more extensive historical account of the origins and development of cooperative banks in nineteenth-century Europe.
6. See, for instance, C. Bosseno, *Crédit Agricole, Un Siècle au Présent, 1894–1994, Tome 1: Des Origines aux Années 1950* (Paris: Hervas, 1994); G. Aschhoff and E. Hennigsen, *The German Cooperative System – Its History, Structure and Strength* (Frankfurt a.M.: Fritz Knapp Verlag, 1995); J. Brazda (ed.), '150 Jahre Volksbanken in Österreich', *Schulze-Delitzsch Schriftenreihe*, 23 (2001); W. Werner, 'Auf der Straße des Erfolges – Zur Geschichte der österreichischen Raiffeisenbewegung von kleinen Ortsgenossenschaften zu international tätigen Netzwerken', *Kooperation und Wettbewerb*, 4 (2005); E. Albert, *Les Banques Populaires en France, 1878–2009; 130 Ans de Coopération* (Paris: Eyrolles, 2008); and J. Mooij (ed.), *Rabobank Matters* (Utrecht: Rabobank, 2009).
7. The practice of charging excessive interest rates was an ordinary characteristic of the era. According to some early reports, annual rates in excess of 30 per cent were not uncommon in Germany; T. W. Guinnane, 'Cooperatives as Information Machines: German Rural Credit Cooperatives, 1883–1914', *Journal of Economic History*, 61:2 (2001), pp. 366–89, on p. 368.
8. Putnam defines social capital as consisting of '*social networks (among individuals) and the norms of reciprocity and trustworthiness that arises from them*'; R. D. Putnam, *Bowling Alone: The Collapse and Revival of American Community* (New York: Simon & Schuster, 2000), p. 19.
9. M. Ghatak, 'Screening by the Company You Keep: Joint Liability Lending and the Peer Selection Effect', *Economic Journal*, 110:465 (2000), pp. 601–31.
10. In Sweden, the *Föreningsbanken Sverige* was more or less forced by the government to convert in 1993 from a cooperative ownership structure to a stock corporation. The transformation in the legal form of *Föreningsbanken* and its subsequent share listing meant the end of the bank's long legacy and identity as a cooperative institution; see J. Körnert, 'Swedish Cooperative Banking in the 1990s: A Decade of Crisis and Transition', in Mooij and Boonstra (eds), *Raiffeisen's Footprint*, pp. 217–30.
11. A striking example is the wave of demutualization of mutual building societies in the United Kingdom in the 1990s; see D. T. Llewellyn, 'UK Building Societies: The Strengths of Mutuality', in Mooij and Boonstra (eds), *Raiffeisen's Footprint*, pp. 231–46.

Since then, these societies adopted riskier business models, faced severe losses in the latest financial crises, went bankrupt or were close to failure.

12. Y. Alexopoulos and S. Goglio, 'Financial Deregulation and Economic Distress: Is There a Future for Financial Co-operatives?', Euricse Working Papers, 001 (2009).

13. As an example, the French *Crédit Agricole* S. A., listed since 2006 on the Euronext Paris, was created to represent all of the Group's business lines and components. As of December 2011, 56.2 per cent of *Crédit Agricole* S. A. was owned by the regional banks that make up the Federation of *Crédit Agricole*, and 38.7 per cent was owned by institutional and individual investors.

14. For instance, the Austrian Volksbanken Group had to change its structure fundamentally in 2011 when it received state aid to compensate for considerable capital losses incurred in Central and Eastern Europe.

15. O. Wyman, *Co-operative Bank, Customer Champion* (London: Oliver Wyman Financial Services, 2008).

16. See M. Desrochers and K. Fischer, 'The Power of Networks: Integration and Financial Cooperative Performance', *Annals of Public and Cooperative Economics*, 76:3 (2005), pp. 307–54. The Dutch Rabobank Group is one of the most centralized systems, whereas the Italian cooperative banking sector is the most decentralized system.

17. See Ayadi et al., *Investigating Diversity in ... Cooperative Banks*, ch. 3.

18. R. Di Salvo, 'The Governance of Mutual and Cooperative Bank Systems in Europe', *Cooperative Studies*, Edizioni del Credito Cooperativo (2003). For instance, the French *Crédit Agricole* Group has a three-tier network, comprising local, regional and central organizations. The Dutch Rabobank has a two-tier network, consisting of local member banks and the central organization. The Italian *banche popolari* system has no national structure at all, with all member banks acting completely independently of each other.

19. This is the case for the Austrian *Volksbanken*, the Finnish *OP-Pohjola* Group and the Dutch Rabobank Group. In these countries, the supervisors have delegated to the respective APEX organizations formal supervisory powers over its member banks. These central institutions themselves are supervised by the national supervisors.

20. The Finnish *OP-Pohjola* Group and the Dutch Rabobank Group have internal support schemes for local cooperative banks with the most far-reaching 'joint liability'. Associations with joint liability allow creditors to make direct claims against the group if the amount owed by the troubled entity is not forthcoming. In effect, joint liability automatically implies a significant degree of pooling among the participating entities.

21. G. Ferri, P. Kalmi and E. Kerola, 'Organizational Structure and Exposure to Crisis among European Banks: Evidence from Rating Changes', University of Bary, Italy, Working Paper (2013).

22. O. Wyman, *The Outlook for Co-operative Banking in Europe 2012: Banking on Values, Building on Agility* (London: Oliver Wyman Financial Services, 2012).

23. P. Kalmi, 'The Disappearance of Co-operatives from Economics Textbooks', *Cambridge Journal of Economics*, 31 (2007), pp. 625–47.

24. Ayadi et al., *Investigating Diversity in ... Cooperative Banks*.

25. C. Gijselinckx and P. Develtere, 'The Cooperative Trilemma: Cooperatives between Market, State and Civil Society', Working Papers on Social and Co-operative Entrepreneurship, WP-SCE 08–01 (2008).

26. A subsidiary of the Austrian Raiffeisenbanken, Raiffeisen Zentral Bank, is listed. BGZ, a 100 per cent subsidiary of Rabobank in Poland, is also partly listed.

27. The Dutch Rabobank pursued the Great Cooperative Debate in the years 1995 through 1997. After intense discussions, it was decided to retain the cooperative identity. It was believed that a different legal format with fairly uncertain effects would diminish the countervailing power of members' influence on the day-to-day business decisions of professionals managing the cooperative banking group. The conviction was that there were great opportunities for a viable and strong cooperative bank with a critical mass amidst private banks. This bank would enrich the banking landscape with a distinctive business model and philosophy, thereby contributing to diversity in banking.

28. Deloitte, *Funding the Future: Emerging Strategies in Cooperative Financing and Capitalization*, Report commissioned for the 2012 International Summit of Cooperatives, Quebec City, 8–11 October 2012.

29. L. Kodres and A. Narain, 'Redesigning the Contours of the Future Financial System', *IMF Staff Position Note*, SPN/10/10 (2010).

30. PA Consulting Group, *Mutually Assured Destruction?* (London: PA Consulting, 2003).

31. For instance, Wyman, *Co-operative Bank*.

32. See J. M. Groeneveld and D. T. Llewellyn, 'Corporate Governance in Cooperative Banks', in Mooij and Boonstra (eds), *Raiffeisen's Footprint*, pp. 19–36. This refers to potential conflicts of interest between managers and owners of a bank. Agency issues arise in any organization in which there is a separation of decision- and risk-taking functions. In the case of cooperative banks, these issues emerge between the management and the members. In the case of shareholder value companies, these issues occur between the management and shareholders.

33. EACB, *60 Million Members in Co-operative Banks: What Does It Mean?* (Brussels: EACB, 2007).

34. EACB, *Cooperative Banks in Europe*.

35. A. W. A. Boot, 'Relationship Banking: What Do We Know?', *Journal of Financial Intermediation*, 9 (2000), pp. 7–25.

36. J. Birchall and L. Hammond Ketilson, *Resilience of the Co-operative Business Model in Times of Crisis* (Geneva: International Labour Office, 2009).

37. United Nations, 'Cooperatives in Social Development and Implementation of the International Year of Cooperatives', agenda item A/66/136 (2011).

38. Deloitte, *Funding the Future*; McKinsey, *McKinsey on Cooperatives* (McKinsey & Company, 2012); Wyman, *The Outlook for Cooperative Banking*.

39. 'Europe's Cooperative Banks: Mutual Respect', *Economist*, 23 January 2010, p. 28.

40. W. Davies, *Reinventing the Firm* (London: Demos, 2009).

41. Kalmi, 'The Disappearance of Co-operatives from Economics Textbooks'; W. Fonteyne, 'Cooperative Banks in Europe – Policy Issues', IMF Working Paper, WP/07/159 (2007).

42. Accountability to shareholders does not operate perfectly or according to a standard textbook regarding the actual drawbacks of the investor-owned model. Many institutional shareholders are arguing that, in practice, their ability to bring inefficient management to task is limited. Besides, institutional investors often do not believe they have significant control, and many believe it is not their function to exercise monitoring and control of the companies in which they hold shares. The discipline of the capital market works very imperfectly for listed banks as well. Companies are not in practice motivated exclusively by the maximization of shareholder value: they may follow a wide variety of objectives and are conscious of a multitude of different stakeholders' interests that at times may conflict with the interests of shareholders.

43. Groeneveld and Llewellyn, 'Corporate Governance'.

44. B. Ensor, *Customer Advocacy 2011: How Customers Rate European Banks*, Forrester report for eBusiness & Channel Strategy Professionals (Cambridge, MA: Forrester, 2012); Wyman, *The Outlook for Cooperative Banking*.

45. Northern Rock, Fortis, UBS and Royal Bank of Scotland are clear examples of this.

46. H. Bonin, 'French Cooperative Banks across Crises in the 1930s and in 2007–2012', in Mooij and Boonstra (eds), *Raiffeisen's Footprint*, pp. 19–36.

47. Wyman, *Co-operative Bank*.

48. L. Laeven and R. Levine, 'Bank Governance, Regulation and Risk Taking', *Journal of Financial Economics*, 93 (2009), pp. 259–75.

49. We have restricted our empirical analysis to European cooperative banking groups for two main reasons. The first one is that reliable data on cooperative banks in other parts of the world are hardly available. Second, cooperative banks in other parts of the world operate in totally different economic, regulatory and social circumstances and differ regarding their development phase and maturity. So the overall analysis would be obscured by situations that differ considerably across continents.

50. In some cases, the consolidated figures were constructed upon request by the author. The data for the Italian *banche popolari* are an example.

51. EACB, *Cooperative Banks in Europe*.

52. In the midst of the recession and ongoing sovereign debt crisis in the second quarter of 2011, only 29 per cent of Europeans believed their bank acted in their best interest; see Ensor, *Customer Advocacy 2011*. According to this survey, the top-rated banks regarding customer advocacy appeared to keep things simple, operate transparently, build trust, and treat their customers benevolently.

53. J. Michie, 'Promoting Corporate Diversity in the Financial Services Sector', *Policy Studies*, 32:4 (2011), pp. 309–23; Ensor, *Customer Advocacy 2011*; Wyman, *The Outlook for Cooperative Banking*.

54. The membership ratio, defined as the percentage of customers that are members, cannot be calculated with great precision. The reason is that not all ECBGs report separate data of customers of (i) local cooperative banks and (ii) other domestic or foreign group subsidiaries. Besides, the customer figures are clouded by double counting.

55. The reason for this decline is the reduced business activity of Nykredit in the mortgage market due to tough competition. Until 2012 customers of Nykredit became members automatically when they got a mortgage loan. Therefore in 2003 Nykredit acquired Totalkredit in order to strengthen its competitive power and win back market shares. In 2012 Nykredit opened up for the opportunity for Totalkredit customers to become members (on a voluntary basis).

56. This can be attributed to a very active membership policy after the finalization of the Great Cooperative Debate in 1998; see Mooij, *Rabobank Matters*.

57. Reasons to become a member are manifold (EACB, *60 Million Members*). It all starts with trust and confidence in the bank. When these elements are present, marketing and brand research show that customers attach great importance to both material and immaterial aspects. For instance, the extent to which customers feel that the bank acts in their interests, the identification with the brand, access to the bank's networks and knowledge, the stability/duration of relationships, the way banks deal with environmental and sustainability issues, the degree of product and price transparency, etc.

58. Ensor, *Customer Advocacy 2011*; Wyman, *The Outlook for Cooperative Banking*.

59. In France ECBGs acquired several private banks over the time sample. The rise in market shares in 2009 was partly due to the merger between Banques Populaires and Caisses d'épargne.
60. CEPS, *Bank State Aid in the Financial Crisis: Fragmentation or Level Playing Field?*, CEPS Task Force Report (Brussels: CEPS, 2010).
61. EACB, *Cooperative Banks in Europe*.
62. Wyman, *Cooperative Bank*.
63. However, some ECBGs do pay limited dividends to members.
64. This impossibility to issue shares on the stock exchange is not a feature exclusive to most non-listed ECBGs, though. The recent financial crisis has demonstrated that quite a number of listed banks were unable to issue shares, when their capital vanished into thin air as a result of substantial losses and write-downs. Instead, quite a few listed banks had to be rescued by some form of state support. Moreover, without a certain profit level, investors will not be inclined to buy additional shares. Consequently, the bank in question will be unable to expand its capital buffer by issuing new shares.
65. A. Cunningham, 'European Cooperative Banks: Moving beyond Issues of Costs and Efficiency', Moody's Special Comment (London: Moody's Investors Service, 2003); Wyman, *Cooperative Bank*; H. Hesse and M. Čihák, 'Cooperative Banks and Financial Stability', IMF Working Paper, WP/07/02 (2007).
66. Laeven and Levine, 'Bank Governance'; S. Mercieca, K. Schaeck and S. Wolfe, 'Small Banks in Europe: Benefits from Diversification?', *Journal of Banking and Finance*, 31 (2007), pp. 1975–98.
67. While in large parts of the literature the volatility of RoA is computed over the full sample period, we use the average $\sigma(RoAi)$ for the period 2002–5 and a four-year rolling time window for $\sigma(RoAi)$ to allow for time variation in the denominator of the Z-score starting in 2006. This approach avoids the situation where the variation in Z-scores over time is exclusively driven by variation in the levels of capital and profitability.
68. Hesse and Čihák, 'Cooperative Banks'.
69. CEPS, *Bank State Aid in the Financial Crisis*.
70. PA Consulting Group, *Mutually Assured Destruction?*
71. A similar pattern emerges for the return on equity (RoE), with one notable exception. In the sub-period 2002–6, RoE*ECBG* was significantly lower than RoE*TBS*. The opposite is true for the time span 2007–11. Over the entire period, RoE*ECBG* and RoE*TBS* were exactly the same (7.8 per cent). The volatility of RoE*ECBG* is consistently lower in every sub-period.
72. J. M. Groeneveld, 'Morality and Integrity in Cooperative Banking', *Ethical Perspectives*, 18:4 (2011), pp. 515–40.
73. Compared to balance sheet totals and equity, the initial write-downs/losses at ECBGs were substantial in a number of cases, but they could absorb these capital losses without substantial state aid. In France, all cooperative banks received support as part of a support package for the entire banking system. It is unknown whether they really needed this support or not. In Austria, the international subsidiary of Volksbanken (Volksbanken International) needed state support in 2010 following severe losses in Central and Eastern Europe. One of the attached conditions was that Volksbanken had to adjust their organizational structure and expropriate the major part of its international activities. In 2012 some cooperative banks operating in Greece, Spain, Portugal and Cyprus were hit hard by the problems in the respective banking sectors and economic recession.

74. This is also in line with the finding of Wyman, *The Outlook for Cooperative Banking*, p. 21, that average retail revenues as a percentage of total revenues of some ECBGs are higher than those of all other banks.

75. M. López-Puertas Lamy, 'Commercial Banks versus Stakeholder Banks: Same Business, Same Risks, Same Rules?', Working Paper prepared for the EACB Award for Young Researchers (2012).

76. J. M. Groeneveld and B. de Vries, 'European Cooperative Banks: First Lessons of the Subprime Crisis', *International Journal of Cooperative Management*, 4:2 (2009), pp. 8–21.

77. Deloitte, *Funding the Future*.

6 Schmidt, Bülbül and Schüwer, 'The Persistence of the Three-Pillar Banking System in Germany'

1. For a definition and classification of 'alternative banks', see the introductory chapters in this volume.

2. A note on terminology is required here: 'Credit institutions' (*Kreditbanken*) is the official term in German banking law, and it is also used in the statistics of the Deutsche Bundesbank, Germany's central bank, to designate private banks.

3. 'Big banks' (*Grossbanken*) is also a quasi-official term used in central bank statistics, designating banks with an extended network of branches. Currently this group comprises four institutions: Deutsche Bank AG, Commerzbank AG, Hypo-Vereinsbank-AG (a subsidiary of the Italian UniCredit Group) and Postbank AG (now a subsidiary of Deutsche Bank AG).

4. For a thorough description and analysis of the developments of the German banking sector over the last decades, see also A. Hackethal, 'German Banks and Banking Structure', in J. P. Krahnen and R. H. Schmidt (eds), *The German Financial System* (Oxford: Oxford University Press, 2004), pp. 71–105. Discussions of German savings banks and of German cooperative banks can also be found, respectively, in R. Ayadi, R. H. Schmidt and S. Carbò Verde, *Investigating Diversity in the Banking Sector in Europe: The Performance and Role of Savings Banks* (Brussels: Centre for European Policy Studies, 2009) on pp. 113–38; and in R. Ayadi, R. H. Schmidt, D. T. Llewellyn, E. Arbak and W. P. De Groen, *Investigating Diversity in the Banking Sector in Europe: Key Developments, Performance and Role of Cooperative Banks* (Brussels: Centre for European Policy Studies, 2010), on pp. 27–42. On German cooperative banks, see also H. H. Kotz and J. Nagel, 'Les Banques du Secteur Coopératif Allemand sont-elles Construites sur un Avantage Comparative Déclinant?', *Revue d'Économie Financière*, 67 (2002), pp. 57–71; and H. H. Kotz, A. Hackethal and M. Tyrell, 'Les Banques Coopératives en Allemagne: Performance et Défis', in *Le Rapport Moral sur l'Argent dans le Monde* (Paris: Association d'économie financière, 2007), pp. 129–41.

5. Some authors have recently coined the term 'dual bottom line institutions' for financial institutions that aspire not only to be profitable but also to serve other purposes at the same time; see, for example, M. S. Barr, A. Kumar and R. E. Litan (eds), *Building Inclusive Financial Systems* (Washington, DC: Brookings, 2007).

6. Examples for the cooperation among private banks are their cooperation in the monitoring and corporate governance of their corporate clients and their cooperation in powerful associations and lobbying groups. As Abelshauser reports in W. Abelshauser, *Kulturkampf: Der deutsche Weg in die Neue Wirtschaft und die amerikanische Heraus-*

forderung (Berlin: Kulturverlag Kadmos, 2003), close intra-industry cooperation has for a long time been a characteristic feature of the German economy, for which close cooperation among large banks is one of the most prominent examples.

7. See K.-H. Fischer and C. Pfeil, 'Regulation and Competition in German Banking: An Assessment', in J. P. Krahnen and R. H. Schmidt (eds), *The German Financial System* (Oxford: Oxford University Press, 2004), pp. 291–349; K.-H., Fischer, *Banken und unvollkommener Wettbewerb* (Wiesbaden: Deutscher Universitätsverlag, 2005); and E. Carletti, H. Hakenes and I. Schnabel, 'The Privatization of Italian Savings Banks – A Role Model for Germany?', *DIW Quarterly Journal of Economic Research*, 74:4 (2005), pp. 32–50.

8. The same critique has also been expressed with respect to *Landesbanken* and their business with medium-sized and large corporations – at least until the public guarantees were abolished as of 2005. In this respect the critique was certainly appropriate.

9. World Bank, 'Commercial bank branches (per 100,000 adults)' (2013), at http://data.worldbank.org/indicator [accessed 1 August 2013].

10. Several studies provide evidence that significant *Hausbank* relationships still existed in the 1990s: see R. Elsas, 'Empirical Determinants of Relationship Lending', *Journal of Financial Intermediation*, 14:1 (2005), pp. 32–57; R. Elsas and J. P. Krahnen, 'Is Relationship Lending Special? Evidence from Credit-File Data in Germany', *Journal of Banking and Finance*, 22:10 (1998), pp. 1283–316; R. Elsas and J. P. Krahnen, 'Universal Banks and Relationships with Firms', in J. P. Krahnen and R. H. Schmidt (eds), *The German Financial System* (Oxford: Oxford University Press, 2004), pp. 197–232; and D. Harhoff and T. Körting, 'Lending Relationships in Germany – Empirical Evidence from Survey Data', *Journal of Banking and Finance*, 22:10 (1998), pp. 1317–53. These studies contradict the earlier view held by J. Edwards and K. Fischer, *Banks, Finance and Investment in Germany* (Cambridge: Cambridge University Press, 1996), i.e. that the *Hausbank* relationship is more of a marketing myth than a relevant business principle.

11. See A. Hackethal, R. H. Schmidt and M. Tyrell, 'Disintermediation and the Role of Banks in Europe', *Journal of Financial Intermediation*, 8 (1999), pp. 36–67, on the methodology of calculating and assessing intermediation ratios – as well as early empirical results for a number of countries. More recent calculations are contained in F. Kirchner, 'Essays on Economic and Financial Systems: An International Comparison' (PhD dissertation, Goethe University, 2012).

12. See F. Allen and A. M. Santomero, 'What Do Financial Intermediaries Do?', *Journal of Banking and Finance*, 25:2 (2001), pp. 271–94.

13. See R. H. Schmidt and M. Tyrell, 'What Constitutes a Financial System in General and the German Financial System in Particular?', in J. P. Krahnen and R. H. Schmidt (eds), *The German Financial System* (Oxford: Oxford University Press, 2004), pp. 19–67, on the meaning and importance of the concept of complementarity in the context of financial institutions and financial systems.

14. The list of those self-declared savings banks that are members of the World Savings Banks Institute, the international association of savings banks, provides a good illustration of this heterogeneity. See also G. Manghetti, 'Do Savings Banks Differ from Traditional Commercial Banks?', in World Savings Banks Institute/ European Savings Banks Group, *200 Years of Savings Banks: A Strong and Lasting Business Model for Responsible, Regional Retail Banking* (Brussels: WSBI/ESBG, 2011), pp. 141–56, on p. 141, on the problem of defining savings banks in a way that would allow distinguishing savings banks from other banks today.

15. Features (iii) to (vii) were applicable in the past or, as the case may be, they are also still applicable today.
16. The German term for these dense networks is *Verbünde*. Since such networks of banks do not exist in Anglo-Saxon countries, there is no term in English that would properly capture the meaning of *Verbünde*.
17. Even in the past, not all national systems of savings banks exhibited all seven features in the same way and to the same extent. One exception is that of Great Britain, where already one hundred years ago the formerly decentralized savings banks were superseded by a single national savings bank. This is why we do not consider the British case in the article.
18. Of course, a trade-off between the disadvantage and the advantage of the institutional set-up has to be found. Without going into details, one might add here that the monitoring function that is performed by certain central institutions of cooperative banking networks serves to limit the negative effects to a considerable extent. For details, see Ayadi et al., *Investigating Diversity in ... Cooperative Banks*, p. 38.
19. Among them are the Bausparkasse (Building Society) Schwäbisch-Hall and the asset management company Union Investment, both among the largest institutions of their kind in Germany.
20. The performance indicators of the central financial institutions of the savings bank group and the cooperative bank group, which are not shown in Figure 6.1, are largely similar to those of the big banks.
21. Y. Altunbas, L. Evans and P. Molyneux, 'Ownership and Efficiency in Banking', *Journal of Money, Credit and Banking*, 33:4 (2001), pp. 926–54.
22. Fonteyne correctly points out that merely comparing performance figures at the level of the institutions would be misleading since it leaves out benefits created at the level of the clients. See W. Fonteyne, 'Cooperative Banks in Europe – Policy Issues', IMF Working Paper, WP/07/159 (2007).
23. T. Beck, H. Hesse, T. Kick and N. von Westernhagen, 'Bank Ownership and Stability: Evidence from Germany', Tilburg University Working Paper (2009).
24. For a sample of 181 large banks (with total assets of at least €10 billion) from 15 European countries, Iannotta et. al. find that cooperative banks have better loan quality and lower asset risk than private banks, while private banks have better loan quality and lower insolvency risk than public sector banks. They do not explore risk proxies of small local banks; G. Iannotta, G. Nocera and A. Sironi, 'Ownership Structure, Risk and Performance in the European Banking Industry', *Journal of Banking and Finance*, 31 (2007), pp. 2127–49.
25. The findings by La Porta et al., which also suggest that private banks are better for economic growth than public banks, were very influential for banking reforms around the world during the last decade; see R. La Porta, F. Lopez-de-Silanes and A. Shleifer, 'Government Ownership of Banks', *Journal of Finance*, 57 (2002), pp. 265–301. However, more recent studies question that their findings can be generalized. For example, Körner and Schnabel find that a negative impact of public ownership on growth is only evident for countries with low financial development and low institutional quality; see T. Körner and I. Schnabel, 'Public Ownership of Banks and Economic Growth: The Impact of Country Heterogeneity', *Economics of Transition*, 19:3 (2011), pp. 407–41.
26. P. Behr, L. Norden and F. Noth, 'Financial Constraints of Private Firms and Bank Lending Behaviour', *Journal of Banking and Finance*, 37 (2013), pp. 3472–85.
27. One cooperative bank, Apo Bank, also reported a loss in 2008. Interestingly, it is an atypical cooperative bank since it is not regionally focused and instead serves two professions, those of doctors and pharmacists, as its clientele.

28. For more details, see Ayadi et al., *Investigating Diversity in ... Cooperative Banks*, and Ayadi et al., *Investigating Diversity in ... Savings Banks*; for more recent developments, see D. Bülbül, R.H. Schmidt and U. Schüwer, 'Savings Banks and Cooperative Banks in Europe' (in French), *Revue d'économie financière* (forthcoming 2013). On cooperative banks in Europe, see also Fonteyne, 'Cooperative Banks in Europe'.
29. An exemption is the abolishment of public guarantees for German *Landesbanken* and local savings banks since 2005.
30. Ayadi et al., *Investigating Diversity in ... Savings Banks*; Ayadi et al., *Investigating Diversity in ... Cooperative Banks*.
31. A critical assessment of the governance of Spanish savings banks after the reforms – and thus of the half-hearted privatization – can be found in H. Mai, *Spain's Cajas: Deregulated, but Not Depoliticized*, EU Monitor, 20 (Frankfurt: Deutsche Bank Research, 2004).
32. For details on this political debate concerning savings banks, see R. H. Schmidt, 'The Political Debate about Savings Banks', *Schmalenbach Business Review*, 61 (2009), pp. 366–92; J. Birchall and H. L. Ketilson, *Resilience of the Cooperative Business Model in Times of Crisis* (Geneva: International Labour Office, 2009); and, more recently, J. Birchall, *Finance in an Age of Austerity: The Power of Customer-Owned Banks* (Cheltenham: Edward Elgar, 2013) for the case of cooperative banks.

7 Giordano and Lopes, 'Alternative Banks in a Dualistic Economy: The Case of Italy before and during the Euro Crisis'

1. J. Williams, 'Determining Management Behavior in European Banking', *Journal of Banking and Finance*, 28 (2003), pp. 2427–60.
2. D. Focarelli, F. Panetta and C. Salleo, 'Determinanti e Consequenze delle Acquisizioni e Fusioni in Italia. Un' Analisi Empirica (1984–1996)', *Banca, Impresa e società*, 18:1 (1999), pp. 63–92.
3. P. Bongini and G. Ferri, *Il Sistema Bancario Meridionale* (Rome and Bari: Editori Laterza, 2005).
4. L. Giordano and A. Lopes, 'Reti Bancarie, Credito e Sistema Produttivo Meridionale', *Rivista Economica del Mezzogiorno*, 23:4 (2009), pp. 827–68.
5. D. Focarelli and F. Panetta, 'Are Mergers Beneficial to Consumers? Evidence from the Market for Bank Deposits', *American Economic Review*, 93:4 (2003), pp. 1152–72.
6. The scores measuring cost and profit efficiency are between zero and one (maximum efficiency); for more details, see L. Giordano and A. Lopes, 'Analysis of the Italian Banking System Efficiency: A Stochastic Frontier Approach', in A. G. S. Ventre, A. Maturo, S. Hoskova-Mayerova and J. Kacprzyk (eds), *Multicriteria and Multiagent Decision Making with Applications to Economic and Social Sciences* (Berlin and Heidelberg: Springer-Verlag, 2012), pp. 20–45.
7. See, for example, S. Grimadi, C. Guagliano and J. S. Lopez, 'L'Evoluzione della Struttura Distributiva delle Banche Italiane dal 2001 al 2006', *Cooperazione di credito*, 195:6 (2007), pp. 7–69.
8. P. Angelini, R. Di Salvo and G. Ferri, 'Availability and Cost of Credit for Small Businesses: Customer Relationships and Credit Cooperatives', *Journal of Banking and Finance*, 22:6 (1998), pp. 925–54; O. Butzbach, 'Il Vantaggio Comparato delle Banche Cooperative nella Letteratura Economica', in A. Giannola, A. Lopes and D. Sarno (eds), *I Problemi dello Sviluppo Economico e del suo Finanziamento nelle Aree Deboli* (Rome: Carocci, 2012), pp. 203–45.

9. Giordano and Lopes, 'Reti Bancarie'.
10. A. Giannola, A. Lopes and A. Zazzaro, 'La Convergenza dello Sviluppo Finanziario tra le Regioni Italiane dal 1890 ad oggi', *Rivista di Politica Economica* (January–March 2013), pp. 145–97.
11. SVIMEZ, *Rapporto sull'economia del Mezzogiorno 2009* (Bologna: Il Mulino, 2009), ch. 12.
12. Ibid.
13. Banca d'Italia, *L'Economia delle Regioni Italiane* (Rome: Banca d'Italia, 2007).
14. O. Butzbach and A. Lopes, 'Mutamento degli Assetti Proprietari e Performance del Sistema Bancario nel Mezzogiorno (1994–2003)', in A. Giannola (ed.), *Riforme Istituzionali e Mutamento Strutturale. Mercati, Imprese e Istituzioni in un Sistema Dualistico* (Rome: Carocci, 2006), pp. 231–51.
15. See Banca d'Italia, *Indagine sul Credito Bancario nell'Area dell'Euro* (Rome: Banca d'Italia, 2010).
16. Ibid.
17. Collateral include financial assets such as shares or debt securities, real estate or even compensatory balances, i.e. the minimum amount of a loan that the recipient must maintain as deposit at the lending bank. It is now obvious that the financial crisis that occurred in 2009, resulting in a decline in securities and real estate values, has reduced the value of collateral and increased risk.
18. J. P. Fitoussi and F. Saraceno, 'European Economic Governance: The Berlin-Washington Consensus', *Cambridge Journal of Economics*, 37 (2013), pp. 479–96.
19. European Central Bank, *Survey on the Access to Finance of Small and Medium-Sized Enterprises (SAFE)* (Frankfurt: ECB, 2012).
20. CONSOB, *Principali Banche Quotate, Aggiornamento Risultati dell'Esercizio 2012 e Tematiche Rilevanti* (Rome: CONSOB, 2013).
21. Banca d'Italia, *Rapporto sulla Stabilità Finanziaria* (Rome: Banca d'Italia, 2013).
22. However, it should be noted that the Bank of Italy is urging banks towards a gradual strengthening of collateral and a progressive increase in the coverage rate of NPL – especially for smaller credit institutions. All this has inevitable consequences for the credit provision to businesses in the medium term.
23. Coefficients of Italian banks remain slightly lower than the other European banks, which in most cases have benefited from substantial public support. In assessing the adequacy of capital ratios, we have to take into account the method of calculation of risk-weighted assets, which for Italian banks are relatively high in relation to total assets.
24. SVIMEZ, *Rapporto 2013*.
25. These data come from the survey conducted by the Bank of Italy (Regional Bank Lending Survey), based on interviews with about 400 financial intermediaries operating in various areas of the country; see Banca d'Italia, *La Domanda e l'Offerta di Credito a Livello Regionale* (Rome: Banca d'Italia, 2012).
26. Ibid.
27. SVIMEZ, *Rapporto 2013*.
28. Ibid.

8 Butzbach, 'Alternative Banks on the Margin: The Case of Building Societies in the United Kingdom'

1. For 'recent' overviews, see H. Ashworth, *The Building Society Story* (London: Franey and Co., 1980); M. Boddy, *The Building Societies* (London: Macmillan, 1980); and M. Boleat, *The Building Society Industry* (London: Allen & Unwin, 1982); for an older but very informative study, S. J. Price, *Building Societies: Their Origin and History* (London: Franey and Co., 1958).
2. H. Bellman, 'Building Societies – Some Economic Aspects', *Economic Journal*, 43:169 (1933), pp. 1–39.
3. J. Holmes, 'People's Future. Building Societies, Co-operative Societies and Model Cottage Societies', *Darlington and Stockton Times*, April 1864, in the London School of Economics Selected Pamphlets collection.
4. W. Chambers, *Building Societies* (1863), in the University of Liverpool Knowsley Pamphlet Collection, p. 5.
5. Ibid., p. 1.
6. As is perhaps inevitably the case in such writings, the story of Chambers's visit is told with many moralistic observations typical of the time, such as when the author notes how, in one of these houses, 'on the parlour-table, like a sun surrounded by planets, lay a handsomely bound family Bible, environed with lesser books in prose and verse; indicating that other feelings besides those of mere animal existence had their proper place in the dwelling'; ibid., p. 13.
7. See Chapter 1 in this volume.
8. Chambers, *Building Societies*, p. 18.
9. Quoted in ibid., p. 24; emphasis added.
10. Ibid., p. 7.
11. Holmes, 'People's Future', p. 3.
12. J. Cook, S. Deakin and A. Hughes, 'Mutuality and Corporate Governance: The Evolution of Building Societies Following Deregulation', ESRC Centre for Business Research, University of Cambridge, Working Paper, 205 (2001).
13. S. E. Platt, *Building Societies Not as They Are But as They Should Be. An Argument for Investors and Borrowers Based on Equity and Mutuality* (London: E. W. Allen, 1877).
14. Quoted in ibid.
15. Ibid., p. 6.
16. Ibid., p. 7.
17. Ibid.
18. Cook et al., 'Mutuality and Corporate Governance'.
19. Platt, *Building Societies*.
20. Ibid., p. 8.
21. Ibid., p. 17.
22. Holmes, 'People's Future', p. 5.
23. Platt, *Building Societies*, p. 14.
24. Chambers, *Building Societies*, p. 15.
25. Platt, *Building Societies*, pp. 10 and 11.
26. See, for instance, P. A. Bongini and G. Ferri, 'Governance, Diversification and Performance: The Case of Italy's Banche Popolari', Milan Bicocca University, Department of Management and Business Administration, Working Paper Series, 02/2008 (2008).
27. Cook et al., 'Mutuality and Corporate Governance', p. 1.

28. P. Hall and D. Soskice (eds), *Varieties of Capitalism: The Institutional Foundations of Comparative Advantage* (Oxford: Oxford University Press, 2001).

29. Bellman, 'Building Societies', p. 7.

30. Ibid.

31. Sir George Stuart Robinson, quoted in ibid., p. 13.

32. J. N. Marshall, R. Richardson, S. Raybould and M. Coombes, 'The Transformation of the British Building Society Movement: Managerial Divisions and Corporate Reorganization, 1986–1997', *Geoforum*, 28:3–4 (1997), pp. 271–88.

33. Ibid.

34. T. J. Gough, *The Economics of Building Societies* (London: Macmillan, 1982).

35. Bellman, 'Building Societies'.

36. D. T. Llewellyn, 'Building Societies and the Financial System', *Building Societies Association Bulletin* (May 1986), pp. 29–42.

37. P. Hardwick, 'Multi-Product Cost Attributes: A Study of UK Building Societies', *Oxford Economic Papers*, 42:2 (1990), pp. 446–61.

38. Marshall et al., 'The Transformation', p. 274.

39. Cook et al., 'Mutuality and Corporate Governance', p. 5.

40. This argument should not be confused with the view that the viability of organizational forms in general, and in banking in particular, must be assessed autonomously from regulations, as if there were some kind of 'natural organizational state' unaffected by state regulation and policies.

41. Cook et al., 'Mutuality and Corporate Governance', p. 17.

42. See, among others, A. Leyshon and N. Thrift, 'The Restructuring of the UK Financial Services Industry in the 1990s: A Reversal of Fortune?', *Journal of Rural Studies*, 9:3 (1993), pp. 223–41; A. Leyshon and N. Thrift, 'Geographies of Financial Exclusion: Financial Abandonment in Britain and the United States', *Transactions of the Institute of British Geographers*, 20:3 (1995), pp. 312–41; A. Leyshon and N. Thrift, 'The Changing Geography of British Banks and Building Society Branch Networks, 1995–2003', University of Nottingham, Working Paper (2006); S. Heffernan, 'The Effect of UK Building Society Conversion on Pricing Behavior', *Journal of Banking and Finance*, 29 (2005), pp. 779–97; Marshall et al., 'The Transformation'; J. N. Marshall, R. Willis, M. Coombes, S. Raybould and R. Richardson, 'Mutuality, De-Mutualization and Communities: The Implications of Branch Network Rationalization in the British Building Society Industry', *Transactions of the Institute of British Geographers*, 25:3 (2000), pp. 355–77; and R. Klimecki and H. Willmott, 'From Demutualization to Meltdown: A Tale of Two Wannabe Banks', *Critical Perspectives on International Business*, 5:1–2 (2009), pp. 120–40.

43. G. Tayler, 'UK Building Societies: "Deregulation" Change Myths', *Services Industries Journal*, 25:6 (2005), pp. 825–43.

44. J. Michie, 'Promoting Corporate Diversity in the Financial Services Sector', *Policy Studies*, 32:4 (2011), pp. 309–23.

45. J. Michie and C. Oughton, 'Measuring Diversity in Financial Services Markets: A Diversity Index', Centre for Financial and Management Studies Discussion Paper Series, 113 (2013).

46. Ibid.

47. It is interesting to note that there are cycles in the scholarly interest on building societies (and on mutuals in general). In the early 1980s the issue of the comparative governance and performance of mutuals with respect to joint-stock banks was discussed extensively, with many scholars drawing on recent and less recent theoretical developments in the

field of agency theory, managerial theories of the firm (in particular Williamson and his hypothesis of managerial expense preference) and property rights theory. P. Barnes, 'The Consequences of Growth Maximisation and Expense Preference Policies of Managers: Evidence from UK Building Societies', *Journal of Business, Finance and Accounting*, 10:4 (1983), pp. 521–30, is a good illustration of this trend. After a decade-long decline in interest, building societies elicited the attention of geographers who, in the late 1990s and early 2000s, investigated the impact of demutualization on socio-economic local development; see, for instance, Leyshon and Thrift, 'The Restructuring'; Leyshon and Thrift, 'Geographies'; and Marshall et al., 'Mutuality, De-Mutualization and Communities'. One important exception is the study by Cook et al., 'Mutuality and Corporate Governance'; one might cite works by Llewellyn as well, such as Llewellyn, 'Building Societies and the Financial System'; and, more recently, D. T. Llewellyn, 'Building Societies and the Banking Crisis', in *Butlers Building Societies Guide* (London: ICAP, 2009). It is only recently, in the post-crisis context, that policymakers and scholars alike have been paying closer attention to the building societies industry and its promises; see Michie, 'Promoting Corporate Diversity'.

48. T. Valnek, 'The Comparative Performance of Mutual Building Societies and Stock Retail Banks', *Journal of Banking and Finance*, 23:6 (1999), pp. 925–38.
49. Barnes, 'The Consequences of Growth Maximization'.
50. Klimecki and Willmott, 'From Demutualization to Meltdown'.
51. H. S. Shin, 'Reflections on Northern Rock: The Bank Run that Heralded the Global Financial Crisis', *Journal of Economic Perspectives*, 23:1 (2009), pp. 101–19.
52. Klimecki and Willmott, 'From Demutualization to Meltdown'.
53. Ibid.
54. Shin, 'Reflections on Northern Rock'.
55. F. Allen and D. Gale, 'Financial Markets, Intermediaries, and Intertemporal Smoothing', *Journal of Political Economy*, 105:3 (1997), pp. 523–46.
56. As Shin argues, Northern Rock was first and foremost a victim of the collapse of wholesale money markets, and therefore does not fit the traditional view of bank runs in the economic literature (as coordination problems among individual depositors); Shin, 'Reflections on Northern Rock'.
57. The British Bankers' Association publishes aggregate data covering the so-called 'Major British Banking Groups', i.e. Santander UK Group (including the retail deposits of Bradford and Bingley), Barclays Group, HSBC Bank Group, Northern Rock plc, Lloyds Banking Group (including Cheltenham and Gloucester plc since October 2007, HBOS since 2010) and Royal Bank of Scotland Group.
58. Heffernan, 'The Effect of UK Building Society Conversion'.
59. Platt, *Building Societies*, p. 14.
60. A feature underlined by Bellman in 1933; see Bellman, 'Building Societies'.

9 Mettenheim, 'The United States: Alternative Banking from Mainstream to the Margins'

1. F. Allen and D. Gale, *Comparing Financial Systems* (Cambridge, MA: MIT Press, 2000), p. 32.
2. Ibid.

3. On free banking in the US, see B. Hammond, *Banks and Politics in America from the Revolution to the Civil War* (Princeton, NJ: Princeton University Press, 1957).

4. For similar claims about London, see P. Dickson, *The Financial Revolution in England: A Study in the Development of Public Credit, 1688–1756* (New York: St Martins, 1967).

5. C. Calomiris, *United States Bank Deregulation in Historical Perspective* (New York: Columbia University Press, 2000).

6. E. White, *The Regulation and Reform of the American Banking System, 1900–1929* (Princeton, NJ: Princeton University Press, 1983).

7. I. Hardie and D. Howarth (eds), *Market-Based Banking and the International Financial Crisis* (Oxford: Oxford University Press, 2013).

8. On bank competition as grounds for reforms, see Allen and Gale, *Comparing Financial Systems*; D. Alhadeff, *Monopoly and Competition in Banking* (Berkeley, CA: University of California Press, 1954); and G. Fischer, *American Banking Structure* (New York: Columbia University Press, 1968).

9. Before the 2008 crisis, Hackethal argued that two interpretations predominated: A. Hackethal, 'How Unique Are US Banks? The Role of Banks in Five Major Financial Systems', *Journal of Economics and Statistics*, 221 (2001), pp. 592–619. The first suggested that the emerging financial paradigm signifies the end of traditional banking and that new policies of bank supervision and regulation are required: see M. Berlin and L. Mester, 'Why is the Banking Sector Shrinking?', Federal Reserve Bank of Philadelphia, Working Paper, 96–18 (1996); F. R. Edwards, *The New Finance: Regulation and Financial Stability* (Washington, DC: AEI Press, 1996); R. E. Litan and J. Rauch, *American Finance for the 21st Century* (Washington, DC: Brookings Institution, 1998); and G. Miller, 'On the Obsolescence of Commercial Banking', *Journal of Institutional and Theoretical Economics*, 154 (1998), pp. 61–73. Another line of scholarship suggested that the end of traditional banking was not foretold and that US banks were well positioned to remain at the centre of financial markets. See J. H. Boyd and M. Gertler, 'Are Banks Dead? Or Are the Reports Greatly Exaggerated?', NBER Working Paper, 5045 (1995).

10. D. Mason, *From Building and Loans to Bail-outs: A History of the American Savings and Loan Industry, 1831–1995* (New York: Cambridge University Press, 2004).

11. R. D. Wadhwani, 'Institutional Foundations of Personal Finance: Innovation in US Savings Banks, 1880s–1920s', *Business History Review*, 85:3 (2011), pp. 499–528.

12. M. H. Kawa and S. Van Bever, 'The Impact of the Financial Crisis on Community Banks: A Conference Summary', Chicago Federal Reserve Bank, Essays on Issues, 272a (2012). Federal Deposit Insurance Corporation, *FDIC Community Bank Study* (Washington, DC: FDIC, 2012).

13. G. Alter, C. Goldin and E. Rotella, 'The Savings of Ordinary Americans: The Philadelphia Saving Fund Society in the Mid-Nineteenth Century', *Journal of Economic History*, 54:4 (1994), pp. 735–67.

14. US Census Bureau, *Historical Statistics of the United States, 1789–1945* (Washington, DC: US Bureau of the Census, 1949), p. 271.

15. D. Hochfelder, '"Where the Common People Could Speculate": The Ticker, Bucket Shops, and the Origins of Popular Participation in Financial Markets, 1880–1920', *Journal of American History*, 93 (2006), pp. 335–58.

16. US Financial Crisis Inquiry Commission, *The Financial Crisis Inquiry Report* (Washington, DC: Government Printing Office, 2011); C. Calomiris and P. J. Wallison, 'The Last Trillion-Dollar Commitment: The Destruction of Fannie Mae and Freddie Mac', *Journal of Structured Finance*, 15:1 (2009), pp. 71–80.

17. The Navy Federal Credit Union is the tenth largest lender.
18. C. Rosenthal, 'Credit Unions, Community Development Finance, and the Great Recession' Federal Reserve Bank of San Francisco, Community Development Investment Center Working Paper Series (2012).
19. This also led to the exposure of major central credit unions to losses in the 2008 financial crisis.
20. Rosenthal, 'Credit Unions', p. 7.
21. H. P. Minsky, D. B. Papadimitriou, R. J. Phillips and L. R. Wray, 'Community Development Banking: A Proposal to Establish a Nationwide System of Community Development Banks', Bard College Levy Economics Institute, Public Policy Brief 3 (1992).

10 Mettenheim, 'BRIC Statecraft and Government Banks'

1. K. von Mettenheim, *Federal Banking in Brazil: Policies and Competitive Advantages* (London: Pickering & Chatto, 2010).
2. R. La Porta, F. Lopez-de-Silanes and A. Schleifer, 'Government Ownership of Banks', *Journal of Finance*, 57:1 (2002), pp. 265–301.
3. E. S. Shaw, *Financial Deepening in Economic Development* (Oxford: Oxford University Press, 1973), and R. I. McKinnon, *Money and Capital in Economic Development* (Washington, DC: Brookings Institute, 1973).
4. B. Steil and R. E. Litan, *Financial Statecraft: The Role of Financial Markets in American Foreign Policy* (New Haven, CT: Yale University Press, 2006).
5. I. Hardie and D. Howarth (eds), *Market-Based Banking and the International Financial Crisis* (Oxford: Oxford University Press, 2013).
6. N. Serra and J. E. Stiglitz (eds), *The Washington Consensus Reconsidered* (New York: Oxford University Press, 2008).
7. C. Conaghan and J. Malloy, *Unsettling Statecraft: Democracy and Neoliberalism in the Central Andes* (Pittsburgh, PA: University of Pittsburgh Press, 1994).
8. L. Sola and L. Whitehead (eds), *Statecrafting Monetary Authority: Democracy and Financial Order in Brazil* (Oxford: University of Oxford Centre for Brazilian Studies, 2006).
9. D. Collier, F. D. Hidalgo and A. O. Maciuceanu, 'Essentially Contested Concepts: Debates and Applications', *Journal of Political Ideologies*, 11:3 (2006), pp. 211–46.
10. F. Allen and D. Gale, *Comparing Financial Systems* (Cambridge, MA: MIT Press, 2000).
11. The terms of this dichotomy are from P. Hall and D. Soskice (eds), *The Varieties of Capitalism: The Institutional Foundations of Comparative Advantage* (Oxford: Oxford University Press, 2001).
12. This distinction is from G. A. Dymski, 'Banking on Transformation: Financing Development, Overcoming Poverty', Paper presented to the UFRJ Economics Institute (September 2003).
13. D. A. Gold, C. Lo and E. O. Wright, 'Recent Developments in Marxist Theories of the Capitalist State', *Monthly Review*, 27:5 (1975), pp. 29–51.
14. This approach is epitomized by K. Polanyi, *The Great Transformation* (New York: Rinehart, 1944); A. Shonfield, *Modern Capitalism* (Oxford: Oxford University Press, 1965); J. Zysman, *Governments, Markets, and Growth: Financial Systems and Politics of Industrial Change* (Ithaca, NY: Cornell University Press, 1983); P. Gourevitch, *Politics in Hard Times* (Ithaca, NY: Cornell University Press, 1986); Conaghan and Malloy, *Unsettling Statecraft*; and Sola and Whitehead (eds), *Statecrafting Monetary Authority*.

15. See Chapter 1.
16. Shonfield, *Modern Capitalism*.
17. C. E. Lindblom, 'The Science of 'Muddling Through', *Public Administration Review*, 192 (1959), pp. 79–88.
18. J. Kirschner (ed.), *Monetary Orders: Ambiguous Economics, Ubiquitous Politics* (Ithaca, NY: Cornell University Press, 2003).
19. S. Hoffmann, *Politics and Banking: Ideas, Public Policy and the Creation of Financial Institutions* (Ithaca, NY: Cornell University Press, 2001).
20. H. Laurence, *Money Rules: The New Politics of Finance in Britain and Japan* (Ithaca, NY: Cornell University Press, 2001).
21. S. Haggard, C. Lee and S. Maxfield (eds), *The Politics of Finance in Developing Countries* (Ithaca, NY: Cornell University Press, 1993).
22. For an overview, see O. Canuto and M. Guigale, *The Day after Tomorrow* (Washington, DC: World Bank, 2010).
23. World Bank, *Brazil: The Industry Structure of Banking Services* (Brasília: June 2007).
24. Although military government ended direct elections for the presidency, governorships and capital (and large) cities, elections for federal and state legislatures and small municipalities continued. See K. von Mettenheim, *The Brazilian Voter: Mass Politics in Democratic Transition, 1974–1986* (Pittsburgh, PA: University of Pittsburgh, 1995).
25. A. Fleury and M. T. L. Fleury, *Brazilian Multinationals: Competences for Internationalization* (Cambridge: Cambridge University Press, 2011).
26. On the liberalization of banking in India, see C. Roland, *Banking Sector Liberalization in India: Evaluation of Reforms and Comparative Perspectives on China* (Heidelberg: Physica-Verlag, 2008); P. Gupta, K. Kochhar and S. Panth, 'Bank Ownership and the Effects of Financial Liberalization: Evidence from India', IMF Working Paper, WP/11/50 (2011); and A. V. Banerjee, S. Cole and E. Duflo, 'Banking Reform in India'. *Brookings Papers on Economic Activity*, 1:1 (2004), pp. 277–332.
27. Wen Jiabao, *Wall Street Journal*, 4 April 2012, p. 1.
28. J. Kornai, *The Socialist System: The Political Economy of Communism* (Princeton, NJ: Princeton University Press, 1992).
29. V. Shih, *Factions and Finance in China: Elite Conflict and Inflation* (Cambridge: Cambridge University Press, 2008).
30. V. Shih, 'Dealing with Non-Performing Loans: Political Constraints and Financial Policies in China', *China Quarterly*, 180 (2004), pp. 922–44; and M. F. Martin, 'China's Banking System: Issues for Congress' (Washington, DC: Congressional Research Service, 2012).
31. See S. V. Lawrence and M. F. Martin, 'Understanding China's Political System', (Washington, DC: Congressional Research Service, 2012), and K. Lieberthal, *Managing the China Challenge: How to Achieve Corporate Success in the People's Republic* (Washington, DC: Brookings Institution Press, 2011) on the ministerial-level importance of executive posts at government banks in China.
32. For an overview of the ownership composition of the largest banking institutions, see Martin, 'China's Banking System'.
33. World Savings Bank Institute, 'WSBI Members' Key Figures' (Brussels: WSBI, 2011).
34. X. Xinliang, 'Corporate Restructuring of Industrial and Commercial Bank of China (ICBC), Motivators and Impacts' (MA dissertation, Nottingham University, 2006).
35. Ibid., pp. 29–30.
36. Martin, 'China's Banking System', p. 16.

37. Ibid., p. 17.
38. V. Shih, 'Big Rock Candy Mountain', *China Economic Quarterly* (June 2010), pp. 26–32.
39. 'According to senior officials from the CBRC, Chinese banks are facing default risks on more than one-fifth of the RMB7,700bn ($1,135bn) loans they have made to local governments across the country; most of these loans were used to fund regional infrastructure projects (*Financial Times*, 08/01/2010). In July 2011, Moody estimated that local government loans can be as high as RMB14.2 trillion, and the NPL ratio for Chinese banks could be 8–12% (*Reuters*, 7/5/2011)'; F. Allen et al., 'China's Financial System: Opportunities and Challenges', NBER Working Paper, 17828 (2010), p. 15 n. 12. See also Martin, 'China's Banking System', p. 31.
40. E. Downs, *Inside China, Inc.: China Development Bank's Cross-Border Energy Deals* (Washington, DC: Brooking Institution, 2011); and D. M. Cimbaljevich, 'China's New Safari into African Development', *Foreign Policy Digest*, 1 May 2010, pp. 1–7.
41. US–China Economic and Security Review Commission, *Report to Congress* (Washington, DC, 2011), p. 46.
42. Downs, *Inside China*, p. 62.
43. N. R. Lardy, 'Sustaining China's Economic Growth after the Global Financial Crisis' (Washington, DC: Peterson Institute, 2012), p. 1: 'contrary to the often repeated assertion, bank loans in 2009–10 did not flow primarily to state-owned companies and that the access of both private firms and household businesses to bank credit improved considerably'.
44. Lawrence and Martin, 'Understanding China's Political System'; and Lieberthal, *Managing the China Challenge*, pp. 50–2.
45. Shih, *Factions and Finance in China*.
46. Shih, 'Dealing with Non-Performing Loans'.
47. S. Shirk, *The Political Logic of Economic Reform in China* (Berkeley, CA: University of California Press, 1993).
48. M. Pei, 'The Political Economy of Banking Reforms in China, 1993–1997', *Journal of Contemporary China*, 7:18 (1998), pp. 321–50.
49. 'Disillusioned Foreign Banks Drift Out Russia', *BARENTSNOVA*, 12 May 2011, at http://www.barentsnova.com/node/1031 [accessed 1 October 2013].
50. Raiffeisen Research, 'CEE Banking Report' (May 2013). p. 56.
51. J. Johnson, *A Fistful of Rubles: The Rise and Fall of the Russian Banking System* (Ithaca, NY: Cornell University Press, 2000); J. S. Abarbanell and A. Meyendorff, 'Bank Privatization in Post Communist Russia: The Case of Zhilsotsbank', *Journal of Comparative Economics*, 25 (1997), pp. 62–96; D. Berkowitz and D. N. DeJong, 'Growth in Post-Soviet Russia: A Tale of Two Transitions?', *Journal of Economic Behavior and Organization*, 79 (2011), pp. 133–43; J. P. Bonin, I. Hasan and P. Wachtel, 'Bank Performance, Efficiency and Ownership in Transition Economies', *Journal of Banking and Finance*, 29:1 (2005), pp. 31–53; and K. Schoors, 'The Fate of Russia's Former State Banks: Chronicle of a Restructuring Postponed and a Crisis Foretold', *Europe-Asia Studies*, 55:1 (2003), pp. 75–100.
52. Raiffeisen Research, 'CEE Banking Report', p. 55.
53. C. P. Rock and V. Solodkov, 'Monetary Policies, Banking, and Trust in Changing Institutions: Russia's Transition in the 1990s', *Journal of Economic Issues*, 35:2 (2001), pp. 451–8.

11 Kumar, 'Cooperative Banks in India: Alternative Banks Impervious to the Global Crisis?'

1. See Government of India's Ministry of Agriculture, 'Report of the High Powered Committee on Cooperatives' (May 2009), at http://agricoop.nic.in/cooperation/hpcc-2009new.pdf [accessed 2 August 2013].
2. See B. Prasad, 'Co-operative Banking in a Competitive Business Environment', *Cab Calling* (October–Decembr 2005), at http://cab.org.in/CAB%20Calling%20Content/Credit%20Cooperatives%20at%20the%20Crossroads%20(Special%20Issue)/Cooperative%20Banking%20in%20a%20Competitive%20Business%20Environment.pdf [accessed 2 August 2013].
3. Narasimham Committee, 'Report of the Committee on the Financial System' (Mumbai: Government of India, 1991).
4. Padmanabhan Committee, 'Banking Supervision' (Mumbai: Government of India, 1995).
5. Tarapore Committee, 'Report on Capital Account Convertibility' (Mumbai: Government of India, 1997).
6. J. Gupta and S. Jain, 'A Study on Cooperative Banks in India with Special Reference to Lending Practices', *International Journal of Scientific and Research Publications*, 2:10 (2012), pp. 1–6.
7. S. L. Kapoor Committee, 'Institutional Credit to Small Scale Industries' (City: Government of India, 1998).
8. J. R. Verma Committee, 'Current Account Carry Forward Practice' (Mumbai: Government of India, 1999).
9. R. Bhaskaran and J. P. Praful, 'Non Performing Assets (NPAs) in Co-operative Rural Financial System: A Major Challenge to Rural Development', *BIRD's Eye View* (December 2000).
10. S. Jain, 'Comparative Study of Performance of District Central Co-operative Banks (DCCBs) of Western India i.e. Maharashtra, Gujarat & Rajasthan for the Years 1999–2000 from the Point of View of Net Profit/Loss', *NAFSCOB Bulletin* (April–June 2001).
11. F. Singh and B. Singh, 'Funds Management in the Central Cooperative Banks of Punjab: An Analysis of Financial Margin', *ICFAI Journal of Management*, 5 (2006), pp. 74–80.
12. V. Mavaluri, P. Boppana and B. Nagarjuna, 'Measurement of Efficiency of Banks in India', University Library of Munich, MPRA Paper, 17350 (2006).
13. V. Pal and N. S. Malik, 'A Multivariate Analysis of the Financial Characteristics of Commercial Banks in India', *ICFAI Journal of Management*, 6:3 (2007), pp. 29–42.
14. A. Campbell, 'Bank Insolvency and the Problem of Non-Performing Loans', *Journal of Banking Regulation* (2007), pp. 25–45.
15. H. K. Singla, 'Financial Performance of Banks in India', *ICFAI Journal of Management*, 7:1 (2008), pp. 50–62.
16. U. Dutta and A. Basak, 'Appraisal of Financial Performance of Urban Cooperative Banks. A Case Study', *Management Accountant* (March 2008), pp. 170–4.
17. M. Levin, 'The Role of Cooperatives in Providing Local Answers to Globalization', Keynote Speech to Tenth National Cooperative Congress, San Jose, Costa Rica, 29 March 2001.
18. A. Sinha, 'Perspectives on Cooperation', valedictory address by Mr Anand Sinha, Deputy Governor of the Reserve Bank of India, at the International Conference on Coopera-

tives, organized by the College for Agriculture Banking, Pune, India, 16–17 November 2012.
19. R. Putnam et al., *Making Democracy Work: Civic Traditions in Modern Italy* (Princeton, NJ: Princeton University Press, 1993).

Mettenheim and Butzbach, 'Conclusion'

1. E. N. White, 'Were Banks Special Intermediaries in Late Nineteenth Century America?', *Federal Reserve Bank of St Louis Review* (May–June 1998), pp. 13–32.
2. A notable exception is H. Hansmann, *The Ownership of Enterprise* (Cambridge, MA: Harvard University Press, 1996).
3. Work in this respect includes D. G. McKillop and J. O. S. Wilson, 'Credit Unions: A Theoretical and Empirical Overview', *Financial Markets, Institutions and Instruments*, 20:3 (2011), pp. 79–123.
4. P. Hall and D. Soskice (eds), *The Varieties of Capitalism: The Institutional Foundations of Comparative Advantage* (Oxford: Oxford University Press, 2001).
5. For a review of banking and finance in the varieties of capitalism literature, see R. Deeg, 'Europe 2020 and Varieties of Capitalism: Complementary or Contradictory?', paper presented at the 18th International Conference of Europeanists, Barcelona, Spain, 20–2 June 2011, and at the Annual Meeting of the American Political Science Association, Seattle, WA, 31 August–4 September 2011.
6. R. La Porta, F. Lopez-de-Silanes and A. Schleifer, 'Government Ownership of Banks', *Journal of Finance*, 57:1 (2002), pp. 265–301.
7. R. Lall, 'From Failure to Failure: The Politics of International Banking Regulation', *Review of International Political Economy*, 19:4 (2012), pp. 609–38.
8. F. Bos, 'Meaning and Measurement of National Accounts Statistics', conference paper for the *World Economics Association Conference on the Political Economy of Economic Metrics* (2013).
9. A. Pettifor, 'The Power to Create Money "Out of Thin Air": Understanding Capitalism's Elastic Production of Money and Moving On beyond Adam Smith and "Fractional Reserve Banking" – a Review Essay of Geoffrey Ingham's *Capitalism*' (London: PRIME Policy Research in Macroeconomics, 2013).
10. For review of Minskyian approaches, see the special issue of *Accounting Economics and Law* (October 2013).
11. Cited by F. Peabody in his 'Introduction' to J. Ford, *Co-operation in New England* (New York: Russell Sage Foundation, 1908), pp. v–xiv, on p. vi.
12. B. Jossa, 'Marx, Marxism and the Cooperative Movement', *Cambridge Journal of Economics*, 29 (2005), pp. 3–18.

INDEX

Caisse D'Epargne Nationale (postal savings bank), 23
Caixa Economica Federal (savings bank), 31, 184, 189–91
Cajas de Ahorro savings banks, 29, 30
Campbell, A., 216
Canning, D., 7, 66
Carbò Valverde, S., 35
Cardoso, President Fernando Henrique, 185, 187, 190
Carnevali, F., 30, 64
CDB (China Development Bank), 193, 202–3
Cen, L., 58
Ceneboyan, A., S. 34, 35
Central Bank of Brazil, 184–5
Central Liquidity Facility (US), 176
Chakravarty, S. P., 35
Chambers, W., 148–9, 152–3
Chinese banking system, 197–204, 208–9
Chiorazzo, V., 68
Christian charity, 15–16
Clinton, Bill, 177
Cohen, E., 14
Coleman, N., 46
Committee on Financial Inclusion, 197
Community Development Financial Institutions, 177
Cook, J., 149, 158
cooperative banks
  access to capital, 65
  and agency theory, 55–63
  business models of, 110
  comparative performance of alternative banks, 33–5
  European cooperative banking groups *see* ECBGs
  founding of, 19–20
  and implications of findings, 227–8, 229, 231–4
  Indian *see under* Indian banking system
  institutional features of, 110
  and Italian banking system, 127–30, 144–5
  modernization of, 31–2
  and three-pillar banking systems, 101–2, 102–5, 111–20
  and US banking system, 170
Cooperative Societies Act (1904), 214

Cornett, Millon, 33, 34, 35, 57
cost-efficiency, 33–4, 127, 129–30, 222
counter-cyclical lending behaviour, 43–9
Coutinho, President Luciano, 192
CRA (Community Reinvestment Act), 170
Crédit Mobilier (special purpose bank), 25
credit unions (US), 175–7
Crespi, R., 35
Cuevas, C. C., 55–6, 57, 60, 61
Cull, R., 45, 46
Cummings-Woo, M., 26
'customer advocacy', 82
customer satisfaction, 82

da Silva, President Luiz Inácio Lula, 185, 188
Davydov, D., 46
DCCBs (district central cooperative banks), 216
De Haas, R., 45–6
de Jonghe, O., 67, 68
de Lima Neto, President Antonio Francisco, 188
de Tocqueville, Alexis, 21
Delestre, Huges, 17
'democratic principle', 111
Demosthenes, 14
Demsetz, H., 54
demutualization, 157–9, 163
dense branch networks, 88, 90
Deshmukh, S. D., 60
development banks, 11–12, 25–6, 55–8, 62, 64–5, 193–4
DeYoung, R., 67–8
Dietrich, A., 34
Dinç, S. I., 57
Dodd–Frank Wall Street Reform and Consumer Protection Act (2010), 1–2, 5
Downs, E., 202–3
DSGV (German Savings Banks Association), 113–14
'dual bottom line' institutions, 75, 77
Duprey, T., 44, 48
Dutta, U., 216
DZ-Bank AG (financial institution), 105, 114, 116

E/A (equity:assets) ratios, 94–5
EACB (European Association of Cooperative Banks), 76

Obama, Barack, 1
Occupy Money Cooperative (US), 177
Office of Thrift Supervision (OTS), 5
Oliver Wyman (consulting group), 32
OMTs (outright monetary transactions), 136
Önder, Z., 46
OTD (originate-to-distribute) models, 68
OTH (originate-to-hold) models, 68
Oughton, C., 5, 159
Owen, Robert, 213
Oxford Handbook of Banking, 4
Özyildirim, S., 46

Pal, V,. 216
Panizza, U., 44, 45
philanthropy, 79, 148–9
Plato, 14
Platt, S. E., 151–2, 153
Plutarch, 14, 15
Polanyi, K., 12–13, 182
political realism, 205, 207, 208
Polo, A., 60
Postal Savings Bank (China), 199–200, 204, 208
postal savings banks, 21–5, 199–200, 204, 208
Praful, J. P., 216
private credit institutions (in three-pillar banking systems), 103
pro-cyclical lending behaviour, 44–8
profit orientation, 106, 107, 120, 151–2
profitability, 34–5, 107, 220–1
Public Bank Initiative (2010), 177
'pure theory of fractional reserve banking', 51–2

Rabobank (cooperative bank group), 29, 31–2, 82, 234
Raiffeisen, Friedrich Wilhelm, 12, 19, 72, 112, 206, 214
Rasmussen, E., 51, 56, 57, 60, 61, 62–3, 66
'regional principle', 107, 110–11
relationship banking, 63–4, 77, 108
Reserve Bank of India (RBI), 194, 195–7, 212, 214–15, 216
revenue diversification, 67–8
risk management, 67–9

RoA (return on assets), 95–6
Roland, K. P., 67–8
Romeu, R., 46
RRBs (regional rural banks), 211
Russian banking system, 205–7, 208–9

Sallie Mae (Student Loan Marketing Association), 173
Sallust, 14
savings banks
    access to capital, 65
    and agency theory, 55–9, 62–3
    and business cycles, 24–5
    business models of, 110–12
    comparative performance of alternative banks, 33–5
    founding of, 17–19
    and implications of findings, 227–8, 229, 231–4
    institutional features of, 110–11
    modernization of, 30–1
    and three-pillar banking systems, 101–2, 103–4, 110–11, 112–21
    and US banking system, 170–2, 178
Schclarek, A., 45, 47, 48
Schmidt, Reinhard, 3
Schulze-Delitzsch, Hermann, 12, 19, 23–4, 72, 112
Seidel, H., 19, 24–5
Select Committee on Securities (1858), 24
Select Committee Report on Savings Banks (1858), 24
Shaw, E., 52
Shih, V., 203
Shin, H., S. 162, 164
Shleifer, Andrei, 57
Shonfield, A., 182
Shulze, Franz, 214
Singh, B., 216
Singh, F., 216
SMEs (small and medium-sized enterprises), 76, 80, 91, 98, 113, 138
Smith, C., 56
SMP (securities markets programme), 136
'social banking', 182
Soskice, D., 229
Sparkasse savings banks, 18–19, 30
special purpose banks, 25–6, 105